RESTRUCTURING THE EUROPEAN STATE

Restructuring the European State

European Integration and State Reform

PAOLO DARDANELLI

McGill-Queen's University Press
Montreal & Kingston • London • Chicago

© McGill-Queen's University Press 2017

ISBN 978-0-7735-5152-7 (cloth)
ISBN 978-0-7735-5253-1 (ePDF)
ISBN 978-0-7735-5254-8 (ePUB)

Legal deposit fourth quarter 2017
Bibliothèque nationale du Québec

Printed in Canada on acid-free paper that is 100% ancient forest free (100% post-consumer recycled), processed chlorine free

McGill-Queen's University Press acknowledges the support of the Canada Council for the Arts for our publishing program. We also acknowledge the financial support of the Government of Canada through the Canada Book Fund for our publishing activities.

Library and Archives Canada Cataloguing in Publication

Dardanelli, Paolo, author
    Restructuring the European state: European integration and state reform/ by Paolo Dardanelli.

Includes bibliographical references and index.
Issued in print and electronic formats.
ISBN 978-0-7735-5152-7 (cloth). – ISBN 978-0-7735-5253-1 (ePDF). – ISBN 978-0-7735-5254-8 (ePUB)

1. European Union. 2. European federation. 3. European Union countries – Politics and government. I. Title.

JN15.D37 2017   321.04094   C2017-904382-X
                                          C2017-904383-8

This book was typeset by Marquis Interscript in 10.5/13 Sabon.

Contents

Acknowledgments   vii

Abbreviations   xi

Introduction   3

1 Conceptualizing State Restructuring   11

2 Theorizing and Testing the Influence of European Integration   29

3 The First Steps   55

4 Widening and Deepening   82

5 A "Europe of the Regions"?   111

6 From a "Europe of the Regions" to "Independence in Europe"   132

7 "Independence in Europe" Takes Centre Stage   176

8 European Integration and State Restructuring: A Realist Bargain Approach   237

Conclusions   253

Appendix   259

Notes   309

References   325

Index   373

Acknowledgments

It is customary to open the preface to a book by saying that it has been a long time in the making. Rarely has this been more appropriate than in this case. As far as I recall, I can trace the origin of my interest in the topic of this book to a childhood conversation sometime in the mid-1970s in Turin, Piedmont, Italy. A relative of my mother's, Pio Giordanengo, a man of considerable cultivation, had joined us for a visit and the conversation touched upon the apparent contradiction between the efforts to revive the local dialect, which started to attract wider support at the time, and the drive toward European integration. My sister, Silvia, observed that the notion of a Europe of the Regions suggested there might not in fact be a contradiction between the two. I am grateful to her for having inspired me.

It would be a long time, however, before I had a chance of devoting time to studying it. My interest was rekindled by the debate on federalism in Italy in the 1990s and the parallel move toward devolution in the UK, with which I became more familiar when I moved to Durham, in the northeast of England, to do a master's degree. The chance came when I embarked on a PhD at the London School of Economics, for which I researched the question of the influence of European integration upon devolution to Scotland. My thesis was subsequently published by Manchester University Press with the title *Between Two Unions: Europeanisation and Scottish Devolution*. Once I recovered from the exhaustion of doing a PhD, widening the scope of my enquiry to other cases was high on my research agenda. It would take another few years, however, before I could do so in earnest.

A grant from the James Madison Trust enabled me to do some of the fieldwork necessary to gather the material for the book. I am very grateful to the Trust for its generous support. Later, a small grant from the Faculty of Social Sciences of the University of Kent funded training in Qualitative Comparative Analysis (QCA) methodology, which has been of great help for the investigation conducted in the book. I thank the Faculty for its support.

In the course of my research I received precious help and support from a number of organizations, to which I am most grateful. I wish to thank in particular: ADVN, Antwerp; Bibliotèque des Sciences Humaines, Université Libre de Bruxelles; Centre Jean Gol, Brussels; Centre Permanent de la Citoyenneté et de la Participation, Namur; Centre Documental de la Comunicació, Universitat Autonoma de Barcelona; Centro de Estudios Andaluces, Seville; Centro de Estudios Avanzados en Ciencias Sociales, Instituto Juan March, Madrid; Departament de Ciencies Poltíques i Socials, Universitat Pompeu Fabra, Barcelona; Departamento de Ciencias Politicas y Relaciones Internacionales, Universidad Autonoma de Madrid; Dipartimento IURA, Università di Palermo; Fondazione Luigi Einaudi, Turin; Institut d'Estudis Autónomics, Barcelona; Institut Emile Vandervelde, Brussels; Institut Jules Destrée, Namur; Liberaal Archief, Ghent; LSE Library, London; Musée de la Vie wallonne, Liège; National Library of Wales, Aberystwyth.

Papers based on the project were presented at the fifth ECPR General Conference, at the fifth PSA Territorial Politics Conference, at the 61st PSA Annual Conference, at the 107th APSA Annual Meeting, and at the 23rd IPSA World Congress, as well as at the Universidad Autonoma de Madrid's Political Science Research Seminar, at the University of Oslo's Political Science Research Seminar, at the University of Berne's Political Science colloquium, and at the University of Kent's Comparative Politics Workshop. I am grateful to the participants in those conferences and seminars for their helpful comments and suggestions.

For their help and advice I would like to thank: Øivind Bratberg, César Colino, Paul Delforge, Frank Delmartino, Kris Deschouwer, Lieven de Winter, Daniel Dustin, Antoni Estupiñá Collet, Paz Fernandez, Fátima Gomez, Mireia Graus Creu, Angustias Hombrado Martos, Bruno Hopp, Simon Krogh, Alexander Libman, Matthew Loveless, Gloria Martinou, Hugh Miall, José Ramón Montero, Edward Morgan-Jones, Fabiola Mota, Klaus-Jürgen Nagel, Wendy Olsen, Jane O'Mahony, Ferran Requejo Coll, Caroline Sägesser,

Ignacio Sánchez-Cuenca, Ben Seyd, Carles Viver i Pi-Sunyer, Andrea Volkens, George Woodcock, and Andy Wroe.

I am grateful to Tom Vandenkendelaere, Marloes van Hooijdonk, and Mareike Thiel for their excellent research assistance.

Special thanks go to Hélène Michel for her friendship and hospitality while researching Belgium, Clive Church for having read and commented on the entire manuscript, and Elizabeth Schächter for cheering me up through the rough patches.

I am very grateful to Jacqueline Mason and to the entire staff at McGill-Queen's University Press for believing in this project and for their impeccable professionalism.

My parents have offered, as always, steadfast support and encouragement, for which I am very grateful to them. My deepest thanks go to my partner, Sue, for her love, assistance, comfort, and humour over the long, hard slog. I dedicate this book to her.

Canterbury, January 2017

Abbreviations

ADVN	Archief en Documentatiecentrum voor het Vlaams Nationalisme
AN	Alleanza Nazionale
ANC	Assemblea Nacional Catalana
APSA	American Political Science Association
BBC	British Broadcasting Corporation
BHV	Brussel-Halle-Vilvoorde/Bruxelles-Hal-Vilvorde
BKV	Belgische Kamer van Volksvertegenwoordigers
CAP	Common Agricultural Policy
CBI	Confederation of British Industry
CDC	Convergència Democràtica de Catalunya
CDH	Centre démocrate humaniste
CD&V	Christen-Democratisch en Vlaams
CHA	Comparative Historical Analysis
CiU	Convergència i Unió
CLN	Comitato di Liberazione Nazionale
CRISP	Centre de recherche et d'information socio-politiques
CSQEP	Catalunyq Sí Que Es Pot
CS	Ciutadans
CT	Constitutional Treaty
CUP	Candidatura d'Unitat Popular
CVP	Christelijke Volkspartij
DC	Democrazia Cristiana
DF	Dansk Folkeparti
DKF	Det Konservative Folkeparti
DRV	Det Radikale Venstre
DSD	Socialdemokraterne

DV	Venstre
ECB	European Central Bank
ECPR	European Consortium for Political Research
ECSC	European Coal and Steel Community
EEC	European Economic Community
EMS	European Monetary System
EMU	Economic and Monetary Union
EP	European Parliament
ERC	Esquerra Republicana de Catalunya
ETA	Euskadi Ta Askatasuna
EU.	European Union
FDF	Front démocratique des francophones
FI	Forza Italia
GDP	Gross domestic product
HI	Historical Institutionalism
ICV	Iniciativa per Catalunya Verds
IMF	International Monetary Fund
IPSA	International Political Science Association
LN	Lega Nord
LSE	London School of Economics
MEC	Mercato Europeo Comune
MLG	Multilevel Governance
MR	Mouvement réformateur
MSI	Movimento Sociale Italiano
NATO	North Atlantic Treaty Organization
N-VA	Nieuw-Vlaamse Alliantie
PC	Plaid Cymru
PCF	Parti communiste français
PCI	Partito Comunista Italiano
PDS	Partito Democratico della Sinistra
PLI	Partito Liberale Italiano
PLP	Parti de la Liberté et du Progrès
PNV/EAJ	Partido Nacionalista Vasco/Euzko Alderdi Jeltzalea
PP	Partido Popular
PP-C	Partido Popular de Cataluña
PPI	Partito Popolare Italiano
PRC	Partito della Rifondazione Comunista
PRI	Partito Repubblicano Italiano
PRL	Parti réformateur libéral
PRLW	Parti des réformes et de la liberté de Wallonie

PS	Parti socialiste [Belgium]
PSA	Political Studies Association
PSB	Parti socialiste belge
PSC	Parti social-chrétien
PS-C	Partit dels Socialistes de Catalunya
PSDI	Partito Socialista Democratico Italiano
PSF	Parti socialiste [France]
PSI	Partito Socialista Italiano
PSOE	Partido Socialista Obrero Español
PVV	Partij voor Vrijheid en Vooruitgang
OICS	Opportunities, incentives, constraints
O-VLD	Open Vlaamse Liberalen en Democraten
QCA	Qualitative Comparative Analysis
csQCA	crisp-set Qualitative Comparative Analysis
fsQCA	fuzzy-set Qualitative Comparative Analysis
QMV	Qualified Majority Voting
RAI	Regional Authority Index
RAI-RSF	Regional Authority Index, regional self-rule
RCC	Royal Commission on the Constitution
RPR	Rassemblement pour la République
RW	Rassemblement wallon
SDP	Social Democratic Party
SF	Socialistik Folkeparti
SNP	Scottish National Party
SP	Socialistische Partij
SP.A	Socialistische Partij-Anders
UDC	Unió Democràtica de Catalunya
UDF	Union pour la démocratie française
UKG	United Kingdom government
UKP	United Kingdom parliament
USA	United States of America
USSR	Union of Soviet Socialist Republics
VB	Vlaams Blok, later Vlaams Belang
VLD	Vlaamse Liberalen en Democraten
VU	Volksunie
VUJO	Volksunie Jongeren

RESTRUCTURING THE EUROPEAN STATE

Introduction

Since 1950, Western Europe has experienced numerous occurrences of state restructuring. In several cases these have seen the creation of a regional level of government to which policy responsibilities previously carried out by central government have been devolved. Over the same period, European integration has led to a significant transfer of power upward to what is now the European Union. Has European integration influenced state restructuring and, if so, how? To what extent has state restructuring been fuelled by integration? These questions were first raised in the mid-1970s and touched upon by many since then but have yet to be fully answered. This book is an attempt to do so.

0.1 THE TOPIC AND THE QUESTIONS

Most Western European states have undergone processes of state restructuring in the post-World War II period. Restructuring has mainly taken the form of a decentralization of power toward sub-central levels of government, which, in some cases, has gone as far as entailing a profound constitutional transformation from unitary structures to federal or quasi-federal ones. This decentralization trend stands in contrast to the long process of centralization of power and nationalization of politics that characterized the European states in the nineteenth century and the first half of the twentieth century (e.g., Sharpe 1979; Caramani 2004, Keating 2013).

It is striking that these cases of state restructuring via decentralization have taken place in European states that have simultaneously been involved in supranational integration, whereby more and more policymaking competences have been transferred to the European Union.[1] Over the last seven decades, millions of citizens in Europe have thus witnessed a profound transformation of the context in which politics and democracy are practised. As Spruyt (2002, 127–8) has remarked, intrastate decentralization and interstate integration are trends of major importance to any understanding of the recent and future evolution of the European state. The same can be said of the connections between the two. Their taking place broadly over the same period has induced a number of observers to note that the European states are increasingly being hollowed out both from below and from above and to postulate a causal link between integration and state restructuring.

The notion that such a link exists is so widely entertained that one can easily find numerous references to it, even in strands of the literature not primarily focused on the effects of European integration on state structures. As early as 1973, Linz (102) noted "It is therefore not surprising that some of the leaders of the periphery look forward to the total destruction of the European system of states … and its substitution by a European federation of 'patries' … in which old and new nations … would become part of a larger polity." Twenty years later, Elliott (1992, 49) wrote: "The development, on the one hand, of multi-national political and economic organizations, and the revival, on the other, of 'suppressed' nationalities and of half-submerged regional and local identities, have simultaneously placed pressure on the nation state from above and beneath. These two processes, no doubt connected in ways that it will be for future generations of historians to trace, are bound to call into question standard interpretations of European history conceived in terms of an inexorable advance toward a system of sovereign nation states." A further twenty years later, Weiler (2012, 910) observed: "Feeding this frenzy for secession and independence in Europe is the premise that all these new states will somehow find a safe haven as Member States of the European Union. Absent that assumption, appetite for independence would be significantly muted, the rough seas of 'going it alone' far more threatening," and lamented: "It would be hugely ironic if the prospect of membership in the Union ended up providing an incentive for an ethos of political disintegration" (911).

Nor are such references confined to the academic literature. A reporter for *Der Spiegel* remarked in 2011 that "The stronger the Brussels-based EU becomes, and the weaker its member states, the louder are the calls by small, long-disadvantaged ethnic groups for self-determination within a Europe of regions" (Mayr 2011). A few years earlier, *The Economist* had argued: "Europe stands at the centre of the plan by the Scottish National Party (SNP) to win next month's election to the Scottish Parliament ... A pledge to seek independence only within the EU has played a big role ... painting a picture of plucky Scotland setting out into the wider world, but within a reassuring European embrace ... Scotland is, of course, only one region in which the EU seems to offer new hope to nationalists ... far from making nation-states redundant, it [the EU] has made it less risky to seek nationhood" (Economist 2007). In the midst of Catalonia's push for a referendum on independence in 2014, *The Economist* returned to the theme, pointing out that the EU has made it "easier for separatists to seek independence within the cocoon of the EU" (Economist 2014).

Yet, despite its prominence in both the academic literature and the mass media, the questions of how and the extent to which state restructuring has been influenced by European integration has not so far been systematically investigated. Hence we still lack a solid understanding of the connections between the two phenomena. This book attempts to answer these questions to help advance our knowledge of the evolution of the state in the context of European integration, on the basis of a comparative analysis since 1950 and across the Western European states. By so doing the book also offers what I believe to be the first comparative account of state restructuring in contemporary Western Europe.

0.2 THE STATE OF THE ART

The broad question of the impact of integration on the politics of state structures started to be addressed in the 1970s (Feld 1975; McAllister 1975; Wolfe 1976; Rudolph 1977; Scheinman 1977; Birch 1978; Sharpe 1979) and has since attracted considerable scholarly interest. In one of the first articles devoted to the subject, Feld asked (1975, 1192): "will politics for regional autonomy be linked to European politics?" Some of the authors who have contributed to this strand of the literature have seen integration as weakening regional demands for self-government. According to Scheinman (1977), for instance, this is because integration is controlled by state governments and because its capitalist character is inimical to regionalist demands for cultural and economic protection. In a second group we find scholars arguing that state restructuring is triggered by cultural conflicts whose roots predate the onset of integration and have been largely unaffected by the latter. European integration and state restructuring should thus be seen as parallel, as opposed to causally connected, phenomena (Kolinsky 1981, 86–94; Urwin 1982; De Bandt 1992, 136; Sharpe 1993, 2).

Quantitative studies have focused almost exclusively on the effects of economic integration and have reached contrasting conclusions. Using demands for regional autonomy as the dependent variable, Van Houten (2003) finds no general evidence of a direct effect of globalization and European integration but leaves the door open to the possibility that more complex, indirect effects might be present. Looking at support for secessionist parties, Sorens (2004) and Brancati (2014) also find no generalized positive correlation with integration. Using fiscal decentralization as the dependent variable, Garrett and Rodden (2003) find a negative correlation with trade integration, whereas Stegarescu (2004) and Baskaran (2010) both conclude that European integration has led to greater fiscal decentralization.

Most of the authors who have considered the connection between the two phenomena, however, have postulated that European integration has a positive – meaning, a facilitating – influence on state restructuring and have identified four main channels through which such an influence operates. First, integration has been seen as fuelling regions' demands for self-government in general terms because it undermines states' sovereignty and their policymaking role. Such demands put pressure on state actors to devolve power to the regions through constitutional reforms (e.g., Rudolph 1977, esp. 544; Kellas 1991, 226–31; Keating 2001, 9–10).

Other authors emphasize that the EU's endorsement of the idea of a "Europe of the Regions" and of the principle of subsidiarity – both of earlier origin but adopted by the EU in the late 1980s–early 1990s – has lent a powerful external legitimation to regional autonomy by making it appear a natural complement to the process of integration. It has also been seen as strengthening the case for regions to acquire – or to increase – governmental powers in order to be able to access EU decision-making (e.g., Anderson 1991, 420; Ladrech 1994, 82; Jones 1995, 294–5; Anderson and Goodman 1995, 617; Loughlin 1996; Börzel 2002, 585–6).

A third major factor discussed in the literature is the effect of cohesion policy (e.g., Marks 1993; Keating 1995; Hooghe 1996; Hix and Goetz 2000, 11; Hooghe and Marks 2001, 81–118; Bartolini 2005, 260–4). The reform of the structural funds in 1988 opened a channel for regional governments to be involved directly in EU policymaking often bypassing the state level. This is seen as having triggered a multifaceted "mobilization and empowerment of subnational governments" (Marks 1993, 407) and having put pressure on state governments to devolve power to the regions. According to Bartolini (2005, 261): "The EU policies have fostered the decentralization trend in most EU countries ... the EU has played an institution-building role for subnational regional strengthening." Hix and Goetz (2000, 11) outline the core mechanism as such: "EU regional policy encourages member states to establish planning authorities at the regional level, which in turn produce demands for a democratization of these structures, and hence the creation of elected regional assemblies and governments" and where these bodies already exist it reinforces the demands "for further delegation of policy competences away from central government."

Last, but perhaps most prominently, European integration has been theorized as leading to state restructuring through the effects of economic integration. By guaranteeing free trade and regulatory uniformity across its member states, the EU makes smaller states economically viable and thus encourages secessionism in those with a high territorial heterogeneity of preferences over public policy (Birch 1978, 336; Meadwell and Martin 1996; Alesina and Spolaore 1997; Alesina et al. 2000; Bolton and Roland 1997, 1066; Alesina and Spolaore 2003, 213–14). As Alesina et al. (2000, 1277) put it: "trade openness and political separatism go hand in hand: economic integration leads to political 'disintegration'"; they also acknowledge, however, that secessions remain costly and difficult processes hence are only likely to take place in the presence of major changes in the "underlying parameters" (1285). As a result, the granting of regional autonomy via state restructuring, rather than secession, is a more likely outcome, on the grounds that "an answer to the trade-off between economies of scale and heterogeneity can be found in a decentralized structure of government" (Alesina and Spolaore 1997, 1046). European integration has thus been widely theorized as having a causal influence on state restructuring in multiple ways but no systematic analysis of whether this is the case has hitherto been carried out.

0.3 THE BOOK

This book is an attempt to investigate the causal connections between European integration and state restructuring in contemporary Western Europe. Its primary objective is to answer the question of whether and how the former influences the latter. A subsidiary question it also tries to answer is the extent to which it does so.

The book develops a conceptualization of state restructuring that distinguishes between bottom-up and top-down forms and puts forward a "Realist Bargain" theory of how these are influenced by integration. The theory is centred on the dynamic of party competition unleashed by regional-nationalist parties' strategy of "independence in Europe."[2] As this dynamic is only present in bottom-up state restructuring, the theory predicts that integration has a significant effect only when restructuring takes a bottom-up form. I test the theory on cases selected across four cross-section levels of analysis and five time points, with focus on thirteen critical junctures of state restructuring and 127 party-election/referendum observations. Through a detailed analysis of party strategies, short- and long-term process tracing, and synoptic comparative analyses, I show that the conceptual and theoretical propositions advanced find strong empirical validation.

In chapter 1, I conceptualize and classify state restructuring. I first develop a new typology of state structures built upon an integrated qualitative and quantitative approach. I then conceptualize state restructuring and distinguish between a strong and a weak form. Subsequently I map the evolution of state structures in Western Europe since 1950 and identify four clusters of cases. Lastly, I explore some key properties of state restructuring, notably the fact that it occurs through critical junctures and tends to follow two distinct dynamics: bottom up and top down. In chapter 2 I develop a theory of how European integration influences state restructuring and explain why I label it realist bargain. I then outline the research design I have adopted, based on a comparative historical analysis (CHA) approach, the procedure through which I have selected the cases for analysis, and the methods I have employed to test the theory.

In the next five chapters I present the findings of an in-depth process-tracing analysis of European integration's influence on state restructuring via the agency of political parties within each critical juncture, divided into five periods. Each of these chapters briefly describes the principal aspects of the process of integration in that period and then analyzes critical junctures of state restructuring occurring within the period. Chapter 3 deals with the first critical juncture of state restructuring in Italy – the implementation of the ordinary regions – and the 1970 constitutional reforms in Belgium. It shows how the Italian process followed a top-down dynamic while the Belgian one conformed to the bottom-up model and that, in line with the expectations of the realist bargain model, there was some Europeanization of state restructuring in Belgium but not in Italy.

Chapter 4 covers the 1980 constitutional reforms in Belgium, the first attempt at devolution in the UK, and the democratization of the French regions. In the first two cases state restructuring followed a bottom-up dynamic while in France it took a top-down form. The fact that Europeanization was absent in France but present, albeit to a limited extent, in Belgium and the UK confirms the theoretical expectations and shows the importance of intervening variables such as party attitudes to "Europe."[3] Chapter 5 examines the third and fourth critical junctures of state restructuring in Belgium, leading to the 1988 and 1993 constitutional reforms that completed the transformation of the country into a federal state. As expected, given the bottom-up nature of the process and the deepening of integration, Europeanization of the politics of state restructuring became more intense and more widespread.

Chapter 6 analyzes the implementation of devolution in the UK, the process leading up to the 2001 constitutional reforms in Italy, and the creation of the regions in Denmark. It shows that state restructuring conformed to the bottom-up model in the first two cases but to the top-down one in the third case. As expected, Europeanization was absent in Denmark but it was significant in the UK and Italy and the agency of regional-nationalist parties played a crucial role in the latter two countries. Chapter 7 focuses on the three most recent critical junctures of state restructuring: the sixth round of constitutional reform in Belgium, the deepening of devolution in the UK in the context of the 2014 Scottish independence referendum, and the reform of the statutes of autonomy in Spain leading to Catalonia's secessionist challenge. All these cases display a bottom-up dynamic and the independence in Europe strategy pursued by regional-nationalist parties played a crucial role.

Chapter 8 and the conclusions sum up the analysis and discuss the significance of its findings. Chapter 8 presents the results of several synoptic comparative analyses and shows that they provide strong empirical support for the conceptual distinction between bottom-up and top-down state restructuring and for the realist bargain theory of how European integration influences state restructuring. These findings underpin the claim that integration has had a significant but punctuated influence on restructuring. In the conclusions I argue that the connections between the two phenomena point to a triple paradox of integration, whereby the latter, although driven by an ethos of ever closer union, actually generates dynamics leading to higher disaggregation, asymmetry, and complexity.

0.4 SUMMARY

European integration and state restructuring are two of the most important processes that have shaped the evolution of politics and government in Europe since the Second World War. The questions of whether the former is causally connected to the latter, and through which mechanisms, have attracted considerable scholarly attention since the 1970s but have not hitherto been systematically investigated. The present book is an attempt to do so on the basis of a comparative analysis across time and space.

The book argues that integration has a very different influence on state restructuring depending on the form the latter takes. Its influence is significant in cases of bottom-up restructuring but virtually absent in cases conforming to the top-down model. This is so because integration affects state restructuring primarily through the dynamic of competition between statewide parties and their regional-nationalist challengers, triggered by the latter's independence in Europe strategy. In aggregate, European integration thus has a punctuated causal effect on restructuring, leading to the emergence of a triple paradox of integration rather than a uniform regime of multi-level governance. This has significant implications for the evolution of politics and democracy in contemporary Europe.

1

Conceptualizing State Restructuring

As a first step in analyzing the connections between European integration and state restructuring, it is necessary to conceptualize the latter. We need to elucidate the nature of state restructuring before we can identify how and to what extent it is influenced by integration. In this chapter I develop such a conceptualization, put forward several typologies of its manifestations, and outline how these typologies have informed the selection of cases for analysis. The chapter is divided into three parts. In the first part I develop a conceptualization of state structures from a static perspective. After reviewing the existing conceptualizations, I put forward a new typology of four categories, built upon an integrated qualitative and quantitative approach. In the second part I conceptualize state restructuring, understood as changes in state structures from a dynamic perspective. In a first section, I identify thirty-two distinct forms of restructuring, grouped into two broad categories: a strong one, in which change brings about a difference of kind, and a weak one, in which change is confined to differences of degree. I then proceed to map the evolution of state structures in Western Europe since 1950 against this conceptual typology and identify four clusters of cases. In the third part I describe three aspects of state restructuring that are key to our understanding of its nature. The first is its occurrence through what we can call "critical junctures." The second one is its being the product of party competition and cooperation, particularly during such junctures. The third and most consequential aspect is that we can identify two distinct dynamics in which it manifests itself – top down and bottom up – marked by different strengths of restructuring and different configurations of party competition and cooperation. As I theorize in the next chapter, and test empirically in the remainder of the book, European integration has had a very different effect depending on which dynamic of state restructuring is at play.

1.1 CONCEPTUALIZING STATE STRUCTURES

The modern state is often defined as a set of institutions exercising sovereign political control over a defined territory (e.g., Burnham 2009). The particular set of institutions within a state can be thought of as its structure. Being highly complex organizations, modern states have of course many different aspects or substructures. The substructure of our concern here is that of the territorial administration of the state and its relations to the latter's central institutions, in particular the presence and nature of subcentral tiers of government. This can be seen as the vertical structure of the state – because it concerns different levels of government, which are typically in a hierarchical relation with each other both constitutionally and territorially – as opposed to the horizontal structure, which concerns such institutions as a bicameral as opposed to a unicameral parliament, a parliamentary vs a presidential system, and so forth. This vertical structure is a principal aspect of the institutional architecture of a state and its fundamental features are typically enshrined in its constitutional document/s.[1]

Unitary vs Federal and Symmetric vs Asymmetric

Traditionally, the fundamental distinction when it comes to states' vertical constitutional structure is that between unitary and federal systems. The former are seen as having a unified constitutional structure in which local government is subordinated to central government, whereas the latter are characterized as compound polities in which two orders of government – general and regional – coexist, coordinated with, but autonomous from, each other (Wheare 1946, 1–15). This traditional dichotomous distinction between unitary and federal has, however, been called into question by the emergence of new forms of federation as well as quasi-federal and hybrid systems (e.g., Rokkan and Urwin 1982, 179–89; Elazar 1987, 33–79; Linz 1997; Watts 2008, 8–18; Loughlin 2013). An increasing number of scholars have abandoned the unitary/federal distinction altogether and conceptualize state structures as a continuum defined by the de/centralization of power (e.g., Treisman 2002; Arzaghi and Henderson 2005; Brancati 2006; Hooghe et al. 2016). Beyond the unitary/federal distinction, state structures also differ in terms of a/symmetry, meaning whether the units of subcentral government all have the same constitutional status and powers – defined as a symmetrical system – or not – i.e., an asymmetrical one. This second aspect has traditionally attracted less attention than the unitary/federal one but has acquired greater prominence in the more recent period (e.g., Tarlton 1965; Keating 1998b; Agranoff 1999; McGarry 2007; Requejo and Nagel 2010). This is because classic federalism was largely symmetrical whereas new federal and quasi-federal structures are often asymmetrical. Like the unitary/federal distinction, a/symmetry is often thought of as a dichotomy but can also be profitably conceptualized as a continuum.

Typologies vs Indices

Reflecting the contrast between the categorical approach and the continuous one, two different methods of mapping state structures comparatively have been put forward. On the one hand, there are qualitative typologies that retain the largely dichotomous distinction between unitary and federal systems (e.g., Rokkan and Urwin 1982, 182; Elazar 1987, 60; Keating 1998a, 115–18; Swenden 2006, 11–18; Watts 2008, 17). On the other hand, several quantitative indices of decentralization and regional authority have been developed (Treisman 2002; Arzaghi and Henderson 2005; Brancati 2006; Hooghe et al. 2016), at the root of which there is a conceptualization of decentralization as a continuous variable. No attempt to combine the two approaches has yet been put forward in spite of the fact that combining them allows us to profit from their respective strengths and thus enhance the analytical purchase of our conceptualizations.[2] On the one hand, quantification can provide a degree of precision that adds rigour to qualitative categories. On the other hand, the latter are still helpful to identify distinct forms of state that are more than mere points on a continuum. In other words, it is useful to think of the continuum as divided by thresholds points beyond which differences of degree become differences of kind.[3] This is the approach I have followed to develop the qualitative-quantitative typology adopted for this book. Before introducing it, I briefly review in the next two sections the most prominent existing typologies and indices and highlight both their strengths and their limitations.

Qualitative Typologies

Rokkan and Urwin (1982, 181–2) developed a four-category typology: unitary states, union states, mechanical federations, and organic federations. Unitary states are characterized by "administrative standardization: all areas are treated alike and all institutions are directly under the control of the centre" (181). In union states, "while administrative standardization prevails over most of the territory, the union structure entails the survival in some areas of variations based upon pre-union rights and infrastructures" (ibid.). Mechanical federalism differs from organic federalism in that the former "is introduced from above by constitutional means ... [whereas the latter] ... is constructed from below, the result of voluntary association by distinctive territorial structures" (ibid.). While the distinction between unitary and union states, on the one hand, and between mechanical and organic federalism on the other hand is a useful one, the distinction between the former two and the latter two, i.e., between unitarism and federalism (both defined broadly) was left unspecified by Rokkan and Urwin. Although the "union state" category implies asymmetry, the latter as a general dimension of state structure was also left unexplored.

Elazar (1987, 33–79) put forward multiple categories of systems with federal features, four of which relate to intrastate structures and are thus relevant for our purposes: legislative unions, constitutionally decentralized unitary states, federations, and federacies. A legislative union is defined as "a compound polity in which the constituent units find their primary constitutional expression through common institutions rather than their own separateness" (48). Decentralized unitary states "constitutionally guarantee their local governments considerable autonomy in some areas" (49), but such local governments are subordinated to the central government. He defined federacies as an asymmetrical federal association of a smaller state with a larger one, "in which any change in the relationship must be determined on a mutual basis by both parties" (54–5).[4] Elazar's approach is useful in drawing attention to the fact that unitary states vary in their degree of static decentralization, but it does not offer a clear definition of the distinction between unitary and federal systems itself. Like Rokkan and Urwin, although his "federacy" category can be seen as an asymmetrical arrangement, Elazar did not explore the a/symmetrical dimension further.

Keating's typology[5] (1998a, 114–15) is based on four categories: federalism, strong regionalism, weak regionalism, and functional federalism. He conceptualizes them as points on a continuum rather than discrete categories but does not provide a concise definition of the properties of each type nor of the boundaries between them. While the distinction between strong and weak regionalism is a useful one, it is left unspecified how exactly the two differ between themselves as well as vis-à-vis federalism. Keating, too, does not categorize a/symmetry either.

Lijphart (1999, 188–9) puts forward a five-category classification, based on two dimensions: federal or unitary, on the one hand, and centralized or decentralized, on the other, plus an intermediate category of semi-federal systems. By attaching a numerical score to each category, he argues the "classification can serve as a quantitative index of federalism" (188). As the index so derived is dependent on the qualitative categories rather than the other way round, however, it cannot be used to identify a quantitative threshold separating unitary and federal systems.

Swenden (2006, 11–18) also proposes four categories: federal, regionalized, unitary decentralized, and unitary centralized. He lists nine characteristics of a federation, including "genuine autonomy" and regions' consent to constitutional change (12). Regionalized states are defined as having "strongly developed local or regional tiers of government with directly elected councils. Unlike the regions of a federation, the regions in a regionalized state remain subordinate to the central government" (14). In contrast, regions in a unitary decentralized state "have fewer legislative, administrative, and/or fiscal powers" (15), while unitary centralized states "have weak or no regional tiers of government at all" (18). Swenden's is arguably the most exhaustive qualitative typology but in it too the boundaries between the different categories are only weakly specified and the a/symmetry dimension is not categorized.

Four categories relevant to intrastate structures are also proposed by Watts (2008, 8–18): unions, constitutionally decentralized unions, federations, and federacies, plus an additional hybrid category. He defines unions as "polities compounded in such a way that the constituent units preserve their respective integrities primarily or exclusively through the common organs of the general government rather than through dual government structures" (10). Constitutionally decentralized unions, in contrast, are "basically unitary in form ... but incorporate constitutionally protected sub-national units of government that have functional autonomy" (ibid.). Federations are "compound polities, combining strong constituent units and a strong general government, each possessing powers delegated to it by the people through a constitution, and each empowered to deal directly with the citizens ... and each with major institutions directly elected by the citizens" (ibid.). As regards federacies, he follows Elazar in defining them as "political arrangements where a smaller unit or units are linked to a larger polity, but the smaller unit or units retain considerable autonomy, have a minimum role in the government of the larger one, and the relationship can be dissolved only by mutual agreement" (ibid.). Watts's typology can be seen as a refinement of Elazar's but, like the latter, it does not offer a definition of the boundary between unitary and federal systems and does not categorize a/symmetry.

Quantitative Indices

Lane and Ersson (1999, 187) were among the first to develop an index measuring "institutional autonomy" in Western Europe. The index is based on scores on four categories (federalism, special territorial autonomy, functional autonomy, and local government discretion), which are added to produce an aggregate score ranging from one to seven.

Treisman (2002) proposes a decentralization index built around six dimensions: vertical, decision-making, appointment, electoral, fiscal and personnel. He does consider the degree to which such an index relates to the unitary/federal distinction but limits himself to noting that two elements of it – whether regional units have what he calls "weak autonomy" and "residual powers" – correlate highly with states' self-description as a federation and Elazar's (1995) list of federal states (Treisman 2002, 29–34). Hence, he does not attempt to identify a threshold between unitary and federal nor does he address the a/symmetry dimension.

Arzaghi and Henderson (2005) build two indices, one of fiscal centralization and one of federalism. The first is based on the share of the central government in total government expenditures while the latter is an average of scores on six dimensions: "(1) official federal versus unitary government structure, (2) election of a regional executive, (3) election of a local executive, (4) ability of the center to suspend lower levels of government or to override their decisions, (5) no, limited, or full revenue raising authority of lower levels governments, and (6) revenue sharing" (1186–8). Like Treisman, Arzaghi and Henderson capture important aspects of the unitary/federal distinction but do not attempt to identify a threshold between the two or to factor in a/symmetry.

Brancati (2006) uses an index of decentralization based on the following variables: the presence of democratically elected regional legislatures, whether regional legislatures have tax-raising powers, whether regional legislatures have exclusive or joint control over education and public order, and whether constitutional change requires regional approval (667–8). Her index has similar strengths to those developed by Treisman and by Arzaghi and Henderson but also the same limitations when it comes to the unitary/federal boundary and the a/symmetry dimension.

Hooghe et al. (2016) put forward the most elaborate and comprehensive index in the form of the Regional Authority Index (RAI). The RAI is meant to capture the two classic dimensions of federalism: "*Self-rule* is the authority that a subnational government exercises in its own territory. *Shared rule* is the authority that a subnational government co-exercises in the country as a whole" (23). The first dimension is operationalized through the following variables: institutional depth, policy scope, fiscal autonomy, borrowing autonomy, and representation. These relate, respectively, to institutional autonomy from the central government, the range of policy competences, the degree of tax-raising and borrowing autonomy, and the degree to which regional office-holders are directly elected – hence independently from other bodies (25). As for shared rule, this captures regions' involvement at central level in law making, executive control, fiscal control, borrowing control, and constitutional reform (26). The index also measures the extent of a/symmetry within each of the two main dimensions. Hooghe et al. build upon many of the insights of previous indices while also going significantly further in terms of the analytical purview of the measures as well as their cross-sectional and cross-temporal scope. It is thus the most exhaustive index currently available. Although it is based on the notions of self-rule and shared rule that are at the heart of the concept of federalism, it does not define how its measures of regional authority relate to the conceptual distinction between unitary and federal states.

In sum, the qualitative typologies and the quantitative indices have developed largely in isolation from each other and little attempt to combine their strengths – and thus minimize their limitations – has been carried out. While the categories of qualitative typologies are often weakly specified and would benefit from a more rigorous definition, the quantitative indices seek to measure aspects of the unitary/federal conceptualization but do not generally attempt to identify a boundary between them. To my knowledge, the only exception is Keman (2001, 205), who puts forward a dichotomous typology of federal/unitary systems in Western Europe based on factor analysis calculations. Scores below zero indicate degrees of unitarism whereas scores above zero measure degrees of federalism, where zero thus constitutes the boundary between the two categories. While a qualitative typology built on quantitative indicators is very much in the spirit of what I am proposing below, Keman's index does not take into account the presence of asymmetrical autonomy – as the scores reported in table A1 show – and therefore does not fully capture a key aspect of state structures that is of considerable interest for the purposes of this book.

A New Integrated Approach

In light of the preceding discussion, the method I have adopted is based on a combination of the two approaches to produce a typology based on Hooghe et al.'s index scores. I depart from Hooghe et al.'s approach in conceptualizing the essence of federal arrangements as the presence of strong self-rule (or regional autonomy) rather than self-rule plus shared rule (or regional authority). This is on the ground that only when deciding for its own citizens without – or with little – interference from the centre or from other regions, can a regional government be considered autonomous. When it contributes to central decisions, in contrast, it is always (unless unanimous consent of the regions is required or bilateral arrangements are in place) dependent on other governments and is thus not autonomous.[6] Self-rule thus more accurately captures *autonomy* as opposed to *authority*. For this reason, I use the RAI regional self-rule scores (hereafter, RAI-RSF) as more valid measures, on the ground that they better "capture the ideas contained in the corresponding concept" (Adcock and Collier 2001, 530).

I focus on three key variables: 1) the presence of strong regional government/s, defined as a RAI-RSF score of at least 13;[7] 2) the proportion of the population living under strong regional government; 3) whether such regional governments are constitutionally incorporated or not.[8] This yields a typology of four categories:

a) unitary state: no regional or macro-local government[9] has a RAI-RSF score higher than 12 hence there is no strong regional government;
b) unitary state with special autonomy: there is one – or more – constitutionally incorporated strong regional governments but such autonomy only concerns up to 10 percent of the country's population;
c) partially federal state: more than 10 but less than 100 percent of the population live under strong regional government;
d) federal state: the entire population live under strong regional government (table A1 summarizes the differences between this typology and those previously put forward by other authors).

1.2 CONCEPTUALIZING AND MAPPING STATE RESTRUCTURING

In broad terms, state restructuring can be defined as a significant change in the way a state is structured. As stated above, the structures of interest in this case are the vertical structures of the territorial administration of the state. For the purposes of this book, state restructuring is thus a form of institutional change related to the vertical structures of the state. Abstracting from the different forms it takes, discussed below, state restructuring is understood here as an overarching concept, as defined by Collier et al. (2012, 223).

Forms and Categories of State Restructuring

On the basis of the typology proposed above, I identify thirty-two specific forms of state restructuring, which can be divided into two broad categories. The first, or strong, category consists of changes that entail a transition from one category to another, leading to a difference of kind. An example of this is a transition from a unitary to a partially federal state. The second, or weak, category is made up of changes that do not entail a transition from one category to another, i.e., changes of degree rather than kind. This would be the case, for example, of a unitary state introducing a tier of weak regional governments. Table A2 outlines the possibilities. When it comes to deciding which form of state restructuring is more significant – i.e., more consequential for the way the state functions – two criteria should arguably be kept in mind: the magnitude of the change and the proportion of the population affected by it. Thus, a transition from a unitary to a federal order is certainly more consequential than a minor increase in the autonomy of macro-local government in a unitary state. It is however more difficult to compare a modest change affecting the entire population of a country with a more radical change affecting only a small proportion of the population. This would be the case, for instance, of the introduction of a tier of weak regional governments for the whole country versus the granting of strong autonomy to a small territory. As explained below, the selection of cases for the analysis performed in this book has been made in the light of these two criteria.

Mapping State Structures in Western Europe since 1950

Applying the preceding conceptualizations, we can develop a cross-sectional and cross-temporal map of state structures in Western Europe.[10] Starting with Austria, this was a federal state in 1950 and is still such today but its regional governments have lost autonomy, from a score of 15 to 14. This is a case of weak restructuring within an unchanged federal order, or type B9.2. Belgium, in contrast, is one of the cases in which state restructuring has been most profound. It was a unitary state in 1950 with a traditional macro-local level of government – the provinces – scoring 10. Through a succession of constitutional reforms, it has transformed itself into a federal state whose component units – regions/communities – score 14 on the RAI-RSF. Belgium is thus a case of restructuring from unitary to federal, or type A1.1. Denmark was a unitary state with special autonomy in 1950. The traditional macro-local government on the mainland – the counties – scored 6 while the Faroe Islands[11] enjoyed strongly autonomous regional government, scored 17. While the Faroes have maintained their autonomy,[12] on the mainland the counties were first granted higher autonomy and later replaced by a new tier of weak regional governments, scoring 7 on the RAI-RSF. This is a case of two-step restructuring resulting in a modest increase in the autonomy of the mainland subcentral governments within an unchanged unitary with special autonomy order, or type B3.1. Finland has undergone a similar evolution. It was a unitary state with special autonomy in 1950, with very weak traditional macro-local units – the provinces – scoring 1 and the strongly autonomous Åland Islands,[13] scoring 17. The latter have maintained their autonomy while on the mainland the provinces have been replaced by a new tier of macro-local units, scoring 6 on the RAI-RSF. This is a case of restructuring resulting in a modest increase in the autonomy of mainland subcentral governments within an unchanged unitary with special autonomy order, or type B6.1.

France was a unitary state in 1950, whose traditional units of macro-local government – the *départements* – scored 7 on the RAI-RSF. Decentralization reforms in the 1980s introduced a tier of weak regional governments – scoring 10 – as well as increased the autonomy of the *départements*, now also scoring 10. France is thus a case of restructuring consisting of parallel reforms modestly increasing the autonomy of subcentral governments within an unchanged unitary order, or types B2.1 and B5.1. Germany was a federal state in 1950, with strong regional governments – the *Länder* – scoring 17. The country has undergone a degree of centralization, notably when it comes to the legislative and financial autonomy of the *Länder*, whose score has dropped to 15. This is a case of restructuring modestly weakening the autonomy of regional governments without altering the federal order of the state, or type B9.2.

Ireland was a unitary state in 1950, with traditional counties as macro-local units of government. They are not scored by Hooghe et al. (2016) because they fall below the population criterion the authors use but their level of autonomy can be estimated at 7. A non-directly elected layer of regional units consisting of consortia of counties has been introduced, scoring 6. In this case restructuring has been minimal as the counties have remained the main intermediate level and the overall autonomy of subcentral governments has not changed, or type B3.1.

Italy was a partially federal state in 1950. Most of the population lived under unitary government and was administered by traditional units of macro-local government – the provinces – scoring 8. The regions of Aosta Valley, Sardinia, Sicily, and Trentino-South Tyrol had a special autonomy status, scored at 12 by the RAI-RSF.[14] Through the implementation of a constitutional provision for the creation of ordinary status regions in the 1960–70s and further reform in the 1990s–early 2000s, strong regional government – scored 15 – has been extended to the entire territory and the distinction between special and ordinary regions has de facto largely disappeared. Italy is thus a case of transition from a partially federal to a federal order, or type A6.1.

The Netherlands was a unitary state in 1950, whose traditional units of macro-local government – the provinces – scored 8. Their autonomy has increased to 10 thus placing the country in the category of modest increase in subcentral autonomy within an unchanged unitary order, or type B5.1. A similar evolution can be observed in Norway. The autonomy of the traditional counties has increased substantially – from 5 to 12 – but the unitary nature of the state has not changed, hence restructuring has taken a B5.1 form.

Portugal was under an authoritarian regime in 1950 with a unitary and centralized structure based on districts, scoring 2. In the wake of democratization in the 1970s, the offshore territories of the Azores and Madeira[15] have been granted strong autonomy – scored 15 – while the mainland districts have been abolished. This is a case of transition from a unitary order to a unitary with special autonomy one, or type A3.1. Like Portugal, Spain was under a highly centralized authoritarian regime in 1950, with a tier of traditional macro-local units – the provinces – scoring 3.[16] With the return to democracy in the 1970s, strong regional governments have been set up – scoring 14 and 15. This has entailed a transformation from a unitary to a federal order, or type A1.1.

Sweden and Switzerland, by contrast, have experienced no change. The former was and still is a unitary state, with traditional macro-local units – the counties – scoring 12. The latter has been throughout a federal state with regional governments scoring 18.

Lastly, the UK was a unitary state with special autonomy in 1950. Great Britain was divided into counties – scoring 10 – while Northern Ireland had a special home rule autonomy status, also scoring 10[17]. Devolution reforms since the 1990s have restored home rule in Northern Ireland[18] and created strong regional governments in Scotland and Wales[19] – scored 14 and 9,[20] respectively. This has entailed a change in the constitutional nature of the state from a unitary system with special autonomy to a partially federal state, or type A5.1. Table A3 summarizes this overview.

Four Clusters of Cases

Four clusters of cases emerge from this mapping exercise. The first is made up of states where restructuring has been absent or minimal. Here we can place Austria, Germany, Ireland, Sweden, and Switzerland. In a second cluster we can place those cases where state restructuring has consisted in increasing the autonomy of traditional macro-local units. The Netherlands and Norway fall into this group. A third cluster comprises cases in which new subcentral governments have been introduced with significant consequences for the functioning of the state but without change in the latter's constitutional order. Denmark and France – as well as, to a lesser extent, Finland – can be placed here. The last cluster is formed by those states that have experienced a constitutional transition, i.e., have moved from one conceptual category of state structures to another. Here we find Belgium, Italy, Portugal, Spain, and the UK. Broadly speaking, the four clusters can be seen as displaying ascending strength of state restructuring.

As discussed above, however, we also need to take into account the percentage of the population affected by restructuring. This is notably the case as regards Portugal, where there has been a change of constitutional order but such change has, in practice, concerned less than 5 percent of the population. Denmark and France, in contrast, although they have not undergone a change of constitutional nature, have experienced state restructuring affecting the entire state population. Hence, in substantive terms, Denmark and France are arguably more significant cases of restructuring than Portugal.[21] As I outline in greater detail in the next chapter, the states I have selected for analysis are thus Belgium, Italy, Spain, and the UK as cases of strong restructuring, and Denmark and France as cases of weak, but significant, restructuring.

1.3 THREE ASPECTS OF STATE RESTRUCTURING

Drawing on the existing literature, we can identify three properties of state restructuring that are key to understanding its nature: a) first, state restructuring takes place through what we can call "critical junctures"; b) second, it is a product of party competition and cooperation; and c) third, there two distinct dynamics through which it manifests itself. I briefly describe them in the following sections.

State Restructuring through Critical Junctures

The main empirical accounts of processes of state restructuring in Western Europe (e.g., Bogdanor 1999; Cotta and Verzichelli 2007, 171–201; Deschouwer 2009, 42–54; Moreno 2001) point out that they have been the product of reforms typically concentrated in discrete and relatively short periods of time. Borrowing the concept of critical junctures employed in historical institutionalism HI (e.g., Lipset and Rokkan 1967, 37–41; Collier and Collier 1991, 27–39; Capoccia and Kelemen 2007), we can call them critical junctures of state restructuring. Although in some cases we find only one critical juncture, in most cases restructuring has been the product of reforms clustered in several critical junctures. Each of these multiple junctures often have distinct characteristics so understanding how state restructuring has come about requires understanding how the decision to restructure was taken in each juncture of the process. In the six states selected for analysis, sixteen main critical junctures can be identified, as follows.

In Belgium state restructuring has been the product of six rounds of constitutional reform taking place in 1970, 1980, 1988, 1993, 2001, and 2013, which I label BE1 to BE6. In Italy we find two critical junctures. The first consisted in the implementation of the ordinary regions in the 1960s and 1970s. The second juncture is the phase marked by the rise of the Lega Nord from the mid-1990s and the response of the statewide parties, which culminated in the constitutional reform of 2001. I label the first IT1 and the latter IT2. In Spain too we can distinguish two main critical junctures. The first one consists in the adoption of the constitutional provision for the creation of autonomous communities in the 1978 constitution and the subsequent establishment of such communities between 1979 and 1983. The second juncture is the revision of the autonomy statute in several regions in the 2000s and 2010s, which in the case of Catalonia has triggered a secessionist challenge with the potential to have a profound impact on the constitutional order of the state. I label the two junctures ES1 and ES2, respectively.

Three junctures can be identified in the UK. The first one is the failed attempt to establish directly elected devolved assemblies in Scotland and Wales in the 1970s.[22] The second one is the successful establishment of the Scottish parliament and the Welsh assembly in the late 1990s. The third one is marked by the drive toward the 2014 independence referendum in Scotland and the subsequent enactment of the Scotland Act 2016 as well as the empowerment of the Welsh assembly culminating in the March 2011 referendum and the Wales Act 2014. These are labelled UK1, UK2, and UK3. In Denmark we find two junctures. The first one consisted in a reduction in the number of counties and their empowerment in 1970. The second was the replacement of the traditional counties with larger regional units in 2007. I label them DK1 and DK2. In France, lastly, we find only one critical juncture: the decentralization reforms of the 1980s, which empowered the *départements* and established directly elected regional councils.[23] It is labelled FR1. Table A4 lists them.

State Restructuring as a Product of Party Competition and Cooperation

A second important insight from the literature is that state restructuring reforms are enacted by political parties engaged in competition, as well as cooperation, with each other. The agency of political parties is the key mechanism that connects structural pressures for change to the actual enactment of reforms. The theoretical literature on ethnic politics and demands for regional self-government places great emphasis on the crucial role played by political parties. Newman argues (1996, 3) that "in most democracies the dominant form of ethnoregional conflict occurs among political parties." Lecours (2000) conceptualizes elite agency such as party strategies as the decisive mechanism through which ethnic identities are politicized and mobilized around demands for regional autonomy. In a similar vein Van Houten (2003) argues: "the most important conclusion ... is that any possible influence of globalization on autonomy demands is mediated by political factors" (132) and "globalization creates pressures and incentives for political actors to change governance structures but electoral and party competition are important intervening factors" (133). Sorens (2009), Alonso (2012), and Amat and Falcó-Gimeno (2014) squarely explain state restructuring as a product of partisan logic. Likewise, the empirical accounts of the main processes of state restructuring cited above also stress the central role played by political parties. To understand state restructuring is thus essential to analyze party agency in the critical junctures through which the process has unfolded.

Two Dynamics of State Restructuring

The last, but most consequential, aspect to consider is what we can call the dynamic that state restructuring takes. I identify two such dynamics and label them "bottom up" and "top down,"[24] respectively. By bottom up I mean a process driven by a demand for self-government coming from one or more regions. This is usually articulated by a competitive challenge brought by a regionalist party – typically a regional-nationalist one[25] – to statewide parties, to which the latter, under certain conditions, react by enacting a reform of the structures of the state. Regional parties are unlikely ever to be in a position to implement state restructuring directly and rely on their challenge to the statewide parties to push the latter toward adopting devolution policies. The challenge presented by a regional-nationalist party should be understood as a dual one. On the one hand, there is the electoral challenge brought to parties that rely significantly on support from the region or regions in which the party/ies operate/s to win office at the state level. Many authors argue that this is the key mechanism through which state restructuring takes place (e.g., Rudolph 1977, 416; Newman 1995; Fearon and Van Houten 2002; O'Neill 2003; Meguid 2008; Sorens 2009; Alonso 2012; Elias et al. 2015).

On the other hand, though, such parties also pose a territorial integrity challenge. This can be explicit, if they have a secessionist position, or implicit, if they have an autonomist position. The latter is on the ground that their nationalist stance implies a claim to self-determination and that independent statehood is the usual way of achieving it, hence an autonomist position always carries the risk of transforming itself into a secessionist one if not satisfied.[26] As such, the territorial integrity challenge brought to bear by regional-nationalist parties affects also those statewide parties that do not heavily rely from an electoral point of view on the region/s where the regional-nationalist parties operate. In response to these challenges, statewide parties implement strong state restructuring as an attempt to see them off, although the effectiveness of such response is open to question (Erk and Anderson 2009). This dynamic typically produces the adoption of forms of "holding together" federalism (Linz 1997), and there is indeed evidence that in the cases of strong state restructuring – i.e., entailing, as defined above, constitutional change – the dynamic, in aggregate terms, appears to have been of the bottom-up variety (Bogdanor 1999; Cotta and Verzichelli 2007, 171–201; Deschouwer 2009, 42–54; Moreno 2001).

To borrow Kingdon's (1995) terminology, the challenge from regional-nationalist parties can be seen to join a *policy* stream (i.e., the demand for devolution) to a *problem* stream (the electoral and territorial integrity threat) and open up a *politics* stream – i.e., pushing a statewide party – as policy entrepreneur, to enact state restructuring reforms.

The opposite dynamic can be observed where state restructuring is the product of a top-down decision by central state actors in the absence of a demand for autonomy coming from the regions themselves. In these cases, party competition and cooperation is restricted to statewide actors and restructuring typically takes a weak form, as defined above. The driver of state restructuring in these cases is not holding together the state but improving the effectiveness and the efficiency of its territorial administration. Denmark and France fit into this category (e.g., Vrangbæk 2010; Schmidt 1990). Table A5 summarizes the salient features of the two dynamics.

While most whole empirical cases – i.e., where the unit of observation is the state as a whole as opposed to a critical juncture – tend to match either dynamic quite closely, it is also possible that different dynamics may characterize different critical junctures within the same overall process at different points in time. Italy appears to be a case in point. While its first critical juncture fits the description of a top-down dynamic, its second one was marked by a bottom-up dynamic (Cotta and Verzichelli 2007, 171–201). The existence of two different dynamics and their presence sometimes within the same overall process underscores the value of performing the analysis at the level of each critical juncture as well as at that of the country, as discussed in the next chapter. Table A6 matches the critical junctures included in the analysis to the type of dynamic.

1.4 SUMMARY

In this chapter I have sought to conceptualize state restructuring. Adopting an integrated qualitative and qualitative approach, I have developed a typology of state structures and how they change over time. A crucial distinction emerging from this classification exercise is that between strong state restructuring, i.e., entailing a change of constitutional status, and weak state restructuring, where a change of constitutional category does not take place. Mapping these conceptual categories against the evolution of state structures in Western Europe since 1950 yields four clusters of cases, on the basis of which, as outlined in the next chapter, I have selected the cases for the analysis performed in the book. I have also identified three aspects of state restructuring that have an important bearing on the questions the book seeks to address. First, the fact that restructuring typically takes place through critical junctures – i.e., distinct phases of reform that mark a turning point in the evolution of the state – calls for a critical juncture-level analysis rather than a country-level one. Even within the same state, such critical junctures often display significantly different features and it is valuable to analyze each of them separately in order to be able to capture as much as possible the nature of the process. Second, within each critical juncture the decision to enact state restructuring is typically the product of party agency in the context of competition and cooperation with other parties. We thus need to analyze party behaviour within those critical junctures to be able to unpack the mechanisms leading to state restructuring decisions. Third, we can identify two distinct dynamics through which state restructuring manifests itself: bottom up and top down. These differ in terms of the presence or absence of demands for self-government, the nature of party competition and cooperation, and the objectives and magnitude of restructuring. As discussed in the next chapter, European integration can be expected to have a very different influence on state restructuring depending on the dynamic the latter takes. To this we can now turn.

2

Theorizing and Testing the Influence of European Integration

In this chapter, after briefly conceptualizing European integration, I theorize how integration may influence state restructuring, and outline the methodology adopted to analyze the connection between the two. I present a realist bargain theoretical model of the causal connections between integration and restructuring. The theory rests on two main claims. The first is that European integration generates different opportunities, incentives, and constraints (OICs) to political parties in relation to state restructuring. The second is that parties react to these OICs to different extents, depending in particular whether they are regional-nationalist or statewide parties. Bearing in mind the distinction introduced in the previous chapter between top-down and bottom-up dynamics of restructuring, the realist bargain theory expects European integration to have a much more significant influence on state restructuring where the latter takes a bottom-up form as opposed to a top-down one. The crucial difference between the two is accounted for by the agency of regional-nationalist parties, which are key actors in bottom-up dynamics but are absent from top-down ones. I label the theory realist bargain because it emphasizes the role played by secessionist challenges and the bargain nature of the interaction between regional-nationalist and statewide parties.

In the third part of the chapter I describe the research design and the methods adopted to test the theory. I designed the study as a comparative historical analysis research, based on a periodization of European integration into five phases and cases selected across four levels of analysis. The main method I employ is qualitative content analysis of parties' rhetorical strategies at the time of elections and referendums within critical junctures of state restructuring, supplemented by synoptic comparative analyses of the *how* and the *to what extent* questions, the first of which performed with a qualitative comparative analysis (QCA) methodology.

2.1 CONCEPTUALIZING EUROPEAN INTEGRATION

For the purposes of this book, I conceptualize European integration as the process of developing what is today the European Union. This encompasses the creation of the institutions of the European Union, the progressive transfer of legal competences to these institutions, the development of public policies based on them, and the accompanying political, economic, social, and cultural effects engendered by the development of the EU. By virtue of such integration, a growing proportion of public policy has come to be made collectively by the EU member states rather than by each of them individually. Following Hix and Høyland (2011, 2–16), this can be thought of as the process of building a suprastate political system.

One aspect of the overall process of European integration that is of particular importance for our purposes here is the effect that the European Union has on its member states, even in areas where no transfer of competences to the EU has taken place, ranging from public policy to institutional setups to electoral campaigning. This is referred to as Europeanization (e.g., Börzel 2005) and is often thought of as the downloading aspect of European integration, as opposed to the uploading of competences and resources from the member states to the EU level.[1]

2.2 A REALIST BARGAIN THEORY OF EUROPEAN INTEGRATION AND STATE RESTRUCTURING

The theory rests on a postulate and four ancillary propositions. The postulate is that, given the centrality of political parties in processes of state restructuring, European integration can be said to influence state restructuring if it affects the agency of political parties in relation to the latter, notably in the critical junctures through which it unfolds. If we accept this postulate, four propositions follow. First, European integration affects party agency because its properties generate opportunities and incentives for parties to engage in restructuring as well as placing constraints on them from doing so.

Opportunities, incentives, and constraints (OICs) can be conceptualized as follows: opportunities are circumstances that facilitate the pursuit of previously adopted goals; incentives are circumstances that induce actors to adopt new goals; constraints are circumstances that constrain actors' ability to pursue their goals.[2] Such OICs vary depending on multiple factors, such as the phase of integration, a party's policy on state restructuring, its ideological position, its attitudes toward Europe, and so forth – hence parties will react to them to a different extent cross-sectionally and cross-temporally. At a general level, second, parties' reaction to the OICs generated by integration can be expected to be determined by two variables: a) the balance between, on the one hand, opportunities and incentives, and, on the other, constraints; b) the salience of state restructuring for a given party (Benoit and Laver 2006, 31–3). Other things being equal, we can expect the more positive the perceived balance and the higher the salience of restructuring, the greater a party's reaction. Third, parties can be expected to react by exploiting the opportunities and the incentives offered by integration in their strategies while minimizing the constraints. In other words, we can expect them to make a *selective* use of the European dimension. Fourth, on the basis of the above postulate and other things again being equal, the more intense parties' exploitation of Europe in pursuit of state restructuring within a given critical juncture, the greater European integration's positive – in the statistical sense – influence on the latter. Developing the theory from these foundations, in the following two sections I first identify what OICs European integration generates in relation to state restructuring and subsequently I analyze how these can be expected to affect the agency of political parties.

Opportunities, Incentives, Constraints for State Restructuring

In order to identify such OICs we need to distinguish between the two dynamics of state restructuring conceptualized in the previous chapter – top down and bottom up – and bear in mind the different types of parties playing a role within them, in particular the distinction between regional-nationalist and statewide parties. All the cases of state restructuring analyzed in this book entail the creation or strengthening of regional governments, so I focus on OICs in relation to granting powers to regional governments.[3] As pointed out in chapter 1, however, regional-nationalist parties play an important role in bottom-up dynamics of state restructuring by articulating a demand for independence. The OICs generated by European integration should thus be understood in relation not only to empowering regional governments but also to seeking (for regional-nationalist parties) or preventing (for statewide parties) independence.

TOP-DOWN DYNAMIC

As seen in chapter 1, three features characterize top-down dynamics of state restructuring: a) statewide parties are the only actors; b) restructuring is weak, i.e., it entails changes of degree rather than of kind; c) parties typically engage in such restructuring to improve the effectiveness and efficiency of public administration, particularly in relation to economic planning and health services, as well as purportedly to bring government "closer to the people" (e.g., Schmidt 1990 on France and Vrangbæk 2010 on Denmark). To theorize the influence of integration in processes characterized by this dynamic we need to understand how the evolving properties of the EU might generate OICs in relation to such motivations.

Considering economic planning first, there are two main ways in which European integration might create opportunities and incentives for state restructuring. The first is through the connection between market integration and regional economic specialization. Based on the experience of the USA, the general expectation among economists was that deepening market integration and monetary union would increase territorial specialization across the EU (e.g., Krugman 1993). Evidence for the period between the mid-1960s and the early 1990s indicates that economic dynamics converged between regions across state borders thus suggesting that specialization might have operated at the level of regions rather than of states (Fatás 1997). In this light it could be argued that economic planning would need to be carried out at regional level to be effective and that directly elected regional governments are better placed than central government bodies to do so. Several authors suggest regional governments endowed with significant powers are necessary in order to enact effective economic development policies in an integrated European market (e.g., Keating 1993, 308; Cheshire 1995, 27; Anderson and Goodman 1995, 614–20). Hence, integration can be seen to generate incentives for granting powers to regional governments in order to make economic planning more effective in an increasingly regionally specialized European economy. While this hypothesis has prima facie theoretical plausibility, I expect the connection to be likely weaker than postulated by these authors, for two reasons.

First, the emphasis on regional economic planning predates the onset of European integration (e.g., Robson 1942) and has declined over time while the latter has deepened (e.g., Hayward and Watson 2009). Regional economic planning appears to be much more a function of the prevailing economic model adopted than of the dynamics of integration. Second, the assumption that directly elected institutions are more effective than functional bodies operating either as deconcentrated units of the central administration or as agencies of traditional local and/or macro-local governments does not seem to be warranted. As will be seen in chapters 3 and 4, in both France and Italy, the cases most often cited in support of the link between planning and regionalization, the emphasis was on democratization rather than planning per se.

The second, and more direct, way in which European integration might generate opportunities and incentives to establish regional governments for planning purposes is through the operation of the EU regional policy, especially since its 1988 reform. The requirement to involve subcentral government in the management of the funds, under the principle of partnership, has been theorized to lead to an empowerment of the regions (e.g., Marks 1993, 407; Keating 1995; Hooghe 1996; Hooghe and Marks 2001, 81–118; Bartolini 2005, 261). From this perspective, integration is seen as generating an incentive to establish regional governments endowed with significant powers in order to manage such funds more effectively and efficiently.

Here again, however, there are three main reasons for scepticism. The first is that the structural funds, like economic planning more generally, can be effectively managed by functional bodies without a direct political legitimation, i.e., unlike the directly elected regional institutions with which we are concerned here. Where new bodies have been set up specifically to manage the structural funds, such as in Ireland, these have been of a functional character. The second is that the geographical areas eligible for funding very often do not coincide with existing regional units and hence do not strengthen the latter as units of decentralized administration. Moreover, the funds' regulations – notably the 75 percent of GDP requirement for objective 1 (later, convergence) funding – offer incentives for defining eligible areas in a way that deliberately does not match regional boundaries. A glaring example is the West and South Wales area, which was purposefully carved out to meet the 75 percent rule (McAllister 2000, 44). Studies that have set out to test the degree to which EU regional policy empowers the regions have found remarkably little evidence of such an empowerment (e.g., Bache and Jones 2000). Likewise, data from the 2007–13 period show that there is no correlation between the level of autonomy and the amount of structural funding a region receives (Chalmers 2013). My expectation is thus that this factor is also a weak motivator for state restructuring, either as an opportunity or as an incentive.

When it comes to the connection between Europe and the organization of health services, this is largely unaddressed in the literature but is potentially of growing salience. Although the EU does not have a formal health policy, its market regulation has increasingly encroached on the way health systems operate (Greer 2006 and 2009; Lamping 2013). Integration could thus potentially be seen as having a bearing on the territorial organization of health services. Costa-i-Font and Greer (2013, 20–4) list four main reasons for health-system decentralization: a) a desire to better match services to the heterogeneity of preferences across the territory; b) a desire to improve the degree of accountability and responsiveness of health service providers; c) in countries facing bottom-up demands for autonomy and/or independence, health services are often devolved as part of a wider package driven by political considerations that are typically unrelated to health policy per se; d) decentralization may favour positive experimentation. In light of these rationales, though, it is difficult to see how integration might generate significant opportunities and incentives to modify existing structures or place constraints on doing so.

In relation to the state restructuring motivation of bringing government closer to the people, European integration is unlikely to generate a significant incentive to do so but it might offer an opportunity. The EU's adoption of the principle of subsidiarity in the Maastricht Treaty has been seen by some authors (e.g., Ladrech 1994, 82; Jones 1995, 294–5) as providing an external legitimation for the devolution of powers toward a regional tier of government, on the ground that the shift of power upward toward the EU level purportedly requires a corresponding shift downward to achieve a balanced provision of public services and maintain citizens' engagement with politics. Top-down state restructuring, however, often entails a transfer of powers to the regional level from lower tiers of government – e.g., in order to achieve economies of scale in the provision of public services – which is difficult to defend from such a balancing argument. This opportunity, therefore, is unlikely to be powerful enough to shape actors' behaviour significantly. By the same token, it is also difficult to identify how Europe might possibly prevent statewide parties from engaging in state restructuring driven by this motivation.

In sum, we can conclude that European integration does not offer powerful opportunities or incentives to statewide parties to enact top-down state restructuring, nor does it place notable constraints on them in doing so. Even in the more recent phases of integration – in which the effect of the structural funds and of the principle of subsidiarity could be detected – they are unlikely to affect their strategies to a significant extent.

BOTTOM-UP DYNAMIC

Processes of state restructuring characterized by a bottom-up dynamic, as argued in the previous chapter, are marked by the following features: a) there are two distinct sets of actors: regional-nationalist parties and statewide ones; b) the process is triggered by a bottom-up demand for self-government – which often includes a secession threat – coming from one or more regions and articulated by the regional-nationalist parties in competition with their statewide rivals; c) restructuring takes a strong form, i.e., entailing a change of kind rather than merely of degree; d) state restructuring is typically enacted by statewide parties as a response to a regional-nationalist challenge. In these cases, European integration generates distinct OICs to the two sets of actors and appreciating the differences between them is essential in order to understand the influence of integration on state restructuring. In theorizing such OICs, the assumption here is that parties are motivated by both policy and office goals (Müller and Strøm 1999) and seek to optimize the trade-off between the two whenever a conflict between them emerges. In terms of state structures policy, the assumption is that regional-nationalist parties' central goal is to maximize autonomy for their region – which, in its strongest form, implies ultimately aspiring to independence[4] – while statewide parties want to retain as much power at the central state level as possible as well as the territorial integrity of the state. In relation to regional-nationalist parties, OICs thus need to be analyzed in relation to their pursuit of autonomy and/or independence while for statewide parties OICs relate to countering such pursuit in order to preserve powers and territory.

Considering regional-nationalist parties first and drawing on the literature on minority nationalism and European integration (e.g., Lynch 1996; De Winter and Gomez-Reino 2002; Jolly 2007; Laible 2008; Elias 2009; Hepburn 2010), we can identify four main ways in which integration offers them opportunities and incentives in their pursuit of autonomy. The first opportunity is related to the erosion of the notion of monolithic statehood. As significant policy-making powers are transferred to the EU level, so further away from the citizens, it becomes easier to cloak a demand for devolution of powers to the regions as a counter-balance to the former, thus conferring to it greater legitimacy and an aura of being in tune with the course of history rather than a backward move, an accusation to which they had long been subjected to in the past. This was particularly the case in the late 1980s to early 1990s, when the EU appeared to embrace the notion of a Europe of the Regions and adopted subsidiarity as one of its guiding principles.

A second opportunity relates specifically to the pursuit of independence. Integration offers a significant opportunity to regional-nationalist parties with a secessionist policy because it embodies the rejection of violence to settle disputes and the primacy given to negotiation and compromise. This is significant because secession still carries considerable stigma in many countries and has historically been associated with violent repression, notably in Spain. From this perspective, EU membership acts as a safeguard against the state's possible temptation to use violent means to prevent a region from seceding, thus removing an obstacle to regional-nationalist parties pursuing a secessionist policy.

A third key factor also relates to the pursuit of independence and can be conceptualized as both an opportunity and an incentive. Economic integration, specifically in the form of the single market and monetary union, makes smaller states more economically viable as it breaks the link between the size of the state and the potential size of the market, as well as guaranteeing regulatory continuity for market actors (Birch 1978, 336; Meadwell and Martin 1996; Alesina and Spolaore 1997 and 2003, 213–14; Bolton and Roland 1997, 1066; Alesina et al. 2000). In other words, it reduces the economic costs of independence and offers regional-nationalist parties the opportunity to counter resistance to independence on economic grounds more effectively. As economic integration increased greatly over time, particularly with the completion of the single market and the implementation of monetary union, we should expect such an opportunity/incentive to be particularly powerful in the most recent periods of integration. The distinction between opportunity and incentive can be thought of as follows. It is an opportunities for those parties that had a long-standing policy of independence, particularly so if this was adopted before the onset of integration, such as in the case of the Scottish National Party (SNP). It should be conceptualized as an incentive, though, for those who traditionally aimed at autonomy within the existing state borders as it gives them an incentive to shift their policy in favour of independence.

Lastly, European integration generates another powerful opportunity/incentive – the distinction is the same as above – for regional-nationalist parties to pursue independence through the biases of its institutional architecture (Birch 1978, 336). The first element of this opportunity/incentive is constituted by the fact that the shift of policymaking responsibilities to the EU level produces an incentive to gain access to decision-making at that level. Because the key decisions are taken by state governments in the Council of Ministers and the European Council, this is effectively an incentive to acquire statehood so as to gain representation in those bodies. The second element is the fact that small states are over-represented in all the key EU institutions, producing a systemic small state bias (e.g., Bindseil and Handtke 1997). In contrast, the channels for regions' direct access to EU decision-making – essentially, the Committee of the Regions – have too weak an influence to constitute a satisfactory alternative. Likewise, regions' access to Council decision-making on behalf of their state is also a weak alternative as such an arrangement only works satisfactorily for regions in symmetrical federal systems such as Germany rather than stateless nations in contexts such as Belgium, Spain, or the UK. The upshot is a strong advantage for statehood over regionhood, hence a powerful opportunity/incentive for regional-nationalist parties to pursue the former rather than content themselves with the latter. The more is decided at the EU level, the greater the incentive to access decision-making at that level so we can expect this factor too to have become stronger over time as integration has deepened.

For the reasons already discussed in relation to the top-down dynamic, I do not regard the EU regional policy as providing significant opportunities and incentives to regional-nationalist parties, either in relation to the pursuit of autonomy or independence. To the extent that a connection can be detected, it could be argued that, once again, it offers an additional incentive to seek statehood. This is on the ground that the crucial negotiations about regional policy occur in the context of seven-year financing packages, which, as Pollack (1995) argues, are "inter-governmental plays" dominated by state actors. Likewise the other factors discussed in the previous section as potentially offering opportunities and incentives to statewide parties to grant powers to regional government might also do so in relation to regional-nationalists' bottom-up demands, but they are likely to be marginal compared to the factors affecting the core objective of maximizing autonomy.

If integration offers powerful opportunities and incentives to regional-nationalist parties to pursue independence, it also creates non-negligible constraints, two of which are particularly significant. The first is that integration embodies an ethos of uniting peoples, which can be construed as militating against a policy of dividing existing states to create new, possibly ethnically defined, ones. From this perspective, the ethos of integration can be used as a rhetorical weapon to undermine calls for independence as it lends itself to a narrative branding such calls as "anti-European" and "against the tide of history." Recalling the first opportunity outlined above, we can thus say that, in ideational terms, integration facilitates demands for devolution but constrains demands for independence.

The second constraint is constituted by the uncertainty surrounding the legal framework governing the creation of new states within the EU. It has long been pointed out in the literature (e.g., Lane 1991) and confirmed by the 2014 referendum campaign in Scotland – discussed in chapter 7 – that there is a distinct possibility that new states born out of secession would find themselves initially outside the EU and would have to apply for membership (e.g., UKG 2013), and thus be subject to a potential veto on the part of the incumbent states from which they have seceded as well as other member states. If so, this would effectively grant incumbent states a veto on unilateral secessions and independence-minded regions would only be able to reap the benefit of EU membership described above in the case of an agreed dissolution of the incumbent state as opposed to secession.[5] In this way, the international and EU legal frameworks can be seen as constraining regional-nationalists' pursuit of independence because they undermine the feasibility of independence in Europe projects.

In a specular fashion, these constraints vis-à-vis regional-nationalist parties constitute opportunities for their statewide competitors as they facilitate the latter's defence of the constitutional status quo. An additional opportunity for statewide parties consists in the fact that regional governments with lawmaking powers are not easily accommodated within the EU decision-making process. No body with a formal stake in EU decision-making represents such regions effectively and alternative channels of representation are less than optimal. The institutional architecture of the EU could thus be seen as militating against the transformation of a state from a unitary to federal order on the grounds that the latter would be less effectively represented in EU decision-making.

In contrast to the situation prevailing in cases of top-down dynamics, European integration can thus be seen to generate much more powerful OICs for state restructuring in contexts of bottom-up dynamics, specifically in relation to the pursuit/threat of independence. It does so essentially vis-à-vis regional-nationalist parties, although what are constraints for them are also opportunities for their statewide opponents. We can also expect such OICs to be more sensitive to the degree of integration, becoming more powerful over time as the latter deepens. If opportunities and incentives on the one hand and constraints on the other may seem almost to cancel each other out and thus have no significant causal effect on state restructuring, the next section argues that this is not the case because the two sets of parties are likely to exploit them to a different extent.

Influence on Party Agency

We can expect all parties to react to the OICs European integration generates in relation to state restructuring in a selective way, i.e., by emphasizing favourable elements and neglecting or dismissing those perceived to be unfavourable. Such a reaction would vary depending on whether the process conforms to a top-down or a bottom-up dynamic as well as on the interplay of other variables, as discussed below.

TOP-DOWN DYNAMIC
We have already seen how the only agents playing a role in top-down forms of state restructuring are statewide parties. We have also seen in the previous section that there are no strong theoretical

reasons to expect European integration to offer significant opportunities and incentives to them to devolve power to a regional level of government or to create constraints on doing so. We should thus expect statewide parties to make little use of the European dimension in their competition over state restructuring. As the hypothesized causal mechanism is largely not at work in these cases, I expect European integration to have a minimal influence on state restructuring where the latter takes the form of a top-down dynamic. State restructuring in these cases is thus a game played entirely within a domestic context. As outlined below, this is tested on the cases of IT1, FR1, and DK2.

BOTTOM-UP DYNAMIC

A very different game and very different expectations about the influence of European integration apply to bottom-up state restructuring. In order to tease out the implications, we need to focus on three variables. The first one is the different strength of the opportunities and the incentives (relative to the constraints) that European integration offers to regional-nationalist and statewide parties, respectively. The more favourable the balance between them, the more likely a party will engage in strategic exploitation of European integration. The second is the asymmetry in the salience of state restructuring to the two sets of parties. The more salient state restructuring is for a party, the more likely it will be to exploit the European dimension in order to bring it about. The third one is a given party's attitudes to Europe.[6] The more positive such attitudes, the more likely the party will be to play the European card.

As we have seen in the previous section, European integration offers powerful opportunities and incentives to regional-nationalist parties to adopt an independentist position and to exploit the European dimension to maximize support for it, i.e., to engage in an independence in Europe strategy. Such opportunities and incentives have become more powerful over time as integration has deepened, hence the attraction of playing the European card has grown. We should thus expect regional-nationalist parties to do so increasingly. As rational actors, these parties will exploit Europe selectively, emphasizing that it makes independence viable and desirable for minority nations while sweeping under the carpet the fact that the EU legal framework makes unilateral secessions difficult. Given that securing independence or at least autonomy for their stateless nation is the paramount objective, if not the very raison d'être, for regional-nationalist parties, we can expect them to play the European card to the full. Their doing so, however, will also depend on their attitudes to Europe and this will vary by party and over time. Parties hostile to the EU and, especially, to the idea of integration itself would find it very difficult to exploit rhetorically what they oppose, in order to advance their other goals. Vice versa, parties with a positive attitude would find it natural to exploit the advantages the European dimension offers them.

In a specular situation to that of the regional-nationalist parties, the fact that the EU legal framework creates constraints on unilateral secessions and that state fragmentation might be construed as running counter to the ethos of European integration, present an opportunity to statewide parties in their effort to deal with a regional-nationalist challenge. Focusing on independence, however, even if from a negative perspective, might backfire for statewide parties as it carries the risk of making it appear mainstream and acceptable – merely difficult in the context of the EU. So statewide parties can also be seen as somewhat constrained in how far they can exploit such an argument. While I expect them to be, like their regional-nationalist counterparts, selective in their exploitation of the European dimension and influenced by their attitudes to it, I also expect them to play the European card to a much lesser extent, due to the effect of the first two variables discussed above. First, because the balance between opportunities and incentives on the one hand and constrains on the other appears objectively less favourable to them than to regional-nationalist parties. Second, because state restructuring generally has a lower salience for the statewide parties, which typically pursue a much wider set of objectives and compete primarily on the left-right spectrum of redistributive politics rather than on the centre-periphery one of territorial politics.

In light of the combined effect of these factors, we can expect regional-nationalist parties to exploit Europe more intensively than statewide parties in processes of bottom-up state restructuring, with a focus on the strategy of independence in Europe. If regional-nationalist parties benefit electorally from such a strategy and are thus in a stronger position to extract state restructuring from their statewide competitors, Europe can be seen to have had a positive

– in the statistical sense – influence on restructuring. This is tested on the cases of BE1-6, ES2, IT2, and UK1-3.

The Theory in a Nutshell

To summarize, the theory runs as follows:

a) Statewide parties only enact strong state restructuring if facing a significant challenge to their electoral position and/or to the territorial integrity of the state.
b) Regional-nationalist parties are the typical actors that pose such a challenge. The stronger the challenge posed by them, the more likely statewide parties will respond by enacting strong state restructuring. The challenge is strongest when regional-nationalist parties put forward a secessionist position, because it poses both an electoral and a territorial integrity challenge.
c) Europe offers more powerful OICs in relation to independence than to devolution.
d) Regional-nationalist parties face a more favourable set of opportunities and incentives versus constraints in relation to independence than statewide parties.
e) Regional-nationalist parties exploit Europe more than statewide parties because of d) and because state restructuring is more salient to them.
f) Parties' exploitation of Europe is selective, i.e., it stresses favourable elements and downplays unfavourable ones, dependent on a positive attitude to the EU and/or to integration and sensitive to the evolution of integration.
g) Regional-nationalist parties that have positive attitudes to integration can be expected over time to shift to a position of independence in Europe and to exploit the European dimension in their rhetorical strategies around it.
h) An independence in Europe strategy is likely to bring electoral benefits to regional-nationalist parties, thus making their challenge to the statewide parties more severe.
i) A more severe regional-nationalist challenge will make strong state restructuring more likely.
j) European integration thus has a positive influence on bottom-up state restructuring via the agency of regional-nationalist parties.

k) Europe offers weak OICs to statewide parties in relation to top-down state restructuring so we can expect them not to exploit it. As regional-nationalist parties are not present in this dynamic of state restructuring, European integration has no significant influence on it.

Why "Realist Bargain"?

I label this a realist bargain (RB) theory of the connection between European integration and state restructuring because of the following properties. First, the theory assumes that the agency of political actors, in this case of party leaders in particular, is dictated by bounded rationality. Actors react rationally to the opportunities, incentives, and constraints generated by the institutional context in which they operate in pursuit of their goals but such rationality is bounded by a number of factors, such as imperfect information, perceptions, and normative preferences.[7] Parties can be generally assumed to pursue a mix of policy and office goals but I hypothesize that regional-nationalist parties give a relative priority to policy while office is more important to statewide parties. Borrowing from the International Relations literature (e.g., Walt 2002), second, I refer to it as "realist" because it emphasizes the centrality of statehood, independence, and territorial integrity and the enduring relevance of the domestic/international dichotomy. European integration has a significant influence only through its connection with the pursuit of independence – and its mirror image, the secession threat – i.e., when the state restructuring game extends into the extra-state dimension. Conversely, when state restructuring is not enacted in response to a secession threat, European integration is largely uninfluential. Third, I refer to it as a bargain in the sense that state restructuring is the product of a competitive "dialectic" between regional-nationalist and statewide parties. To understand how European integration influences state restructuring it is thus crucial to appreciate the sequencing at the heart of its bottom-up version and the central role played within it by the competitive game between the two sets of parties. In this respect, the theory advanced here conforms to the model of "typological theory" discussed by George and Bennett (2005, 233–62).

Although the multilevel governance (MLG) theory does not aim to offer a fully specified theory of how Europe affects state restructuring, it has become the prevailing lens through which the connections between Europe and the regional level of politics are looked at (e.g., Marks 1993; Marks et al. 1996; Piattoni 2010). Its claim that integration empowers the regions, in spite of its vagueness, has been particularly influential and has spurred a considerable literature (e.g., Martin and Pearce 1993; Garmise 1997; Smyrl 1997; Bache and Jones 2000). It is thus valuable to see how the RB theory advanced here compares to the MLG approach. Four main elements of contrast are worth emphasizing. At the most basic level, RB offers a falsifiable specification of how integration influences state restructuring – hence the most significant form of regional empowerment – while MLG confines itself to observing that EU regional policy empowers the regions and that state governments are no longer the only actors in the multilevel EU polity. MLG, in particular, fails to draw a distinction between the process of state restructuring as defined here and relations between regional and central governments in contexts where institutional change is absent. Second, RB emphasizes the two-step, indirect way in which integration affects state restructuring and the crucial role played by regional-nationalist parties while MLG implicitly assumes a direct effect on the regions. Third, RB stresses the enduring relevance of the domestic/international dichotomy as underlined by the important role the pursuit of independence and the threat of secession play. According to the fluid world MLG posits, this would have lost importance. Fourth, and most important, while MLG also tends to assume a broadly uniform process of Europeanization and empowering, RB expects the mechanism activating a causal effect of integration on state restructuring to be present only in some countries and only at some points in time. As a result, far from being uniform, we can expect its effects to be highly uneven and punctuated.

2.3 TESTING THE THEORY: RESEARCH DESIGN AND METHODS

In this second part of the chapter I outline the research design and the methods that I have adopted to test the realist bargain theory. In the first section I explain the rationale for the adoption of a CHA approach based on long- and short-term process tracing. In the second section, I develop a periodization of integration in five phases and provide a stylized description of their salient features. In the following section, I illustrate the selection of cases across four levels of analysis. In the fourth section, I justify the choice of content analysis of parties' rhetorical strategies as the principal data gathering method. In the last two sections, I explain the methodology adopted to perform synoptic comparative analyses of the *how* and the *to what extent* questions.

A Comparative Historical Analysis Approach

Both European integration and state restructuring are phenomena that unfold over extended periods of time while the latter also occurs to a different extent and in different forms across political systems. To study the causal connections between them we thus need to perform a cross-temporal and cross-spatial analysis. A CHA approach based on long- and short-term process tracing is particularly suited to this task. According to Mahoney and Rueschemeyer (2003, 10), CHA is characterized by "a concern with causal analysis, an emphasis on processes over time, and the use of systematic and contextualized comparison." The concern with causal analysis sets it apart from historical-orientated work that seeks to provide an account of events but without engaging in the task of ascertaining whether and to what extent there is a causal relations between explanans and explanandum. The emphasis on temporal analysis enables the researcher to capture the unfolding of processes over time through particular attention played to aspects such as timing, duration, and sequencing, which may lead apparently similar causal factors to produce different outcomes. Systematic and contextualized comparison allows for a rigorous testing of hypotheses while benefiting from deep and contextually sensitive knowledge of the cases under analysis (10–15). The approach has much in common with historical institutionalism (Steinmo et al. 1992), although scholars working within HI tend to be more interested in how relatively stable institutions influence a range of outcomes, public policy in particular, rather than in how institutions themselves change over time, which is my concern here.

CHA typically employs an analytical technique known as process tracing, defined by Collier (2011, 823) as "the systematic examination of diagnostic evidence selected and analyzed in light of research questions and hypotheses posed by the investigator." For the purposes of this book, process tracing is employed both long- and short-term. Long-term, it is applied to the analysis of the unfolding of an entire process of state restructuring, which, as seen above, often entails several critical junctures. Within each of these junctures short-term process tracing is employed to identify the mechanisms that led to the enactment of state restructuring reforms at that point in time. Collier identifies four types of process-tracing tests – "Straw-in-the-Wind"; "Hoop"; "Smoking-Gun"; "Doubly Decisive" – according to the standards of necessity and sufficiency one applies for accepting or rejecting the postulated inference.

As mentioned in the introduction, the book aims to answer primarily the question of *how* integration influences restructuring and secondarily the question of the extent to which it does so. Accordingly, the realist bargain theory is tested in a two-step fashion. The first step consists in testing whether regional-nationalist parties exploit the European dimension in relation to state restructuring during critical junctures as hypothesized by the theory. This is a test of *how* European integration influences state restructuring, based on the mechanisms put forward by the theory. The second step consists in testing the extent to which state restructuring has advanced as a result of regional-nationalists' exploitation of the European dimension. This is a test of the *extent to which* European integration has influenced state restructuring.

The *how* question is given precedence for two reasons. First, it is logically prior to the question of *to what extent* and is a crucial aspect of establishing causality. As Marx et al. (2014, 117) argue, answering the *how* question should be at the heart of comparative analysis. Second, it can be answered in a more robust way as the degree to which political parties exploit the European dimension in their rhetorical strategies lends itself to being measured with relative precision. The *to what extent* question, by contrast, is harder to answer with a high degree of confidence because it is very difficult to isolate the effect of European integration from that of many other variables.[8] Any answer to this second question, thus, can only be tentative. In other words, regional-nationalist parties' exploitation of the European dimension is a necessary, but not a sufficient, condition for European integration to have an influence on state restructuring. In the terminology of the process tracing literature, the theory faces a smoking-gun test on the first question and a hoop test on the second one (Van Evera 1997, 32; Collier 2011, 825; Mahoney 2012, 578).

Five Phases of Integration

As European integration has unfolded over time its properties have also evolved. While a number of fundamental traits of the EU have remained relatively stable since its inception as the Coal and the Steel Community (ECSC) in 1952, important aspects have changed considerably and the OICs it generates for state restructuring have likewise changed too. As state restructuring has been a product of critical junctures taking place at a particular point in time, in order to successfully capture the possible influence of integration we need to identify the properties of the EU at that particular point in time. While all periodizations are fraught with difficulties and are necessarily based on somewhat arbitrary boundaries (e.g., Green 1992; Besserman 1996), they are nevertheless necessary in order to identify different phases of the process of integration.

The periodization I have adopted distinguishes between five periods, labelled T_1 to T_5 (table A7). Their stylized features are as follows. The first period corresponds to the early phase of the process of integration, between 1952 and 1972. The period had four main characteristics: a) it was marked by so-called negative integration, i.e., a focus on removing barriers to trade to achieve the completion of a customs union, with only minimal flanking policies of positive integration beyond the common agricultural policy; b) territorially, the EU was constituted by the six founding members, i.e., Belgium, France, (West) Germany, Italy, Luxembourg, and the Netherlands; c) in institutional terms, decision-making was dominated by the Commission and the Council, the latter operating by unanimity, with only a consultative role for the still indirectly elected European Parliament (EP).

In the second period, from 1973 to 1984 the EU experienced a series of crises but also of important new developments: a) integration was no longer essentially negative but started to develop in new directions, in particular in the field of regional policy and monetary cooperation; b) the six founding members were joined by Denmark, Ireland, and the UK after the first enlargement; c) institutionally, although the Commission-Council axis continued to dominate, the formalization of the European Council meetings and the shift to direct election of the European Parliament were important developments.

In the third period, from 1985 to 1993, integration underwent a significant acceleration, with the signing of the Single European Act in 1986 and the Maastricht Treaty in 1991. In this phase the focus of integration moved on to the completion of the single market and the development of accompanying policies, notably in the social and territorial cohesion fields, which also included an apparent endorsement of the idea of a Europe of the Regions. Territorially, the EU expanded to the south, admitting Greece, Portugal, and Spain, while from an institutional point of view it witnessed the activism of the Commission led by Jacques Delors and the beginning of the empowerment of the European Parliament.

In the following period, from 1994 to 2004, the key features can be summarized as follows: a) the focus of integration shifted to the completion of monetary union and the accompanying efforts in many countries to meet the qualifying criteria; the social dimension of integration failed to develop as supporters expected while states' control over regional policy was tightened; b) the Union expanded to the north, taking in Austria, Finland, and Sweden; c) the Commission lost the central role it enjoyed under Delors, leaving the Council in a more dominant position while the European Parliament saw its power increasing markedly.

In the most recent period, from 2005 to today, the key characteristics of the Union underwent yet more significant change: a) EU politics became overwhelmingly concerned with the crisis in the eurozone and the wider economic depression; b) the Union expanded dramatically to the east, eventually encompassing twenty-eight countries; c) the adoption of the Lisbon Treaty further strengthened the role of the EP primarily at the expense of the Commission but the politics of the eurozone crisis also brought to the fore the role of the European Council and of its most powerful members – notably Germany – leading to an overall rise of intergovernmentalism. The overall level of integration increased from one period to the next. Table A7 summarizes these features.

Four Levels of Units of Analysis

The selection of cases is based on the principle that in qualitative analysis with a small number of cases it is desirable, if at all possible, to increase the number of cases by disaggregating the small number of macro cases into a larger number of micro cases (e.g., Collier 1993, 111–12; King et al. 1994, 217–28). On this basis, I employ a cascading case-selection strategy leading to the selection of units of observation across four levels. At the first level, as already mentioned in the previous chapter, the units of analysis are the six states that have experienced significant state restructuring since 1950: Belgium, Italy, Spain, and the UK as cases of strong restructuring, broadly speaking conforming to the bottom-up dynamic, and Denmark and France as cases of weak restructuring following the top-down dynamic.

State restructuring, however, as I have already argued, typically takes place through what we can call critical junctures, the properties of which often vary widely within the same country. It is thus important to disaggregate the first-level units into a number of critical junctures, which constitute the second-level units of analysis. As seen in chapter 1, and summarized in tables A4 and A6, we can identify sixteen such junctures, twelve of which conforming to the bottom-up dynamic and four to the top-down dynamic. As the realist bargain theory postulates very different effects of European integration on state restructuring depending on the dynamic the latter displays, the bottom-up critical junctures can be considered the treatment cases while the top-down ones constitute the control cases. Two of them took place before the state in question joined the EU so have been excluded from the analysis.[9] Given space constraints, BE5 has also been excluded due to its limited importance. This leaves the thirteen critical junctures listed on the right hand side of table A8 as the second-level units of analysis, ten of which are of the bottom-up variety and three of the top-down one. In terms of time period, two fall in the first (BE1, IT1), three in the second (BE2, FR1, UK1), two in the third (BE3, BE4), three in the fourth (DK2, IT2, UK2), and three in the last one (BE6, ES2, UK3) – as shown in table A9.

Within each of these critical junctures party competition over state restructuring and the exploitation of the European dimension in relation to it has focused on the key elections and referendums taking place in that period. As detailed in the empirical chapters, in some cases the relevant elections were general elections while in others they were regional elections. Likewise, some referendums were statewide while others were regional. As listed in the third column of table A13, I have identified twenty-three such elections and referendums. These constitute the third-level units of analysis. Lastly, at the time of these elections and referendums a number of political parties engaged in campaigning and deployed their rhetorical strategies to gain a competitive advantage over their rivals. The most significant parties taking part in these contests have been selected for analysis, significance being generally operationalized as having secured more than 5 percent of the seats in parliament[10] in the previous election. The observation of each party campaign at each election/referendum time thus constitute the fourth-level units of analysis. As listed in the fourth column of table A13, 127 of them have been selected.

Content Analysis of Rhetorical Strategies

Parties engage in campaigning through what we can call "rhetorical strategies." Following Schimmelfennig (2003, 199), I conceive of rhetorical strategies as "the strategic use of arguments." Through their choice of arguments parties try to attract support for themselves and their core policies.[11] If such strategies resonate with voters and bring electoral rewards to a party, the latter would be in a stronger bargaining position vis-à-vis its competitors and therefore more likely to achieve its policy objectives. It is within their overall rhetorical strategies that parties may decide to exploit the European dimension in relation to state restructuring. In order to ascertain the degree to which they do so, it is necessary to analyze such strategies.

The main available sources on parties' rhetorical strategies during elections and referendum campaigns are documents such as electoral manifestos and other party publications, and media reports of campaign events such as leaders' speeches, as well as the secondary literature. Such sources can be analyzed quantitatively or qualitatively. Quantitative methods perform automated counting of word frequency and generally rest on salience theory, according to which parties are assumed not to oppose each other directly but to emphasize different aspects in their campaign, expressed through a different choice of words. While these methods have performed well on the task of measuring parties' left-right positioning, they are less satisfactory on more complex issues that cut across the left-right divide such as state restructuring (e.g., Budge 2001, 90; Adamson and Johns 2008, 136–7).

For the purposes of this book, I have thus chosen qualitative content analysis, with statements as the basic unit of measurement. Three aspects of party campaigning content have been analyzed: a) the position in relation to state restructuring; b) the attitudes to European integration and to the EU; c) the degree to which the European dimension has been exploited in relation to state restructuring. With regard to the latter, the quantity of statements linking the two and the nature of the link established have been analyzed to estimate the intensity (how strongly the link between Europe and state restructuring was made) and the direction (whether it was used in favour of or against it) of linking.[12]

Synoptic Comparative Analyses of "How"

Through the process of disaggregation described above, the six largest units of analysis have been broken into thirteen critical junctures at the macro level and 127 party-election/referendum observations at the micro level. To test how the realist bargain theory performs across them, we can formulate a number of hypotheses in relation to each level of analysis.

At the macro level of critical junctures the theory postulates that significant exploitation of the European dimension in relation to state restructuring only occurs in bottom-up dynamics. As these are characterized by high constitutional significance and a strong role played by regional-nationalist parties, we can specify the following hypotheses:

MacroH1: high constitutional significance of state restructuring is a necessary condition for European integration to have an influence on it.

MacroH2: a strong role played by regional-nationalist parties is a necessary condition for European integration to have an influence on it.

MacroH3: high constitutional significance and a strong role played by regional-nationalist parties are jointly sufficient conditions for European integration to have an influence on state restructuring.

At the micro level of parties-election/referendum observations the theory postulates that regional-nationalist parties will adopt an independence in Europe position and exploit the European dimension around it, dependent on positive attitudes to integration and sensitive to the phase of integration while statewide parties will exploit Europe to a very limited extent. The following hypotheses can thus be derived:

MicroH1: regional-nationalist parties with a traditional autonomist policy will shift to an independentist policy over time, and exploit the European dimension around it to a significant (*europ-i*: >0.5) extent.

MicroH2: being a regional-nationalist party is a necessary condition for a party to exploit the European dimension in relation to state restructuring to a significant (*europ-i*: >0.5) extent.

MicroH3: a radical constitutional position is a necessary condition for a party to exploit the European dimension in relation to state restructuring to a significant (*europ-i*: >0.5) extent.

MicroH4: a positive attitude to integration is a necessary condition for a party to exploit the European dimension in relation to state restructuring to a significant (*europ-i*: >0.5) extent.

MicroH5: a high level of integration (*integ*: >0.5) is a necessary condition for a party to exploit the European dimension in relation to state restructuring to a significant (*europ-i*: >0.5) extent.

MicroH6: being a regional-nationalist party with a radical constitutional position and positive attitudes to integration and operating at a time of high integration are jointly sufficient conditions for a party to exploit the European dimension in relation to state restructuring to a significant (*europ-i*: >0.5) extent.

To test these hypotheses, the evidence presented and discussed in chapters 3–7 has been analyzed synoptically with QCA methods. QCA seeks to combine the strengths of both qualitative and quantitative approaches by using deep, case-focused knowledge to analyze complex causation and reach parsimonious modest generalizations. The causal connections between conditions and outcomes[13] are conceptualized in terms of set relations, whereby membership in the set of cases displaying the outcome is analyzed in relation to membership in the set of cases sharing the condition/s. This is done by identifying which conditions or configurations of conditions are necessary and/or sufficient to produce the outcome under investigation (Ragin 2008; Schneider and Wagemann 2012). It is therefore a particularly useful method to test the hypotheses formulated above.

Two main variants of QCA have been developed: crisp-set (csQCA) and fuzzy-set (fsQCA) (Rihoux and De Meur 2009; Ragin 2009; Schneider and Wagemann 2012). The principal difference between them is that in csQCA conditions are dichotomized – coded 0 or 1 – while fsQCA is centred on the notion of degrees of membership in sets and allows for a more fine-grained measurement of conditions and outcomes. Crisp-set QCA is a powerful instrument for the analysis of necessity and sufficiency where conditions and outcomes can be effectively dichotomized while fsQCA is preferable where a more sensitive analysis is needed.

Given the nature of the two main units of analysis under investigation – the critical junctures at the macro level and the party-election/referendum observations at the micro level – I have performed two QCA synoptic comparative analyses: a macro csQCA analysis of critical junctures and a micro fsQCA analysis of party-election/referendum observations. Within each of them, I have tested for both necessity and sufficiency. The results are presented and discussed in chapter 8.

Synoptic Comparative Analysis of "To What Extent"

If the realist bargain theory is correct, three observable implications should follow in terms of the extent to which European integration has influenced state restructuring:

a) Regional-nationalist parties that have exploited the European dimension should have derived electoral benefits from doing so. *Ceteris paribus*, those who have exploited Europe to a significant extent (*europ-i*: >0.5) should have been more successful than those who have failed to do so. This has been assessed on the basis of parties' electoral results.
b) In the regions in which regional-nationalist parties have exploited the European dimension to a significant extent (*europ-i*: >0.5), mass support for independence in Europe should have increased following them doing so. This has been assessed on the basis of public opinion surveys and referendums results.
c) Regional-nationalist parties' exploitation of the European dimension should have – via a) and b) – led to stronger state restructuring. *Ceteris paribus*, countries in which regional-nationalist parties have exploited Europe to a significant extent (*europ-i*: >0.5) should have experienced stronger state restructuring than those in which regional-nationalist parties have failed to do so. This has been assessed on the basis of a qualitative analysis of the strength of restructuring, in light of the integrated qualitative-quantitative approach outlined in the previous chapter.

As already mentioned, measuring the extent to which European integration influences state restructuring via the agency of political parties faces severe methodological limits, chiefly that of isolating the effect of Europe from that of many other factors. While it is still a worthwhile exercise, the testing of the above implications can only be of the hoop test variety and the limitations of the inference that can be derived from it should accordingly be kept in mind. The results are presented and discussed in chapter 8.

2.4 SUMMARY

The causal connections between European integration and state restructuring can be theorized as a realist bargain model. The model is built on four main cornerstones. First, Europe generates different OICs for statewide parties and regional-nationalist parties, respectively, to engage in state restructuring. Second, these OICs are more favourable to the latter set of parties than to the former and lead them over time to adopt a strategy of independence in Europe. Third, the electoral and territorial integrity challenges brought to bear by regional-nationalist parties campaigning for independence in Europe triggers a competitive dynamic that leads statewide parties to enact state restructuring to contain such challenges. Fourth, as regional-nationalist parties are only present in bottom-up dynamics of state restructuring, the theory expects European integration to have a causal influence only in the latter cases. I label the theory realist bargain because it emphasizes the role played by secessionist challenges and the bargain nature of the interaction between regional-nationalist and statewide parties.

To test the theory I have developed a comparative research design across time and space based on a CHA approach. On the temporal axis, I periodize European integration into five phases while on the spatial axis I selected cases across four levels, from six states at the most macro level to 127 party-election/referendum observations at the most micro one. The testing has been conducted on the basis of a detailed qualitative content analysis of party campaigns within each critical junctures supplemented by synoptic comparative analyses of the *how* and *to what extent* questions, respectively. Chapters 3 to 7 present the detailed qualitative content analysis, while chapter 8 reports and discusses the results of the synoptic analyses.

3

The First Steps

The first period analyzed covers the initial phase of European integration, from the establishment of the European Coal and Steel Community in 1952 to the first enlargement in 1973, and the first steps of state restructuring in Italy and Belgium. After a brief summary of the development of integration and of the key features of the European Union in this period, the chapter analyzes the first critical junctures of state restructuring in the two countries, which led to the implementation of the ordinary regions in Italy and the first "federal" constitutional reforms in Belgium. The evidence reviewed in the chapter confirms the classification of these two critical junctures put forward in chapter 1. The implementation of the regions in Italy followed the top-down pattern while the Belgian reforms were the product of a clear bottom-up dynamic. In line with the theoretical formulations of the realist bargain model, no Europeanization of state restructuring took place in Italy while a modest, but significant, exploitation of the European dimension was evident in Belgium. As expected, this was largely the product of the agency of regional-nationalist parties.

3.1 THE DEVELOPMENT OF INTEGRATION

In this early period, the EU presented both features that would remain relatively constant over the entire process of integration as well as others that would change profoundly. Considering the latter first, the common element among them was their modest extent compared to later developments. In many ways the EU was naturally a much more limited organization than the one we are familiar with today. This was most notably the case in terms of geographical extension – the original six founding members – and the overall depth of integration. The original objective of the European Economic Community set up in 1958 was to achieve a customs union by removing tariffs and quotas on trade between its members. In its first two decades integration was therefore primarily negative in character, i.e., concerned with removing obstacles to trade rather than developing policies of positive integration (Scharpf 1996), with the exception of the Common Agricultural Policy (CAP), established in the early 1960s. The regulatory activity of the Union was consequently very limited, and this was reflected in a modest legislative output. Likewise, expenditure was also significantly smaller than today and heavily taken up by CAP spending.[1] The decision-making process was dominated by the Commission and the Council while the European Parliament,[2] which was not directly elected at the time, had only a marginal, consultative role. The balance of power between the Commission and the Council saw the former in the ascendancy under the presidency of Walter Hallstein leading on to a reassertion of Council hegemony following the empty-chair crisis and the Luxembourg compromise of 1965–66 (Dinan 2014, 104–8). The national veto was well entrenched in the Council as its decisions were based on unanimity. Integration generally enjoyed diffuse public support, although within a context of low political salience, known as the "permissive consensus" (Lindberg and Scheingold 1970, 41). At the party level, though, there was a division between right-of-centre parties broadly in favour and left-of-centre ones – particularly those on more radical positions – largely critical if not openly hostile (e.g., Hix 1999).

On the other hand, three important aspects that would come to characterize the subsequent development of integration were already prominent in this period. The first is the focus on market integration. The pursuit of an ever more integrated market based on the so-called four freedoms (of goods, capital, services, and people), as set out in the Treaty of Rome, was established as the fundamental objective of integration and has remained such to the present day. To enforce these freedoms, the EU started to build a distinct international legal order that would acquire in time traits of a domestic body of law, supervised by the supranational European Court of Justice (e.g., Alter 2002). Third, the institutional setup of the EU created a substantial bias in favour of the smaller states, which enjoyed over-representation in the key institutions.[3] Some of the EU features that generate opportunity and incentives for state restructuring, as discussed in the previous chapter, were thus already present, if *in nuce*, in this early period.

3.2 ITALY: THE IMPLEMENTATION OF THE ORDINARY REGIONS

Brief Historical Overview

No single, overarching political system ruled what is today's Italy between the fall of the Western Roman Empire in AD 476 and the creation of the Kingdom of Italy in 1861.[4] When the movement for national unification, or *Risorgimento*, got under way from about 1820 onward, it did not have an institutional legacy to rely upon or to free itself from. This contrasts, for instance, the situation of Germany, the other prominent case of nineteenth century national unification.[5] Hence, those at the helm of the Risorgimento had essentially a blank canvas when it came to the structure to give to the state they were helping to build. Not surprisingly, then, a vigorous debate between those advocating federalism and those favouring a unitary state took place in the period leading up to the establishment of the Kingdom of Italy and in the formative years of the new state. Although Count Cavour and most of the other liberal-conservative leaders who led the unification process were personally sympathetic to ideas of local autonomy and limited centralization, a number of factors conjured up to lead to the structuring of the Kingdom of Italy as a unitary state.[6] An 1865 law, effectively extending Piedmont's law of 1859 to the entire state, granted municipalities and provinces little autonomy and made them subject to central government's control exercised through the institution of the prefect (Pavone 1964, 189–91; Ragionieri 1967, 157). It would set the country on a unitary and centralized path for over a century.

The first stirrings of a new regionalism started to emerge in the wake of the First World War. In 1920–21 Prime Minister Giovanni Giolitti abandoned his previous hostility to regional government and voiced support for directly elected regional institutions exercising competences transferred to them from both the central government and the provinces (Ragionieri 1967, 185–6). The Partito Popolare Italiano (PPI), a Catholic party established in 1919, was openly regionalist. A report adopted at the party's third congress in 1921 called for directly elected – by universal suffrage[7] and proportional representation – regions with lawmaking and tax-raising powers. Such regions would be autonomous entities free from state supervision and have competences in agriculture, education, infrastructure, industry, labour, and social services (186–8). According to Ragionieri, "fino a quel momento nella storia italiana nessuna proposta regionalistica aveva trovato una formulazione altrettanto chiara ed esplicita" (187).[8] It was probably not a coincidence that the party's leader, Luigi Sturzo, was from Sicily, a region with a strong autonomist tradition that would later play a crucial role in the introduction of regional government in Italy (La Loggia 1955, 54; Ragionieri 1967, 181–3). In the same period an autonomist movement also emerged in the other main island, Sardinia, which led to the foundation in 1921 of the Partito Sardo d'Azione, or Sardinian Action Party (Sechi 1970; Hepburn 2009). At the other end of the country, the areas annexed in 1918, South Tyrol and the Julian Venetia, were granted a special administrative regime and linguistic rights for German-speakers and the speakers of Slavic languages, respectively (Weibel 1971, 26–7). Regionalist ideas made their way into central government too, as in 1921 a parliamentary committee charged with studying the reform of public administration recommended decentralization on a regional basis (26). Such ideas would soon be stifled, however, by the rise of fascism, which by the mid-1920s established an authoritarian and rigidly centralized regime, leaving no space for regional or local autonomy (Adorni and Francia 1998, 176; Fontana 1973).

As a reaction to the centralization of the fascist regime, support for federalism and other forms of territorial autonomy was widespread within the resistance movement. The movement's umbrella organization, the Comitato di Liberazione Nazionale (CLN), or National Liberation Committee, itself adopted a regional structure, partly as an organizational device and partly out of ideological commitment (Ragionieri 1967, 191–2). Among the political forces represented on the CLN, the Partito d'Azione, or Action Party, a liberal-radical party, had a federalist position embedded within a vision of a federal Europe (Rotelli 1967, 57). When the first government fully issued from the resistance took office in June 1945, however, it faced secessionist movements in the Aosta Valley, South Tyrol, and Sicily, with the involvement of France and Austria, respectively, in the first two cases. The government's response was to grant autonomy statutes to the three regions, with the Sicilian one the first to be fully implemented in May 1946 (Rotelli 1967, 67; Weibel 1971, 155, 293).

Therefore regional autonomy had de facto already been introduced by the time the constitutive assembly gathered to draft a new constitution in summer 1946. The assembly's committee charged with drafting the section on the structure of the state was divided on the question of regionalization, as much within parties as between them, with those in favour of regional autonomy having a narrow majority, although the balance of forces was reversed in the assembly as a whole. Despite much internal disagreement on regional governments and the extent of their autonomy, the positions of the two main parties – the Democrazia Cristiana (DC), or Christian democracy, and the Partito Comunista Italiano (PCI), or Italian Communist Party – were distinct enough: the former (the heirs of the interwar Italian Popular Party) were generally in favour of regional governments with primary legislative powers and some fiscal autonomy while the latter were only prepared to contemplate forms of administrative decentralization, especially so as far as the mainland was concerned (Rotelli 1967, 297–9).

The roots of the DC's support for regionalization were in the association between regional autonomy on the one hand and democracy and freedom on the other, in opposition to the centralized authoritarianism of the fascists. As such regional autonomy was seen as a middle way between centralization and full-blown federalism, which was perceived as opening the way to secessions (275–84). The PCI, by contrast, was officially "contrario ad ogni forma di organizzazione federativa dello Stato"[9] (252n99). Although the party often couched its opposition to federalism – as well as other forms of regional autonomy with primary legislative powers – in terms of the defence of national unity against secessionist threats, it is clear that the core motivation was quintessentially ideological, viz. that regional autonomy would allow pockets of conservative resistance to stymie the process of socioeconomic transformation that the party intended to carry out upon gaining office at the central level (250–6). Although less monolithically so than its fellow party on the left, the Partito Socialista Italiano (PSI), or Italian Socialist Party, essentially shared the same view (257–8).

Such divisions between the main parties in the assembly interacted with international developments and their repercussions on domestic politics. In January 1947 the committee submitted to the assembly a full draft providing for some special autonomy regions and ordinary autonomy for the others, but both of them would be granted legislative and executive powers. By the time the assembly started debating the draft in late May 1947, a government crisis had occurred which saw the PCI and the PSI expelled from government in the context of the incipient Cold War confrontation between the USA and the USSR (Rotelli 1967, 314–15; Ginsborg 2003, 111–13). This would dramatically change the two parties attitudes to the regions because by then they saw them, as Rotelli (1967, 325) put it, "Adesso che il Partito comunista e il Partito socialista erano stati estromessi dal governo, le Regioni offrivano alla sinistra prospettive nuove di lotta politica."[10] The left's change of position altered the preference distribution in the assembly, leading to the emergence of a majority in favour of regionalization. This was still rather timid support, though, and the assembly made significant amendments to the draft, striking off, in particular, exclusive legislative powers for the ordinary regions (326–31). The constitution thus laid out a two-type structure of five special statute regions – Aosta Valley, Friuli-Julian Venetia, Sardinia, Sicily, and Trentino-South Tyrol – possessing, on paper, strong autonomy and fifteen ordinary statute regions with much more modest competences.

The special statute regions either were already in operation or would be established speedily.[11] The implementation of the ordinary regions, in contrast, would prove to be a lengthy and contested affair. A major DC victory in the crucial 1948 election led to the party's unchallenged hegemony over parliament and the executive and the long-term exclusion of the PCI and the PSI from government. Such dominance, and the fear that the regions – especially those of the central red belt – could become a bastion of left-wing power, led to much DC's foot-dragging on the issue. With the exception of a 1953 law laying out the organs the regions would have, no other implementing law was passed throughout the decade (Bassanini 1970, 9; Leonardi et al. 1981, 100). Toward the end of the 1950s, however, several factors conspired to change the situation and lead to the so-called *centro-sinistra*, or centre-left, phase of Italian politics in the context of which the implementation of the ordinary regions would at last take place. The two most important factors were the erosion in support for the DC, which forced it to seek wider coalitions, and the progressive distancing of the PSI from the PCI in the wake of the Soviet invasion of Hungary in 1956, which made the former, for the first time, a possible coalition partner for the DC (Pryce 1963, 250). The crucial election of this critical juncture was that of April 1963, to which we now turn.

The April 1963 Election

PARTIES

Three parties played an important role in this election and its aftermath: the DC, the PSI, and the PCI. After winning an absolute majority in 1948, the DC remained the largest party in parliament and the dominant actor in the executive throughout the 1950s, governing either alone or in coalition with small centrist parties such as the Partito Socialista Democratico Italiano (PSDI), the Partito Liberale Italiano (PLI), and the PRI (Partito Repubblicano Italiano) (Ignazi 2010, 50–6).[12] In the 1958 election, the party secured 45.8 percent of the seats in the Chamber of Deputies, the lower house of parliament, almost double the figure for the second largest party, the PCI (Mackie and Rose 1974, 220–1).

As already seen, the PSI was initially closely aligned with the PCI. It was excluded from the government alongside the latter in the May 1947 crisis and joined the communist party in a so-called Fronte Popolare, or People's Alliance, for the 1948 election. After 1956, though, the party broke its close alliance with the PCI and moved gradually closer to the DC. In 1962, the socialists offered for the first time their outside support to the Christian democrats, in exchange for a reformist program, including in particular the nationalization of the electricity industry and the implementation of the ordinary regions. In the 1958 election it gained 14 percent of the seats in the lower house (ibid.).

The PCI was the main opposition party, controlling 23.5 percent of the seats in the lower house after the 1958 election (ibid.). Since its expulsion from government in 1947, the party had been considered uncoalitionable by the DC and its allies and as a threat to democracy by a substantial portion of public opinion. Being able to ally itself either with the DC or, at least theoretically, with the PCI, the PSI was the pivotal actor in the party system and was thus able to leverage that position to secure programmatic concessions beyond what its electoral weight would have allowed.

POSITIONS ON STATE RESTRUCTURING

The DC devoted a prominent section of its manifesto to the regions, claiming original ownership of the idea of regionalization and committing itself to taking further steps toward their implementation while arguing that this should be done on the basis of a cautious step-by-step approach, to ensure conditions of political stability – meaning no risk that communist-controlled regions might pose a threat for the DC-led central government – were in place (DC [1963] 1968, 1479). In its campaign the party stressed these points further. The implementation of the regions was made subject to a clear democratic choice on the part of the PSI. In a speech during the campaign, the leader of the party, Aldo Moro, argued that only "condizioni di più sicura stabilità democratica"[13] would make possible the creation of the regions (quoted in SS 1963a; also Pansa 1963). He defined regionalization as "la più grande riforma dello Stato democratico"[14] (quoted in Pansa 1963) and argued that it would only be possibile if it did not lead to democratic instability: "Vogliamo le regioni, ma in una situazione di stabilità politica per impedire l'azione disarticolante del pci"[15] (quoted in Pansa 1963; also LS 1963; Pryce 1963, 251; La Palombara 1966, 81). Hence, he argued "Le regioni non sono per ora, sono per il domani, quando coraggiose, storiche decisioni del psi saranno state prese"[16] (quoted in Pansa 1963). Although the party devoted two sections of its manifesto to economic planning and to the problem of the economic development of the south, respectively, no mention was made in either section of the role regional governments would play (DC 1968, 1484–5, 1492–3) and little emphasis was put on it in the campaign.

The PSI stressed that the implementation of the regions was a *conditio sine qua non* for its participation in a governing coalition (Nenni 1963, 123–4; La Palombara 1966, 75; D'Angelo Bigelli 1971, 292, 304; Leonardi et al. 1981, 101). In a televised address in the closing stages of the campaign, the party's leader, Pietro Nenni stated that negotiations with the DC would have to start again "dalle regioni e dalle leggi agrarie"[17] (De Luca 1963). The PSI's support for the implementation of the regions was primarily on democratic, rather than economic planning, grounds. Although Nenni did argue for regionalization in relation to economic planning on other occasions (Nenni 1963, 123, 149), he did not make the link in his televised address (De Luca 1963). Antonio Giolitti, the chief architect of the socialists' economic program, did not see the implementation of the regions as playing a significant role in his vision for a structural reform of the economy (Scroccu 2012, 185–92). Although the PSI viewed the regions also as instruments of economic planning, it primarily saw them as "an effective means of opposing the authoritarian and centralized state" (La Palombara 1966, 79).

The PCI criticized the timidity and the contradictions of the first *centro-sinistra* government, especially the failure to carry out all the reforms it had announced, with the partial exception of the nationalization of the electricity industry. It denounced the *centro-sinistra* as a strategy intended primarily to divide the labour movement and called for a union of the left to defeat the DC (PCI 1963, 2). Like the socialists, the PCI envisaged a role for the regions in economic planning but built its case for them primarily on democratic grounds. It did so in the first programmatic section of its manifesto, headlined "Per la democratizzazione dello Stato,"[18] arguing that the state apparatus was still largely the one left behind by the monarchy and the fascist regime. Its full democratization entailed "l'attuazione urgente delle Regioni a statuto normale e il pieno sviluppo delle autonomie locali"[19] (PCI 1963, 3; also Höbel 2010, 337–8). In contrast, the section devoted to "democratic economic planning" confined itself to calling for the creation of agricultural development agencies on a regional basis (PCI 1963, 3). The only democratic party that was explicitly hostile to the implementation of the regions was the PLI, as, according to its leader, regionalization would lead to a "smembramento del paese"[20] (SS 1963b).

ATTITUDES TO, AND STRATEGIC USE OF, EUROPEAN INTEGRATION

The DC was strongly in favour of European integration, a stance the party presented as closely linked to the Atlantic alliance as the two fundamental pillars of Italy's foreign policy under Christian democratic stewardship (Masala 2004, 109–12; Conti and Verzichelli 2005, 84–5). The party's manifesto devoted a section to "the unity of Europe," in which it argued that the integration of the continent was "un fine da perseguire con tutti gli sforzi"[21] (DC [1963] 1968, 1508). In the course of the campaign, the DC foreign minister stated that never was the building of a united Europe more needed (LS 1963). The PCI also associated European integration with the Atlantic choice but approached it from the opposite position, one of firm hostility (Conti and Verzichelli 2005, 89–91; Maggiorani 1998). The party's manifesto denounced "tutti i limiti e i pericoli, economici e politici, di un europeismo e di un processo di integrazione economica prigionieri delle strettoie e della piattaforma politico-militare del MEC"[22] (PCI 1963, 2) and branded the latter a "gabbia entro cui l'Italia è costretta ad accettare la direzione dei gruppi internazionali più reazionari"[23] (4). The party called for a revision of the Treaty of Rome to dismantle the structures of the Common Market and extend economic cooperation to the socialist and neutral countries, and beyond Europe (4).

Although sharing some of the doubts expressed more forcefully by the communist party, the PSI had long adopted a less hostile position, for instance abstaining in the parliamentary vote to ratify the Paris treaty rather than voting against it (Conti and Verzichelli 2005, 98). In the late 1950s and early 1960s, the PSI's attitudes toward integration were at the centre of its general moderation and rapprochement with the DC, not least because the latter had made the socialists' acceptance of Europe and NATO a *conditio sine qua non* of deeper collaboration between the two parties. In the course of the 1963 campaign, Nenni stated that the socialists claimed "una funzione d'avanguardia nel movimento democratico per l'unità"[24] (quoted in De Luca 1963). The party was thus on a position of cautious support for integration, which has been defined as "functional Europeism" (Conti and Verzichelli 2005, 80–1). None of the parties, however, linked in any way the implementation of the ordinary regions and the process of European integration.

ELECTION OUTCOME

The results of the election were a setback for the DC and a victory for the PCI and, especially so, the PLI, while the PSI lost ground slightly. The DC lost considerable support, especially in the northern part of the country, and declined from 45.8 to 41.3 percent of seats.[25] In contrast, the PCI made a significant advance, gaining almost three percentage points – from 23.4 to 26.3 – in its share of seats. Even more emphatic was the PLI's victory. The party doubled its share of the vote and climbed from 2.8 to 6.2 percent of seats. The PSI lost only marginally, declining from 14 to 13.8 percent of the seats (Pryce 1963).

The fact that the DC suffered a setback while the PSI managed on the whole to hold its ground strengthened the two parties' resolve to deepen the collaboration between them under the aegis of the *centro-sinistra* strategy. As the implementation of the regions was a key plank of the latter, the election outcome brought the prospect closer. In the same direction went the victory of the other great advocate of regionalization, the PCI. The emphatic victory of the PLI, on the other hand, is likely to have been dictated by opposition to the *centro-sinistra*'s nationalization policy rather than to the implementation of the regions and, given the still relatively small size of the party, did not have enough weight to alter the balance of forces now coalescing in favour of the creation of the ordinary regions.

The Implementation of the Ordinary Regions

After a DC single-party interim government and laborious negotiations, in late 1963 an agreement was finally reached between the DC and the PSI for a so-called *centro-sinistra organico* – i.e., for the PSI's formal entry into a governing coalition with the DC rather than merely offering external support. The text of the agreement among the four parties that would form the government – DC, PSI, PSDI, and PRI – emphasized their objectives of democratic development, economic planning, and the modernization of state administration (DC, PSI, PSDI, and PRI, 1963, 7–8). In the section on democratic development, the commitment to the implementation of the ordinary regions figured prominently and was expressed as follows: "Nell'ambito dell'attuazione della Costituzione assume particolare rilievo la creazione delle regioni a statuto ordinario. I partiti sono d'accordo che tra i primi atti di governo siano ripresentate ... le leggi istitutive delle regioni a statuto ordinario, in esse compresa la legge elettorale."[26] (DC, PSI, PSDI and PRI 1963, 6). In the section on economic planning and the closing of the development disparities between the different areas of the country, however, no mention was made of the role the regions could play (13–16).

Despite the official commitment to implement the regions early in the new parliamentary term, strong resistance within the ranks of the governing parties remained and it was only in March 1967, under the third *centro-sinistra* government led by Aldo Moro, that an outline agreement on the electoral law for the regional councils was reached (Degl'Innocenti 2004, 35). In a parallel move, regional economic committees were set up in September 1964. These were, however, functional bodies made up of representatives of local government, the field administration of the state, employers, and trade unions and under the direction of the central Ministry of Budget and Economic planning (LU 1964a,b; Degl'Innocenti 2004, 38-9; Selan and Donnini 2009, 272-9).[27]

The electoral law for the regional councils was finally adopted in February 1968, with the support of the governing coalition and the PCI and the opposition of the PLI and the neo-fascist Movimento Sociale Italiano (MSI) (LS 1968; Leonardi et al. 1981, 102). A second law laying out the financing arrangements for the regions was adopted in May 1970 and the first elections for the regional councils were held in June of the same year. A series of decrees in January 1972 transferred from the state administration to the regions a number of competences and the corresponding infrastructure and personnel. After several rulings of the Constitutional Court that upheld a restrictive interpretation of the regions' autonomy, a second decree completed the transfer of competences in 1977 (Putnam et al. 1993, 21-6).

The regional institutions established by this legislation followed a model of parliamentary government, with regional councils directly elected on the basis of proportional representation and executive bodies responsible to them. The regions were granted competences in a wide range of areas, principally health and related social services, housing, and urban planning, as well as some aspects of agriculture, culture, education, environment, policing, public works, transport, and tourist infrastructure. Significantly, the regions received no wider economic planning powers beyond those pertaining to urban planning, reflecting the strong reservations that many who supported the regions on democratic grounds had vis-à-vis regional planning (La Palombara 1966, 116-17). While in the areas of their competences the regions were formally granted primary legislative powers, in practice their lawmaking autonomy was severely restricted by the fact that competences had been devolved in a fragmented fashion, rather than by coherent policy fields, and by the presence of extensive framework state legislation, with which regional law had to comply. Central government also retained a veto over regional legislation. A similar picture was painted by the funding arrangements, which left the regions with little fiscal autonomy and heavily dependent on central funds (King 1987, 337; Putnam et al. 1993, 21–6).

The reform had only lukewarm public support. Asked in 1963 whether the implementation of the regions would bring more harm than good, 31 percent had a positive opinion, 22 percent had a negative one, and 30 percent had no opinion (Putnam et al. 1993, 58). After the completion of the devolution process, in 1981, the corresponding figures were 31, 18, and 8, respectively (ibid.).[28] In the same year, only 35 percent were satisfied with regional government, a figure dropping to less than 20 percent in the southern regions (54–5). Hence, the reform was carried out in the absence of any significant demand for autonomy coming from the regions themselves or any challenge from regionalist parties. This was also due to the fact it consisted of a long-delayed implementation of a constitutional provision rather than a new policy development. In a sense the creation of the regions was preordained, and the onus was not so much on those wanting it but on those resisting it.

Summary

In line with Italy's characterization as a paradigmatic example of *partitocrazia* (e.g., Cotta and Verzichelli 2007, 35–64), the politics of the implementation of the ordinary regions was heavily dominated by the political parties and totally dependent on the tempo of their competition and cooperation. Such parties were exclusively statewide ones, which engaged in regionalization primarily for ideological and partisan reasons. From an ideological point of view, the principal motivation was to complete the process of democratization of the state by bringing government closer to the people and reversing the centralization bequeathed by the fascist period. While this was stressed in particular by the parties of the left it also resonated significantly within the ranks of the DC. Economic planning was only a secondary motivation, as evidenced not least by the fact that the regional bodies eventually established had only modest powers in economic planning while the main role in the latter was performed by the regional planning committees with a very different institutional status (see also Putnam et al. 1985, 346; Pieraccini 2000, 238–40).[29]

The constitutional significance of the reform was also limited in that, although the regions were granted primary legislative powers, a property of strong autonomy as discussed in chapter 1, the exercise of these was effectively restricted to such an extent that it almost deprived them of substance. The RAI-RSF scoring of the ordinary regions – below 13 until 1998 – confirms this assessment (Hooghe et al. 2016, 477). The first critical juncture of state restructuring in Italy thus followed closely a top-down dynamic and, as expected, was not Europeanized to any discernible extent. As no political party linked the European dimension and the implementation of the ordinary regions, either in relation to the "full democratization" objective or the "more effective economic planning" one, the reform process enfolded entirely within a domestic dimension.

3.3 BELGIUM: THE FIRST CONSTITUTIONAL REFORM

Brief Historical Overview

In spite of a long tradition of provincial autonomy, including the short-lived federation of the United Belgian States,[30] the Belgian state created in 1830 was a unitary and rather centralized political system inspired by the French administrative model. The law on local government of 1836 gave considerable autonomy to the municipalities but made the provinces mere administrative districts, supervised by a governor appointed by central government (Pirenne 1948–52d, 50–1). French – which was at the time the language of the educated classes, hence also of the restricted electorate, throughout the country – was made the only official language.

Starting from around 1840 a social movement emerged in the northern part of the country directed at revitalizing the Dutch language and securing its use in public affairs. The movement would soon be known as Vlaamse Beweging, or the Flemish Movement, and the northern provinces collectively referred to as Flanders.[31] The establishment's response to the rise of the Flemish Movement was to reluctantly grant progressively wider language rights to Dutch speakers without changing the constitutional order of the state. Meanwhile, the growing assertion of Flanders led to the progressive emergence of a Walloon regional consciousness in the southern half of the country.[32] The deepening linguistic tensions between the two communities were compounded by religious and partisan differences. The Flemish provinces were strongly Catholic while the industrial areas of Wallonia, where most of the French-speaking population lived, were fiercely secular. With the rise of the socialist party in the late nineteenth century, this was reflected in starkly different electoral outcomes. While all bar one of the deputies returned in Flanders in 1894 were Catholic, for instance, all the socialists and the liberals were elected in Wallonia (Mabille 2011, 173).

In the context of the crystallization of two distinct regional communities, demands for a federal reform of the state – or for administrative separation, as it was usually referred to at the time – started to be voiced. Interestingly, these came initially from Francophones operating within the emerging Walloon Movement rather than from the *flamingants*, as the activists in favour of the Dutch language were known (De Vroede 1975, 40; Delforge 1999, 282; Destatte 1999, 16–18).[33] Such suggestions, however, remained very marginal in the political debate. The Flemish movement radicalized and acquired a clear nationalist character in the years immediately before and during the First World War, culminating in a declaration of independence for Flanders by radical activists in December 1917 (Hermans et al. 1992, 238–9). In the interwar years, "the Flemish question was the fundamental political issue in Belgium" (Kossman 1978, 630). Two language laws enacted in 1932, which defined the borders of the regions and strengthened the principle of unilingualism within them, represented a major step in the territorialization of the language question "on the road to administrative separation along linguistic lines" (McRae 1986, 29).

In this context, calls for a federalization of Belgium became more widespread, notably among the Flemings, and led to the first bills being introduced to parliament in 1931 and 1938 (Herremans 1962a, 6). The establishment was still largely hostile, however, as reflected in the report of a study group on state reform set up in the wake of the 1936 election, which rejected federalism "on the grounds that it would pose too great a threat to the integrity of the Belgian state" (Murphy 1988, 120) and advocated instead cultural autonomy based on two advisory cultural councils. A similar support for cultural autonomy and rejection of federalism was the core conclusion of the 1958 report of the Harmel Centre, a new reform study group set up ten years earlier (Herremans 1961a; Murphy 1988, 130). But pressure for a restructuring of the state continued to grow in both regions and demands for constitutional reform acquired a larger following. Two Flemish mass demonstrations in Brussels in 1961 and 1962 led to the adoption of four laws in 1962–63 that permanently fixed the language border and adjusted the language regime applicable north and south of it (De Vroede 1975, 84; McRae 1986, 151). The laws marked the culmination of the long process of building two uniformly unilingual – as well as culturally and politically self-conscious – regions and paved the way for the constitutional reforms of 1970.

In both Flanders and Wallonia demands for constitutional reform came to be voiced primarily by new regional parties, the nationalist Volksunie (VU), or People's Union, and the regionalist Rassemblement wallon (RW),[34] or Walloon Rally, respectively, which challenged the traditional, ideology-based, statewide parties, i.e., the Christian democrats, the socialists, and the liberals. The rise of these parties took place against the backdrop of a wider transformation of the Belgian party system under way since the early 1960s. This was marked by the declining salience of the church-state cleavage and a corresponding rise of the ethno-linguistic one amid a progressive erosion of the postwar consociational settlement. The Leuven crisis[35] exacerbated tensions between the two language communities and triggered an early general election in March 1968. The election ushered in a critical juncture in the evolution of the Belgian state: it created a political situation in which constitutional reforms could no longer be avoided (Verdoodt 1976, 4; Lamberts 2004, 73).

The March 1968 Election

PARTIES

The challenge of the regionalist parties and the Leuven crisis led to a split of the largest and most dominant party, the Christian democrats, into two separate parties, the Christelijke Volkspartij (CVP) in Flanders and the Parti social-chrétien (PSC) in Wallonia (Lamberts 2004, 73–80). This was the first step in a process that, within ten years, would lead to a division of the Belgian party system into two entirely separate regional party systems. Thus party competition in the election took place in both Flanders and Wallonia between two regional and two statewide parties. The former included the Volksunie and the CVP in Flanders and the RW and the PSC in Wallonia. The liberals (Parti de la Liberté et du Progrès/Partij voor Vrijheid en Vooruitgang, hereafter PLP) and the socialists (Parti Socialiste Belge/Belgische Socialistische Partij, hereafter PSB) made up the latter. The CVP and the PSC were together the largest party family and were virtually indispensable in any governing coalition (Timmermans 1994, 121; Lamberts 2004, 80). The PSB was the second largest party and a regular participant in coalitions but with a less central status in the system. The PLP was the traditional third party and had participated in fewer coalitions so had a more marginal system status (Mabille and Lorwin 1977; Rudd 1988; Deschouwer 2009, 77–83). The VU and the RW were outsider parties with a radical constitutional agenda and were largely considered uncoalitionable (Dewachter et al. 1977, 250).

POSITIONS ON STATE RESTRUCTURING

The parties divided themselves in three groups on the question of constitutional reform. The new regional parties, the VU and the RW, were calling for Belgium to become a federal state (VU 1968a, 68; 1968b, 13; 1970a, 4; 1970c, 3; Menu 1994a, 86; RW 1968, 6; 1969, 4). The dominant parties in the two main regions, the CVP in Flanders and the PSB in Wallonia, supported the introduction of forms of regional autonomy but rejected federalism (CVP 1968, 34–5; PSB 1968, 3, 8; Menu 1994c, 161–2). The liberals mounted a strong defence of the unitary state, arguing instead for decentralization in favour of the traditional provinces (PLP 1968a, 10–11, 17–18, 47–50, 62–3). The Francophone Christian democrats were also hostile to regionalization, although less strongly so than the liberals (PSC 1968, 26–7).

The Volksunie had an explicitly nationalist outlook and had long made autonomy for Flanders within a federal Belgium its central objective (CRISP 1961, 7–8; 1966, 11–12; De Winter 1998). Its 1968 program was centred on Flanders's right to self-determination (VU 1968b, 5; Menu 1994a, 104). Self-determination had to be achieved through a transformation of Belgium into a federation of two units each possessing a large degree of autonomy as well as fiscal resources. In keeping with the traditional Flemish position, it firmly rejected the notion of Brussels as a third community and any enlargement of its bilingual area (VU 1968a, 68; 1968b, 13; Menu 1994a, 86). The party argued that a federal constitutional order was the only one able to satisfy Flanders's national aspirations and provide a solution to the political crisis created by the conflicting interests of the two communities (VU 1968a, 68; 1968b, 6; 1968c). It presented the stakes of the election as a stark choice for Belgium: either a constitutional reform leading to a federal system or full application of the rules of democracy, whereby the Flemings would reap the rewards of their being 60 percent of the population (VU 1968a, 69).

The RW had been formed in 1968 just in time to fight the general election. It was the result of a union between the Parti wallon founded in 1965 and several other organizations active within the Walloon Movement (Buelens and Van Dyck 1998, 51–2). The party was explicit in its support for Walloon autonomy and in its desire to provide a counterweight to Flemish nationalism. Its 1968 manifesto presented the party's program thus: "Ce Rassemblement a pour objectif fondamental d'arrêter la marée nationaliste flamande et de tenir en échec sa volonté de dominer l'Etat belge"[36] (RW 1968, 6). Its key policy demand was a legal recognition of the existence of the Walloon community, to be realized through the creation of a Walloon assembly possessing significant powers as well as the introduction of parity rules between the two communities in the state institutions (ibid.). The RW's position was elaborated in its second congress, held in March 1969, when the party called for Belgium's transformation into a federal system of three regions, to which would be devolved major policy responsibilities. The state would retain exclusive powers in foreign affairs, defence, currency, customs, religion, and the highest level of the judiciary. Matters such as economic and social policies, public finances, transport and communications, and judicial matters would be concurrent powers whereas all other powers would belong to the regions (RW 1969, 4). The RW's position was thus very similar to that of the Volksunie, with the important difference that the former envisaged a federal system of three units – i.e., with regional status for Brussels – whereas the latter saw a federal Belgium as the union of two communities.

As the traditionally dominant party in Flanders, the CVP had long been sympathetic to the demands of the Flemish Movement (Wils 1992) but tried to reconcile them with its status as Belgium's natural party of government. The difficulty in doing so had posed severe challenges to the party on several occasions. In 1936 it reorganized itself into two largely autonomous wings and tried to reach an agreement with the Flemish nationalists. With the rise of the Volksunie in the late 1960s, the CVP came again under considerable pressure and had to face deep internal divisions on the constitutional question. If the Flemish wing of the party had to counter the competitive challenge of the Volksunie and was thus inclined to support ideas of cultural autonomy on a regional basis, the Walloon wing, in a minority position in its region, was deeply hostile to them (Lamberts 2004, 72). The Leuven crisis brought the tensions to a breaking point and led to the decision by the two wings of the party to fight the election separately on the basis of different platforms (73).

In the campaign for the 1968 election, the CVP presented its newly Flemishist status as a decision to take charge of the political leadership of the Flemish people (CVP 1968, 1–2). The party acknowledged that there was a problem of coexistence between Flemings and Walloons and therefore that the unitary nature of the Belgian state had to give way to a new structure based on the recognition of two cultural communities (34). Although its leader, Gaston Eyskens, had been an early advocate of federal ideas,[37] the party fell short of embracing federalism as support for the unitary state was still strong within its ranks. The CVP thus called for the devolution of important legislative and executive responsibilities to regional bodies based on the principles of cultural autonomy as well as homogeneity of language and culture in the two communities (35).

As a "still Belgian" party, the PSB had also faced mounting internal tensions on the constitutional issue in the course of the 1960s. Its internal balance was specular to that of the CVP: it had always been in the minority in Flanders but long dominant in Wallonia. For both ideological and partisan reasons, the Flemish wing of the party had always been cool toward Flemish nationalism and its demands for autonomy. The Walloon wing, in contrast, after having been initially hostile to regionalist ideas came round to a position of cautious support. In 1967 the Walloon socialists reaffirmed their support for regional institutions for the whole of Wallonia against suggestions put forward in favour of provincialism and of creating five regions, as proposed by the Flemish socialists (Destatte 1997, 299). The party thus campaigned on a moderate platform that tried to reconcile the two tendencies. Acknowledging that the resolution of the so-called community question was a prerequisite to addressing the economic problems of the country, it advocated both economic regionalism and cultural autonomy. On the one hand, it argued that Belgium was primarily made up of three regions, hence the country's problems had to be tackled through economic planning at the regional level carried out by three regional planning offices (PSB 1968, 1–3; Menu 1994c, 161–2). On the other hand, it also endorsed the principle of full cultural autonomy and proposed the creation of two cultural councils with consultative powers (PSB 1968, 8; Menu, 1994c, 161-2). It also expressed support for the general principle of decentralization and deconcentration of the state administration, in the name of simplification and of bringing government closer to the citizens (PSB 1968, 2).

At the opposite end of the spectrum, the still unitary PLP mounted a strong defence of the constitutional status quo. Given its traditional status as the party of the bourgeoisie drawing support from all regions of the country, the liberals had always adopted a unitarist position on constitutional matters (Rudd 1988, 184). When the party renewed itself and adopted a new name in 1961, its commitment to a unitary state in opposition to the federalist ideas that had by then acquired a wider audience became a key plank of its position. It scored a resounding victory in the 1965 general election on that platform (De Vroede 1975, 13; Rudd 1988, 187, 194, 204). The PLP presented the 1968 election as a crucial choice between extremism and separatism on the one hand and unity and patriotism on the other (PLP 1968a, 10, 63; Coombes and Norton-Taylor 1968, 66; Dewachter 1987, 297, 327-8). It attacked the federalist ideas espoused by the VU as destined to lead to a breakup of the country, damage the economy, and foster intolerance (PLP 1968a, 11, 17-18, 62). Instead, the party proposed to resolve the community question through a wide-ranging institutional reform that, while preserving Belgium's unitary character, would decentralize power to the provinces – rather than creating new community/regional institutions – and give citizens a greater say in the political process (IBID., 47-50; 1969).

Lastly, the Walloon Christian democrats, traditionally a minority in the south of country, had long opposed regionalist ideas and found themselves at odds with their Flemish fellow party members (Lamberts 2004, 72). Having split from the latter, the PSC was thus free to voice its opposition to federalist ideas. Its 1968 manifesto made clear the party "entend garder la cohésion nationale des structures publiques et privées et est adversaire du fédéralisme"[38] (PSC 1968, 26). The heightened community tensions had to be addressed through a new national pact negotiated on a basis of equality, which would introduce the principle of parity between the communities for all matters that touched on their vital interests as well as a fair allocation of public expenditure (2, 6, 25). Echoing the liberals' position, the PSC argued that the desire for autonomy should be met by decentralizing powers to local and provincial governments rather than by creating regional institutions (26–7). The parties defending a unitarist position thus advocated decentralization to the provinces as a tactic to deflect support for regionalist ideas while avoiding appearing overly conservative in their constitutional stances.

ATTITUDES TO, AND STRATEGIC USE OF, EUROPEAN INTEGRATION

All six parties were strongly in favour of European integration, but with significant differences between the Christian democrats, the liberals, and the socialists on the one hand and the VU and, to a lesser extent, the RW on the other. The traditional parties were all in favour of a deepening of the mainstream process of integration – i.e., as then practised within the EU – with the aim of completing the internal market, developing common policies in the economic, social, and scientific fields, and strengthening the European institutions (CRISP 1969b, 10–11). The PLP manifesto explicitly mentioned the creation of a United States of Europe as the ultimate goal (CVP 1968, 29–30; PSC 1968, 14, 33; PLP 1968a, 59; PSB 1968, 10; Loeb 1969, 10–11). The VU, in contrast, saw integration as a radical process of transformation leading to a federal *Europa der volkeren*, or Europe of cultural nations, whereas integration EU-style tended to underpin the traditional state order within which stateless nations such as Flanders were trapped (VU 1968b, 15–16; 1970c, 3, 6; Menu 1994a, 104; Maes 2009; CRISP 1969a, 4, 13; 1973, 3; Lynch 1996, 120). The RW also supported the idea of a Europe of the Regions but gave it a primarily economic, as opposed to ethnic, connotation and saw it more as a natural evolution of integration than a radical break with the existing state order (RW 1969, 4; CRISP 1969a, 4, 13).

The differences in attitudes toward integration were largely mirrored in the degree to which parties exploited the European dimension in relation to state restructuring. The VU presented the internal federalization of Belgium as the other side of the coin of the process of federalizing Europe, arguing that the two should go hand in hand, so that each nation and region could freely choose its political and socioeconomic structures. The integral federalization of Belgium would be the first step in that direction (VU 1968b, 6, 12, 15–16; 1970b; 1970c, 3, 6; Menu 1994a, 104). The VU thus exploited the European dimension in two main ways. First, by arguing that the transfer of sovereignty to regional units was the logical corollary of sovereignty transfers upward to the EU (VU 1970c, 3). Second, by stressing that an autonomous Flanders in a federal Belgium would not be isolated because it would be part of an emerging Europe-wide federal order. The existence of a common EU market, notably, would eliminate any economic dislocation deriving from federalization and the fact that the concept of socioeconomic region started to be endorsed by the EU was presented as a vindication of the party's stance (3, 6). According to Maes (2009), "We always saw Europe as the replacement of Belgium after the autonomy we would get for Flanders" while Lynch (1996, 116) argues: "The VU has consistently attempted to use European integration as a process to legitimize federalism and the necessity of state reform in Belgium" (see also Herremans 1962a, 11; 1962b, 21; 1962c, 14–16; CRISP 1964, 13; 1966, 11–12; Rifflet 1967, 11–12).[39]

The RW also placed its demands within a European context but made less of a conscious effort to exploit the latter to buttress its case for federalism. Its call for federalism at the 1969 congress, as seen above, was based on the grounds that federalism would combine autonomy with union, initially within the Belgian context and "après-demain, avec les autres régions d'Europe"[40] (RW 1969, 4; see also Rifflet 1967, 11–12). On the same occasion, the party stressed its demand for "l'accélération de la politique d'intégration européenne sur la base des régions"[41] (RW 1969, 4; see also CRISP 1975, 14). This was in line with the traditional stance of the Walloon Movement. As early as 1939, some figures in the Walloon Movement had started to make links between Belgian federalization and the federalization of Europe (Delforge 1999, 300). In 1949 the Walloon National Congress voted a motion linking the demands of the Walloon Movement to European federalism (CRISP 1959, 4; Herremans 1962a, 8; Joris 1998, 95). The following year, a commentary on the Schuman Plan in *Wallonie libre* expressed fears that economic integration would damage Wallonia. It called for Wallonia to be represented in the negotiations and that the treaties be based on the "droit des régions plutôt que sur le droit des Etats"[42] (quoted in Destatte 1997, 246). The program of the Parti wallon des Travailleurs, created in 1965, linked the achievement of domestic federalism to the federation of the European nations (CRISP 1967, 16; Destatte 1997, 287). *La Wallonie dans l'Europe*, a manifesto signed by prominent figures in March 1968, argued that the completion of the customs union would not automatically produce harmonious economic development across all Europe's regions, notably as regarded the recovery of the old industrial ones. On the contrary, the wider economic space would exacerbate territorial imbalances. In that context, the creation of regional institutions and the representation of regional interests at the European level would be vital (WdE 1968, 3).

From an opposite perspective to that of the VU and the RW, the PLP saw European integration as being antithetical to federalization in Belgium, on the grounds that the former was outward-looking and unifying while the latter was inward-looking and divisive, and used the European dimension to some extent to undermine support for constitutional reform (PLP 1968a, 19; 1968b, 7; 1969). The PLP argument reflected a widepsread view at the time (Rifflet 1967, 11–12). The CVP, the PSC, and the PSB made no connections between the European dimension and state reform in their campaign.

ELECTION OUTCOME

The VU and the RW were the clear winners of the election. The former increased its tally of seats in the Chamber of Representatives by two thirds (from twelve to twenty) and overtook the liberals to become the third largest party in Flanders. This was also the highest number of votes ever obtained by a Flemish nationalist party (Fraeys 1969, 278, 280). The RW tripled its share of the vote in Wallonia and increased its seats in the lower house from two to seven. These results were also by far the best any Walloon regionalist party had ever achieved (280). The liberals lost one seat overall in spite of higher support in Wallonia, dragged down by heavy losses in Brussels (277–8, 282).[43] The result was particularly disappointing for the party, which, as we have seen, had performed strongly in 1965. The socialists also lost ground, shedding five seats compared to the previous election, due to a drop in support in Brussels and Wallonia, which outweighed modestly higher support in Flanders (277–8, 282). The biggest losers were the two newly autonomous Christian democratic parties, which had to surrender a total between them of eight seats compared to 1965 (CRISP 1968, 24–5). This was a bitter defeat for the CVP in particular, whose newly acquired Flemish identity failed to resonate with the voters (Coombes and Norton-Taylor 1968, 69; Fraeys 1969, 278). An analysis of electoral behaviour showed that the growth in support for the VU and the RW had come primarily at the expense of the CVP and the PSB, respectively. Two thirds of voters lost by the CVP defected to the VU, while half of those lost by the PSB in Wallonia shifted their vote to the RW. The same analysis also showed that the language issues were the primary drivers of electoral behaviour in both Flanders and Wallonia (Fraeys 1969, 290–1; see also Quévit and Aiken 1975, 38–42; Nielsen 1980, 83). Exploitation of the European dimension thus went hand in hand with electoral success for the VU and the RW.

In terms of the constitutional question, these results constituted a major boost for the federalist option versus the defence of the unitary state and put serious pressure on the established parties, primarily the CVP and the PSB, to carry out some form of constitutional reform that would address, at least in part, the demands for regional autonomy. As two contemporary British observers remarked: "some kind of federal system might be the only eventual alternative to permanent deadlock, ineffective government or even worse" (Coombes and Norton-Taylor 1968, 71). This created the political conditions within which the 1970 reform took place.

The 1970 Constitutional Reform and Its Implementation

The government that eventually emerged after the election – a coalition of Christian democrats (both parties) and socialists – had a reform of the state at the top of its agenda. Prime Minister Gaston Eyskens stated in his inaugural declaration to parliament that the government was committed to granting full autonomy to the two main cultural communities and warned that "De Staat moet dus zijn organisatie herzien"[44] (BKV 1968, 5). In the same speech, he also linked the reform of the Belgian state to the process of European integration, twice stressing that "Maar dit België moet tegelijkertijd meer regionaal en meer Europees zijn"[45] (ibid.). A committee mostly made up of parliamentarians, and also including the oppositions, was set up and by February 1970 achieved an outline agreement on the key principles of cultural autonomy and regionalization, although it could not reach a compromise on the thorny question of Brussels's status (Zolberg 1977, 127). In presenting the key lines of the reform to parliament, Eyskens famously declared: "De unitaire Staat, met zijn structuur en zijn werkwijze zoals die thans door de wetten nog geregeld zijn, is door de gebeurtenissen achterhaald. De gemeenschappen en de gewesten moeten hun plaats innemen in vernieuwde staatstructuren die beter aangepast moeten zijn aan de eigen toestanden van het land"[46] (BKV 1968, 5).

A package of constitutional amendments was approved in December 1970, with five key elements. First, the official recognition of four linguistic areas: Dutch (Flanders), French (most of Wallonia), German (the easternmost part of Wallonia), and bilingual (Brussels). Second, the establishment of two communities – Flemish and Francophone – with lawmaking powers over cultural and educational matters. The communities would be governed by a council made up of the members of parliament for the respective language group but would not possess executive bodies, their decrees being executed by central government. Third, the creation of three regions – Flanders, Wallonia, and Brussels – whose competences and institutions would be set by subsequent implementing legislation. Fourth, such implementing legislation would be subject to a special majority requirement, defined as a majority within each language group – each member of parliament being allocated to a language group – and a two-third overall majority in each chamber. Five, a series of safeguards for the French-speaking minority were introduced, including a requirement for equal representation in the executive and an alarm-bell procedure that effectively gave the Francophones a veto on legislation perceived to be detrimental to their interests (Dunn 1974, 153–60; Zolberg 1977, 127–9).

Even though these reforms fell well short of introducing federalism, they did mark the end of the traditionally unitary nature of the Belgian state and set in motion a dramatic process of state restructuring. According to Nandrin (1997, 13), the 1970 reform was the decisive moment in the process of state transformation. The Flemish minister who steered the package through parliament, Leo Tindemans, referred to them as "federalization without federalism" (quoted in Zolberg 1977, 127). They essentially reflected a compromise between the two main parties, and – by virtue of their dominant position within their respective language communities – between Flanders and Wallonia, the former securing cultural autonomy for Dutch speakers and the latter obtaining the prospect of a regional structure for Wallonia. The liberal party voted in favour of the reforms in parliament, thus helping to achieve the necessary majorities, but did not have a significant impact on the outcome. The regional parties, on the other hand, were formally excluded from the negotiations – as "structural opposition parties"[47] – but had a significant indirect influence on the reforms through the competitive pressure they put on the two main parties.[48]

Although only limited public opinion data are available for this period, it appears that a significant gap in support for the reform existed between the party elites and the electorate. A 1966 survey found that only 9 percent of respondents citing the language issue among the five most important problems for the country considered federalization as the solution (Verdoodt 1976, 5).

Summary

True to Belgium's reputation as a *particratie*, the politics of state restructuring in this phase was totally dominated by the political parties (Dumont 1977, 532; Covell 1982, 452). By contrast to Italy, though, the trigger to the reform was the rise of startup regional parties with a radical constitutional agenda, which posed an electoral challenge to the incumbent statewide parties. The demand for a restructuring of the state was at the heart of this challenge and led the statewide parties to embark on a reform of the state as an attempt to counter such a threat.[49] The VU and the RW thus played the crucial role of *zweeppartij*, or whip party, vis-à-vis their mainstream competitors (Rudolph 1977, 409; Dewachter 1987, 300; Joris 1998, 12; De Winter and Dumont 1999, 198). Although the constitutional implications of the reform might appear rather modest at first glance, it is important to bear in mind that it was intended to be the first step in a long process of state reorganization and that its significance as a constitutional turning point was not lost on the contemporaries. This first critical juncture of state restructuring in Belgium thus conforms closely to the bottom-up dynamic conceptualized in chapter 1. Although the politics of reform was only moderately Europeanized overall, the pattern of parties' exploitation of the European dimension was a revealing one. Both the VU and the RW exploited Europe to strengthen the case for state restructuring, while the PLP also did so, albeit to a lesser extent, from a negative position. In contrast, the CVP and the PSB, in spite of their positive attitudes to both state restructuring and Europe, did not link the two in their strategies.

3.4 GENERAL SUMMARY

The features of the first critical junctures of state restructuring in Italy and Belgium largely confirm the conceptual classifications and theoretical expectations developed in the previous chapters. In both countries political parties played a dominant role, enacted the reforms according to heavily partisan motivations and in the face of only lukewarm public support. The dynamic of the two processes, however, were very different. While in Italy it took a top-down form, in Belgium it followed a clear bottom-up dynamic. From the perspective of the realist bargain model of the connections between European integration and state restructuring, the consequences were manifest and closely in line with the theoretical expectations. While Europeanization was absent in Italy, it was modest, though significant, in Belgium. Already in this early phase of European integration, parties such as the VU and the RW played the European card in their rhetorical strategies and appeared to reap electoral benefits from doing so. Their discourse prefigured in an embryonic form those displayed much more intensively by similar parties in later periods. The CVP and the PSB, on the one hand, and the PLP, on the other, also behaved according to the theoretical expectations.

4

Widening and Deepening

In this period both European integration and state restructuring widened and deepened. The second phase of integration saw the EU enlarging from six to nine members as well as developing new policies and institutional arrangements that marked a significant change compared to the previous period. State restructuring deepened in Belgium, with the enactment of the second constitutional reform in 1980, and widened to the UK and France, with the first attempt at devolution to Scotland and Wales in 1979 in the former and the democratization of the regions in 1982 in the latter. The Belgian and British critical junctures followed the bottom-up model of restructuring while the French one was unmistakeably top-down. Broadly in line with the theoretical expectations, there was no Europeanization in France while there was some in Belgium and the UK. The patterns of Europeanization in the latter two cases, however, illustrate the complex determinants of parties' propensity to strategically link integration and state restructuring, especially the role played by attitudes to the EU and to integration.

4.1 THE DEVELOPMENT OF INTEGRATION

This phase of European integration goes from the first enlargement in 1973, when Denmark, Ireland, and the UK joined, to the Fontainebleau summit of 1984, which resolved the UK budgetary question and opened the way to a new phase. It is generally considered a difficult period for the EU, if not the lost decade of integration (see Dinan 2014, 132–94 for an overview). The economic context was particularly difficult, due to oil crisis–induced recessions in

1973 and 1979 and to the monetary turmoil unleashed by the collapse of the Bretton Woods system earlier in the decade. Integrating the new members also proved difficult, with the UK holding a referendum on withdrawal in 1975, and Greece, which joined in 1981, also behaving awkwardly.

These difficulties, however, led to the development of new policies that would acquire a prominent role in the subsequent phases of integration. The stormy international monetary environment spurred the intensification of monetary integration, culminating in the launch of the European Monetary System in 1979 (Apel 1998, 24–44). The wider economic disparities across regions evident in the enlarged Union stimulated the adoption of a policy of territorial cohesion in the shape of the European Regional Development Fund established in 1975 (Wallace 1977).

On the institutional front, too, significant developments took place. Two of them were to prove especially consequential for the subsequent course of integration: the emergence of the European Council and the direct election of the European Parliament. Starting in 1974 the meetings of the heads of government of the member states were given a more regular and structured nature in the form of the European Council (Dinan 2014, 151–4). Around the same time, the decision to shift to direct elections for the European Parliament was taken, leading to the first European election in 1979. Despite the adverse circumstances, European integration thus deepened and started to take on positive features in this period, belying characterizations of it as the dark ages of integration. The institutionalization of the European Council reinforced the ascendancy of the intergovernmentalist approach to decision-making that had prevailed since the empty chair crisis, as seen in the previous chapter.

4.2 THE UK: THE FIRST DEVOLUTION ATTEMPT

Brief Historical Overview

The United Kingdom came into being as a product of England's drive to establish political control over the whole of the British Isles. This was achieved through a series of unions, taking different forms, which saw first Wales, then Scotland, and lastly Ireland being merged with England into what from 1800 onward has been called the United Kingdom.[1] Prior to its incorporation into England in the mid-sixteenth century, Wales had never been a political unit as such and, following union, it did not have a distinct status of any kind until late in the nineteenth century (Morgan 1963). Scotland, by contrast, was an independent kingdom from the ninth century until 1707, and its union with England,[2] unlike the others, was negotiated rather than imposed (McLean and McMillan 2005, 13–60). Under the terms of the Treaty of Union,[3] it secured the right to maintain its own institutions of the Presbyterian Church of Scotland, the legal and educational systems, and local government. The English-dominated Kingdom of Ireland was then merged with the Kingdom of Great Britain to form the United Kingdom in 1800. The constitutional nature of the UK in the nineteenth century has been described as a union state, meaning a unitary state with a single lawmaking parliament but with a special status for some parts of the country based on pre-union rights (Rokkan and Urwin 1982, 11; McLean and McMillan 2005, 1–11).

The question of the nature of the relations between the territories incorporated through the successive unions and the English core first acquired political salience in the 1880s, as a result of the rise of Irish nationalism and Gladstone's proposal of home rule for Ireland (Bogdanor 1999, 19–54; McLean and McMillan 2005, 91–112).[4] The central government's response to the pressure coming from Scotland's demands – support for home rule was much weaker and more controversial in Wales – was to go some way toward accommodating them without compromising the sovereignty of parliament and political control over public policy. The way chosen to do this was to establish in 1885 a territorial department to deal with Scottish affairs – the Scottish Office – headed by a Scottish secretary of ministerial rank. The Scottish Office was to run the administration for Scotland and its secretary to be the "voice of Scotland in government" and the "voice of government in Scotland." Its administration was moved from London to Edinburgh in 1939. From 1907 to the 1950s, sections of government departments with specific responsibility for Wales were set up, which were then subsumed into the Welsh Office in 1964–65 (Bogdanor 1999, 111–16, 157–62; McLean and McMillan 2005, 115–17).

In the interwar period, nationalist parties were formed in both Wales and Scotland, the Plaid Genedlaethol Cymru (PC), or National Party of Wales, and the Scottish National Party (SNP), respectively. In 1949 a civil society petition, the Scottish Covenant, demanding a devolved parliament attracted around two million signatures – out of a total Scottish population of five million (Bogdanor 1999, 139). Meanwhile, the first ever opinion poll on the issue, conducted in 1947, found a three-quarters majority in favour of self-government for Scotland (Mitchell 1996, 149). Support for the SNP and PC rose significantly in the 1960s, leading to high-profile victories in by-elections in 1966–67. In their wake the government set up a commission of enquiry, later known as the Kilbrandon Commission, charged with examining the constitutional structure of the UK in the context of the new demands for self-government coming from Scotland and Wales. The Commission reported in 1973, with a majority of members recommending the establishment of directly elected regional assemblies for Scotland and Wales (RCC 1973; Bogdanor 1999, 171–7).

From the October 1974 Election to the March 1979 Referendums

PARTIES

Four parties were the key actors in the politics of state restructuring in the 1974–79 parliament: the two main statewide parties – Labour and the Conservatives – and the two regional-nationalist ones, the SNP and the PC. The Labour Party came first in the October 1974 election, winning 319 seats on 39 percent of the vote, an increase of 18 seats and two percentage points on the previous election. The Conservative party secured 277 seats on 36 percent of the vote, a drop of 20 seats and two percentage points compared to the previous election. Labour thus won the election and was able to form a government with a narrow majority of three seats in the House of Commons. The SNP achieved a spectacular success in Scotland, winning 30 percent of the vote and 11 of the 71 Scottish seats. The PC performed less strongly than the SNP, securing only three of the 36 Welsh seats on 11 percent of the vote in Wales (Butler and Kavanagh 1975, 295–6, 345–53).

POSITIONS ON STATE RESTRUCTURING

With support for the nationalist parties at an all-time high in Scotland and Wales,[5] the question of their constitutional status took centre stage in the 1974–79 parliament (Jaensch 1976, 307, 318–19; Esman 1977, 264–5; Jones and Keating 1982, 189). Achieving autonomy for their respective nations was at the heart of both parties' program, although such autonomy was defined in different ways. The SNP was committed to independence, defined in the party's constitution as "the restoration of Scottish national sovereignty" (reproduced in Brand 1978, 305). An independent Scotland would remain within the Commonwealth and retain the queen as head of state. The SNP envisaged winning a majority of the Scottish seats in a general election as a mandate for negotiating secession (SNP 1979, 14–15; Lynch 2002, 146–53; Mitchell et al. 2011, 19–20).

The emergence of the Labour Party's policy to establish a Scottish Assembly created a strategic dilemma for the SNP (Drucker 1976; Kauppi 1982; Levy 1986; Lynch 2002, 146–53; Mitchell et al. 2011, 20). On the one hand, an assembly could be seen as a useful stepping-stone: it would have made it easier for the SNP to win a majority of the seats and on that basis to claim a mandate for secession. On the other hand, with mass support for independence still very low, there was a high risk that "the establishment of a Scottish Assembly might satisfy the electorate sufficiently to postpone the achievement of independence indefinitely" (Macartney 1981, 18). The SNP was torn by this dilemma but narrowly decided in favour of devolution at its 1976 conference, on the ground that, in the words of its parliamentary leader, "Scotland must be prepared to build on whatever devolution can be wrung out of this Government" (quoted in Mbadinuju 1976, 296; see also Lynch 2002, 147–8 and Mitchell et al. 2011, 20). The party's support for devolution was steadfast, and its campaign for the 1979 referendum was unambiguously for a Yes vote (Macartney 1981).

The PC was more ambiguous as to what constitutional end goal it was pursuing. It advocated "full self-government for Wales" (PC 1979, 1; McAllister 2001, 131–7) without specifying whether that meant sovereign statehood or home rule within the UK. The party had traditionally been more concerned with the defence of Wales's cultural and linguistic distinctiveness rather than with its constitutional status. The wider Welsh nationalist movement too had traditionally aimed for an equal status with England within the UK rather than separation (Bogdanor 1999, 144–65). Devolution thus presented much less of a dilemma for the PC than it did for the SNP, and the party supported it in parliament and in the 1979 referendum campaign (Jones and Wilford 1983).

The rise of the regional-nationalist parties in Scotland and Wales was particularly threatening to the Labour Party, which had become dependent on the votes from the two regions to win general elections.

Leading into the October 1974 election for the first time the party published separate Scottish and Welsh manifestos and promised to "create elected assemblies in Scotland and Wales" (Craig 1990, 251). Once in office, the party moved speedily and set forth its proposal in the *Our Changing Democracy: Devolution to Scotland and Wales* white paper published in November 1975.[6] The white paper proposed directly elected assemblies for both Scotland and Wales, the first one with primary lawmaking powers – in areas such as education, health, and social services – and the second one with secondary legislative and executive powers only. Both assemblies would be elected by the first-past-the-post system and be financed by a block grant from the Treasury. A Scotland and Wales bill incorporating the proposals was introduced to parliament in late 1976 but fell victim to a defeated guillotine motion in February 1977. After a tactical agreement with the Liberal Party, later that year the government introduced two separate bills, which became the Scotland Act 1978 and the Wales Act 1978. Due to pressure from anti-devolutionists from within its own ranks as well as from those of the opposition, a clause was incorporated into the Act making its implementation subject to endorsement by at least 40 percent of the Scottish and Welsh electorates – as opposed to voters – in regional referendums (Bogdanor 1999, 179–89). The divisions within the party came to the fore in the campaign for the referendum in Scotland, in which Labour divided into three groups and displayed greater hostility toward the SNP – supposedly its ally in the campaign – than toward the Conservatives (Macartney 1981; Dardanelli 2005a, 33–4).

As traditional defenders of unionism, the Conservatives had long been hostile to devolution (Mitchell 1990). Under the Heath leadership, however, the party modified its position and expressed support for the principle of devolution although it took no steps toward implementing it when it was in office in 1970–74 (Greenwood and Wilson 1978, 162–5). For the October 1974 election, the Conservatives also published separate manifestos for Scotland and Wales and promised to set up an – indirectly elected – assembly for the former but only increased powers for the Secretary of State and the Welsh Office in relation to the latter (Craig 1990, 234–5). Under the new Thatcher leadership and in the context of Labour's devolution policy, the party adopted a two-pronged strategy. On the one hand, it continued to support devolution in principle, at least where Scotland was concerned. On the other hand, it opposed Labour's policy as a flawed model and the vast majority of its MPs voted against the bills in parliament (Bogdanor 1980, 89–91). The party maintained such a position in the referendum campaigns. While in Wales it simply campaigned for a No vote, in Scotland it urged voters to reject the Scotland Act 1978 while assuring them that this would not spell the end for devolution, thus hinting that the Conservatives would put forward a sounder model in the future (Mitchell 1990, 88–9; Dardanelli 2005a, 38–9).

ATTITUDES TO, AND STRATEGIC USE OF, EUROPEAN INTEGRATION

The SNP was deeply hostile to the EU, which it saw as a centralizing and undemocratic force, bent on imposing uniform policies across Western Europe and wipe out cultural differences. The party's official position was that an independent Scotland would attempt to renegotiate its membership of the EU and would put the results of such negotiations to a referendum, although the majority of the party simply favoured withdrawal (SNP 1979, 28; Lynch 1996, 32–7; Mitchell 1998b, 111–17; Dardanelli 2003, 274–6). The party indirectly linked membership of the EU and independence insofar as only an independent Scotland would have been in a position to renegotiate the terms of its membership. Access to EU decision-making was at the heart of this vision as the party committed itself to seeking "a seat in the Council of Ministers, appropriate representation in the European Parliament and other EEC institutions" (SNP 1979, 28). The SNP, however, did not exploit the European dimension in its campaign for a Yes vote in the referendum (SNP 1979, 11–14; Bochel et al. 1981; Macartney 1981; Dardanelli 2005a, 29–30, 34–6).

PC was less hostile to the EU and was positive toward alternative forms of integration (Wyn Jones 2009, 136–8). Although it had campaigned for a No in the 1975 referendum on the UK's membership of the EU, shortly afterward it called for "full national status for Wales inside the European Communities" (quoted in Lynch 1996, 71), a status that would have given Wales direct access to the EU decision-making process. In the manifesto for the 1979 election the party position was summarized as such: "Plaid Cymru is totally opposed to the concept of a centralized European state and will work for the creation of an [sic] Europe where self-governing communities co-operate fully with one another" (PC 1979, 2; also Lynch

1996, 71–2; Mitchell 1998b, 111–17; McAllister 2001, 145–9; Elias 2009, 49–53). The manifesto also linked self-government and the European dimension by arguing: "only Plaid Cymru can be relied upon to win any measure of self-government for our country. Plaid Cymru will also fight for a stronger voice for Wales in the EEC Parliament and institutions while we remain part of the EEC." (PC 1979, 2). In a similar way to the SNP, though, the party failed to appeal to the European dimension to bolster its support for devolution in the 1979 referendum campaign (Jones and Wilford 1983).

The Labour Party was deeply divided about Europe. At the time of the 1975 referendum, the leadership was divided but mostly in favour while the grassroots were largely opposed. Afterward, the party accepted the reality of membership but divisions remained. The roots of this hostility were in the perception of the EU as a capitalist organization, both in political and economic terms, and in the constraints it put on the pursuit of socialist policies in the UK (Byrd 1978, esp. 130–4, 145–6; LAB-S 1979, 24–5; LAB-W 1979, 24–5; George and Haythorne 1996, 110–11; Daniels 1998, 74; Baker et al. 2008, 95–7). Some Scottish pro-devolution leaders made an explicit link between EU membership and Scotland's self-government, but to the majority of the party the European dimension appeared largely disconnected from devolution and Labour did not make any attempt to exploit it in the referendum campaigns (Macartney 1981; Dardanelli 2005a, 34–6; Jones and Wilford 1983).

The Conservatives were the "party of Europe" in the 1970s, having taken the UK into the EU in 1973 and having campaigned vigorously for a Yes vote in the 1975 referendum (Ashford 1980, esp. 103–10). In the eyes of the party the EU was seen as a primarily economic organization, bringing positive effects on the country in terms of market opportunities and enhanced competition (CON-S 1979, 32–3; CON-W 1979, 32–3; Ashford 1980, 112; Morris 1996, 130; Baker et al. 2008, 97–9). Of the four parties, the Conservatives were the one seeing the most significant links between EU membership and devolution, but the prevailing view was that the connection was a negative one. The direct election of the European Parliament and the prospect of a directly elected Scottish assembly, for instance, were seen as raising the spectre of over-government. More fundamentally, the drive to create lawmaking bodies at the regional level was running counter to the secular movement for integration embodied by the European Union. From this perspective, the Conservatives and the business organizations, which joined them in the No campaign, made some limited use of the European dimension to undermine the rationale for devolution in the Scottish referendum campaign (Dardanelli 2005a, 39–40, 57–8).

REFERENDUM OUTCOMES AND THEIR AFTERMATH

The referendums, held on 1 March 1979, resulted in an overwhelming rejection of devolution in Wales and a narrow endorsement in Scotland. In the former, 20 percent of voters supported an assembly against 80 percent rejecting it, on a 59 percent turnout. In Scotland 51.6 percent voted Yes and 48.5 voted No, on a 63 percent turnout. As a percentage of the electorate, this meant that 33 percent endorsed the Act against 31 percent rejecting it. If we take into account that the 40 percent rule created an incentive for opponents of devolution not to vote, rather than vote No, and the distribution of preferences among those who did not vote, however, it is clear that the Scotland Act 1978 was also rejected (Dardanelli 2005a, 62–73). The percentage of the electorate having endorsed devolution in the two regions falling much shorter of the required threshold, the implementation of devolution was effectively blocked. This triggered a no-confidence vote initiated by the SNP and the Conservatives, which brought the government down on 28 March.

In the subsequent general election, held in May, the SNP suffered a major defeat and the PC also lost ground. The former saw its share of the vote in Scotland collapse from 30.4 to 17.3 percent and lost all but two of its MPs. The latter lost about three percentage points in the vote share but managed to retain two of its three MPs. The Labour Party was also decisively defeated, losing over two percentage points in electoral support and fifty seats. The Conservatives scored a resounding victory, gaining over eight percentage points in voters' support and sixty-two seats (Butler and Kavanagh 1980, 353–4). The incoming Conservative government repealed the Scotland Act and the Wales Act within a month of entering office (Bogdanor 1999, 191). The 1979 referendums and the election thus killed devolution and the issue would remain off the mainstream political agenda for the entire decade that followed. The failure of the SNP and PC to exploit Europe to their advantage could be seen to have contributed to the failure of state restructuring in this juncture (Dardanelli 2005a, 75–81).

Summary

As mentioned in chapter 1, although this first devolution attempt in the UK failed, it was close enough to succeeding that it is reasonable to consider it a critical juncture under the so-called possibility principle (Mahoney and Goertz 2004). Taken as a whole, the juncture conforms clearly to the bottom-up model. Party competition was central to the process. Devolution was put forward by the Labour Party as a reaction to the challenge presented by the rise of the SNP (and, to a much lesser extent, PC), which was posing both an electoral threat, given Labour's reliance on the Scottish vote, and a territorial integrity threat to the UK state, given its secessionist position. The politics of devolution was thus played between one – or two – regional-nationalist parties and two statewide ones. The partisan nature of devolution, however, was tempered by the direct involvement of the affected electorates via referendums. Although the referendum clause itself had been introduced in the bills as a result of partisan infighting, the voice given to the electorate was nonetheless highly significant and, as it turned out, decisive for the fate of the reform.

The significance of restructuring also corresponds to the bottom-up model as the powers the proposed Scottish Assembly would have had were of considerable consequence, including primary legislative powers in a number of policy fields. Devolution was clearly seen as a major constitutional reform that would profoundly affect the nature of the UK, as Bogdanor (1999, 1) put it: "Devolution is the most radical constitutional change this country has seen since the Great Reform Act of 1832." The bottom-up model admittedly fits the Welsh component of the reform package less well as the challenge presented by PC was much less serious and the proposed assembly would only have executive powers. If we were to consider Wales in isolation, we would have to conclude that the dynamic was more top down than bottom up. However, because the devolution proposals for Wales were clearly an addition to those put forward to address the Scottish question,[7] and the latter was unequivocally a bottom-up dynamic, the entire process had a primarily bottom-up nature.

Although modest overall, the patterns of Europeanization displayed confirm the theoretical expectations of the realist bargain model. The Conservative campaigners for a No in the referendums, in a manner reminiscent of the Belgian liberals in the late 1960s, enlisted the European dimension to undermine the appeal of devolution and independence, thus confirming the scope for Europe to be used negatively to oppose state restructuring, while the pro-devolution Labour Party failed to play the European card to its advantage. The two regional-nationalist parties adopted different strategies: while the SNP did not exploit the European dimension to buttress its call for a Yes vote, PC did so, albeit to a moderate extent. The two parties' attitudes to integration, as opposed to the existing EU, appear to account for this divergence. While both were critical of the EU, PC, in a similar vein to the VU and the RW in Belgium, had a positive view of an alternative form of integration while the SNP did not distinguish between integration as such and the actual EU in its hostile stance. This shows the role played by perceptions and attitudes as an intervening variable between the opportunities and incentives offered by integration and parties' decision to exploit it in relation to state restructuring.

4.3 BELGIUM: THE SECOND CONSTITUTIONAL REFORM

As the constitutional reforms of 1970 only established the main principles of the new structure of the state, passing the implementing legislation was a key stage before the new structures could operate. Given that this legislation, as mentioned, required special majorities, the process of implementation proved to be long and fraught with difficulties. A stark contrast emerged in particular between the speedy implementation of cultural autonomy, put into practice in the first parliamentary term after the changes in the constitution, and the delay concerning regionalization. In 1974 the government set up advisory regional institutions intended to prepare the full implementation of the regions, which would last until 1979 (Brassinne 1999, 309). In the period 1976–78 a series of negotiations between parties representing the two main communities took place and managed to reach agreements – such as the Egmont Pact of 1977 – which however foundered in parliament due to intraparty frictions (MacMullen 1979, 335; Covell 1982; Mabille 2011, 309–11). Prime Minister Tindemans's resignation in October 1978 prevented the implementation of a new agreement, known as the Stuyvenberg, and led to the December 1978 election.

The December 1978 Election

PARTIES

In the course of the 1970s, the Belgian party system underwent further dramatic changes. After reaching a peak of support at the 1971 election and brief spells in office as part of broad coalitions later in the decade, the community parties experienced a decline. This was terminal in the case of the RW, which suffered a series of splits from 1976 onward and saw its support more than halve in the 1977 election, a defeat from which it would never recover (Buelens and Van Dyck 1998, 66; Delforge 2003, 21–5). The VU defended its positions better but was damaged by its participation in government in 1977–78 and, especially, its endorsement of the Egmont Pact, to which large sections of Flemish public opinion were hostile (De Winter 1998, 42). This led a group of hardliners to break away from the party to found a more radical one, the Vlaams Blok (VB), or Flemish Bloc (Mabille 2011, 311). The decline of the community parties took place in the context of a further division of the traditional statewide parties into separate regional ones. In 1972 the liberal party followed the lead of the Christian democrats and split into the Flemish Partij voor Vrijheid en Vooruitgang (PVV), or Party of Freedom and Progress, and what would become after several incarnations the Francophone Parti réformateur libéral (PRL),[8] or Liberal Reformist Party (Rudd 1988, 189–92). Just before the 1978 election it was the turn of the socialists to split, giving birth to the Parti socialiste (PS) on the Francophone side and the Socialistische Partij (SP) on the Flemish one (Delwit 1994, 32–3).

By the time of the election, then, the old statewide party system had completed its transformation into two separate party systems all made up of regional parties. The PS would quickly emerge as the dominant party in Wallonia and, as such, as a key actor in the politics of state restructuring as the principal representative of one of the communities, while the two liberal parties played a very different role to that of the old PLP. Whereas the latter had been the champion of Belgian unitarism in the 1960s, the new parties would welcome former members of the community parties and adopt a strong regionalist profile. The PRL was the first to do so, as symbolized by the fact that its first leader, Jean Gol, was a former RW member (Rudd 1988, 191), while for the PVV the Flemishist turn would come, as we will see in the next chapter, in the early 1990s.

POSITIONS ON STATE RESTRUCTURING

The VU was critical of the 1970 reforms, which, it argued, had blocked the Flemish majority at the central level without granting Flanders significant autonomy in return. A genuine federal transformation of the state was necessary both to tackle the economic crisis and to preserve democratic freedom and diversity in the country. The party thus demanded "een Vlaamse staat in een Belgische bondstaat"[9] (VU 1978, 3) based on a single parliament and executive, with authority over the whole Flemish region as well as the Flemish community in Brussels. It also called for this parliament to have as wide a range of competences as possible and its own tax-raising powers, warning against a form of pseudo-federalism that would leave the most important levers of power in the hands of the parity-based central government (3–4).

The RW also maintained its federalist position and argued that autonomy for Wallonia was a precondition to tackling the economic crisis, under the banner "La condition institutionnelle du redressement économique: le fédéralisme intégral"[10] (RW 1978, 17). It highlighted the contrast between the rapid implementation of the cultural communities, the focus of Flemings' demands, and the fact that the regions provided for in the constitutional amendment of 1970, a key Walloon demand, had still not been implemented. The party demanded the creation of three directly elected regional assemblies with equal lawmaking powers, regional executives responsible to such assemblies, and autonomous funding and administrative services. The two cultural communities and the three regions would then delegate a certain number of competences to the central government (RW 1978, 18; also Covell 1981, 208).

The former statewide parties clustered together supporting a completion of the state reform, although they refrained from labelling it federalism. The CVP argued that a harmonious cohabitation of the communities and the regions within the Belgian state was only possible if a comprehensive reform was carried out (CVP 1978, 21–3). It stressed that the authority of the state had to remain strong and well-organized and warned against those who wanted to hollow out the central institutions of the state (see also Menu 1994b, 277). At the same time, communities and regions needed a framework of autonomy within which to exercise both legislative and executive competences and the provinces had to be retained as a level of coordination between the regions and the municipalities. The party also stressed that a settlement of the Brussels question was the most important precondition to a successful completion of a new round of reforms and that this rested, among other things, on a recognition of the Dutch-speaking character of the Brussels suburbs.[11] Although the party acknowledged the existence of the regions, the philosophy underlying its proposals was clearly based on the recognition of two main cultural-linguistic communities rather than three regions (CVP 1978, 21–3).

The PVV was more positive toward the institution of the region, committing itself to pursuing a "bloiend Vlaams gewest in een modern België"[12] (PVV 1978a, 22) in negotiations on a completion of the reform of the state. The latter should lead to each level of government having a directly elected assembly and an executive responsible to it, and the number of such levels should be limited to three, implying the abolition of the provinces (1978a, 23; 1978b, 12). The newly autonomous SP stressed its enduring commitment to internationalist ideals and promised: "Wij willen geenszins de nationalistiche toer op gaan"[13] (SP 1978, 2). It supported a thorough reform of the state able to address the calls for greater autonomy but, at the same time, it warned that the need for important national competences in the judicial, economic, social, financial, and monetary fields as well as in foreign affairs and defence will continue to exist in the future (64–5). For the sake of simplicity and efficiency, and in contrast to the long-standing policy of the unified socialist party, it called for a two-unit structure, thus emphasizing the cultural-linguistic dimension over the regional one. Each community assembly should be directly elected, have its own executive and possess adequate fiscal resources while the provinces should be rethought (SP 1978, 64–5; MacMullen 1979, 336).

The Francophone parties focused in particular on the implementation of the regions. The PS and the PSC – as well as the Front démocratique des francophones (FDF) – issued a joint declaration promising to make their entry into a governing coalition dependent on a commitment to implement the regions and calling for wider powers for the regions in fields such as water supply, transport, tourism, economic development, and scientific research (PS-PSC-FDF 1978; Covell 1982, 464). The PS put considerable emphasis on the need to reach a pacification between the communities while at the same time defending the interest of the French speakers, arguing "qu'une solution véritable au contentieux communautaire passe par une régionalisation plus accentuée"[14] (PS 1978, 2) while the PSC placed regionalization within a call for a wider reform of the political system: "l'Etat central est encombré de problèmes qui seraient mieux réglés au niveau des régions et des communautés"[15] (PSC 1978, 2).

The PRLW was on a very similar line: "Le P.R.L.W. veut structurer la Belgique d'une manière simple, efficace, sans dépenses supplémentaires, en rapprochant le pouvoir publique du citoyen"[16] (PRLW 1978, 8). On this basis, the territorial structure of the state should have only three tiers: the municipality, the region, and the state. The Walloon region should have a parliament and an executive responsible to it as well as economic powers sufficient to enact an autonomous economic development policy. To do so it should also possess its own financial resources (9). The major change relative to 1968 was thus the absence of a unitarist position or a defence of the status quo. All parties seemed to agree that the latter could not be a stable institutional setup and was just a staging post toward some form of federal order.

ATTITUDES TO, AND STRATEGIC USE OF,
EUROPEAN INTEGRATION

All parties remained strongly supportive of European integration, although the community parties maintained their vision of an alternative Europe and some criticisms of the EU started to be voiced by the left. The CVP put a lot of emphasis on the European dimension, presenting the "versnelde opbouw van Europa"[17] (CVP 1978, 1) as one of the three fundamental axes of its program. It welcomed the entry into force of the European Monetary System as the first step toward an economic and monetary union, and saw the shift to direct elections for the European Parliament as the first step in the democratization of the EU, a process that ought to lead to a European federation (CVP 1978, 36–8; see also Menu 1994b, 277). The PVV put forward a very similar line, calling for a liberal and democratic Europe, not merely a Europe of technocrats and business people. It should be based on a constitution enshrining the separation of powers and majority voting, and should aim for a full economic and monetary integration and a common foreign policy (PVV 1978a, 25–7; see also 1978b, 13, and Menu 1994d, 230). The PRLW also put considerable emphasis on integration, headlining a section of its manifesto "Pour une Wallonie européenne"[18] (PRLW 1978, 31). In it the party outlined a program in ten points including a stronger role for the Commission and the Parliament, the adoption of a charter of rights, the achievement of monetary union with the creation of a parallel European currency, and common policies on energy, environment, and external relations (31–2).

The PSC devoted less attention to Europe in its manifesto but expressed general support for integration and, in particular, for the two main steps forward being taken at the time – the implementation of the European Monetary System and the first direct election for the European Parliament – calling for "une Europe unie au plan politique, forte au plan économique et progressiste au plan social"[19] (PSC 1978, 11). The two socialist parties, though generally supportive of integration, were critical of the weakness of democracy and of the social dimension. The francophone PS hailed the direct election of the EP as the first step in the building of a genuinely democratic European community and called for the parliament to be granted additional powers in the economic and social spheres (PS 1978, 17). Its counterpart in Flanders devoted a section of its manifesto to "Vlaanderen in Europa," in which it stressed the SP's commitment to a more progressive and integrated Europe, on the grounds that many problems related to employment, environment, technological development, and industrial and monetary policies could only be tackled effectively within a European framework. The party felt, however, that the existing EU fell significantly short of its aspirations and, although the introduction of direct elections for the European Parliament was a significant step forward, more progress had to be made in the direction of a more social and more democratic Europe (SP 1978, 56–9).

The VU and the RW continued to put forward an alternative view of integration. The former did not pay attention to Europe in its manifesto but maintained its commitment to a *Europa der volkeren* (VU 1978; Lynch 1996, 119–23; Maes 2009). At its fourth congress in November 1980, the youth wing of the party, or VUJO, adopted a resolution calling for "politiek zelfbestuur voor de Staat Vlaanderen,"[20] initially within a confederal Belgium and in time within a "gekonfedereerd Europa der volkeren"[21] (VUJO 1980, section 3, 1). The latter called for a "different Europe" based on a strengthened regional and social dimensions and independence from both the USA and the USSR in international relations (RW 1978, 70–3).

Compared to the 1968 election, parties linked European integration and state restructuring much less. In spite of its enduring commitment to a *Europa der volkeren*, the VU did not actually exploit the European dimension in the 1978 manifesto to bolster its demand for a Flemish state. More in line with its previous stance, the RW placed its demands for Wallonia's autonomy in a European context in which the regions would play a key role but did not explicitly use the latter to support such demands (70–3). In a similar vein, the CVP stressed its support for a development of EU regional policy and the need to further develop and recognize the regions but did not make any direct linkages between the European dimension and the process of constitutional reform in Belgium (CVP 1978, 38). In contrast with the PLP's attempt in the previous election, the liberal parties did not link Europe and state reform either, nor did the socialist parties.

ELECTION OUTCOME

Tindemans's calculations in calling an early election only a little more than a year after the previous one were widely interpreted as intended to weaken the VU and strengthen the CVP's position as Flanders's representative in the era following the Egmont-Stuyvenberg negotiations with the Francophone parties on the state reform (e.g., Irving 1979, 253–4). By that yardstick, the election outcome was a mixed one for the CVP. On the one hand, the party lost ground slightly in terms of votes, although it did gain an extra seat[22] (Fraeys 1979, 16, 23). On the other hand, the VU suffered a major defeat, losing almost five percentage points in electoral support and surrendering nearly a third of its seats – down from twenty to fourteen (Irving 1979, 254; Fraeys 1979, 18, 23). The PVV was the one that profited the most from the losses of the VU, gaining nearly three percentage points and five seats while the SP declined slightly, losing one seat (Irving 1979, 254; Fraeys 1979, 18, 23). There was more stability on the Francophone side. The PS lost two percentage points and three seats while the PRLW also lost two percentage points but managed to retain its tally of seats. The PSC was the main beneficiary, gaining one seat, while the RW after the heavy losses in the previous election declined further and surrendered another seat (Fraeys 1979, 16–17, 20).

The overall picture was one of heavy defeat for the community parties and broad stability among the mainstream ones, with marginal strengthening of the CVP – and of the wider Christian democratic family – vis-à-vis the PS, so also of the Flemings vis-à-vis the Francophones. On this occasion, thus, the VU's and RW's failure to exploit the European dimension effectively was associated with electoral losses for both parties. In terms of state restructuring, the elections pointed to the existence of broad support for a completion of the reforms started in 1970 and a rejection of more radical options in a context in which the electorate was much more preoccupied with the state of the economy than with the constitutional question (De Ridder et al. 1978, 92; Irving 1979, 254; MacMullen 1979, 336). That cleared the way for the 1980 package of constitutional reforms.

The 1980 Constitutional Reforms

The 1980 reforms – comprised of a number of constitutional amendments as well as two institutional laws enacted over the same period – were essentially a completion of the process started in 1970 and a revision of some of its provisions, notably as regards the implementation of the regions. As Irving put it, "these regional institutions, together with their precise powers, have been at the heart of the constitutional debate of the last ten years" (1979, 251). The key points of the reforms were threefold: a) a reform of the communities; b) the implementation of two regions; and c) a clarification of the legal standing of the decrees issued by the communities and the regions vis-à-vis the laws of the state. The cultural communities lost their "cultural" adjective and their responsibilities were broadened to include so-called personalizable policy areas, such as healthcare and social service, with competences in these areas also extended to Brussels. Such communities were given their own executives bodies responsible to the community councils, although the latter remained composed of state parliamentarians rather than being directly elected.

The Flemish and Walloon regional governments were set up and given lawmaking powers over a range of policy areas – including economic development, energy, environment, housing, labour, territorial planning, and water supply – although with a number of matters still reserved to the central government. Like the communities, the regions were also to be governed by indirectly elected councils made up of state parliamentarians and executives responsible to them. Flanders decided not to establish regional bodies but to have the community council and executive also exercise the competences of the region so that only one set of Flemish institutions would exist. This was in line with the traditional Flemish focus on the community rather than the region. No such merger of the two bodies took place on the Francophone side so that Walloon institutions were set up alongside those of the French community. The implementation of the regions laid down in the 1970 constitutional amendment was still incomplete, though, because no agreement was reached on the question of Brussels; it was decided to proceed with the implementation of the two main regions, leaving a solution to the Brussels question for a later date.

The last main element of the reform package was the introduction of the principle of legal parity between the decrees of the communities and the regions and the laws of the state, so that no hierarchy existed in law between them (Covell 1981, 212–15; Mabille 2011, 312–17). Like the previous package of reforms, this one too was passed by a coalition of the mainstream parties – this time including the liberals – without participation from the community parties (Covell 1981, 205, 214).

A significant gap between the preferences of the political parties and those of the mass public was still present. In 1975, only just over a third of voters supported a transformation of the state in a federal direction in both Flanders and Wallonia, while around 50 percent (46 among the Flemings and 54 among the Walloons) wanted to preserve a unitary state (McRae 1986, 119). In 1979, only 24.5 percent in Flanders and 24 percent in Wallonia were in favour of a federal state, whereas 24.8 and 38 percent, respectively, supported the status quo (Delruelle-Vosswinckel and Frognier 1980, 23–4). By 1982 public support for federalism, however, had grown to 42 percent among the Flemings although it had declined to 30 percent in Wallonia (McRae 1986, 119).

Summary

The politics of state restructuring in Belgium in this second juncture continued to be dominated by political parties, without significant involvement from the electorate and also seemingly at odds with the latter's preferences. Although in a less clear-cut fashion than the first juncture, the process leading to the 1980 reforms followed a bottom-up dynamic. If the electoral rise of the VU and the RW had by then run its course, their role as *zweeppartijen* was still being felt, in two main ways. First, this second round of reform was largely an implementation and a completion of the constitutional reforms adopted in 1970 and could thus be seen as the long-term effect of the dynamic at play in the first juncture. Second, the regional-nationalist challenge ultimately led to the traditional statewide parties to fall apart and give way to new regional parties, thus embedding a permanent community logic into the party system/s. Confirming the interpretation given of their 1970 predecessors, the reforms enacted in this second juncture were of significant constitutional consequence. The implementation of the regions, in particular, unmistakeably transformed the old unitary architecture of the state and, if it did not deliver a federal order as such, it clearly laid the ground for it. The patterns of parties' exploitation of the European dimension broadly support the theoretical expectations but in a very weak form. The degree of overall Europeanization was minimal, with the VU largely failing to link Europe and state restructuring and the RW only doing so very tamely. Interestingly, the former statewide parties followed in the footsteps of their predecessors and did not link the European dimension and state restructuring despite their positive attitudes to both.

4.4 FRANCE: THE DEMOCRATIZATION OF THE REGIONS

Brief Historical Overview

The rule of the kings of France was expanded and consolidated in the late medieval and the early modern period through the successive incorporation of territories up to the so-called natural borders of the Rhine in the east and the Alps and the Pyrenees in the south (Price 2005, 54–95). The territories that came under the sovereignty of the king, known as *provinces* and *pays*,[23] had disparate constitutional statuses, those of older conquest typically being formally incorporated into the kingdom and those of more recent acquisition being linked to it on the basis of a feudal contractual relation with the king (Mousnier 1974, 471–2). The newer provinces typically retained a certain number of privileges and liberties, for instance in taxation matters, and a provincial assembly. The field administration of the state consisted of many different types of territorial units, whose boundaries did not coincide (Bazoche 2008, 14–16). Against this background, in the seventeenth century the monarchy started a drive to secure its control of the realm and make its administration more efficient and effective (41–2). Central to this effort was the introduction of the *intendants* in the first half of the century. These were a corps of officials tasked with representing the full spectrum of royal powers in the provinces, unlike the previous administrators who tended to have sectoral competences (Mousnier 1980, 484–544). Provincial liberties were gradually reduced in favour of absolute royal power, as symbolized by the fading away of the provincial estates, thus building a progressively more centralized state administration (Mousnier 1974, 473–4).

At the outset of the Revolution, in 1789–90, the patchwork of traditional units was replaced with a uniform tier of districts, the *départements*, the epitome of the rational unit of territorial administration (Bazoche 2008, 57–60). In 1800, under Napoleon's consulate, each *département* was placed under the authority of a prefect appointed by central government and charged with the execution of its policies in the area (Chapman 1955, 17–32). The Napoleonic reforms completed the process of centralization and "condemned all local self-government" (Kohn 1955, 35). The Revolution did not mark a watershed in this respect as the centralization achieved under the *Ancien Régime* was perpetuated and deepened by the republic, whose fundamental ideological underpinning was the Jacobin notion of the "one and indivisible republic."[24]

From the early nineteenth century onward, the territorial structuring was thus based on two principles: "that the centre should control the periphery and that there should be equal treatment of citizens across the national territory" (Elgie 2003, 212). Because resistance to the revolution was often linked to the defence of regional interests (Martin 1996, esp. 127–35), regionalism was associated with opposition to the principles of the republic and thus viewed as reactionary. Centralization was not without its detractors, however, and throughout the nineteenth century calls for decentralization were sometimes heard, and not only from the right wing of the political spectrum (Grémion 1987, 237–8; Bazoche 2008, 85–161). A movement of cultural regionalism also emerged toward the end of the century (Bazoche 2008, 75–83). At the same time, though, the Third Republic was engaged in a process of "nationalization of the masses," to borrow Mosse's (1975) phrase, intended to turn "paesants into Frenchmen" (Weber 1979). Neither criticism of centralization nor cultural regionalism had much political effect, though, leaving aside the establishing in the 1870s and 1880s of elected assemblies for the *départements* and the municipalities.

The acquisition of the masses to the notion of a French "civic nation" as theorized by Renan ([1882] 1947) was successful, and minority nationalism of the type emerging elsewhere in Europe failed to establish itself in the areas possessing a distinct ethnolinguistic heritage (Loughlin 1985). Regional groupings of *départements* were put in place by various branches of the state administration but their boundaries did not coincide thus reproducing a patchwork reminiscent of the late *Ancien Régime* (Bazoche 2008, 166). The first attempt to create a uniform tier of multipurpose regional units was made by the Vichy government in 1940–41, but it was not fully implemented (199–200).

In the postwar period, the emphasis given to economic planning and concerns about the relentless growth of Paris (Gravier 1947) led to a renewed focus on functional decentralization, whose first significant manifestation was the creation of regional districts for planning purposes in 1955–56 (Hansen 1968, 74–7). The boundaries of these regions were deliberately drawn not to match those of the old provinces but rather to define rational units of regional administration. In 1960 these units were given a wider remit beyond economic planning and renamed *Circonscriptions d'action régionale*, or regional action districts. In 1964, as already seen, advisory regional development committees were set up in each region and the prefects based in the regional capital given the title of regional prefect (82–4). By this time, support for decentralization had become increasingly widespread, marked by Charles De Gaulle's endorsement in a March 1968 speech (Dumont 2004, 46). De Gaulle's proposal for a constitutional amendment creating regions governed by indirectly elected assemblies failed, however, in a referendum in April 1969, in spite of broad public support for the principle of regionalization (Machin 1978, 144–5; Bazoche 2008, 207). In 1972 eventually, the regional action districts were renamed regions and given an indirectly elected assembly, made up of departmental assembly members. The regional prefect was tasked with executing the assembly's decisions (Schmidt 1990, 93–5; Bazoche 2008, 208). Such postwar regionalization was characterized by Wright (1979) as "the triumph of the functional approach."

The Presidential and Parliamentary Elections of May–June 1981

PARTIES
The French party system is the runup to the 1981 elections has been characterized as the *quadrille bipolaire* (Knapp and Wright 2006, 255–6; Sauger 2010, 8–9), being dominated as it was by four large

parties of approximately equal strength, divided into two alliances. The ruling centre-right majority was formed by the Gaullist Rassemblement pour la République (RPR), or Rally for the Republic, and the liberal Union pour la démocratie française (UDF), or Union for French Democracy. The main opposition parties were the Parti socialiste (PSF), or Socialist Party, and the Parti communiste français (PCF), or French Communist Party.

As the heir to the Gaullist tradition, the RPR represented the dominant political force of the Fifth Republic and had been in power since 1958 (Bourricaud 1977). In the 1978 parliamentary election it obtained 150 seats after receiving 23 percent of the vote in the first round. The UDF had been founded in 1978 as a federation of several smaller parties supporting President Valéry Giscard d'Estaing. Although throughout the Fifth Republic the non-Gaullist centre-right had always been the junior partner on the right, the UDF as the party of the president had gained in stature in the late 1970s. In the 1978 election it gained 121 seats and 21 percent of the vote in the first round. The presidential alliance formed by the RPR, the UDF, and smaller allies narrowly won the 1978 election and formed the third government of Raymond Barre, in office from April 1978 to May 1981. For the 1981 presidential election the RPR and the UDF presented their own candidates, respectively Jacques Chirac and Valéry Giscard d'Estaing, in the first round. After Chirac failed to go through to the second round, the right rallied behind Giscard d'Estaing. For the subsequent parliamentary election, the two reformed their electoral cartel, under the banner Union pour la nouvelle majorité.

Since its refoundation in 1971, the PSF had become the largest party on the left and the main challenger to the ruling centre-right (Bell and Criddle 1984). In the 1978 parliamentary election it gathered a 23 percent share of the vote in the first round and secured 104 seats. Once the dominant party on the left, the PCF declined in the 1970s but was still a significance force. Its tally in the 1978 election was 21 percent support in the first round and 86 seats. Since 1972, the PSF and the PCF had been allied in a Union of the Left cartel under PSF leadership. The socialist leader Mitterrand was the joint Union candidate in the 1974 presidential election (Machin and Wright 1977). The left parties reverted to presenting their own candidates in the first round of the 1981 presidential election, François Mitterrand for the PSF and Georges Marchais for the PCF, but unified in supporting Mitterrand in the second round. The two parties then formed a presidential majority alliance for the subsequent parliamentary election.

POSITIONS ON STATE RESTRUCTURING
Since the failure of De Gaulle's proposals for regionalization in the 1969 referendum, the RPR proceeded cautiously in the field of decentralization. Pompidou, De Gaulle's successor as president, was hostile to regional government on the ground that it posed a threat to national unity and such position determined the limited extent of the 1972 reforms mentioned above (Mény 1974, 67). In its manifesto for the 1981 parliamentary election, the RPR expressed support for the principle of decentralization but stressed the role of *départements* and municipalities rather than that of the regions. Although it called for "Le pouvoir de décision doit appartenir aux élus locaux dans tous les domaines concernant le cadre de vie des citoyens"[25] (RPR 1981, 18), it did not endorse the direct election of regional assemblies, confining itself to arguing that the regions should have full responsibility for the "réalisation d'équipements collectifs"[26] (ibid.). Revealingly, however, the manifesto devoted the first fourteen pages to a wide-ranging criticism of the presidential program but it refrained from criticising the latter's decentralization objectives (1–14).

Although Giscard d'Estaing had been elected on a decentralist platform in 1974, once in office his government took little concrete action and the president himself grew increasingly hostile to the idea of regionalization (Machin 1978, 139–40, 149n10; Schmidt 1990, 96–8). The fact that local vested interests were particularly strong within the UDF ranks was an important factor in shaping the party's attitudes (Machin 1978, 140–1). In a May 1980 interview, reflecting on his achievements as president and his objectives for a new mandate, Giscard d'Estaing did not mention decentralization or regionalization (LE 1980). Likewise, his book published during the campaign for the 1981 presidential election, and intended to defend the record of his presidency, devoted a section to decentralization but did not mention regionalization (Giscard d'Estaing 1981, 175–9).[27] The joint RPR-UDF platform for the parliamentary election argued in favour of a decentralization of power to the regions, the *départements*, and the municipalities, calling in particular for a "vraie réforme régionale ... de manière à donner aux établissements publics régionaux la pleine responsabilité de la réalisation des équipements publics, ainsi que de larges attributions en matière d'aide aux P.M.E. et à l'artisanat, d'emploi et de formation, d'urbanisme ou d'expression culturelle."[28] (RPR-UDF 1981, 16), falling short, however, of endorsing the direct election of the regional councils.

Despite being the heirs to the Jacobin tradition of high centralization, the parties of the left reoriented their position significantly in the 1970s (Schmidt 1990, 100). As early as 1972, their Union de la gauche common program included the democratization of the regions through assemblies directly elected by proportional representation. An advisory social and economic council would sit alongside the assembly (Bazoche 2008, 255–6). The left's success in the local elections in 1977 and 1978 gave it control over most of the two tiers of local government and produced a political context highly favourable to the decentralization reforms (Grémion 1987, 241–2). PSF-sponsored bills introduced in 1974 and 1980 proposed the direct election of the regional councils, in line with the 1972 common program of the left, and the granting to the regions of autonomous fiscal resources as well as a modest expansion of their powers (Schmidt 1990, 101–3). Decentralization featured prominently in Mitterrand's manifesto for the 1981 presidential election, proposition no. 54 of his *110 propositions pour la France*: "The decentralization of the state will be a priority. The regional councils will be elected by popular vote and their government assured by a president and a cabinet. Corsica will have a special status" (PSF 1981). The PCF also supported decentralization in general and the direct election of the regional councils in particular, although they were less prominent in its program than in the socialist one (Schmidt 1990, 103–4). Its manifesto for the 1981 presidential election did not mention decentralization (PCF 1981).

Over the course of the 1970s, thus, a degree of convergence among the parties on decentralization had taken place but the regions remained somewhat controversial, with divisions running between the parties as well as within them (Schmidt 1990, 99). In the 1981 campaign, however, party competition between left and right focused overwhelmingly on the economy rather than decentralization and although the parties of the right did not support the direct election of the regional councils, they did not feel strongly about it and did not campaign against it.

ATTITUDES TO, AND STRATEGIC USE OF, EUROPEAN INTEGRATION

Although Europe attracted a low degree of politicization in the campaign (Hutter and Kerscher 2014, 275), most parties expressed support for integration, albeit with some noticeable differences between them. The PSF supported the democratization of the EU institutions and the development of social policies, within a call for "Une France forte dans l'Europe indépendante"[29] (PSF 1981, 12; see also Bound and Featherstone 1982, 171–6; Guyomarch et al. 1998, 91–2; Cole 1999, 72–5). The RPR called for "une Europe forte et efficace"[30] but stressed that this had to be on the basis of "la souveraineté et l'autorité démocratique des États"[31] (RPR 1981, 21; see also Knapp 1994, 418–22; Guyomarch et al. 1998, 85; Shields 1996, 91–3). The joint program with the UDF for the parliamentary elections stated: "la construction européenne doit être renforcée"[32] and within it the economic, monetary, and social cohesion between the member states should be deepened and new common policies in the fields of energy and industry developed (RPR-UDF 1981, 1). UDF's Giscard d'Estaing had been strongly pro-integration, albeit from an intergovernmental and state-centric perspective, during his presidency and reiterated this position in the campaign (Giscard d'Estaing 1981, 257–62; see also Guyomarch et al. 1998, 82–3). The PCF, in contrast, criticised the PSF for supporting European integration (PCF 1981, 4) but did not put forward a position of its own, although its stance was generally a hostile one (Bound and Featherstone 1982, 183–6; Guyomarch et al. 1998, 94).

As noted above, regionalization was the most controversial aspect of decentralization on the ground that opponents often saw it as a potential threat to the unity of the country. From this perspective, some elite figures, such as Michel Debré, were against the creation of strong political regions, because they associated them to radical plans for a federal Europe of the Regions (Quermonne 1963, 871–3; Hansen 1968, 77; Dupuis 1974, IX). Once it became clear, though, that regionalization would be limited and could hardly be construed as a threat to the nation, the European dimension faded away from the politics of decentralization. In the 1981 campaign, none of the parties made any links between European integration and decentralization (RPR 1981; Giscard d'Estaing 1981; RPR-UDF 1981; PSF 1981; PCF 1981).

ELECTORAL OUTCOMES

The presidential election was a clear victory for Mitterrand. After coming second in the first round, the socialist candidate won the presidency in the second round against Giscard d'Estaing with 51.75 percent of the vote versus 48.24 percent on an 85 percent turnout (Hainsworth 1981, 440–2). The socialist triumph was magnified in the parliamentary election, in which they secured the most emphatic victory of their history, winning 283 seats and thus achieving an absolute majority in the National Assembly. Although the PCF benefited from its alliance with the PSF in the second round, it still had to surrender almost half of the seats it had in the previous parliament. The right was severely defeated too, down to 82 seats for the RPR and 64 for the UDF, against the 150 and 121, respectively, they had obtained in 1978 (447). The elections ushered in a PSF-PCF coalition government led by Prime Minister Pierre Mauroy with a two-thirds majority of seats in the National Assembly, the first left-wing government of the Fifth Republic. As Hainsworth put it, "The presidential and parliamentary elections of 1981 radically altered the face of French politics" (448).

The 1982–83 Decentralization Laws

With such a solid parliamentary majority and decentralization being dubbed *la grande affaire du septennat*, or the great measure of the presidential term (Defferre in Philipponneau 1981, 7), the government moved speedily to implement the reforms. Prime Minister Mauroy was in favour of a more ambitious regionalization, but Mitterrand was wary of the regions and Mauroy had to scale back his ambitions (Bazoche 2008, 259). A first law enacted in March 1982 established the regions as *collectivités territoriales*, or units of subcentral government, governed by an assembly directly elected by universal suffrage and an executive responsible to the assembly. It gave them responsibility to "promouvoir le développement économique, social, sanitaire, culturel et scientifique de la région et l'aménagement de son territoire"[33] (Law 82-213, art. 59) and removed the supervisory and executive powers held by the regional prefects.

Subsequent laws enacted in 1983 set the principles governing the transfer of competences and the attribution of financial resources, conferring to the regions responsibility for building and maintaining secondary schools and providing vocational training (Dumont 2004,

33-4, 46-7). A further law enacted in 1986 laid out the rules governing the functioning of the regional assemblies, based on those of the departmental councils, and in March 1986 the first regional elections were held (48). Law 82-213 and another law enacted in July 1982 also created a Corsican Assembly and established a special statute for the island's regional institutions, albeit one not radically different from that of the other regions (Savigear 1989, 100-3).

The laws of 1982-83 also removed the prefects' supervisory and executive role in relation to the *départements*, transferring them to their elected councils, thus strengthening considerably the role of the *départements* within the overall structure of the country's territorial administration. As the laws also established that there would be no legal hierarchy between the regions and the *départements*, they effectively left the latter as the main level of subcentral government in the country, although interpretations of the relative power of each differ (Schmidt 1990, 118-20). In spite of mass attitudes to decentralization being generally positive, there was very little demand for regional autonomy even in the regions with a distinctive ethnolinguistic heritage (Machin 1978, 144-6).

Summary

The French decentralization reforms of the early 1980s, and their regional component in particular, conform neatly to the top-down model. The reforms were enacted with the objective of improving the functioning of the territorial administration of the state and democratize its institutions. The protagonists of the politics of decentralization were all state-wide parties, facing neither a challenge from regional-nationalist parties nor strong public demand for regional autonomy. Moreover, the reforms were limited in scope, especially as regards the regional tier, essentially confining themselves to democratizing the regional assemblies, without substantial changes to their policy autonomy and their role within the overall territorial administration of the state. The reforms left the *départements* as the main subcentral tier of government, thus falling well short of altering the constitutional nature of the state. As expected, given the top-down nature of the process, state restructuring in France in this phase saw no Europeanization. Parties made no linkages between European integration and decentralization so the politics of reform was played out entirely in a domestic dimension.

4.5 GENERAL SUMMARY

The evidence reviewed in this chapter provides additional support to the conceptual and theoretical framework of the book. In all three cases, parties were the dominant actors in the process, although in the UK this was tempered by the involvement of the electorate through referendums, which ultimately led to the failure of state restructuring in this juncture. The UK and Belgium, on the one hand, and France, on the other hand, however, followed different dynamics. While in the former two cases state restructuring was a response to the challenge posed by regional-nationalist parties, in the latter the drivers of reform were very different, thus underpinning the conceptual distinction between bottom-up and top-down restructuring.

Conforming to the theoretical expectations, no linking of the European dimension and the decentralization reforms could be observed in France, while a modest degree of Europeanization took place in the UK and Belgium. In these two cases positive exploitation of Europe was only adopted by the regional-nationalist parties while their statewide rivals – including the newly regionalized Belgian parties – failed to do so. However, the fact that both the VU and, to a large extent, the SNP also failed to play the European card shows that regional-nationalist parties' propensity to strategically link European integration and state restructuring is determined in a complex way. While the lower profile of integration in this phase can perhaps account for the general feebleness with which parties exploited it in relation to state restructuring, other factors were also at play. In the case of the SNP in particular, attitudes to the EU and to integration appear to have played a crucial role. In a specular fashion, the Conservatives' use of Europe to undermine support for devolution, although modest, confirms the potential for the European dimension to be used in a negative way by centralist parties with a positive attitude to the EU.

5

A "Europe of the Regions"?

This third phase saw a major relaunch of the process of European integration after the difficult period of the 1970s–early 1980s. It was marked by ambitious treaty reforms and the drive to complete the single market, culminating in the formal birth of today's European Union in 1993. The period also witnessed an intensification of the links between the European and the regional level of government, leading some to suggest that the EU embraced the notion of a Europe of the Regions. Somewhat ironically, though, in these years there were fewer critical junctures of state restructuring than in others and they were confined to one country only, Belgium, where the third and fourth rounds of constitutional reforms completed the country's transformation into a fully fledged federation. In the wake of the earlier stages of state reform, these junctures continued to follow a bottom-up dynamic. Linkages between the European dimension and state restructuring became stronger and more widespread although attitudes to the EU and to integration remained an important intervening factor.

5.1 THE DEVELOPMENT OF INTEGRATION

The period between the Milan summit of 1985 and the entry into force of the Maastricht Treaty as well as the inauguration of the single market in 1993 is usually described as the relaunch phase of integration after the stagnation of the 1970s and early 1980s (for an overview, see Dinan 2014, 195–249). While the contrast between the two periods is often overplayed – as seen in the previous chapter, important steps in integration took place in the 1970s – it is undeniable that major developments characterized this period, leading to a qualitative change in the speed and depth of integration. Spain and Portugal were also admitted in 1986, thus completing the EU's enlargement toward the south.

In policy terms, the most important initiative was the single-market program. Intended to complete the building of an integrated internal market, the program targeted the elimination of technical, regulatory, and other non-tariff barriers to trade within the EU. Laid out in a Commission white paper issued in 1985, endorsed at the Milan summit of the European Council in the same year and implemented from 1987 onward, the program consisted of about 300 measures to be enacted by the end of 1992. Throughout those years, achieving the 1992 objectives became the paramount aim of the EU. Although the program had broad support from across the political spectrum, many harboured doubts as to its potential negative effects. Such doubts crystallized around three aspects, concerning the environment, labour, and the peripheral regions, respectively. As regards the first aspect, environmentalists worried that the increased economic activity unleashed by the program together with a lightening of the regulatory regime brought about by the increasing application of the mutual recognition principle would inflict severe damage on the environment, at a time when green concerns were acquiring greater salience across Europe. In a similar vein, trade unions and the left-of-centre parties traditionally linked to them were concerned that a freer and more unified European market would strengthen the hand of employers versus that of employees and engender a race to the bottom in standards of social protection. Lastly, many feared that such a market would also lead to the further concentration of economic activity in west-central Europe, thus bringing about an impoverishment of the peripheral regions.

To counter such fears and underpin support for the single market program, the EU embarked on an effort to develop flanking policies in these areas. The protection of the environment was given a formal treaty basis with the entry into force of the Single European Act in 1987, thus laying the ground for the development of an EU environmental policy (Lenschow 2005, 306–12). In the social sphere, the EU committed itself to the building of a "social Europe" that would complement the economic focus of the single-market program. The inclusion of the Social Charter in the Maastricht Treaty symbolically marked the culmination of this drive, although the actual policy achievements fell short of what many advocates of a social Europe had hoped (Leibfried 2005, 246–9). In the field of territorial cohesion, the regional policy that had been initiated in the mid-1970s underwent a major transformation with the reform of the structural funds in 1988. Funding was doubled, oversight by the Commission strengthened and a set of principles introduced thus turning, in the view of many analysts, what was little more than a side-payment mechanism into a genuine common policy (Allen 2005, 218–19). Among the principles introduced was that of partnership, requiring state governments to work in partnership with their regional and local counterparts as well as so-called social partners such as employers and unions in drafting the development plans submitted to the EU for funding. More broadly, the European institutions, the Commission in particular, invoked more frequently a Europe of the Regions to refer to this partnership between the European and the regional level of policymaking, thus appearing to embrace a notion that, as seen in the previous chapters, had often had a connotation of radical alternative to the Europe of the States embodied by the EU (Hooghe 1996; Loughlin 1996).

In the institutional domain, the period saw equally significant developments. As already mentioned, the Single European Act, the first major amendment of the 1957 Treaty of Rome, came into force in 1987. Among its most significant provisions were the adoption of the cooperation legislative procedure, which gave for the first time the European Parliament a formal stake in lawmaking, and the introduction of a qualified majority voting procedure in the Council. Both innovations were explicitly linked to the single-market program and applied principally to the legislative measures needed for its implementation. The volume of the latter and the broadening of the EU policymaking scope led to a marked increase in the legislative output of the EU and its domestic impact, also leading to a significant growth in the volume of lobbying targeting the European institutions. The Commission under the presidency of Jacques Delors was a major policy actor in this phase, leading many to consider it as the golden age of the Commission. The activism of the Commission and the growing influence of the Parliament marked a considerable reshaping of the EU institutional triangle away from the overwhelming dominance of the Council that had prevailed in the previous two decades.

Mass attitudes also underwent a significant evolution. After a long period in which a permissive consensus prevailed, the resonance given to the single-market program ensured that Europe hit home for the first time. While the salience of integration grew so did public support for it, in particular as regards a positive perception of the gains to be derived from membership, reaching a peak in 1991 (Hix and Høyland 2011, 108).

5.2 BELGIUM: THE THIRD AND FOURTH CONSTITUTIONAL REFORMS

As seen in the previous chapter, the initial reforms laid the foundations for a radical transformation of the state but left a number of key issues unresolved. Prominent among them was the question of Brussels.[1] The 1980 reform established the principle that Brussels would be a region like Flanders and Wallonia but left open the issue of its exact boundaries and the nature of its institutions. The policy competences of the regions created by the latest reform were still object of intense debate; there was significant pressure for a widening of them, particularly in the field of education. A dispute regarding the village of Voeren/Fourons, located on the linguistic border, also continued to fester, eventually bringing the government down and leading to the early general election of December 1987.[2]

The December 1987 Election

After having gone through a dramatic process of separation in the 1968–1978 period, the two distinct party systems that emerged from that process experienced a period of consolidation in the 1980s. On the Flemish side, the CVP lost support but retained its position as the largest party in the region, polling 34.6 percent of the vote in the 1985 election.[3] After a period of decline, which saw it being overtaken by the PVV as the second party, the SP regained ground and was comfortably in second position in the wake of the 1985 election, in which it received 23.7 percent of the vote. The PVV moved in the opposite direction and suffered a major setback in the 1985 election, when it polled 17.4 percent of the vote, a loss of almost four percentage points compared to the previous election. Despite a certain erosion in support, the VU held on to its fourth place, winning 12.7 of the vote in the 1985 election.[4] In Wallonia, the virtual disappearance of the RW led to the consolidation of a three-party system. The PS strengthened its position as the largest party, gaining almost 40 percent of the vote in the 1985 election. The PSC declined and lost the position of second largest party to the PRL, the two parties scoring 22.6 and 24.1 percent, respectively, in 1985.[5]

POSITIONS ON STATE RESTRUCTURING

As Mabille (2011, 341) put it, "la campagne électorale de l'automne 1987 fut largement dominée par des thèmes relatifs au contentieux communautaire."[6] Among the Flemish parties, the CVP presented itself as a champion of a thorough federalization of the state. Pointing out that such a large process ought to be implemented in a gradual way, it argued: "De staatshervorming van 1980 was een eerste belangrijke stap in deze richting. Zij moet nu worden verdiept en voltooid"[7] (CVP 1987, 11). It then argued that the new parliament – which had been given the power to amend the constitution – had a unique opportunity to carry the process forward. The reformed constitution would usher in a "volwaardige federale staat waarin de Vlaamse gemeenschap over ruime autonomie beschikt"[8] (ibid.). In addition to a definitive fixing of the language border, the party was calling for the wholesale devolution of education and scientific research as well as parts of economic policy. The explicit objective of HS was "een maximale bevoegdheidsoverdracht naar de Vlaamse gemeenschap met behoud van de economische en monetaire unie en van een omkeerbare, doorzichtige en louter aanvullende nationale solidariteit"[9] (ibid.). This should be accompanied by a reform of the central institutions of the state, notably the Senate, which should become a "senate of the communities" (11–12). Additionally, it expressed support for the principle of subsidiarity, arguing in favour of decentralization toward the provinces and the municipalities within Flanders, and for each level of government to be fiscally responsible (11).

The SP argued that the 1980 reform had to be rethought and adjusted, on the basis that "Het algemeen uitgangspunt is de politieke instellingen aan te passen aan de verwachting naar meer autonomie"[10] (SP 1987, 8). The party called for the organization of the state to be simplified and clarified, based on a clear allocation of competences to the various levels of government and the creation of effective solidarity mechanisms between the different areas. Two key steps in that direction would be the abolition of bicameralism and the direct election of the regional parliaments (ibid.). The federated entities should be given residual powers over all matters not explicitly assigned to the federal level, which would include the competences necessary for the preservation of the country's economic and monetary union together with foreign affairs, defence, justice, social security, and law and order (ibid.). The bilingual Brussels area should be confined to the traditional nineteen municipalities and the two communities should be on an equal footing within its institutions (ibid.).

The PVV was also committed to further reform of the state in a federal direction: "De onvoltooide staatshervorming van 1980 moet verdiept worden om zo te komen tot een werkbaar federaal model, voorwaarde voor het voortbestaan van het Belgisch staatsbestel waaraan we gehecht zijn"[11] (PVV 1987, 6). From this perspective, the party argued for a significant devolution of power to the communities and the regions, notably in the field of education, and the granting to them of financial responsibility (ibid.). The PVV also sided with the other Flemish parties in calling for a special status for Brussels, which would respect the existing language border and would allow for institutional power-sharing between Flemings and Francophones (ibid.).

The VU manifesto was focused on the question of state restructuring to a much greater extent than those of the other parties. Like them, the VU expressed strong support for deeper reform of the state, calling for a "grondige hervorming, met een zo groot mogelijk zelfbestuur"[12] (VU 1987, 2). The main principles it emphasized included the inviolability of the language border, the right to power-sharing for the Flemings in the Brussels institutions, and the need for fiscal autonomy for each community (2–4). It went somewhat further than the traditional parties, though, in envisaging the communities as the central actors in the process: "De vraag mag niet zijn, welke bevoegdheden overgedragen worden naar de Gemeenschappen. Het zijn de Gemeenschappen die na overleg moeten beslissen, wat ze nog aan de nationale regering overlaten en hoe de financiering daarvan zal geregeld worden"[13] (2). In line with this, it called for the direct election of the Flemish Council – the governing organ of the Flemish community – and for the powers of the federal institutions to be restricted to those necessary for the maintenance of an economic and monetary union, with all other powers granted to the communities (3). Arguing that the 1970 and 1980 reforms were deficient because they were adopted without the involvement of the VU, the party committed itself to playing a strong role in the forthcoming reform, which it presented as a condition for the latter to be successful (ibid.).

Among the Francophone parties, the PS criticised the Martens VI government for its alleged pro-Flanders bias and contrasted it with its core proposal: "une réforme cohérente, claire, simple et équilibrée de la Belgique: le fédéralisme intégral"[14] (PS 1987, 27). Under this label, the party called for a simplification of the structures of the state, a clear division of competences between tiers of government, residual competences to be attributed to the regions, no legal supremacy of state law over regional and community law, and the implementation of the Brussels institutions as a third fully fledged region (27–8). In policy terms, such "integral federalism" would entail the devolution to the regions and the communities of a wide array of competences and the corresponding fiscal resources (ibid.). If these demands were broadly in line with those of the other parties, the PS went further in calling for the regions and the communities also to have full and direct responsibility for international relations within their sphere of competences (29). According to the party, "Le fédéralisme intégral est désormais, qu'on le veuille ou non, la seule voie possible pour remédier aux dysfonctionnements de plus en plus graves qui caractérisent l'Etat belge et qui risquent de le mener, soit à l'éclatement, soit à la flamandisation complète "[15] (30).

The PRL put emphasis on simplifying the structures of the state. It called for the implementation of the regional institutions for Brussels, a clarification of the division of competences between the government tiers and the fusion of the institutions of Brussels and Wallonia into a single set of institutions representing all Francophones, along the lines of the merger carried out in Flanders (PRL 1987, 78–80, 43–4). Such simplification had to be accompanied by the devolution of further powers to the regions and the communities, while preserving the political, economic and monetary union of the country (ibid.).

The PSC also stressed the need to simplify the structures of the state, as well as better respect the interests of Francophones (PSC 1987, 35). It advocated a "fédéralisme d'union, c'est-à-dire en faveur d'une autonomie plus grande des régions et des communautés associée à la mise en place de mécanismes renforçant l'Etat central"[16] (36). This had to be achieved through a clarification of the division of competences across the different levels of government as well as greater cooperation and solidarity between them. The Brussels regional institutions should be set up, the community and regional councils should be directly elected, and the Senate should be transformed into a federal chamber in which the two communities would be on an equal footing (36–8). Distancing itself from the other parties, however, it stressed its opposition to the devolution of education to the communities, making it subject to the introduction of safeguard guaranteeing freedom of education, i.e., support for Catholic schooling (ibid.).

There thus was among the parties a broad agreement that the 1980 reform needed to be completed and extended for the state to work effectively and the tensions between the two communities to be reduced. The distance that could be observed in the previous period between the VU and the RW, on the one hand, and the traditional parties, on the other, had largely disappeared. The VU was still on a distinctly more radical course than the other parties, but less so than previously. There was also broad convergence – leaving the Brussels question aside – between the Flemings and the Francophones on the main guidelines for the next constitutional reform. The federal model that had been rejected by the mainstream parties in the 1960s and 1970s, was by then the accepted common ground. The fact that all parties had become regional parties, of course, was an important factor in this evolution of positions. There also was broad agreement on which competences should be devolved to the communities and the regions, education chiefly among them (although the PSC was still reluctant on this point).

ATTITUDES TO, AND STRATEGIC USE OF,
EUROPEAN INTEGRATION

In addition to expressing broad support for European integration (VU 1987, 8), the VU placed the reform of the Belgian state fully in a European dimension: "Wij beschouwen de nationale bevoegdheden als een voorlopige overgangsregeling tot op het ogenblik dat de Europese integratie een feit wordt en de Gemeenschappen rechtstreeks binnen het Europees verband kunnen opereren"[17] (3). In the context of the growing importance of policymaking at the EU level linked to the single-market program, the VU argued: "is het van hoog belang dat Vlaanderen een rechtstreekse vertegenwoordiging krijgt in de Europese instellingen"[18] (8).

The CVP displayed its customary strong support for European integration, reminding voters that the Christian democrats were the founders of Europe and that a strong Europe was needed more than ever to address the multiple challenges of the contemporary world (CVP 1987, 12). The party supported a strong European Commission, the granting of fuller powers to the European Parliament, and the development of political cooperation in the direction of a common foreign and security policy backed by adequate financial means (ibid.). It also called for a strengthening of the social dimension and a development of environmental policy. It had a positive view of the single-market program, pointing out that it presented a "unieke kans voor Vlaanderen dat in het hart van Europa ligt"[19] (3). The party linked the federal reform of the state and European integration, arguing that "Dit nieuwe Vlaanderen en België gaan aldus hun Europese toekomst tegemoet"[20] (11). In relation to Brussels, the CUP pointed out that in addition to being the capital of the country and of the Flemish community, it was also the capital of Europe, claiming "Ons federalistisch ideaal kadert volledig in de Europese eenmaking"[21] (ibid.). It also suggested that a federal Belgium could be a model for Europe: "Het kan ook een voorbode zijn hoe in het toekomstige Europa volken met mekaar moeten samenleven"[22] (12).

The SP was strongly in favour of integration: "De Vlaamse socialisten streven naar een open en progressief Europa in federale zin"[23] (SP 1987, 8). The party also supported the single-market program but warned that it had to be accompanied by other measures if it was not to lead to an even greater concentration of capital in the hands of a few. Among the measures advocated were common energy and environmental policies, greater economic coordination among the member states, especially as regards employment conditions, industrial policy and consultation with social partners (ibid.). The SP put particular emphasis on the development of social and regional policies at the EU level, without which "Zoniet zal de marktintegratie de kloof tussen rijk en arm in Europa alleen maar vergroten"[24] (ibid.). It also called for an increase in the EP's powers and the development of a common foreign and security policy. It did not link, however, the European dimension to the reform of the Belgian state.

The PVV also maintained its long-standing strong support for European integration: "Vlaanderen en België kunnen slechts een rol spelen in de wereld binnen een Europese Gemeenschap die stoelt op de liberale principes: vrij verkeer van personen, goederen, diensten en kapitaal"[25] (PVV 1987, 8). The completion of the single market and the achievement of monetary union would be the best tools through which to achieve such liberal objectives (ibid.). The party, though, made no linkages between European integration and the domestic state reform.

Among the Francophone parties, the PS expressed strong support for integration while at the same time deploring the state of the European Union (PS 1987, 50). It was supportive of the single-market program but warned that "des mesures d'accompagnement sont nécessaires pour que le marché intérieur n'accentue pas les déséquilibres sociaux et régionaux"[26] (51). From that perspective, the party called for a reform of the agricultural policy and higher expenditure on scientific research and the structural funds, in the context of a reform of the EU budget, as well as for the development of a European foreign and defence policy (ibid.). From an institutional perspective, the socialists put forward a radical program consisting in the creation of a real European parliament, a real European government through the convening of a European constituent assembly charged with the drafting of a European constitution to be ratified by national referendums (52–3). The PS did not explicitly link integration and state reform, save for its call for the regions and the communities to be involved in EU policymaking in the areas of their competence and its support for a Europe of the Regions (29, 51).

The PRL also expressed strong support for integration: "Une Europe forte et unie est indispensable. Les Libéraux ont toujours été à la pointe du combat pour l'unification européenne"[27] (PRL 1987, 85). The party supported the development of the research, agricultural and regional policies of the EU and was committed to the achievement of a single currency (ibid.). In a similar vein as the PS, it did not make strong links between the European dimension and the reform of the Belgian institutions but did connect the European and the regional level in the following way: "La construction européenne doit par ailleurs s'appuyer sur la reconnaissance du fait régional. L'Europe des régions répond à un souci d'efficacité, de réalisme et à la volonté des citoyens"[28] (125).

The PSC devoted little attention to Europe in its manifesto, confining itself to stating that "le P.S.C. est attaché à la poursuite de la construction européenne"[29] (PSC 1987, 34). Although it did not make strong links with the reform of the state, it attacked the vision of some of its rivals by warning that "Le P.S.C. s'oppose à un modèle d'organization confédérale où l'Etat belge est progressivement vidé de sa substance en attendant l'Europe des régions"[30] (36).

Linkages between Europe and state restructuring were thus more intense and more widespread than in the previous periods. After its failure to do so in 1978, the VU was again the party linking Europe and state reform most strongly and the question of direct access to EU decision-making featured prominently in its discourse. The fact that the CVP, the PS, and the PRL also placed reform in a European context and endorsed the concept of a Europe of the Regions is noteworthy though it should not be taken at face value. On the one hand, it testifies that the European institutions' apparent embrace of the notion was successful in making it feed through into mainstream political discourse. On the other hand, this was a sanitized and watered-down version of the Europe of the Regions idea rather than the one with radical connotations advocated by the regional-nationalist parties.

ELECTION OUTCOME

The 1987 election recorded one of the lowest rates of electoral volatility since the introduction of proportional representation in 1919. Although results differed markedly between the two language regions, within each of them stability largely prevailed (Fraeys 1988, 3–4). In Flanders, the CVP continued its decline, losing over three percentage points in electoral support and six seats in the Chamber of Deputies, while the PVV gained a little over one percentage point in its vote share and managed to win three additional seats. The SP and the VU won broadly the same share of votes as in 1985 and kept their previous tally of seats in the lower house. With 43 seats out of 212 in the latter, though, the CVP remained by far the largest Flemish party, followed by the SP with 32, the PVV with 25, and the VU with 16 (10, 13–14). Given the broadly similar positions of the CVP and the PVV and the stability of the other two main parties, the results did not have a significant impact on the Flemish parties' alignment on the reform of the state.

The clear winner among the Francophone parties was the PS, which gained 4.5 percentage points in Wallonia and five additional seats in the Chamber of Deputies compared to the previous election. The PRL and the PSC both declined marginally and had to surrender a seat in the lower house. With forty seats in the Chamber, the PS consolidated its position as the dominant party in the southern half of the country, followed by the PRL with twenty-three and the PSC with nineteen (10, 16–17). Party alignment on state restructuring in the Francophone camp remained therefore broadly stable, with an even clearer leading role for the PS. Rhetorical use of Europe in connection with state restructuring was not meaningfully associated with electoral gains or losses. Given the complex arithmetic of Belgian politics, the results of the 1987 election in Flanders and Wallonia largely cancelled each other out and left the CVP and the PS, as usual, as the dominant actors on the two sides of the linguistic divide, paving the way for the forthcoming reform of the state to reflect a compromise between their respective preferences.

The 1988–89 Constitutional Reforms

There were two sides to the constitutional reforms of 1988–89. On the one hand, they reflected the broad consensus among the parties. With some exceptions, powers over education were transferred to the communities (with guarantees written in the constitution to assuage the PSC's opposition), while extensive competences over industrial policy, transport, and infrastructure were devolved to the regions. This shifted the balance of power decisively in favour of the communities and the regions vis-à-vis the central state. The communities and the regions were also given increased financial resources to match their new responsibilities so that around a third of public spending came under their control (Deschouwer 2009, 52–3; Mabille 2011, 343–5).

On the other hand, the agreement on Brussels was a carefully crafted compromise between the clashing demands of the Flemings and the Francophones. The regional status of Brussels mandated by the 1980 constitutional amendment was at last enacted, bringing it effectively on an equal status with Flanders and Wallonia, as the Francophones wanted. In a concession to a core demand of the Flemings, though, its territorial extension was kept within the existing boundaries, thus leaving several municipalities with a high percentage of Francophones in the monolingual Flemish region. In another compromise between the two communities mirroring that reached in 1970 for the central institutions of the state, Flemings were given parity with Francophones in the Brussels regional executive and key decisions in the regional assembly were made subject to a double majority requirement, i.e., a majority within each of the two language groups (Deschouwer 2009, 52–3; Mabille 2011, 343–5).

While these reforms represented a major step forward in the process of state restructuring in Belgium, a number of key aspects were left still to address. Four of them were especially prominent. First, the direct election of the community and regional councils, to give them full democratic legitimacy and autonomy from the institutions of the central state. Second, a transformation of the Senate into a chamber of the communities and regions, to allow it to represent the federated units at central level. Third, the question of the international extension of the communities/regions' competences so that the latter would have the power to conduct international relations and sign treaties within their sphere of competence. Lastly, a reversal of the principle of distribution of powers between the central state and the communities/regions, whereby the latter would have residual competences. The remainder of the 1987–1991 parliament was dominated by negotiations among the government parties on these issues, but no agreement was possible and the VU's withdrawal from the governing coalition triggered the resignation of the prime minister and the calling of early elections in November 1991 (Mabille 2011, 345–9).

The November 1991 Election

As seen above, the 1987 election did not produce dramatic results. The shape of the two party systems on the eve of the 1991 election was thus broadly the same as before the previous election. The only two changes of some significance were the further decline of the CVP in Flanders and a strengthening of roughly the same magnitude for the PS in the French-speaking part of the country. Although still very minor in electoral terms, the extreme right nationalist Flemish party Vlaams Blok and the Francophone green party Ecolo have been included in the analysis because, as we will see, they made major advances in the election and established themselves as important actors within their respective party systems.

POSITIONS ON STATE RESTRUCTURING
Party positioning was broadly similar to that observed for the 1987 election, with high convergence among the mainstream parties and across the linguistic divide in favour of a completion of the reform process and the achievement of a genuine federal institutional architecture. The VU and, particularly so, the VB, however, distanced themselves from this convergence and took a distinctly more radical stance, the former advocating confederalism and the latter calling for Flanders's independence.

The CVP defended the reforms already implemented and called for their completion, notably through the direct election of community/regional assemblies and appropriate financing mechanisms. Further competences could be devolved but it was important not to endanger the economic and monetary union of the country and the functionality of the state, although communities/regions should have international recognition and be granted treaty-making powers in the policy areas under their responsibility (CVP 1991, 2–3, 9–10; also Menu 1994b, 498).

The SP advocated a simplification and a democratization of the structures of the state, making community and regional assemblies directly elected, reforming the Senate, and clarifying the division of competences among the state, the communities, and the regions. Residual competences should be granted to the communities/regions but all competences should be enumerated as far as possible. The communities should have international relations powers in their sphere of competence whereas international relations in the policy areas allocated to the regions should remain with the central state in order to preserve the economic and monetary union of the country and meet EU requirements (SP 1991, 84–6; also Menu 1994c, 479–80).

The PVV called for the achievement of a real federal state through the direct election of the community/regional assemblies, a clearer division of competences, the creation of a genuine constitutional court, and international recognition and treaty-making powers for the communities/regions (PVV 1991, 2, 6–7). It also advocated a thorough reform of social security, including transferring some competences to the regions and privatizing others (2).[31] After the election, the party underwent a refoundation and a change of name to Vlaamse Liberalen en Democraten (VLD). The new party, which had been joined by former VU members, radicalized its position on constitutional matters, its founding manifesto including a commitment to bring about "een zelfstandig Vlaanderen in een federaal België en een federal Europa"[32] (VLD 1992, 1).

With the mainstream parties embracing federalism and the rising challenge from a more radical position brought about by the VB, the VU went beyond its traditional federalist position and advocated a confederal model. This would entail further devolution of power to the two communities leading to a transformation of Belgium into a confederation between a Flemish and a Walloon state (VU 1991, 1). Each state would have as much autonomy as possible – including over social security – subject only to minimal confederal standards, which would be set at the European level in the long term. The mechanisms of fiscal transfers between them would have to be fundamentally changed and the Flemish state would acquire international recognition and treaty-making powers for the policy areas within its competence (VU 1991, 1–3; also 1993, 11, 13).

At the most radical end of the spectrum, the VB expressed an extreme nationalist and secessionist position. Its manifesto branded Belgium a "historische vergissing," or historical mistake, and stated: "Vlaanderen moet dus een geografisch kleine maar sterke onafhankelijke staat worden in Europa, met Brussel als hoofdstad"[33] (VB 1991, 2; Govaert 1992, 20). Secession could take place peacefully and the VB saw itself as a pressure group pushing the other parties to take steps toward independence in a similar vein in which the VU conceived of its role in the 1960s and 1970s. Independence would bring substantial economic benefits, as it would put an end to the subsidies flowing to Wallonia through the Belgian tax system, and would save the Flemish character of Brussels, increasingly threatened by its recognition as a third region (VB 1991, 2–3). An independent Flemish state should then strive for closer integration with the Netherlands through a series of treaties leading to the setting up of a confederation (4).

Among the Francophone parties, the PS placed considerable emphasis on the reform of the state and called for a completion of the process started in 1988 so that Belgium would become a real federal state. The key steps to be taken concerned the direct election of the community/regional assemblies and a further reallocation of responsibilities to them. Residual competences should be assigned to the communities and the regions, state competences should be enumerated, and the communities/regions should be granted external relations and treaty-making powers matching their domestic competences. Control of agriculture, trade, and local and provincial governments should also be transferred to the regions (PS 1991, 2–3).

The PRL and the PSC, in contrast, devoted much less attention than the PS to state restructuring. The former expressed support for the direct election of the community/regional assemblies and the regionalization of agriculture but was firmly opposed to a devolution of social security (PRL 1991, 3, 10, 14). The latter confined itself to stigmatizing demagogy and nationalism and reiterating its call for the achievement of a "fédéralisme d'union" (PSC 1991, 1).

Ecolo called for the forthcoming reform of the state to address four main issues: the direct election of the community/regional institutions, the international extension of the competences of the communities and the regions, the granting to the latter of residual competences, and a reform of bicameralism at the centre with greater differentiation of composition and roles between the lower and the upper chamber. It was opposed, however, to a further devolution of powers to the communities/regions in the fields of social security, agriculture, and international cooperation (ECO 1991, 50–2).

ATTITUDES TO, AND STRATEGIC USE OF, EUROPEAN INTEGRATION

The mainstream Flemish parties continued to display their traditional strong support for European integration inspired by the federal ideal of a union of the existing states. The CVP, the PVV/VLD, and the SP were all committed to deeper integration, calling for a greater democratization of EU institutions and decision-making, and further policy development (CVP 1991, 16; PVV 1991, 8; SP 1991, 103–5; Menu 1994c, 483). In line with their positions on the left-right spectrum, the CVP and, especially, the SP put emphasis on the need to develop a stronger social dimension (CVP 1991, 16–17; SP 1991, 103–5; Menu 1994c, 483) while the PVV/VLD stressed the completion of economic and monetary union, the widest possible application of the four freedoms, and a reform of agricultural policy (PVV 1991, 8). The CVP also called for regions and cultural communities to receive a clearer recognition in the Maastricht Treaty but stopped short of endorsing the idea of a senate of the regions for the sake of preserving a transparent institutional structure for the EU (CVP 1991, 17). Although criticism of the Maastricht Treaty for not going far enough in many of these respects was expressed, the three parties all voted in favour of its ratification in parliament (Deschouwer and Van Assche 2008, 79). While the CVP and the PVV/VLD made no direct linkages between the deepening of European integration and the federalization of Belgium,[34] the SP used Europe to underscore its federalist position, arguing that integration was making further redistribution of responsibilities among the regions, the state, and the Union necessary but it was also rendering independence outdated (SP 1991, 103–5; Menu 1994c, 479–80).

The VU, in contrast, was much more critical of the EU's evolution and vocal in its advocacy of an alternative form of integration. The party called for the construction of Europe to be based on integral federalism and the principle of subsidiarity. Further transfers of competences to the EU would have to be matched by strengthened democratic control through real decision-making powers for the European Parliament and a European government made accountable to it (VU 1991, 3; 1993, 7, 41, 50). The cultural communities and regions of Europe should have an important role through representation in an upper house of the European Parliament and direct access to the European Court of Justice. In the medium term, these communities and regions, rather than the existing states, should become the building blocks of a European federation (VU 1991, 3; 1993, 7, 9, 52). Given these preferences, the VU was naturally disappointed with the Maastricht Treaty, which it saw as ushering in an arrogant technocratic system, and voted against the treaty in the ratification process (Lynch 1996, 130; Deschouwer and Van Assche 2008, 80).

Also in contrast to the mainstream parties, the VU strategically exploited the European dimension to press for the full federalization of Belgium. It presented its goal as making Flanders "een deelstaat van een confederatie die nu nog Belgisch is, maar straks Europees"[35] (VU 1991, 2) and saw its striving for "minder België, meer Vlaanderen en meer Europa"[36] (VU 1993, 7) as part of a Europe-wide struggle. It argued that the dynamics created by a directly elected Flemish parliament and by integration would lead to more competences being transferred to Flanders at the same time as the remaining competences of the Belgian state would be taken over by Europe, thus making the transition to Flanders's independence in Europe inevitable (ibid.). Hence: "Dit is du seen nieuwe ordening van Europa. In die ordening is België overbodig"[37] (VU 1993, 9).

The VB was ambivalent toward integration and critical of the Maastricht Treaty. On the one hand, it supported Europe's drive to acquire the capabilities in the military, economic, and cultural spheres to guarantee its peace and freedom, and called explicitly for a European defence community to replace NATO in the long term. On the other hand, it warned against the homogenizing effects of Europeanization and called for a strict application of the principle of subsidiarity (VB 1991, 10). Like the VU, its vision was for a confederal *Europa der volkeren*, not the Europe emerging from the Maastricht Treaty (see also Laible 2008, 68, 121–48), hence it voted against the treaty's ratification in parliament (Lynch 1996, 130;

Deschouwer and Van Assche 2008, 80). The VB placed Flanders's independence within the framework of the EU but, unlike the VU, did not exploit the latter to bolster support for it (VB 1991, 2).

On the Francophone side, the PS maintained its strong support for integration, endorsing more majority voting, legislative co-decision between the Council and the European Parliament, and greater accountability of the European Commission to the latter (PS 1991, 47). It called, however, for deeper economic integration to be complemented by a strengthening of the social dimension: "Un lien doit aussi exister entre la réalisation de l'Union économique et monétaire et les progrès en matière d'harmonisation fiscale et sociale"[38] (ibid.; also Menu 1994c, 483). It also expressed support for a strengthening of the links between the EU and the regions "pour que les Régions et les Communautés soient pleinement associées au processus de décision européenne"[39] (PS 1991, 48).

The PSC's position was in line with its traditional enthusiasm for integration. It expressed support for the then European Community to become a real political and economic European Union with increased policymaking competences (PSC 1991, 2). Its vision was resolutely federalist, as it called for the EP to become a fully fledged parliament with legislative co-decision rights, more majority voting in the Council, the transformation of the European Commission into a European government, and the development of a common foreign and defence policy (PSC 1991, 23). Ecolo also adopted a strongly pro-integration position: "Notre objectif reste une Communauté de type fédéral ('Europe des Régions')." (ECO 1991, 97). From that perspective, it advocated a democratization of the EU institutions, via a strengthening of the European Parliament, a European Commission responsible to it, the creation of a senate of the regions, and the adoption of a constitution but expressed fears that the treaty under negotiation (Maastricht) would fall short of these objectives[40] (50, 97). The PRL did not take position on European integration in its manifesto but continued to be a strong supporter and voted in favour of ratification of the Maastricht Treaty in parliament (PRL 1991; Rudd 1988, 205–6; Deschouwer and Van Assche 2008, 79). With the exception of Ecolo's references to a Europe of the Regions and a senate of the regions, none of the Francophone parties made any links between European integration and the restructuring of the state in Belgium.

ELECTION OUTCOME

Even more so than in the past the outcome was markedly different in the north and in the south of the country, testifying to a deepening divergence in electoral behaviour (Fitzmaurice 1992, 180; Mabille 2011, 358). In Flanders, the VB was the clear winner of the election while the VU, the SP, and the CVP were the main losers. The VB tripled its share of the vote and multiplied its representation in the Chamber of Deputies by six, from two to twelve seats. The VU, in contrast, lost over three percentage points in electoral support and over a third of its seats in the lower house, dropping from sixteen to ten seats. The SP and the CVP both lost over four percentage points, ending up with a record low share of the vote, and had to surrender four seats each. The PVV made a small advance and gained one seat in the Chamber, its second-best-ever result. With thirty-nine seats in the lower house, the CVP remained the largest Flemish party, followed by the SP with twenty-eight, the PVV with twenty-six,[41] the VB with twelve, and the VU with ten (Fraeys 1992, 138–43). In terms of the politics of state restructuring, these results pointed in two directions. Among the mainstream parties, the simultaneous weakening of the CVP, traditionally the most vocal on autonomy demands, and of the SP, the most reticent, largely cancelled each other out. Among the nationalist parties, the VB's overtaking of the VU marked a significant radicalization of the nationalist vote, although the fact that the former's constitutional position was associated to extreme right policies, notably on immigration, contributed to its marginalization.

Electoral volatility was lower among the Francophone parties but the same pattern of shifting support from the mainstream to fringe parties could be observed. The major difference is that such a shift benefited the left wing in Wallonia and Brussels whereas it went to the right wing in Flanders. The PS, the PRL, and the PSC all lost votes and seats while the green party Ecolo scored a major victory. The PS lost almost five percentage points and five seats in the Chamber of Deputies, while the PRL and the PSC lost three and one percentage points and had to surrender the same number of deputies, respectively. Ecolo tripled its share of the vote and of the seats in the lower house. In the new parliament, the PS remained the largest Francophone party with thirty-five seats in the Chamber, followed by the PRL with twenty, the PSC with eighteen, and Ecolo with ten (Fraeys, 1992: 138, 144–6). Given the broad agreement among the Francophone parties on the contours of the next reform of the state, these results had little effect on the politics of state restructuring south of the linguistic border. On this occasion, parties' exploitation of the European dimension was actually associated with electoral losses.

The 1993 Constitutional Reforms

In spite of their losses in the election, the government that took office in March 1992 was composed by the two Christian democratic and the two socialist parties. In the course of negotiations with the VU and the two green parties – needed to achieve the supermajorities required to change the constitution – a new set of reforms was agreed and implemented in 1992–93. Known as the St Michael's Agreement, the reform package completed Belgium's transition toward a fully fledged federal architecture, as symbolized by the amended art. 1 of the constitution now reading: "Belgium is a federal state composed of Communities and Regions." The key missing element of the direct election of the community/regional assemblies was implemented and the latter were given new competences, notably in the field of agriculture, trade, and scientific research. The communities/regions were granted foreign relations and treaty-making powers within their domestic competences, on the basis of the principle *in foro interno, in foro externo*. One of the constitutional amendments also granted them residual competences and provided for the enumeration of the powers of the state but made it subject to implementation by law.[42] The bulk of tax-raising powers and social security, though, remained under the control of the central state (Deschouwer 2009, 53–4; Mabille 2011, 362–7).

Like previous ones, this package of reforms too reflected a compromise between the two communities and between their respective largest parties and was thus closest to the preferences of the CVP and the PS. From a longer term perspective, however, these reforms were almost a perfect realization of the VU's and the RW's platforms of the late 1960s, thus showing that, to paraphrase Newman (1995), the regional-nationalist parties advocating a federal reform of the state had lost the electoral battles but had effectively won the policy war. As at previous points in the process, there continued to be only weak public support for a federalization of the state, even in Flanders.

A 1992 poll found that 30 percent of Flemings supported federalism against 44 percent preferring a unitary constitutional order (De Winter and Frognier 1997, 172–3).

5.3 SUMMARY

In line with the earlier steps in the process, these two critical junctures of state restructuring in Belgium continued to be entirely dominated by the political parties, with little direct involvement of the electorate and only weak public support. Both junctures conformed to the bottom-up model and replicated in particular the features of the second one, in that they should be seen as the long-wave effect of the original 1970 reform. Party competition took on a peculiar form, with the decline of the regional-nationalist parties being compensated by the disappearance of the statewide parties, leading to a situation in which there was a broad convergence among parties over state reform, apart from the issue of Brussels, because a regionalist logic had become entrenched across the party systems. This also meant that electoral results had little impact on parties' ability to implement reform as defeated parties were often still needed to have a sufficiently broad coalition to enact constitutional change.

In line with expectations, the VU exploited the European dimension to a growing extent in this phase and was a clear outlier in doing so. Reflecting the growing importance of EU decision-making, the issue of gaining direct access to it started to feature prominently in the VU's discourse. Among the other parties, though, linkages between the European dimension and state restructuring were less widespread and less intense in 1991 than in 1987. The former statewide parties behaved very much like their predecessors in generally neglecting the European dimension in their strategies, in spite of their positive attitudes to both the EU and state reform. The contrast in the intensity with which the VU and the VB exploited Europe is also instructive and, insofar as it can be imputed to the latter's attitudes to integration, confirms that a negative stance on integration is a powerful barrier to a party's use of Europe in relation to state restructuring even when such a party has a secessionist position.

6

From a "Europe of the Regions" to "Independence in Europe"

After the dramatic acceleration of the previous decade culminating in the ratification of the Maastricht Treaty in 1993, in the subsequent period the pace of integration slowed down and the EU focused both on consolidating the recent achievements and on preparing the next steps rather than embarking in new directions. Developments that had been hoped for in the previous phase – chiefly those of a Europe of the Regions and of a social Europe – failed to materialize, leading to a certain disillusion both at the elite and mass levels. State restructuring, by contrast, made major advances in the UK, Italy, and Denmark. After the first attempt of the 1970s and a false-dawn election in 1992, devolution to Scotland and Wales was implemented in the UK in 1997–99. The rise of the Lega Nord in Italy opened a new critical juncture of state restructuring that led to the enactment of a wide-ranging constitutional reform in 2001. In Denmark a radical structural reform was adopted in 2004, replacing the traditional counties with a new tier of regional governments. State restructuring in the UK and Italy conformed to the bottom-up model while the Danish reform followed a top-down dynamic. As expected, in Denmark no party linked Europe and state restructuring whereas Europeanization was significant in both the UK and Italy. Confirming the theoretical expectations further, regional-nationalist parties accounted for the lion's share of such Europeanization strategy in the two countries and the latter was closely tied to positions advocating independence in Europe.

6.1 THE DEVELOPMENT OF INTEGRATION

This phase of European integration spans the period from the entry into force of the Maastricht Treaty to the eastern enlargement and the signing of the Constitutional Treaty (CT) in 2004. It was characterized by the consolidation of the single market and the efforts to prepare the Union for the two major challenges of the new century: monetary union and enlargement to the east.

Following a currency crisis in 1993, the commitment to monetary union enshrined in the Maastricht Treaty entered a crucial implementation stage in 1994, with the start of the so-called Stage 2 of the Economic and Monetary Union (EMU). The overriding focus in this stage was on states' effort to meet the EMU convergence criteria relating in particular to inflation, public deficit, public debt, and currency stability. As many of the countries that intended to join the first wave of EMU were far from meeting these criteria at the outset, they had to make a major convergence effort, entailing in most cases significant fiscal austerity. While the initial expectation was for only a small group of countries – understood to be comprised of Germany, France, and the three Benelux states – to be in the first wave, the political dynamic in countries such as Italy and Spain determined that in the end no fewer than eleven countries adopted the euro in 1999 (Dinan 2014, 275–83).

In other areas of policymaking some trends that had emerged in the previous phase of integration slowed down and were even partially reversed. After the rush to adopt close to 300 directives to put into effect the single-market program, the volume of legislation declined sharply and attention shifted to addressing the backlog in implementation. The importance of cohesion policy in terms of budget allocation continued to grow, but more in relative terms – i.e., vis-à-vis agricultural spending – than in absolute terms. The loss of state control over the structural funds, which a number of political scientists had detected in the 1988 reform, was partially reversed in the subsequent 1993 reform, in which the role of the Commission was curtailed and those of state governments strengthened (Sutcliffe 2000). The vision of a social Europe complementing economic and monetary integration largely failed to materialize, leading to disappointment among left-of-centre politicians and public opinion (Leibfried 2005, 246–56). The most significant policy development outside monetary integration was arguably the incorporation of the Schengen agreement on the elimination of internal border checks into the *acquis communautaire* in 1997. The borderless area ushered in by Schengen became one of the most visible sign of the progress of European integration.

Such policy developments were overshadowed by preoccupation with the second overriding objective of integration in this phase: enlargement. A small scale enlargement took place in 1995 with the entry of Austria, Finland, and Sweden but the *pièce de résistance* was undoubtedly enlargement to the east, to take in the countries of the former Soviet bloc and heal the Cold War division of Europe. Debate centred on the questions of the timing and scope of the enlargement, as well as the preparation the prospective new members had to undergo to ready themselves for membership. After protracted negotiations, Cyprus, the Czech Republic, Estonia, Hungary, Latvia, Lithuania, Malta, Poland, Slovakia, and Slovenia joined in May 2004 (Sedelmeier 2005).

Enlargement also put on the table the question of which institutional reforms had to be carried out by the EU to be able to cope successfully with a much larger and more heterogeneous membership. Institutional reforms had also been made more pressing by concerns with the emergence of a democratic deficit, which manifested itself in particular in the troubled ratification of the Maastricht Treaty (Dinan 2014, 231–47). Three main items featured on the agenda: the size of the European Commission, the operation of the so-called qualified majority voting in the Council, and the extension of the co-decision legislative procedure under which the European Parliament is an equal co-legislator with the Council. Two amending treaties, the Treaty of Amsterdam of 1999 and the Treaty of Nice of 2003, were primarily intended to address these questions but ultimately fell well short of addressing them satisfactorily. Reforms were made more urgent by the 1999 crisis of the European Commission, which saw the body resigning *en masse* to avoid a near-certain motion of censure by the European Parliament, and the continual decline in turnout for the European Parliament elections, which was raising questions about the latter's legitimacy as its powers kept being increased with each round of treaty revision. As a response, the European leaders decided to launch an ambitious reform process intended to lead to the adoption of a constitution for the EU. Drafted through the novel method of a convention, the Treaty establishing a

Constitution for Europe, better known as the Constitutional Treaty, was signed in October 2004 (Dinan 2014, 270–5).

Links between the EU and the regions, which had received a major impetus in the 1980s and early 1990s, continued to develop but fell short of the most enthusiastic expectations. The principle of subsidiarity enshrined in the Maastricht Treaty was welcomed by regionalists as a counterweight to the threat of centralization the deepening of integration was seen as posing. It was also seen as giving a European legitimacy to demands for devolution of powers to regional and local governments at the domestic level, although the scope of its enunciation in the treaty was confined to EU-state relations. In a similar vein, the Committee of the Regions started operating in 1994 as a consultative body to the decision-making institutions, along the lines of the role played by the Economic and Social Committee since 1958. Its mixed membership – i.e., bringing together representatives of subcentral governments with vastly different powers – and its advisory role, however, meant that it fell well short of the hopes regionalists had had of a senate of the regions at the EU level. It became clear that the EU institutions' understanding of a Europe of the Regions was only a pale reflection of the radical vision entertained by regionalists and regional-nationalists (Christiansen 1996).

In addition to the developments mentioned above, other factors conjured up to generate a sense of disillusion with the EU at the level of mass opinion following the enthusiasm generated by the Europe 1992 program. The economic and currency crises of the early 1990s, which struck the European countries as they were about to complete the single market, undermined confidence in economic integration as a one-way street of rising prosperity and smooth adjustment. At the same time, the violent breakup of Yugoslavia amid a dramatic resurgence of virulent nationalism also shattered belief in both supranational integration in general and the emergence of a postnational popular identification with the EU in particular. This was reflected in a marked decline in mass support for the EU (Hix and Høyland 2011, 108).

6.2 UK: THE IMPLEMENTATION OF DEVOLUTION

Following the rejection of devolution in the March 1979 referendums and the defeat of the Labour Party and the SNP, as well as of

PC, in the subsequent general election, the issue of devolution was removed from the political centre stage for most of the 1980s. The Thatcher government repealed the Scotland Act and the Wales Act 1978 and abandoned the distinction it had previously drawn between opposition to Labour's proposals but support for the principle of devolution, ruling out any form of self-government for Scotland. This was in spite of the fact that the party witnessed a continuous decline in Scotland, a decline that many observers attributed primarily to its stance on devolution (Kendrick and McCrone 1989; Seawright 1999). Labour maintained a commitment to a Scottish assembly in the 1983 and 1987 elections, but the issue was low on the party's agenda. The SNP itself underwent a period of crisis and a change of leadership in the early 1980s, which weakened its capacity to challenge the statewide parties.

Devolution started to regain political salience in the wake of the 1987 election, which saw the Conservatives defeating the Labour Party for the third time in a row at the UK level but losing over half of their seats in Scotland (Butler and Kavanagh 1988, 327–30; Bennie et al. 1997, 50). Significant developments took place both within the political parties and beyond. Under the leadership of Gordon Wilson, the SNP sought to react to the 1979 debacle and the subsequent crisis by moderating the party's stance and widening the appeal of independence. Central to this objective was a radical rethinking of its attitudes to the EU and the relation between the latter and independence. The party went from a commitment to withdrawing an independent Scotland from the EU, subject to a referendum vote, to making EU membership the cornerstone of its self-government policy. At its 1988 conference the SNP adopted a policy of independence in Europe, i.e., entailing secession from the UK but continued membership of the EU as an additional member state. In Wilson's words, "I wanted to make it easier for people to vote for the SNP and for independence [and] I saw Europe as a counterweight to London" (2000). Shortly afterward it scored its first significant political victory on the new platform when Jim Sillars, a strong advocate of independence in Europe, took the former Labour stronghold of Glasgow Govan in a by-election in November 1988. Around the same time, the Campaign for a Scottish Assembly, an association of grassroot devolutionists, drafted a Claim of Right for Scotland, which was signed by many prominent figures in March

1989 and led to the setting up of a broad-based Scottish Constitutional Convention later in the same year. Under the impulse of its Scottish branch, the Labour Party decided to join the convention with the aim of arriving at a set of proposals acceptable to a broad range of pro-devolution actors, which the party would commit itself to implementing when returned to office at Westminster. Labour played a major role in the Convention and when the latter published its proposals for a Scottish parliament in 1990, it adopted them as official party policy. On the eve of the 1992 general election the question of devolution, particularly with regard to Scotland, had thus returned to the centre stage of British politics.

The April 1992 Election

PARTIES

The shape of the party system presented two very different faces at the UK and at the Scottish level, respectively. In the UK as a whole, the party system was still the traditional two-and-a-half affair. The Conservatives were the first party, having won the 1987 election with 376 seats against 229 for Labour, equivalent to 58 and 35 percent, respectively. The distance in terms of votes, although less dramatic, was also significant: 42 percent for the Conservatives to 31 percent for Labour. The Social Democratic Party (SDP)-Liberal alliance polled 23 percent but, being penalized by the first-past-the-post system, only secured twenty-two seats (Butler and Kavanagh 1988, 283; 1992, 1–22). In Scotland, however, Labour was by far the dominant party, having won fifty out of seventy-two seats (69 percent) on a 42 percent share of the vote while the Conservatives were a distant second, with ten seats and a 24 percent share of the votes, and the SDP-Liberal alliance a close third, with nine seats and 19 percent electoral support. The SNP was the fourth party, polling 14 percent but, being also penalized by the electoral system, only won three seats (Bennie et al. 1997, 50). In Wales too, Labour was by far the largest party, having won twenty-four out of thirty-eight seats (63 percent) on a 45 percent vote share in 1987. The Conservatives obtained eight seats and a 29.5 percent share of the votes, while the SDP-Liberal alliance and PC both won three seats, on an 18 percent and 7 percent, respectively, share of the votes (Butler and Kavanagh 1988, 284).

POSITIONS ON STATE RESTRUCTURING

The SNP focused its campaign on its independence in Europe policy, under the slogan "Independence in Europe – Make it Happen Now!" claiming that it was "the only policy which will bring stability to Scotland ... Independence is the immediate, logical and clear cut answer to the question of how Scotland should be governed" (SNP 1992a, 2). The party was almost as hostile to devolution as it was to the constitutional status quo, arguing that the former "would results in endless feuds with Westminster" (ibid.). This was in line with the attitude it had adopted to the Scottish Constitutional Convention, from which it had withdrawn when the latter decided to work on a single proposal for a devolved parliament.

PC supported the establishment of a Welsh parliament "with full national status within Europe" (PC 1992, 44, also 7, 43). The creation of a parliament would be accompanied by electoral reform and the adoption of a written constitution and a bill of rights: "Each individual in a self-governing Wales will be a citizen of Wales and of Europe" (44). Although the party's aims were still formulated in rather ambiguous terms, it seems clear that the constitutional status it sought was essentially one of independence in Europe.

The Labour Party supported devolution. Its Scottish manifesto stated that it "will immediately introduce legislation to establish an elected Scottish Parliament. Labour's legislation will be firmly based on the proposals agreed in the Scottish Constitutional Convention" (LAB-S 1992, 6). The Convention's 1990 report *Towards a Scottish Parliament* called for the establishment of a Scottish Parliament elected by proportional representation, and with significant economic and some fiscal powers, in addition to the policy areas that were already within the purview of the Scottish Office. There were three main differences with the proposals that had been put to the referendum in 1979. First, the body would be called a parliament rather than an assembly. Although largely symbolic, the change was significant in that there had been in the 1970s a close association between the term assembly, as offered by the Scotland Act 1978, and a lesser form of devolution compared to a parliament (e.g., Dardanelli 2005a, 64). To match the terminology employed, the proposed parliament would have wider powers and more ample autonomy than the 1970s assembly would have had (Mitchell 1998a). Lastly, but perhaps most significantly, it would be elected by proportional representation rather than the first-past-the-post system. The proposals concerning Wales had a much lower profile in the manifesto, the party confining itself to stating: "Within the lifetime of a full parliament we will establish a directly elected Welsh Assembly" (LAB-W 1992, 8). The assembly would take over most of the functions carried out by the Welsh Office and be responsible for matters such as education, housing, and planning (ibid.).

The Conservatives, by contrast, supported the status quo and attacked devolution as a "slippery slope" to secession. Prime Minister John Major warned that Labour's devolution policy was putting the United Kingdom "in danger" (quoted in Bennie et al. 1997, 71) while the party's manifesto also emphasized the risk to the unity of the country: "We can all make our contribution to the success of the United Kingdom; and we must keep that kingdom united" (CON-S 1992, 2). Devolution had to be rejected because it would pose a threat to such unity: "Any proposals for constitutional change must be judged by the extent to which they would strengthen or undermine the Union. We are not willing to jeopardise the integrity of the United Kingdom" (50). With regard to Wales, "Conservatives believe that all forms of constitutional and political separation could put Wales onto a dangerous road to economic and social secession from the United Kingdom" (CON-W 1992, 8).

ATTITUDES TO, AND STRATEGIC USE OF, EUROPEAN INTEGRATION

Party attitudes to the EU had changed profoundly compared to the late 1970s. As we have seen, the SNP undertook a radical conversion from deep hostility to enthusiasm, not only fully accepting Scotland's membership of the European Union but actually turning the latter into the cornerstone of its independence policy. According to the party's leader when the policy was adopted, "independence in Europe" was a "first class way of pushing the advantages of political independence without any threat of economic dislocation" (quoted in Lynch 1996, 38). Beyond the economic dimension, the SNP also saw Europe as removing secession's negative association with separation and isolation, as well as giving an independent Scotland direct access to the increasingly important EU decision-making process (Lynch 1996, 37–49; Dardanelli 2005a, 86). The party exploited the European dimension to the full in its 1992 campaign, presenting the election as a "choice to go forward into the mainstream of Europe, or be stuck in a backwater of Britain" (SNP 1992a, 1) taking advantage of the fact that "Meanwhile – as confirmed by eminent legal opinion – as a successor state to the United Kingdom, Scotland continues to be part of the European Community" (3). The manifesto also stressed that independence would give Scotland "a direct, powerful voice in Europe and the wider world" (1992a, 2; also 1992b, 4–7).

PC also displayed a positive attitude, advocating "a confederal Europe with Wales taking full part" (PC 1992, 3) and attacked the two main parties for being "obsessed with the sovereignty of the United Kingdom" (5). The party was in favour of increased powers for the existing European Parliament and the creation of a senate of the nations and regions alongside it (46). The European dimension was placed at the heart of the manifesto to strengthen support for self-government. The devolution trend taking place elsewhere in Europe was favourably contrasted with the over-centralization of the UK (3, 5, 6, 24). The large increase in the powers of the EU and the advantages of direct membership were exploited to make a powerful case for access to EU decision-making: "Wales must have a direct and equal voice in the institutions of the European Community. If Wales is to survive as a vibrant and confident society we must win full national status within the Community" (14, also 45, 50).

The Labour Party had also abandoned its previous hostility to the EU and was supportive of integration, in particular of the EU's emerging social dimension and the growing investment in cohesion policy (LAB-S 1992, 6; LAB-W 1992, 6; George and Haythorne 1996, 111–12; Daniels 1998; Dardanelli 2005a, 91). The party placed Scotland in a European context and stressed the importance of giving it a voice in Europe: "Labour is determined to give Scotland a place at the centre of European affairs. As part of Scotland's evolving role in Europe, we will establish a representative office in Brussels and seek appropriate representation for Scotland in European institutions" (LAB-S 1992, 23). Concerning Wales, Labour supported the election of its representatives in the Committee of the Regions as opposed to their appointment by central government (LAB-W 1992, 6). It did not, however, exploit the European dimension to bolster support for a Scottish parliament and a Welsh assembly.

The Conservatives' attitudes toward the EU moved in the opposite direction to those of Labour, the SNP, and PC. From being the party of Europe in the 1970s, it had become an increasingly Eurosceptic party from the late 1980s onward. While it was supportive of the single-market program and ratified – after an epic battle in parliament – the Maastricht Treaty, it was hostile to the EU's growing supranationalism and, especially, its nascent social dimension as embodied by the Maastricht Treaty's Social Charter. Although the party was still in favour of integration overall, it put strong emphasis on respect for the principle of subsidiarity (CON-S 1992, 3–4; Morris 1996, 131–5). The Conservatives made a considerable effort to appeal to the European dimension to undermine the case for devolution and independence for Scotland, stressing two points in particular. First, that any form of separation would go against the spirit of integration: "To begin to erect barriers of any kind on this island would be to defy the trend towards greater European integration and cooperation" (CON-S 1992, 50). Second, that constitutional change would weaken Scotland's voice in Brussels: "Through the United Kingdom, Scotland is able to wield greater influence in the European Community than would otherwise be the case ... Scotland's voice [in the EU] will be weakened by the creation of a separate Scottish Parliament" (49, also 7). In contrast, no reference to the European dimension was made in relation to the constitutional status of Wales (CON-W 1992).

ELECTION OUTCOME

The election results painted a different picture in Scotland compared to the rest of the UK, Wales included. UK-wide, despite a loss of votes and seats relative to the previous election, the Conservatives were returned to office with 336 seats – a reduced overall majority of 21 – compared to Labour's 271 seats, on a 42 and 34 percent share, respectively, of the popular vote (Butler and Kavanagh 1992, 285). In Wales too, the Labour Party made advances both in terms of votes and seats while the Conservatives lost support. PC increased its vote share slightly and won an additional seat (287). In Scotland, on the other hand, the Labour Party lost over three percentage points in electoral support and had to surrender one seat while the Conservatives, rather unexpectedly, increased their share of the vote and gained one seat. The best relative performance in Scotland was that of the SNP, which raised its vote share by over half – from 14.1 to 21.5 percent – compared to 1987, even if it did not manage to increase its tally of seats (ibid.). In this instance, thus, exploitation of the European dimension was associated with electoral success, although this was much more the case for the SNP than for PC.

The SNP results threw sharp light on how difficult it was for the party to overcome the first-past-the-post system's inbuilt bias in UK general elections, thus raising the attractiveness of a Scottish parliament in the eyes of the party. Labour's defeat, though, meant that the prospect for devolution had receded for another parliamentary term once again. If the election outcome was disappointing for the SNP – as well as for the Labour Party – at a deeper level the party could be seen as having scored a significant victory in terms of public attitudes to independence. The latter had by then majority support among nationalists, with over 40 percent in favour of independence in Europe. Among Labour voters, even more significantly, independence had overtaken the status quo as the second most popular constitutional option, with the bulk of support for it also being accounted for by the "in Europe" option (Brand and Mitchell 1994).

The May 1997 Election

POSITIONS ON STATE RESTRUCTURING

All three parties maintained broadly the position they had in 1992, but with some significant changes. The SNP based its campaign again around the theme of independence in Europe but, for the first time, made it subject to endorsement by the people in a referendum (SNP 1997, 9). It described independence as "the only way in which Scotland can put its wealth to work and care for its people again" (5) and criticised Labour's proposals as "New Labour's scheme for a Scottish assembly is fatally flawed, and will deliver no real power … Only the SNP offers a clear, logical and achievable blueprint for progress" (9).

PC called for a "powerhouse parliament," arguing that only a parliament with lawmaking and tax-raising powers could deliver what Wales needed, whereas Labour's devolution proposals would still leave the region dependent on Westminster legislation. Hence, in a referendum on constitutional reform, "the options must include full self-government in Europe and an elected Parliament with law-making powers" (PC 1997, 6). The party envisaged a two-phase process of constitutional change, with a lawmaking parliament being the first step and in a second step: "A self-governing Wales could then take its place among the nations of Europe and the world with an independent place in the European Union, Commonwealth and United Nations" (8).

The Labour Party's commitment to devolution was reinforced by the accession of John Smith to the leadership of the UK party in the wake of the 1992 election. A Scotsman and a long-time supporter of devolution, he considered it to be the "settled will of the Scottish people" (quoted in Wright 1997, 143). After Smith's death in 1994, Tony Blair continued the same policy, endorsing the second report of the Constitutional Convention, presented in 1995. The party then decided to put the issue to a referendum after the general election with the later change of having two questions, one on establishing the parliament and the other on granting it tax-varying powers (Jones 1997). Labour's manifesto confirmed the commitment: "For Scotland we propose the creation of a parliament with lawmaking powers, firmly based on the agreement reached in the Scottish Constitutional Convention, including defined and limited financial powers to vary revenue and elected by an additional member system." (LAB-S 1997, 32). The party remained opposed to independence and kept portraying it in negative terms as a policy bringing political isolation, economic damage, and social disruption to Scotland, though with much less hostility than in the 1970s (Hassan and Lynch 1999, 13). Labour also maintained its commitment to establishing a Welsh assembly but made it subject to endorsement by the people in a referendum: "We will, with the consent of the people of Wales, legislate for a Welsh assembly" (LAB-W 1997, 32).

The Conservatives stuck to their dogged defence of the status quo. The party attacked both the principle of devolution to Scotland – as a first step to the break up of the UK – and the proposed tax-raising powers. John Major wrote in the party's manifesto that "the menace of separatism – introduced through the Trojan Horse of devolution – would blight the lives of Scots for generations to come" (CON-S 1997, 2), while the Scottish leader of the party, Michael Forsyth, argued: "nor do we need any lessons in patriotism from those who trumpet their attachment to Scotland's interests while pursuing – directly or indirectly – separatist policies whose consequences would be to detach us from the United Kingdom and impoverish our people for generations to come" (4). Mr Forsyth was also at the forefront of the party's attacks against the so-called tartan tax during the campaign (Bennie et al. 1997, 72). In a similar vein, the party's Welsh manifesto stressed: "We must protect our constitution and unity as a nation from those who threaten it with unnecessary and dangerous change" (CON-W 1997, 3). It branded an assembly "divisive and wasteful" (4) and warned that it would be "the greatest threat to that stability and security that we have ever had to face in Wales ... [it] would begin the process of unravelling the Union and could lead to the break up of the United Kingdom" (53).

ATTITUDES TO, AND STRATEGIC USE OF, EUROPEAN INTEGRATION

The SNP manifesto was focused on the advantages that independent membership would bring and did not articulate a detailed position on integration, confining itself to supporting an extension of the powers of the European Parliament vis-à-vis the Commission and the Council (SNP 1997, 30). The party continued to exploit Europe intensely to bolster the case for independence as, according to its spokesperson, "the whole concept of a small country in Europe has become a powerful argument for us ... Europe is a powerful campaigning tool for the SNP" (Pringle 2000). The manifesto stressed that "Scotland, on independence, will automatically become a full member of the European Union" (SNP 1997, 7) and benefit from full access to its decision-making institutions: "We will have full voting power in the European Council and the Council of Ministers. These representatives would be in a position to advocate on Scotland's behalf with the right of veto over any decisions affecting Scotland's vital national interests. This is a far cry from the present powerlessness we endure, and some considerable distance from the still powerless observer status that Labour proposes under its devolution plans ... Scotland's representation in the European Parliament would double on Independence" (30).

Europe was even more front and centre in the PC campaign. Throughout its manifesto, the party emphasized that its commitment to the establishment of a Welsh parliament had to be understood in a European dimension: "Plaid Cymru is the only party which stands for a law-making Parliament for Wales with a voice in Europe" (PC 1997, 6). The theme of transforming Wales from the periphery of the UK to the heart of Europe was repeatedly pointed out: "a Powerhouse Parliament does more than just hand back democracy to Wales, it also puts us at the heart of Europe ... A Powerhouse Parliament will put Wales at the heart of a new Europe of the Nations and historic Regions – no longer left on the furthest edge of the UK listening to the Euro-squabble of middle England" (2); "Only Plaid Cymru has the record of consistently challenging the historical forgery that is the British state and of projecting a vision that reunites Wales with its European destiny" (9). In a similar vein to the SNP's, the party stressed in particular that its policy would allow Wales to get access to the top table of EU decision-making: "it must be allowed to develop its own direct link with the European Union, where so many decisions are taken today which affect the vital interest of Welsh industry and agriculture" (5). The prospect of monetary union would only reinforce such a need, which the constitutional status quo was unable to address: "In fact, the demands of political and monetary union in the EU force a decision between the small union – the UK – and the larger union – the EU ... Our constitutional relationship with Europe, via a Westminster government which is skewed toward the priorities of South-east England, has thwarted a full transformation of our economy. In particular, it has stood between Welsh needs and the structural and regional funds of the EU" (9).

Labour displayed a positive attitude toward European integration and contrasted its stance to the growing Euroscepticism of the Conservatives. The party stressed in particular its support for the completion of the single market, enlargement to the east, and the UK's signing up to the Maastricht Treaty's Social Charter, while promising a referendum on the country's adoption of the euro, were a set of economic conditions to be met (LAB-S 1997, 38–9; LAB-W 1997, 37–8). Although the Labour Party generally saw Europe as a context facilitating the case for devolution in the 1990s (Dardanelli 2005a, 91–3), it did not link the two in its manifesto, either in relation to Scotland or to Wales (LAB-S 1997, 32; LAB-W 1997, 32–3).

The Conservatives took a cautious stance on integration, supporting the UK's continuing involvement in the EU but making clear their rejection of moves toward federalization and the building of a social Europe, arguing that they wanted to be "in Europe but not run by Europe" (CON-S 1997, 39). One of the key passages in the manifesto committed the party to "Develop Europe as a partnership of nation states – ensuring that Britain retains a stable relationship within Europe but outside any federal structure that might emerge, and outside Social Chapter and employment legislation that would damage our competitive, enterprise economy" (38; also CON-W 1997, 50). Although to a lesser extent than in 1992, the Conservative party continued to exploit Europe to undermine the case for devolution to Scotland. Its Scottish manifesto argued that devolution would weaken, rather than strengthen, Scotland's voice in the EU: "Scotland...through the Union has been able to punch far above her weight in Europe and on the wider world stage" and committed the party to "retain Scotland's strong voice inside the institutions of the EU – rejecting the devolution and separation proposals of our opponents which would inevitably marginalise that voice" (CON-S 1997, 38-9, 47). John Major also linked European integration and devolution in the campaign, branding them as two faces of the same process of "power draining away from Westminster" (*Times* 1997) and warning "there are 72 hours in which to save the Union, 72 hours to make sure that the system of Government that has prevailed in this country for a very long time is protected and enshrined ... not broken up and divided in one direction toward the EU and the other to a devolved Parliament across the United Kingdom" (*Times* 1997). With regard to Wales, however, the Conservative manifesto only briefly mentioned that devolution "would marginalise Wales in Britain and in Europe" (CON-W 1997, 53).

ELECTION OUTCOME

In contrast to 1992, the election results painted the same picture in the UK as a whole as well as in Scotland and Wales. The Labour Party won office for the first time since 1979 on a landslide victory. It received 43 percent of the votes and won 418 seats in the House of Commons (63 percent), the largest number the party had ever had. Compared to the previous election, Labour gained almost nine percentage points in vote share and 145 seats. The Conservatives' defeat was a mirror image of Labour's triumph, losing over 11 percentage points in support and 178 seats, to leave the party with only 125 seats (25 percent) on a 31 percent share of the vote (Butler and Kavanagh 1997, 255).

Labour was the undisputed winner in Scotland and Wales too, gaining six and seven additional seats on a 46 and a 55 percent, respectively, share of the votes. The SNP managed to double its number of seats to six, although its electoral support increased only slightly to 22 percent. PC also gained a marginally higher share of the votes but did not increase its tally of four seats. In a most dramatic result, the Conservatives were wiped out in both Scotland and Wales, losing eight and nine percentage points in support, respectively, and all their seats (256).

On the wave of its electoral triumph, the Labour Party was able to form a government with a huge majority in the Commons and quickly passed legislation to fulfil its commitment to hold a two-question referendum on the establishment of a Scottish parliament with some tax-raising powers.

The September 1997 Referendums

In stark contrast to the divisions prominent in 1979, the pro-devolution parties conducted a unified campaign for the 11 September referendum in Scotland (*Scotsman* 1997b,c,e,f; McCrone and Lewis 1999). Central to the unity of the pro-devolution camp was a rapprochement between Labour and the SNP, on the basis of a discourse playing down the differences between independence and devolution and presenting the latter primarily as an alternative to the Tory-imposed status quo rather than as an antidote to secession, as it had been the case eighteen years before. The efforts of the leaders of the Labour Party in Scotland, Donald Dewar, and of the SNP, Alex Salmond, played a crucial part in this respect, having concluded that "absolute unity is the only way to guarantee the result they seek" (*Scotsman* 1997g).

On the other side of the argument, the Conservatives, unlike in 1979, did not receive support from the business organizations and fought the No corner in almost complete isolation (McCrone and Lewis 1999, 24). Remarkably, the rapprochement between Labour and the SNP took place in spite of the fact that No supporters still centred their attacks on the risk that devolution would lead to secession. In the last stages of the campaign, the prominent anti-devolutionist Tam Dalyell declared that "a Scottish parliament would be the first step on the motorway-without-an-exit to a Scottish state that is separate from England" (*Scotsman* 1997a). In the crucial phase of the campaign, Michael Ancram, the Conservatives' constitutional spokesman and leader of the Think Twice group, argued that "within ten years, you would see an enormous cesspool of resentment build up which can only play into the hands of nationalism and the separatist movement" (*Scotsman* 1997d; see also Thatcher 1997).

The Conservatives also directed their attacks against the dangers of the tartan tax. This latter line of attack did have some success as it was probably instrumental in delivering lower support for the tax-varying powers than for the principle of devolution itself, though it did not stop those powers from being endorsed. In contrast, the main line of attack centred on the breakup of the UK totally failed to produce the outcome the No campaign had achieved in 1979. Support for devolution held steady throughout the campaign and turned into a strong endorsement in the referendum: 74.3 percent of the electorate voted Yes on the question of whether a Scottish parliament should be established and 63.5 percent approved granting it tax-varying powers (Surridge and McCrone 1999; Curtice 1999). Although Europe featured less prominently in the campaign, as the SNP focused on supporting devolution rather than advocating independence, it had an important indirect effect. By contributing to making independence preferred to the status quo among the electorate, the SNP's policy of independence in Europe removed the interaction effect between attitudes to independence and attitudes to devolution that loomed large in the 1979 referendum and played a key role in the endorsement of devolution in 1997 (Dardanelli 2005b).

The campaign for the Welsh referendum, held a week after the Scottish vote, followed a similar pattern although there were greater divisions within the Labour Party on the merits of the devolution proposals on offer. Labour, Plaid Cymru, and the Liberal Democrats conducted a unified Yes campaign with the Conservatives being the main force on the No side. Given the disparities in the powers offered to Wales in comparison to Scotland, PC was even more in a dilemma than in 1979 on whether to support devolution or not. Eventually the party concluded that an assembly would still constitute progress relative to the status quo and played a full part in Yes for Wales. The Yes side stressed modernization and democratization while the No campaign emphasized the threat to the unity of the UK and the wasteful nature of a "toothless" body (McAllister 1998, 157–8; Wyn Jones and Lewis 1999, 42–3). Public opinion was much more divided than in Scotland and the referendum result delivered the thinnest of endorsements: 50.3 percent of voters supporting the establishment of an assembly on a 50.2 percent turnout (McAllister 1998; Wyn Jones and Lewis 1999; Wyn Jones and Trystan 1999).

The Implementation of Devolution

Following the referendums, the Labour Party initiated legislation to set up a Scottish parliament and a Welsh Assembly leading to the enactment of the Scotland Act 1998 and the Government of Wales Act 1998. The Scotland Act established a Scottish parliament and an executive, possessing extensive primary legislative competences and a limited tax-varying power. The Scottish parliament would be elected every four years through a version of the additional member system, combining 55 percent of the seats allocated in single-member constituencies and 45 percent allocated through district lists. The executive, headed by the first minister, would be accountable to the parliament and be politically responsible for the civil service administration previously overseen by the Scottish Office. The parliament would have the power to enact primary legislation in all policy areas not reserved to the UK parliament by the Act. In practice this meant that the parliament was granted lawmaking powers primarily in the fields of agriculture, education, healthcare, housing, law and order, local government, and most aspects of transport. The main source of funding would be a block grant from the central Treasury, but the parliament was given the power to modify the rate of income tax by plus/minus three percent (Bogdanor 1999, 202–9).

By contrast, the Government of Wales Act provided for an assembly possessing executive responsibilities only and no fiscal powers. The assembly would be directly elected by a mixed member system similar to the Scottish one – though with a different balance between the two election channels – and work on a hybrid basis combining elements of the cabinet system and the local government committee model. The assembly would have executive competences over a wide range of areas including agriculture, education, healthcare, housing, local government, social services, transport, and the Welsh language (209–13). The two acts thus granted a high degree of autonomy to Scotland and less extensive but still not negligible autonomy to Wales, turning the UK into a partially federal state, as conceptualized in chapter 1.

Summary

This second critical juncture of state restructuring in the UK once more conformed to the bottom-up model. The challenge presented to the Labour Party by a resurgent SNP was a crucial factor in inducing the former to join the Scottish Constitutional Convention and committing itself to enacting devolution afterward. The establishment of a Scottish parliament with primary lawmaking powers in a wide range of policy fields was a reform of major constitutional significance as the debate in the 1970s had already hinted at. As in the earlier period, the Welsh component of the reform was closely linked to the dynamic of the Scottish devolution and largely subordinate to it.

A key difference with the previous juncture, and one that goes a long way to explaining their different outcomes, was the extent to which the politics of state restructuring was Europeanized. The SNP radically changed its attitudes to the EU and, together with PC, played the European card to the full. In the discourse of both parties, gaining access to decision-making at the EU level was a central theme. By contrast, while the Conservatives made significant negative use of the European dimension to undermine devolution, the Labour Party made little effort to exploit Europe to advance state restructuring, in spite of its positive attitudes to both. The new strategy brought significant electoral payoffs for the SNP but was even more successful in terms of its effects on public opinion. By linking independence to Europe, the move made it mainstream to the point that it became the second most popular constitutional option at mass public level by 1997.

6.3 ITALY: THE 2001 CONSTITUTIONAL REFORM

The ordinary regions implemented in the 1970s were widely judged in the following decade to have fallen short of the vision of regional autonomy put forward by the framers of the constitution (e.g., Putnam et al. 1985, 341–50; King 1987, 336–7). In several regions of the north – Veneto, Piedmont, and Lombardy in particular – regionalist parties started to emerge whose program included a demand for their respective regions to be granted the same level of autonomy enjoyed by the regions with a special autonomy statute – which in the north included Aosta Valley, Trentino and South Tyrol,[1] and Friuli-Julian Venetia (Allievi 1992, 36; Woods 1992; Biorcio 1997, 41–4). The European elections gave these parties an incentive to cooperate and both in 1984 and 1989 they formed an electoral alliance. It was on the latter occasion that the cartel known as Alleanza Nord scored its first significant success in the crucial region of Lombardy, the heart of the north as well as Italy's economic powerhouse and its most populous region (Biorcio 1997, 50). Under the leadership of the Lombard League, later that year six regionalist parties formed a new, federally structured, party named Lega Nord (LN), or Northern League (54). The new party scored a major success in the 1990 regional election, winning 19 percent of the votes and fifteen seats in Lombardy, making it overnight the second largest party in the region (ibid.). The rise of the Lega Nord took place in the context of a crisis of Italy's postwar political regime, marked by the transformation of the PCI, formerly the largest communist party in Western Europe, and the break out of a major corruption scandal (e.g., Bull and Newell 1993, 206–7; Cotta and Verzichelli 2007, 48–52).

The April 1992 Election

PARTIES

On the eve of the 1992 election, the Italian party system continued to display the traditional features that had characterized it since the late 1940s. It was a highly fragmented party system, with three main parties and a number of smaller ones. The Christian democrats were still dominant, having obtained 34 percent of the vote in the 1987 election. The old communist party had split in 1991, the bulk of it transforming itself into a social-democratic party, the Partito Democratico della Sinistra (PDS), or Democratic Party of the Left, while a hardline faction broke away to create the Partito della Rifondazione Comunista (PRC), or Refounded Communist Party. The PCI had won a 26 percent share of the vote in the previous election. The socialist party, allied with the Christian democrats since the mid-1960s, was the third largest party, scoring 14 percent in the 1987 election (Ignazi 2010, 56–60).

POSITIONS ON STATE RESTRUCTURING

The Lega Nord fought its first nationwide election on a platform of a federal reform of the state. Somewhat surprisingly, given its nature as a federation of regional leagues, it was not envisaging the existing regions becoming the constituent units of the proposed federation, calling instead for the creation of three so-called macro-regions: North, Centre, and South. The macro-regions would have competence notably over economic policy while defence, justice, law and order, and the currency would be responsibilities of the federal authorities. The role of the existing regions and who would control the other areas of public policy was left unspecified in the program. The LN's campaign put emphasis on federalism and the macro-regions as a battle cry rather than as detailed policy proposals (LN 1991; CdS 1992b; Allievi 1992, 44–5; Bossi and Vimercati 1992, 154–70; Savelli 1992, 181; Agnew 1997, 113). The DC expressed cautious support for a development of the ordinary regions in the context of a wider institutional reform, focusing in particular, as per its manifesto, on strengthening their financial autonomy and widening their legislative competences: "Lo sviluppo dell'istituto regionale costituisce uno degli obiettivi prioritari della DC per la prossima legislatura"[2] (DC 1992, 19).

The PDS went further than its traditional rival and supported a deeper reform of the state in a federal direction. Its manifesto called for: "Tutto ciò che non è riservato alla grande legislazione nazionale va attribuito alle Regioni, così che il nostro diventi uno Stato quasi federale"[3] (PDS 1992, 3–4). In a similar vein, the PSI placed further devolution of powers to the regions at the heart of its vision for a reform of the state and called for a "regionalismo autenticamente politico ai limiti del federalismo"[4] (PSI 1992, 27–8). This would entail lawmaking competences in a wider range of policy areas, genuine fiscal autonomy, and a simplification of the allocation of responsibilities between the state, the regions, and local authorities (28).

ATTITUDES TO, AND STRATEGIC USE OF, EUROPEAN INTEGRATION

All three statewide parties were strongly in favour of European integration, with only minor differences between them. The DC placed considerable emphasis on its pro-integration profile, headlining its manifesto *Una proiezione internazionale per la politica italiana* (an international outlook for italian politics) and devoting its first part to the party's contribution in the achievements of European integration (DC 1992, 1–3; CdS 1992a,c; Bull 1996, 150–1).

The PSI emphasized its enthusiasm for integration, heading the first section of its manifesto "Toward a Federal Europe" and claiming that the Maastricht Treaty was a major step in that direction (PSI 1992, 1). The PDS and the LN paid less attention to integration in their manifestos but were also strongly supportive, albeit with somewhat less enthusiasm in the latter's case (PDS 1992; LN 1991; Savelli 1992; Conti and Verzichelli 2005, 102–6). All of them supported ratification of the Maastricht Treaty (Quaglia 2008, 67–9). The LN did not link the European dimension and its proposed federalization of the state directly in its program but elsewhere did link Europe and state reform to allay fears that federalism would divide Italy. A book performing the role of an extended manifesto argued that "Il federalismo che terrà unita l'Europa non potrà dividere l'Italia"[5] (Savelli 1992, 181). The notion that shifts of powers downward to the regional level and upward to the European level were two sides of the same coin featured prominently in the LN's discourse in this period and also appeared to resonate with its supporters (Allievi 1992, 25, 35–6, 43; Bossi and Vimercati 1992, 194–204; Diamanti 1993, 101; Gilbert 1993, 104–5, and 1995, 58–9; Ruzza and Schmidtke 1993, 22fn18; Desideri 1995, 83). The DC made a negative appeal to the European dimension in its campaigning to argue that further devolution would go against the logic of European integration (DC 1992; CdS 1992a,c). The PDS and the PSI did not link integration and state reform (PDS 1992; PSI 1992).

ELECTION OUTCOME

All three main statewide parties lost ground in the election. The DC lost five percentage points and twenty-six seats in the Chamber of Deputies compared to the 1987 election. The PDS suffered even more heavily, dropping ten percentage points and surrendering seventy seats in the lower house (compared to the PCI's tally in the previous election). The PSI's results were less negative, down one percentage points and two seats compared to the previous election. The clear winner of the election was the Lega Nord, which scored 8.65 percent of the popular votes overall but between 14 and 27 percent in Lombardy, Veneto, and Piedmont, thus increasing its seats in the lower house from one to fifty-five (Donovan 1992; Bull and Newell 1993; Besson and Bibes 1993). Analyses of vote change between 1987 and 1992 showed that most of the support obtained by the Lega came from the DC and, to a lesser extent, the PCI (Biorcio 1997, 64–5). The success of the LN thus injected a powerful impetus for a restructuring of the state, although electoral support for the Lega did not automatically signal support for a federalization of the state. An August 1991 survey, for instance, showed that 30 percent of LN sympathizers in Lombardy – and 70 percent overall – rejected the idea of creating a Republic of the North (LS 1991). In this case a modest exploitation of the European dimension by the LN went hand in hand with significant electoral advances for the party.

The March 1994 Election

PARTIES

The 1992 election and the adoption of a new electoral system by referendum the following year triggered a profound transformation of the Italian party system and brought to an end what would soon come to be referred to as Italy's first republic. The most significant changes were the demise of the DC, which had been the hegemonic party for more than forty years, and the emergence of Silvio Berlusconi's party Forza Italia (FI), which would be a key political actor for the next twenty years, as well the demise of the PSI and the transformation of the neofascist MSI into the more moderate Alleanza Nazionale (AN), or National Alliance (Gilbert 1995; Cotta and Verzichelli 2007, 52–64). The new mixed-member electoral system, allocating 75 percent of the seats in single member constituencies, was a radical change from the previous, very proportional, list system and gave incentives to parties to form electoral alliances. Three such alliances contested the 1994 election: one on the left led by the PDS, another on the right bringing together Forza Italia, Alleanza Nazionale, and the Lega Nord, and a smaller, centrist one around the Partito Popolare Italiano (PPI), or Italian People's Party, the main rump of the former DC.

POSITIONS ON STATE RESTRUCTURING

The PDS placed the reform of the state at the top of its programmatic commitments, calling for a "regionalismo forte, di ispirazione federalista ... che è cosa ben diversa tanto da un mero decentramento dello Stato, quanto dall'idea di una disgregante confederazione di Repubbliche"[6] (PDS 1994, 6). It did not, however, detail what such strong regionalism would entail. FI focused on the financial relations between levels of government and proposed the adoption of a radical form of fiscal federalism. Under the plan the power to tax would be taken away from the state and devolved entirely to regional and local governments, which would then transfer a quota to the central government to pay for the latter's discharge of its functions, to be restricted to matters of national interest. The number of government tiers should be reduced and the allocation of responsibilities to them should be governed by the principle of subsidiarity (FI 1994, 23). The LN maintained the idea of creating three macro-regions but it too focused primarily on the fiscal dimension. Its proposal shared the key elements of that put forward by FI, whereby tax-raising powers would be granted exclusively to regional and local governments and these would then transfer a quota to the macro-regions and to the federation to finance their operation and policies (LN 1994, 2–3). As in 1992, the party's proposals were still lacking details on the proposed new constitutional architecture of the state.

The PPI's manifesto expressed support for regional and local autonomy and a rejection of all forms of centralism but was short on concrete proposals for change beyond a generic call for the regions to have effective decision-making capacities and fiscal autonomy (PPI 1994, 7).

ATTITUDES TO, AND STRATEGIC USE OF,
EUROPEAN INTEGRATION

Attitudes to the EU displayed more diversity than two years earlier. While the PDS, the PPI, and, to a lesser extent, the LN maintained their traditionally strong support for further integration in a federal direction, FI, although broadly positive, was more cautious and hard nosed. The PDS's manifesto argued: "L'opzione europea è per l'Italia una scelta prioritaria e irreversibile ... non vi è per l'Italia alcuna possibilità di un moderno sviluppo economico e sociale se non entro il processo di Unione Europea"[7] (PDS 1994, 10). On that basis, the party called for further integration beyond that achieved with the Maastricht Treaty, addressing the EU's democratic deficit, and developing a genuine common monetary policy and a social dimension as well as enlarging toward the north and the east (ibid.). The PPI continued to express the enthusiasm of its predecessor, headlining the relevant section of its manifesto "Un progetto federale per una forte Europa"[8] (PPI 1994, 5). In it the party called for closer integration with a federal objective and the enlargement of the EU to new members, and argued that Italy, by virtue of its historical role in integration and its national interests, should be at the forefront of this process (6). Even if it placed less emphasis on it, the LN also expressed strong support for further integration: "La Lega Nord è chiaramente favorevole all'Europa unita. Solamente un'Europa unita può infatti affrontare i problemi e le sfide dei prossimi decenni"[9] (LN 1994, 23; see also Agnew 2002, 173). In contrast, although FI subscribed to the process of European unification, it stressed much more the need to bolster Italy's role within it and to defend its national interests, calling also for a deeper and clearer application of the principle of subsidiarity (FI 1994, 21). None of the parties, however, linked European integration and the reform of the state.

ELECTION OUTCOME

The right-wing alliance centred on Forza Italia scored an emphatic victory in the election, gaining 46 percent of the vote in the single-member constituencies and securing an absolute majority of 366 seats in the Chamber of Deputies, against the 33 percent of the popular vote and 213 seats won by the left-wing alliance led by the PDS. The centrist alliance led by the PPI came a very distant third, with only 16 percent support and 46 seats in the lower house. For the PPI itself, the results represented a catastrophic defeat, as the party only managed to win 29 seats in the Chamber against the 206 the DC had won two years before (Bull and Newell 1995, 87). Within the winning alliance, the LN emerged as the single largest party, more than doubling its tally of seats from 55 to 117. However, this was due to the votes it received from supporters of its allied parties in the single-member constituencies, whereas in the proportional vote support for the party actually fell, primarily to the benefit of FI (Biorcio 1997, 75–82).

In terms of their significance for the prospect of a restructuring of the state, these results thus painted a Janus-faced picture. On the one hand, the LN had gained a major representation in parliament and access to the central government, something regional parties – even those such as the LN that operate in several regions – rarely achieve. Moreover, the leading party in the coalition, FI, was ostensibly committed to a federal reform of the state. On the other hand, many in the LN interpreted the result as a setback for the party and viewed FI as a rival more than an ally (ibid.). Moreover, the National Alliance, the third party in the coalition, represented a sector of public opinion traditionally favouring centralism and was hostile to radical reforms, especially in the fiscal field, that the regions of the centre and the south, more dependent on state transfers, might perceive as detrimental to their interests. The fate of state reform thus hinged on the sincerity of FI's commitment and the solidity of the alliance between the latter and the LN. Both of them soon proved to be lacking.

Following the victory of the right-wing alliance in the 1994 election, the first cabinet led by Silvio Berlusconi took office in May but fell in the following December after the LN withdrew from the governing coalition, in the wake of disappointing results in the June election for the European Parliament. The party's decision appears to have been dictated by the fear of losing ownership of the reform of the state within a potentially mortal embrace with Forza Italia (ibid.). Meanwhile, the defeat of the centrist choice made by the PPI in 1994 triggered a reconsideration of the party's options and eventually led to the decision to ally itself with the PDS within a centre-left alliance known as L'Ulivo, or Olive Tree. The fall of the interim government led by the technocrat Lamberto Dini in January 1996 opened the way to a new general election in the spring.

The April 1996 Election

PARTIES

Three main actors contested the April 1996 election: the centre-left L'Ulivo, an alliance led by the PDS and including the left-of-centre Christian democrats and the Greens[10]; the centre-right cartel comprising of Forza Italia and the National Alliance, renamed Polo per le libertà, or Freedom Pole; and the Lega Nord, now standing on its own.

POSITIONS ON STATE RESTRUCTURING

The issue of state reform featured prominently in the campaign and in the party manifestos. LN made federalism, again, the cornerstone of its manifesto, although its proposals seemed to prefigure a confederal rather than a federal system and once again many aspects of how the new political system was meant to operate were left unspecified. The party called for the wholesale transfer to the federated states of the bulk of competences, personnel, and resources, leaving to the (con)federal government only coordination and control responsibilities as well as core functions such as defence, financed by transfers from the federated states. The party did not explicitly state so, but its discourse implied that the federated states would be macro-regions such as the North – increasingly referred to as "Padania" – rather than the existing regions and left unclear whether the relationship between such macro-regions and the regions would be federal or not (LN 1996, 1–4). Although no mention of independence for Padania was made in the manifesto, the LN was becoming more tolerant of secessionist opinions within its ranks and its leader increasingly made threats to the effect that the North would seek independence if the other parties blocked the (con)federal reform it demanded (Biorcio 1997, 84–6).

The Ulivo's program was structured around eighty-eight proposals, the first fourteen of which concerned institutional reforms. The third and fourth proposals dealt more specifically with the territorial structure of the state and the autonomy of subcentral governments.

According to the alliance, its proposals were based on the principles of local self-government and cooperative federalism (UL 1995). The Ulivo proposed a major expansion of the legislative responsibilities of the regional assemblies, devolving to them all lawmaking powers not expressly reserved for the central parliament. The regions would also be granted full autonomy in adopting their own statutes and form of government (subject only to the constitution), would have control over local government, and be free from central government's control. Such wide-ranging devolution of power would be complemented by a transformation of the Senate into a chamber of the regions, composed of representatives of regional institutions and possessing equal powers with the lower house on legislative matters affecting the regions (ibid., tesi no. 3 and 4).

FI maintained a commitment to fiscal federalism, but it presented it as simply an increase in the fiscal autonomy of regional and local governments rather than a genuine federal reform of the state, and gave less prominence to it than in the previous campaign (FI 1996, 3).

ATTITUDES TO, AND STRATEGIC USE OF,
EUROPEAN INTEGRATION

Attitudes to European integration remained broadly positive, although with a major difference in emphasis between the LN and the Ulivo on the one hand and Forza Italia on the other. The LN claimed "la Lega Nord considera l'Europa come la cornice primaria della propria azione politica"[11] (LN 1996, 24). In relation to the 1996 intergovernmental conference, the party supported the inclusion in the treaty of the principles of self-determination for all peoples, of local autonomy, and of protection of all linguistic and cultural identities. It was also in favour of the expansion of the EU's remit in the fields of justice and home affairs as well as in that of foreign and security affairs, whereas it was cautious on the question of enlargement, arguing for the application of a criterion of "affinity of traditions" (24–6). The LN exploited the European dimension considerably. Echoing a traditional theme of the Europe of the Regions discourse, it claimed that the unitary state was increasingly a relic of the past, too small to deal with the big economic and environmental challenges and at the same time too large to govern closely to citizens' needs and identities (24). The Lega focused in particular on the risk that the North would be cut off from core Europe if Italy failed to qualify for the third stage of monetary union,[12] despite being one of the continent's most prosperous areas: "È vitale evitare l'esclusione della Padania da un'istituzionalizzazione di un 'nucleo solido' al quale essa è intimamente legata"[13] (24, also 1–2). The alternative, not explicitly spelled out but hinted at, was for Padania to seek membership of such a European core on its own, leaving the rest of Italy outside. The party also called for a new interpretation of the principle of subsidiarity, expressly including the regional and local levels, and a strengthening of the Committee of the Regions as a first step in its transformation into a second chamber of the European Parliament, as a chamber of the regions (25).

The Ulivo pointed out the importance of the 1996 revision of the Treaty of Maastricht as a turning point between further integration and a watering down of the Union, stressing Italy's crucial role in promoting the former. The alliance called for a completion of monetary union, the development of political integration, in particular in the field of foreign affairs and security, wider application of qualified majority voting, greater legislative powers for the EP, and the removal of states' veto rights on treaty amendments, as well as enlargement to new members (UL 1995, tesi no. 24 and 25). It linked Europe and state reform only indirectly, arguing that decentralization was consistent with the process of European integration and calling for the Committee of the Regions to be granted a binding legislative role in matters affecting regional governments (ibid., tesi no. 3 and 24).

In stark contrast to such strong support expressed by its main rivals, but broadly in line with the coolness displayed in the 1994 election campaign, the FI manifesto, dubbed *Contratto con gli Italiani*, or Contract with the Italians, did not put forward a position on integration nor did it link it to state restructuring (FI 1996).

ELECTION OUTCOME

The centre-left Ulivo alliance won the election, receiving 42 percent of the vote and winning 285 seats in the Chamber of Deputies, but fell short of an overall majority. The centre-right Polo secured 246 seats in the Chamber on a 40 percent share of the vote. The LN saw its representation in the lower house shrink to 59 members but was the most voted single party in the north of the country, with peaks of 29 percent in Veneto and 25 percent in Lombardy (Biorcio 1999, 60). The party interpreted this as a vindication of the decision to radicalize its constitutional position and go it alone.

The election ushered in an Ulivo government led by Romano Prodi, which, however, had to rely on the external support of PRC to command a majority in the lower house. Although this was clearly a fragile position for the government to be in, the political constellation was arguably the most favourable to a restructuring of the state since the 1960s. Such a reform was a central plank of the governing coalition's program and the latter's resolve was spurred by the threat of a resurgent and radicalized LN, determined to exploit the freedom of manoeuvre afforded to it by being in opposition (see also Newell 1996, 109–10). Although its representation in parliament declined, in terms of electoral support the LN's strategy of exploiting the European dimension was associated on this occasion with positive payoffs.

The Decentralization Laws and the 2001 Constitutional Reform

In the course of 1996, the LN radicalized further, developing a notion of Padanian nationalism and engaging in a mobilization campaign intended to rally voters and sympathizers to its by then openly secessionist position (Biorcio 1997, 94–103; Diamanti 1997, 65–6). Most prominently, it held a three-day demonstration along the river Po "for the independence of Padania," culminating in a "declaration of independence" for Padania in Venice on 15 September 1996. In February 1997, it officially changed its name to Lega Nord – Per l'indipendenza della Padania. The fear of Padania being excluded from core Europe if Italy failed to qualify for the first wave of monetary union was an important determinant of this strategy (Luverà 1997; Berlucchi 1997, 363; Cento Bull and Gilbert 2001, 108–9; Agnew 2002, 178). This European dimension also resonated with the Lega's militants: two thirds of the participants at the river Po demonstration favoured an independent Padania within the EU (Biorcio 1997, 94), although support for secession remained low among the wider population in the North (Diamanti 1996; Berlucchi 1997, 366; Beirich and Woods 2000, 138).

The government reacted to these developments by putting in motion its restructuring program, in a two-pronged way. On the one hand, it set about enacting a package of ordinary laws through which all powers that could be devolved to the regions within the framework of the existing constitution could be so transferred. On the other hand, it aimed to amend Title V of the constitution to entrench the new organization of the state (Baldi 2006, 88). A 1997 law, known as the Bassanini law after the minister who promoted it, introduced a form of administrative federalism based on the principle of subsidiarity, whereby the regions would be the primary administrative agencies of the state, including in policy fields under the legislative competence of the central government, and would transfer further down the territorial scale of administration those functions better executed at that level. On the basis of the Bassanini law, administrative competences in the fields of agriculture, economic development, labour market, public transport, and retail were devolved to the regions together with the transfer of personnel to carry them out (Rampulla 1997; Gilbert 2000; Baldi 2006, 88–91). In the fiscal sphere, two laws enacted in 1997 and 1999 created a regional business tax and replaced most of the grants with which the regions had hitherto been funded with a share of the state's taxes such as income tax and VAT, thus increasing the transparency of their financing system as well as, to some extent, their fiscal autonomy (Baldi 2006, 92–3).

With regard to amending Title V of the constitution, the government initially aimed to include it within a broader package of reforms to be agreed with the opposition in an ad hoc parliamentary committee known as the Commissione Bicamerale. After the latter's demise in the face of its inability to reach an agreement, the government pursued reform unilaterally, adopting a first constitutional law in 1999 and a second one in 2001, just before the end of the 1996–2001 parliament. The second law was then endorsed in a referendum in October 2001 by 64 percent of the votes cast, on a turnout of 34 percent (Amoretti 2002, 126).[14]

The first law modified the institutional setup of the regions, notably strengthening their constituent autonomy, and introducing a presidential element in their form of government, with the direct election of the president of the region.[15] The 2001 constitutional law reversed the principle governing the allocation of lawmaking competences, enumerating those reserved to the central state and leaving residual competences to the regions. By so doing, the constitutional amendment expanded the legislative remit of the regions, mainly in the form of shared competences in the fields of education, foreign affairs, labour market, and trade. By virtue of their residual competences, the regions would also be granted on paper exclusive lawmaking responsibilities over agriculture and industry, housing and urban planning, regional and local infrastructure, social services, and transport, although the exact allocation was left to a subsequent implementing law to define. Taken together these reforms strengthened considerably the competences and the autonomy of the ordinary regions and eliminated almost completely the asymmetry between them and the special status regions (Baldi 2006, 93–7). Turning Italy into a de facto federal state, as defined in chapter 1, they marked a key turning point in the process of state restructuring.

Summary

This second critical juncture in Italy's state restructuring was thus very different from the first. Whereas the implementation of the ordinary regions in the 1960s and 1970s conformed to the top-down type, the juncture analyzed here displays clear features of the bottom-up model, both in terms of party competition dynamic and of the constitutional significance of the reforms. The challenge brought to the statewide parties by the rise of the Lega Nord, a regional rival with a radical constitutional agenda, was the central factor in the process. The constitutional reforms eventually enacted moved the system close to a fully fledged federal order, a major change compared with the weak institutions created in the previous period.

The influence of the European dimension was also markedly different compared to the first critical juncture. Whereas in the 1960s the implementation of the ordinary regions was a purely domestic affair, this second round of state restructuring was significantly influenced by European integration. The European dimension had always been important to the LN's discourse on federalism and became particularly so as the party shifted toward a secessionist stance in 1995–97. The particular focus of the linkage was that the prospect of Italy being excluded from the first wave of monetary union was exploited by the LN to bolster support for the independence of the North, on the grounds that Padania would easily qualify on its own and was being held back by the rest of Italy. Although support for independence remained low among the wider electorate, the strategy appeared to resonate with the Lega's sympathizers and it is likely to have contributed to it becoming the best supported party in the North in the 1996 election. In turn, the extent of popular support for the Lega in such an important part of the country on that occasion is likely to have provided the final push for the Ulivo coalition to implement the reform of the state it had outlined in its manifesto.

6.4 DENMARK: THE CREATION OF THE REGIONS

Brief Historical Overview

Denmark emerged as a unified kingdom toward the end of the tenth century. Following the introduction of absolutism in the mid-seventeenth century (Jespersen 2011, 46–51), territorial administration was reformed in 1662 when the medieval fiefdoms were replaced by forty-nine *amter*, or counties, headed by an *amtmand*, or prefect. The number of counties fell steadily over the following century, until a major reform in 1793, intended to make them more uniform in size, set their number at eighteen. In the course of the nineteenth century, indirectly elected county councils were set up, which were responsible for the administration of the county together with the prefect. The prefect acted as the president of the county council as well as the chief executive of the county's administration. From 1960 onward the county councils were directly elected every four years. The responsibilities of the county tier grew considerably in the 1960s, hand in hand with the development of healthcare and other social services, which together with the maintenance of local roads, constituted the counties' main responsibilities. The counties were primarily funded through a property tax. With the growing importance of the counties in the delivery of welfare state services, a debate developed concerning their status (DCB 2014). An official report issued in 1966 recommended a reform of the system, which was then enacted in 1967 and implemented in 1970. The reform reduced the number of counties from twenty-four[16] to fourteen, transferring executive responsibility from the prefect to the county mayor elected by the council, and increasing their responsibilities as well as their revenue-raising powers (Picard 1983, 541–4; Hansen 1993, 313; Christensen 2000, 392–4).

After the 1970 reform, the bulk of service delivery was entrusted to county and municipal governments, leaving few areas of domestic policy still delivered directly by the central state administration, primarily law and order, postal and telecommunication services, and university education (Nissen 1991, 191). The aim was to replace service delivery by sectoral field agencies of the central administration with delivery by multipurpose local and county governments (Hansen 1993, 312). The most important county functions after the 1970 reform were management of hospitals and provision of related healthcare services, as well as responsibility also for district planning, some social services, secondary schools, environment, and transport (Nissen 1991, 190–1; Hansen 1993, 313–14; Mouritzen 2011, 59). They were funded primarily by a share of state taxes on income and land, whose importance increased over time, and a declining share of block grants (Nissen 1991, 191; Mouritzen 2011, 59–60).

As the demand for welfare services grew considerably in the wake of the 1970 reform, expenditure and personnel almost doubled in the counties in the 1970s and 1980s (Nissen 1991, 193; Tonboe 1991, 19–25). According to Tonboe (24), the reform led to a "decentralized *local* welfare state." In the 1980, although state taxes provided 70 percent of public financing, only 32 percent of total public expenditure at point of delivery was disbursed by the central state administration, the rest being accounted for by the municipalities (54 percent) and the counties (14 percent) (23, 28). The growth in municipal and county expenditure made tax autonomy at subcentral level controversial and led to increasing efforts by central government to control it (25–32). With reference to the counties, Nissen argued that citizens did not identify with them: "There has never been any popular demand for regionalization" (1991, 197).

Already in 1988, the then Conservative prime minister wondered whether a country of the size of Denmark needed three levels of government (Nissen 1991, 195; Mouritzen 2010, 26). As central and local governments could not be questioned, the debate focused on the intermediate level of the counties. Support for the idea of abolishing them and transferring their responsibilities to the central and local levels appeared attractive to many but little serious debate ensued (Nissen 1991, 195–6; Mouritzen 2010, 21–2). According to Nissen (1991, 197), the prospect of the completion of the single market was seen by some as an additional reason for abolishing the counties and re-establishing direct state delivery, in the name of national integration, presumably in the face of what could be perceived as the tendencies toward fragmentation unleashed by the single market. But an official commission reporting in 1998 concluded that the country's territorial structure was efficient and sustainable in the face of foreseeable future challenges (Bundgaard and Vrangbæk 2007, 498; Mouritzen 2010, 26).

The November 2001 Election

PARTIES

The Danish party system was highly fragmented on the eve of the 2001 election, being composed of two main parties, three mid-sized ones, and a number of smaller parties. A key determinant of such fragmentation was the highly proportional electoral system (Elklit 1999, 137-8). The largest party was the centre-left Socialdemokraterne (DSD), or Social Democratic Party, with sixty-three seats in the Folketing, the 179-member unicameral parliament. The centre-right liberal party, Venstre (DV), was the other main actor, having won forty-two seats in the previous election. Both parties had roughly maintained their representation in the Folketing compared to the previous parliamentary term. Det Konservative Folkeparti (DKF), or Conservative People's Party, was the third largest party with sixteen seats but had suffered a heavy defeat in 1998, losing almost half of its MPs. Three smaller parties completed the set of significant actors. The far-left Socialistik Folkeparti (SF), or Socialist People's Party, had thirteen MPs, the same number as the right-wing Dansk Folkeparti (DF), or Danish People's Party. The SF had the same number of seats in the previous parliament whereas the DF, having been founded in 1995, was at its first parliamentary experience. Its tally of thirteen seats thus represented a considerable achievement. The centre-left, social liberal Det Radikale Venstre (DRV), a traditional ally of the social democrats, had seven seats, slightly down from the previous election (Aylott 1999; Biugan 1999; Elklit 1999; Elmelund-Præetskær et al. 2010, 123-8).

POSITIONS ON STATE RESTRUCTURING

No significant public debate on state restructuring took place before the election and the issue did not feature prominently in the campaign, which was dominated by immigration and security instead (Mouritzen 2010, 26-7; Qvortrup 2002, 206-8; Andersen 2003, 188-90). The Progress Party - the predecessor of the DF, founded in 1972 - was the first to call for the abolition of the counties but its proposal did not attract much support at the time, soon after the adoption of the 1970 reform (Christiansen and Klitgaard 2008, 52). The DF then followed in its footsteps since its reorganization in 1995 (Krogh 2011, 320). In its 2001 manifesto the party reiterated its position in the following terms: "Det er meningsløst, at et lille land som Danmark har tre forvaltningsniveauer. Amtskommunerne skal derfor nedlægges"[17] (DF 2001, 27). In the counties' stead, the party advocated forms of intermunicipal cooperation and for the healthcare sector, particularly the hospital infrastructure, to be managed centrally (27, 53). By the late 1980s, the conservatives too had moved to that position, with their leader openly calling for the abolition of the counties in 1991 (Christiansen and Klitgaard 2008, 56). The rationale for this was that doing away with the counties would lower the costs of public administration and reduce the risks of overtaxation of households and businesses. In a 2000 position paper, the party called for the abolition of the counties, focusing again on the tax-raising aspect – "den amtslige struktur og skatteudskrivning er uhensigtsmæssig og overflødig. Tre skatteudskrivende led er en hæmsko for en dynamisk udvikling af den offentlige service"[18] – and arguing that their functions could be performed more effectively by the municipalities themselves, by larger regional units or by the state (DKF 2000, 11). In its 2001 manifesto, however, the party did not include a reform of the state's structure in its policy proposals (DKF 2001).

Both the DF and the conservatives had a very limited power base in the county councils, so little partisan interest in their preservation. The liberals largely shared the conservatives' agenda of making public administration more efficient and reduce taxation but had a strong position in the county councils and the smaller municipalities – more dependent on the counties than the larger ones – so had traditionally been hostile to a reform threatening their power base in local government and the unity of the party (Nissen 1991, 196; Bundgaard and Vrangbæk 2007, 498; Mouritzen 2010, 24, 38; Krogh 2011, 322). Not surprisingly, their manifesto was silent on the question of the structure of the state (DV 2001). The DSD, with an equally strong presence in municipal and county government, were also traditionally opposed to a change in the structure of the state (Nissen 1991, 196; Bundgaard and Vrangbæk 2007, 498; Mouritzen 2010, 24, 38; Krogh 2011, 322). The DSD did not devote much attention to the state structure in its manifesto but included a mention of a greater role for the counties in the management of hospital waiting lists (DSD 2001, 5). Neither the DRV nor the SF put forward a position on state reform (DRV 2001; SF 2001).

ATTITUDES TO, AND STRATEGIC USE OF,
EUROPEAN INTEGRATION

Coming shortly after the 2000 referendum on the adoption of the euro, Europe did not feature prominently in the campaign (Knudsen 2008, 157). The DF, however, devoted a great deal of attention to it in its manifesto and – in line with its traditional stance (159–60) – expressed strong criticism, seeing integration as a threat to Denmark's sovereignty and democracy as well as being contrary to what the majority of Europeans wanted (DF 2001, 14, 40). A key passage stated: "Dansk Folkeparti er modstander af Den Europæiske Union, og vi bekæmper alle forsøg på skabelsen af en europæisk forbundsstat"[19] (39). The party strongly defended the maintenance of Denmark's opt-outs won at Maastricht[20] and the country's veto in EU decision-making (25, 36, 39, 44). It equally strongly opposed the adoption of an EU constitution, arguing that, should this take place, the party would demand Denmark's immediate withdrawal from the EU. It also called for its withdrawal from the Schengen agreement (40–1, 44). More generally, it argued for a reduction in the EU's sphere of activity and budget, a curbing of the powers of the European Commission and Parliament in favour of the Council of Ministers, and a more cautious admission of new members (41–4). The conservatives devoted much less attention to the EU but displayed a positive attitude, in particular with regard to the development of a common security and defence policy, arguing that Denmark's opt-outs should be scrapped (DKF 2001, 2). Venstre, by contrast and in spite of its being among the most pro-EU parties in Denmark, did not refer to the EU in its manifesto (DV 2001). Both the liberals and the conservatives had traditionally been pro-EU (Aylott 1999, 66; Knudsen 2008, 156–8).

Although the social democrats devoted little space to Europe in their manifesto, they put forward a generally positive approach to the EU and its enlargement to the east but a negative assessment of its agricultural policy, vowing to fight for its reform (DSD 2001, 4, 16–17, 23). The social democrats had been broadly in favour of integration but also suffered divisions on the issue, and tensions between the party's position and opinions among its core electorate (Aylott 1999, 75–6; Biugan 1999, 172; Knudsen 2008, 156). The DRV expressed a pro-EU outlook, calling for Denmark to be a full member of the EU without reservations, i.e., by scrapping its opt-outs (DRV 2001, 1). Like the DSD, the DRV had also been divided on Europe in the past but moved in a more positive direction over time (Knudsen 2008, 158–63). The SF, traditionally opposed to the EU but also in the process of moderating its stance (158–9), failed to express a position on the EU altogether (SF 2001). None of the parties linked Europe and state reform.

ELECTION OUTCOME

The election was a major success for Venstre, which increased its representation in the Folketing to fifty-six seats, up fourteen on the previous election, on a 31 percent share of the vote. It was the first time since 1920 that the liberals had the largest number of MPs. The People's Party was the other main winner of the election, increasing its tally of MPs by nine to a total of twenty-two, on 12 percent electoral support, while the social liberals also did well, gaining two additional seats to a total of nine. The social democrats, by contrast, were the main losers, seeing their support drop by almost nine percentage points and surrendering eleven seats. The conservatives and the socialists, with sixteen and twelve seats respectively, roughly maintained their representation. After eight years of rule by the social democrats and the social liberals,[21] the election thus marked a sharp swing to the right, so much so that the right–of-centre parties – DV, the DKF, and the DF – together commanded a majority in parliament for the first time since the introduction of universal suffrage in 1918 (Qvortrup 2002; Andersen 2003). Following the election, the liberals and the conservatives swiftly formed a coalition government led by Venstre's Anders Fogh Rasmussen, with external support from the People's Party. State reform did not feature in the coalition agreement between the two governing parties (Mouritzen 2010, 26–7).

The Breakthrough of the Reform

With the conservatives and the People's Party already won over to the case for reform, the liberals were the pivotal actor. The conservatives tried to persuade them early in the life of the new parliament to address the issue but did not get very far, the government confining itself to tightening its supervision of the counties and the municipalities (Bundgaard and Vrangbæk 2007, 498). In June 2002, however, Dansk Industri, the peak business organization, called for the counties to be abolished, and received support from *Berlingske Tidende*, the country's leading conservative newspaper, as well as a respected think tank (Bundgaard and Vrangbæk 2007, 498; Christiansen and Klitgaard 2008, 60–77). Initially, the government, and Venstre in particular, rejected the suggestion, with Minister of Interior and Health Lars Løkke Rasmussen stating in parliament later that month that "regeringen har ingen planer om at foretage ændriger i den kommunale struktur"[22] (quoted in Christiansen and Klitgaard 2008, 13).

Over the following six weeks, however, the media debate intensified, with *Berlingske Tidende* publishing the results of an opinion survey showing that the abolition of the counties was favoured by a majority of the population, and supportive interventions by some liberal leaders presenting a structural reform as a solution to the problem of high taxation (Bundgaard and Vrangbæk 2007, 499; Christiansen and Klitgaard 2008, 60–77). The Amtsrådsforeningen, or Association of County Councils, traditionally an important policy actor (Nissen 1991, 194; Tonboe 1991, 25; Mouritzen 2010, 24–5), was divided on the issue and did not mobilize against the reform (Bundgaard and Vrangbæk 2007, 499–500). Although most of the liberal leadership, including Prime Minister Fogh Rasmussen,[23] tried to close the debate when the parliament returned from its summer recess, it had acquired such momentum that it was difficult to stop.

The other parties jumped in, with the conservative parliamentary group formally demanding that the counties be abolished and the opposition social democrats and social liberals proposing the creation of a commission to study the issue (Bundgaard and Vrangbæk 2007, 500). Soon after, the government reacted by announcing the appointment of a Strukturkommissionen, or Commission on the Administrative Structure, to examine possible reforms, specifically the pros and cons of moving to only two tiers of elected governments (Bundgaard and Vrangbæk 2007, 502–3; Mouritzen 2010, 27). The commission reported in January 2004, presenting a set of reform options, ranging from fewer and larger counties to the latter's abolition (Mouritzen 2010, 28).[24] In the meantime, the conservatives and the People's Party had presented their own proposals calling for the intermediate tier of directly elected governments to be eliminated altogether (Krogh 2011, 323).

In its prospectus of April 2004, the government proposed abolishing the counties and transferring most of their responsibilities to the state and to the municipalities, while five regions would be created to run hospitals. The regions would be directly elected but with no taxation powers (Regeringen 2004; Bundgaard and Vrangbæk 2007, 509; Christiansen and Klitgaard 2008, 116–45; Mouritzen 2010, 29). Within the space of less than two years, the government, and the health minister in particular, thus went from ruling out any top-down reform to championing a radical version of it (Bundgaard and Vrangbæk 2007, 509; Mouritzen 2010, 36). The main centre-left parties, the social democrats and the social liberal party, were opposed and favoured the counties retaining their competences and their tax-raising powers, but the People's Party offered its support to the government's proposal thus putting the latter in a position to secure a majority in parliament (Bundgaard and Vrangbæk 2007, 509; Mouritzen 2010, 29). The government held negotiations with the opposition parties but an agreement could not be reached so in late June it settled for a pact with the People's Party instead. The final compromise reached saw the regions being given some additional functions but no taxation powers (Bundgaard and Vrangbæk 2007, 510–15; Mouritzen 2010, 29–30; Krogh 2011, 324–6).

Throughout its 773-page report, the Strukturkommissionen only referred to the European dimension twice, to point out that international – including EU – rule-making would likely increase demands on local governments (SK 2004, 538), and that the counties were facing pressures for coordination as a result, among other factors, of EU legal harmonization (560). Europe or the EU were not mentioned once in the government document (Regeringen 2004). The only way in which the European dimension played a role was that during the key phase leading to the establishment of the Strukturkommissionen, Denmark held the rotating EU presidency and the latter's demands on the prime minister's time and attention have been seen by some as one of the factors that led him to the decision to appoint the commission (Bundgaard and Vrangbæk 2007, 502).

The February 2005 Election

POSITIONS ON STATE RESTRUCTURING
Following the agreement on state restructuring, the government decided to call an early election, ostensibly to receive a clear mandate

on the implementation of the reform ahead of the local elections. This time, therefore, the reform did feature in the campaign, although the focus was still on immigration and valence issues related to welfare services and most parties gave the reform a low profile in their programs (Pedersen 2005; Andersen 2006). Venstre mentioned the reform in the section of its manifesto devoted to healthcare, arguing that the soon-to-be established regions would provide hospital care of the highest quality thanks to their size and economies of scale (DV 2005, 6). The conservatives gave it greater prominence, including it among the principal achievements of the outgoing liberal-conservative government and devoting a whole section of the manifesto to it. The party claimed that "den største og vigtigste reform af den offentlige sektor i mange år"[25] would strengthen local democracy and improve service delivery, giving citizens greater value for money (DKF 2005, 7). The social liberals called for the regions to be given tax-raising powers and for them to engage in active economic development policies in collaboration with universities and companies. It also criticised the government's reform on the ground that it would reduce municipalities' autonomy (DRV 2005, 1–2). Somewhat surprisingly, the DF did not mention it in its manifesto, nor did the social democrats or the socialists (DF 2005; DSD 2005; SF 2005).

ATTITUDES TO, AND STRATEGIC USE OF,
EUROPEAN INTEGRATION

Despite the looming vote on the Constitutional Treaty, Europe once again did not feature prominently in the campaign (Kelstrup 2013, 26). Venstre made no references to the EU in its manifesto (DV 2005). The conservatives put forward a common line with the liberals, stating that the two parties would recommend a Yes vote in the planned referendum on the ratification of the Constitutional Treaty and, more broadly, would follow the lines of the framework agreement "Denmark in the enlarged EU" reached with the social democrats, the socialists, and the social liberals (DKF 2005, 14). The DF maintained its hostile attitude, arguing that the treaty would push the EU in the direction of a United States of Europe and calling for its rejection (DF 2005, 1). The social democrats, on the other hand, made no references to the EU (DSD 2005) while the socialists confined themselves to taking a positive approach to the regulation of chemicals proposed by the European Commission (SF 2005, 6–7).

The social liberals once again confirmed themselves as Denmark's most pro-integration party, supporting the Constitutional Treaty and Turkey's entry to the EU as well as the scrapping of the country's opt-outs (DRV 2005, 1). Again, no party made any connection between Europe and the reform of the state.

ELECTION OUTCOME

The election results were broadly positive for the government. Although Venstre suffered a small drop in support, down two percentage points and four seats compared to the previous election, both the conservatives and the People's Party made advances, gaining two seats each. The social democrats suffered another setback, losing three percentage points in electoral support and five seats compared to 2001. The far-left socialists also lost support, albeit marginally, while the social liberal party was the main winner of the election in relative terms, nearly doubling its share of the vote and its number of MPs to a total of seventeen (Pedersen 2005; Andersen 2006). As these results kept the strength of the extended governing coalition – i.e., including the DF's external support – unaltered and further weakened the main opposition party, the government was returned to office shortly afterward under the continuing leadership of Fogh Rasmussen.

The Creation of the Regions

The incoming government proceeded speedily with the implementation of the reform, enacting seventy-two new laws in 2005 and 2006 (Andersen 2010, 49). Together with an amalgamation of the municipalities, the reform abolished the 350-year-old counties and replaced them with five regions. Their borders and the location of the regional capitals were decided centrally by the government (Mouritzen 2010, 32). The regions were primarily entrusted with running public hospitals and providing related healthcare services. Additionally, they were given responsibilities in the fields of economic development, environmental protection, social services, and transport (Mouritzen 2010, 30). On the basis of this portfolio of competences, the regions were expected to be responsible for about 9 percent of public expenditure, thus a lower level than the former county tier (Andersen 2010, 51).

The law setting up the regions tightly constrains them in their organization and operation and provides for them to be financed through earmarked grants from central and local governments, thus leaving them with very little autonomy vis-à-vis the central state and the municipalities, as well as with opaque accountability vis-à-vis the citizens (Andersen 2010, 51–2; Krogh 2011, 315). Additionally, in situations where the municipalities and the regions have a common responsibility for the tasks and a disagreement between them arises, it is the municipalities that have the power to make the final decisions (Krogh 2011, 314). Although larger than the municipalities, the regions have less powers and autonomy than the former and are in a junior position vis-à-vis them (Andersen 2010, 51, 62–3). This situation has led Krogh (2011) to argue that the regions are inefficient, in the sense that they have a low capacity to adapt to future challenges and that they were so designed as a result of pressure dictated by partisan considerations on the part of the conservatives and the People's Party.

Although the reform strengthened the local level of government, its overall effect was, on balance, a centralizing one, as the main competence of the former counties – hospital healthcare – is now much more tightly controlled by central government (Andersen 2010, 53). In this respect, the Danish reform bears more than a passing resemblance to the reform carried out in Norway earlier in the decade, whereby hospital healthcare was taken away from the counties and entrusted to five regional boards under the control of the central government (Baldersheim and Fimreite 2006, esp. 768; Baldersheim and Rose 2010, esp. 93; Hagen and Kaarbøe 2006).

Summary

In the modern period, the structure of territorial administration in Denmark has been closely linked to the development of the country's welfare state. In Blom-Hansen's (2010, 52) words, subcentral tiers became "the implementing agency of the welfare state" and Mouritzen (2010, 21) points out that "no local governmental system plays a similar role in any country in the world." Because local government plays such an important role, a reform of its structure and operation bears great importance for the functioning of the political system. This was particularly the case with the structural reform analyzed here, given its scope and complexity. According to Bundgaard and Vrangbæk (2007, 491), "This so-called 'structural reform' has been described as the greatest public sector reform ever undertaken in Denmark."

Yet, such an important reform was never object of an extensive public debate or featured prominently in election campaigns. Although it appears to have had the backing of a majority of the population, it was enacted and implemented in a very elitist fashion, with little citizen involvement. It was dictated by efficiency calculations and a desire to increase the system capacity of subcentral government (Mouritzen 2010, 33–5) rather than as a response to citizens' demands. Party competition on the reform was played entirely among statewide parties and the reform, although extensive, has not changed the constitutional nature of the state. Furthermore, if the creation of regions might superficially be interpreted as an instance of decentralization, the reform actually had a centralizing net effect. The Danish reform can be thus seen as a paradigmatic example of a top-down dynamic of state restructuring, as defined in chapter 1.

In line with the theoretical expectations, the European dimension did not play a role in the dynamic of the reform. Not only did it not feature in party campaigns but it was also largely absent from the more technical reports of the government and of the Strukturkommissionen. The analysis conducted here thus confirms Mouritzen's – one of the members of the commission – assessment, according to which, "the rationale of the Danish reform is not in any way cast in terms of the needs arising from internationalization, globalization or Europeanization or similar processes" (2010, 36). Given the importance of local government to the functioning of the Danish political system and the fact that increasingly the EU has a direct impact on it (Andersen 2010, 65; Martinsen 2013, 196–9), this is particularly remarkable.

6.5 GENERAL SUMMARY

The critical junctures of state restructuring in the UK and Italy were thus very different from the Danish one: while the former two provide a clear illustration of the bottom-up model, the latter is an equally clear example of a top-down dynamic. While in all cases party competition was central to the process, in the UK and Italy the electoral and territorial integrity challenge brought to bear by regional-nationalist parties such as the Scottish National Party and the Lega Nord played a crucial role in leading the Labour Party and the Ulivo, respectively, to enact restructuring, whereas in Denmark competition was among statewide parties only. While devolution in the UK was, broadly speaking, a continuation, albeit in different circumstances, of the 1970s' process, it is noteworthy that in Italy this juncture differed markedly from the earlier one, in line with the classification introduced in chapter 1. Confirming the above characterization, the regional institutions created by the British and Italian reforms were much more powerful and constitutionally significant than those established in Denmark.

The patterns of Europeanization closely matched the theoretical expectations. Parties' strategic use of Europe in relation to state restructuring was prominent in both the UK and Italy but absent in Denmark. This is almost exclusively accounted for by the agency of the regional-nationalist parties, which adopted an independentist policy and actively exploited the European dimension around it. The radical change underwent by the SNP between the 1970s and the 1990s – from hostile neglect to the embrace of independence in Europe – provides a powerful illustration of the opportunities and incentives at play. Reflecting the further deepening of integration in this phase and the looming prospect of monetary union, access to decision-making at the EU level and, in LN's case, remaining in the hard core of members were at the heart of their discourse. In contrast, the limited positive – in the statistical sense – linkage of Europe and state restructuring by statewide parties was no more intense than the negative use made by parties such as the Conservatives in the UK and the DC in Italy, despite the fact that many of them were supportive of both.

7

"Independence in Europe" Takes Centre Stage

The most recent phase of integration paints a contrasting picture. On the one hand, integration deepened further, particularly in the eurozone, in reaction to the economic and sovereign debt crisis that broke out in 2008. On the other hand, this led to unprecedented public backlash against Europe and a deepening chasm between eurozone members and the rest of the EU, which culminated in the UK's vote to leave the EU in June 2016. Against this backdrop, new critical junctures of state restructuring took place in three countries. In Belgium, a sixth round of state reform in 2011–13 led to yet more devolution of powers to the communities and the regions. Rising support for the SNP in the UK after 2007 led to the 2014 independence referendum and further devolution of powers to Scotland, thus deepening the constitutional transformation of the UK. In Spain, the reform of the regional statutes of autonomy from 2003 triggered an ongoing secessionist challenge in Catalonia that has the potential to lead to a significant constitutional change for the country as a whole. In all three cases, state restructuring has taken a bottom-up dynamic, in which regional-nationalist parties with an independentist agenda have played a crucial role. In line with expectations, these parties strategically exploited the European dimension to a considerable degree to bolster their policies while their rivals largely failed to do so. Somewhat surprisingly, the deep crisis of integration had little visible effect on these strategies, with parties' discourse following very closely the patterns displayed in previous periods.

7.1 THE DEVELOPMENT OF INTEGRATION

This phase of European integration covers the most recent period, from the big bang enlargement of 2004[1] and the failure of the Constitutional Treaty in 2005 through the 2008–13 economic and financial crisis to the 2016 Brexit vote. This was again a difficult period for the EU, marked by two challenges in particular. The first was the struggle to reform the "constitutional" and institutional setup of the Union in the wake of the failure of the Constitutional Treaty. The second was dealing with the severe problems generated by the deep economic and financial crisis, particularly in the eurozone, and their multiple economic, political, and institutional ramifications.

Ratification of the Constitutional Treaty foundered on its rejection in referendums in France and the Netherlands. This shattered the dreams of a constitutional moment for the EU and of greater popular engagement, through the convention method. After a period of reflection, the treaty was repackaged as the Lisbon Treaty but, tellingly, the more overtly constitutional elements and the convention method of negotiation were dropped (although the text of the Lisbon Treaty was still largely that drafted by the Convention) and ratification by referendum abandoned by almost all states. In symbolical constitutional terms the Lisbon Treaty was a step back but in substantive terms it was a major step forward, as it provided for a further strengthening of the European Parliament, the extension of qualified majority voting, and an enhanced role for the European Council. After a difficult ratification process, the treaty entered into force in November 2009 (Dinan 2014, 307–16).

While the treaty was still in the process of being ratified, the financial crisis sparked by the collapse of the US so-called subprime market reached Europe and plunged the continent into a deep economic recession. The recession soon proved itself particularly serious for the European Union because it triggered a sovereign debt crisis in several peripheral members of the eurozone and threatened the very survival of monetary union and of European integration itself (328–49). Several countries had to submit themselves to an official bailout program organized by the EU and the IMF, while others, such as Spain, narrowly escaped that fate but voluntarily enacted wide-ranging austerity and deep structural reforms. The emphasis on financial stability was given legal form in the adoption, outside the EU legal framework but with a view to eventually including it in the latter, of the Fiscal Stability Treaty in 2012, laying down strict budget limits.

The promise by President of the European Central Bank (ECB) Mario Draghi in July 2012 to do "whatever it takes" (Wilson et al. 2012), later formalized in the explicit commitment by the ECB to provide unlimited financial support to any eurozone country undergoing a bailout program through Outright Monetary Transactions proved to be a turning point in the crisis. Together with the creation of the European Stability Mechanism, also in 2012, it succeeded in allaying fears of a breakup of the eurozone, thus bringing financial markets back to stability. By spring 2014, the yields on the sovereign debt of the countries most affected by the crisis were back to pre-2008 levels. If the financial crisis was past its worst by then, deep scars in the economic fabric of the eurozone remained, particularly in the form of record-high unemployment in several countries.

The deep recession and the unpopular austerity programs, perceived to having been dictated by Brussels, led to a steep plunge in public support for European integration, particularly in those countries most affected by the crisis (PRC 2014, Braun and Tausendpfund 2014). The deepening of integration within the eurozone and the belief held by many that monetary union had at best been badly designed and was at worst a historical mistake also deepened the psychological divide between the eurozone and the rest of the EU. This was particularly in evidence in the UK, in which it helped creating the conditions for Brexit (Cameron 2014). Throughout the EU, the crisis also led to an unprecedented degree of politicization of European integration, with Europe becoming – often for the first time – a salient issue in domestic elections as well as in the European Parliament election held in May 2014. The popular backlash against integration translated into a major surge in support for Eurosceptical parties, which secured their highest ever representation in the eighth European Parliament (Hennig et al. 2014). The 2014 EP elections took place against the backdrop of the most serious confrontation between the West and Russia since the end of the Cold War, over the annexation of Crimea and the wider Ukraine crisis (Sakwa 2014). The UK's vote to leave the EU marked a watershed in the history of integration and ushered in a period of deep uncertainty for the Union and for Europe as a whole.

7.2 BELGIUM: THE SIXTH REFORM OF THE STATE

With the election of the regional parliaments in 1995, Belgium's transformation into a federal state achieved its completion. As soon as the new bodies were elected, they generated fresh impetus toward a further reform of the state, with the Flemish parliament playing a prominent role. Shortly after its first direct election and at the instigation of the executive headed by Luc Van den Brande, the Flemish parliament set up a commission on institutional reform (Pagano 2000, 14). Around the same time, a group of scholars started to draft a constitution for Flanders (Brassinne 1997). The report of the commission was endorsed in March 1999, when the parliament approved five resolutions by a large majority (Pagano 2000, 7; De Winter and Baudewyns 2009, 296; Mabille 2011, 390). The resolutions called for a set of ambitious reforms. First, and most controversially, for a shift to a two-unit federal structure centred on Flanders and Wallonia, thus implying the demotion of the Brussels region and of the German-speaking community. Second, for the two main federated units – i.e., Flanders and Wallonia – to have constitutive autonomy, residual competences, and financial autonomy. Third, for a further wide-ranging devolution of powers to those units in the fields of agriculture, communications, development aid, healthcare, labour market, scientific research, international trade, and transport (Pagano 2000, 10; De Winter and Baudewyns 2009, 296; Mabille 2011, 390). The European dimension was not extraneous to this drive. In a note to parliament from the Flemish government, Van den Brande argued that European integration was reducing the importance of the Belgian economic and monetary union and thus opened the way to more autonomy for Flanders, notably in fiscal matters (Pagano 2000, 14). Although the Francophone parties rejected the Flemish resolutions, the renewed pressure for state reform was not to go away.

In the course of the 1999–2003 parliament, the conjunction of the Flemish demands and of the financing needs of the Francophone community pushed the two sides, under the leadership of the liberal-socialist government of Prime Minister Guy Verhofstadt, toward negotiating a new reform package. Following a series of political agreements, two special laws were enacted in July 2001, through which competences over agriculture, international trade, and local government were devolved to the regions and the latter's fiscal autonomy was marginally increased. The laws also renewed the financing arrangements for the communities and laid the basis for the devolution of some elements of aid development and election regulations (Nassaux 2002; Mabille 2011, 395–7). Known as the fifth reform of the state, this package went some way toward satisfying Flanders's demands, as expressed in the 1999 resolutions, but was seen as falling well short of fully meeting them. It proved controversial among the Flemish parties, with the CVP and the VB voting against, and the VU divided (Mabille 2011, 397).

The limited extent of the 2001 reform led to a radicalization of Flemish nationalism, within which the independence option gradually gained mainstream support (De Winter 2006, 93). Symptomatic of this trend was the manifesto published by the think tank In de Warande in November 2005, titled *Manifest voor een zelfstandig Vlaanderen in Europa*, or Manifesto for an Independent Flanders within Europe (IdW 2006; see also Pagano et al. 2006). The manifesto argued that the existing federal architecture of the Belgian state was no longer fit for purpose, for three main reasons: the growing economic, political and social differences between Flanders and Wallonia, the persistently high level of fiscal transfers from the former to the latter, and the unsatisfactory status of Brussels. In its stead, the manifesto called for Flanders and Wallonia to become independent member states of the European Union. As the title of the manifesto indicates, the European dimension was at the heart of the think tank's reflections and proposals: "the wide competences the EU has already acquired and will take over still, only stimulate and facilitate the transformation of both Flanders and Wallonia into independent states, both members of the European Union as successors to Belgium" (IdW 2006, 195). The need for Flanders and Wallonia to access EU decision-making was particularly emphasized: "It is of great and ever increasing importance that Flanders and Wallonia should be involved more in the decision-making process of the EU ... It is necessary for Flanders and Wallonia to be able to let their voices fully be heard in the European debate" (195–6), on the grounds that only states are full actors in EU decision-making and a Europe of the Regions would remain at best a distant prospect.

The fallout from the 2001 reform and the new political climate in Flanders had a significant effect on the party system in the north of the country. The divisions over the reform proved to be fatal to the already weakened Volksunie, which split into two in September

2001, the right-wing of the party giving birth to the Nieuw-Vlaamse Alliantie (N-VA), or New Flemish Alliance (Govaert 2002; Mabille 2011, 401). Although initially in a weak position, the N-VA, as we will see below, would become by the end of the decade the dominant party in Flanders. Following its breakthrough in the 1991 election, the Vlaams Blok continued to grow relentlessly until it became the largest Flemish party in the 2004 regional election, when it received close to a quarter of the votes and secured 32 out of 124 seats (Tréfois and Faniel 2007a, 17). In November of that year, in the wake of a ruling by the Court of Cassation confirming that the party had broken the law on racist and xenophobic actions, the Vlaams Blok decided to dissolve itself and reconstitute as Vlaams Belang, or Flemish Interest, thus maintaining the same initials (18–19).

The other two main Flemish parties, also underwent significant, if less dramatic, changes. In 2001 the CVP changed its name to Christen-Democratisch en Vlaams (CD&V), or Christian Democratic and Flemish, thus emphasizing its Flemishness. The liberal party, which had changed from PVV to VLD in the early 1990s, further changed its name to Open VLD (O-VLD) in 2007 following a merger with a smaller party (2, 32). The socialist party too underwent a significant transformation in the 2000s, including the adoption of a new name – Socialistische Partij-Anders (SP.A), or Socialist Party-Different – and the setting up of an electoral cartel with Spirit – the former social-liberal wing of the Volksunie – for the 2003 and 2007 elections (33–42).

The June 2007 Federal Election

PARTIES

On the eve of the June 2007 federal election, the Flemish party system had the following shape. The electoral cartel between the CD&V and the N-VA, set up in 2004, was the largest political force, having won 26 percent of the vote in the 2004 regional election. With 24 percent support, the VB was a close second, and the largest single party, followed by the liberals and the socialists, which both polled around 20 percent in the election. The CD&V/N-VA cartel, the VB and the SP.A had all strengthened their position compared with the previous election while the VLD had lost support.

Significant change also took place among the Francophone parties. In 2002 the liberal party joined in a federation with the FDF and two smaller parties to give birth to the Mouvement réformateur (MR), or Reformist Movement (Tréfois and Faniel 2007b, 6–7). In the same year, the PSC also changed its name to Centre démocrate humaniste (CDH), or Democratic Humanist Centre, thus renouncing its Christian democratic heritage and pursuing a deliberately centrist strategy (28–9). The balance of forces among the Francophone parties, by contrast, remained broadly stable. The socialists continued to be the dominant party, having obtained 37 percent of the vote in Wallonia and 29 percent in Brussels in the 2004 regional elections. The MR retained the second place traditionally held by the liberals, with 24 percent in Wallonia and 28 percent in Brussels in 2004. The CDH was the smallest of the three main parties, with 18 percent in Wallonia and 12 percent in Brussels in the regional election. The green party Ecolo polled less than 10 percent in both regions but has been included in the analysis because it made a major advance in the 2007 election (10, 18, 32, 37, 41).

POSITIONS ON STATE RESTRUCTURING

Since its 2001 rebranding and its subsequent electoral alliance with the N-VA, the CD&V emphasized its Flemishist character and radicalized its constitutional position. Under the heading *Meer Vlaanderen*, or more Flanders, the manifesto stated that the party wanted to develop the Flemish "state" further and had committed itself to working with its N-VA partner toward a further reform of the federation in a confederal direction: "Ten gronde wil CD&V een duidelijke, doorzichtige staatsinrichting waarbij het zwaartepunt, zowel qua bevoegheden als qua middelen, bij de deelstaten kmot te liggen ... Dus kiest CD&V ondubbelzinnig voor een verdere confederale evolutie waarin de bevoegheden van de federale overheid afgelijnd worden en alle andere bevoegheden de deelstaten toekomen"[2] (CD&V 2007a, 59; also 2007b, 14). Based on the 1999 resolutions of the Flemish parliament, the CD&V called for competences in the fields of healthcare, family support, employment, transport, telecommunications, and scientific research to be devolved to the regions as well as greater control over personal and business taxation. The guiding principle was "dat Vlaanderen een eigen sociaaleconomisch, fiscaal en financieel beleid kan voeren, op maat van de Vlamingen"[3] (2007a, 59; also 2007b, 15). The party committed itself to maintaining solidarity with the French-speaking part of the country but demanded a strict application of the language laws, notably in the Brussels suburbs, and the splitting of the Brussels-Halle-Vilvoorde (BHV) electoral and judicial district (2007a, 59; 2007b, 15).[4]

In line with the manifesto it adopted at its birth in 2001 (N-VA 2001), the N-VA went farther than its partner and openly called for independence "Het uiteindelijke doel van de N-VA is Vlaanderen als onafhankelijke staat in een democratisch Europa"[5] (N-VA 2007, 6). In the short term, it argued that, in order to clear the numerous blockages in the system, a further reform of the state was necessary. It committed itself not to join a governing coalition unless such a reform was included in the program. In alliance with the CD&V the party wanted to shift Belgium toward a confederal constitutional architecture, through the implementation of the 1999 resolutions of the Flemish parliament, the splitting of the BHV district, and a clearer division of competences between the centre and the regions (7–8).

The VB maintained its traditional unambiguous call for Flanders to secede from Belgium and become an independent republic: "Het Vlaams Belang is de enige partij die resoluut en consequent opkomt voor Vlaamse onafhankelijkheid"[6] (VB 2007, 3). Independence was presented as the only solution for Flanders to escape the political and economic straitjacket of the Belgian state and enjoy the sovereignty to which it was entitled to as a nation. An independent Flemish state would have Brussels as its capital, with some linguistic and cultural facilities for the Francophone population. In the meantime, linguistic facilities for the Francophones living in the Brussels suburbs should be phased out and the BHV electoral district split (4).

Since its transformation into the VLD in 1992 the Flemish liberal party had been stressing its Flemishist character; this was further reinforced in the early 2000s, when it was joined by four former VU members (Breuning and Ishiyama 1998, 12; Tréfois and Faniel 2007a, 24–32, 43–5). At its congress in 2002, the party called for a wide range of policy areas to be regionalized and, for the first time, advocated a confederal evolution for Belgium (Tréfois and Faniel 2007a, 25). In its manifesto for the 2007 federal election, however, the O-VLD put forward a more moderate stance. It supported a further reform of the state but one that, while giving more autonomy to Flanders, would also preserve a strong federal government and foster greater cooperation between the two. It explicitly stated: "Open Vld verzet zich gegen separatisme"[7] (O-VLD 2007, 16). In a work program adopted earlier that year, the party accepted keeping solidarity transfers between the regions and between individuals provided these were based on objective and transparent parameters. On the other hand, and in line with the other parties, it argued that the linguistic situation in the Brussels periphery was increasingly difficult and it called for the language facilities to be phased out and the BHV district to be split (Govaert 2007, 15).

The manifesto of the SP.A and its electoral agreement with Spirit focused on economic and social issues and devoted little attention to the constitutional question. It opposed independence for Flanders and expressed support for the transfer to the regions of some competences in the field of employment and transport but did not put forward a comprehensive blueprint for a further reform of the state or take a position on the division of the BHV district (SP.A 2007a, 2007b; SP.A-Spirit 2007; Govaert 2007, 15). With the exception of the socialists, there was thus a broad consensus in Flanders about the desirability of a further reform of the state, which would give greater autonomy to the communities/regions and shift Belgium in a confederal direction.

Positions were very different among the Francophone parties. Unlike in previous critical junctures, none of them advocated further devolution of power to the regions and the communities, and their campaigning was focused on a defence of the status quo, particularly with regard to social welfare transfers and the rights of the Francophons living in the Flemish periphery of Brussels (see also De Winter and Baudewyns 2009, 294). The PS wanted social welfare to remain a federal competence, warning that removing solidarity between the regions would destroy the federal state (PS 2007, 74, 150). In the name of improving the overall functioning of the state, it called for a strengthening of the role of the federal government in the provision of some social services and a reform of the Senate into a genuine representative of the communities and the regions (PS 2007, 151–2; Coosemans 2007, 7). Not only did the party defend Brussels's existence as a fully fledged region but it argued in favour of its enlargement to include the *communes à facilités* as well as in favour of retaining the BHV district (PS 2007, 152–5; Coosemans 2007, 7). The MR was even less supportive of further state restructuring, instead focusing its manifesto on the need to reform the institutional architecture of the Francophone part of the country, chiefly by merging the institutions of the Walloon region and of the French community, to improve the quality of government and reduce waste

(MR 2007, B2; Coosemans 2007, 8). It was also opposed to the splitting of the BHV district (Govaert 2007, 16).

In a similar vein to the PS, the CDH defended the federal status quo against the confederalist or secessionist temptations of the Flemish parties, arguing in favour of a *fédéralisme de coopération*. From that perspective, the party called for a strengthening of the federal institutions, notably through a reform of the Senate, and the retention of unified systems of social welfare and employment relations. The BHV district could only be split if the boundaries of the Brussels region were enlarged (CDH 2007, 203–8; Coosemans 2007, 8–9). Ecolo argued that the federal system had reached an equilibrium point and a new reform should be focused on improving its functioning rather than shifting additional powers to the communities/regions. The party rejected any attempts to further weaken the federal government and reduce fiscal transfers between the regions (ECO 2007a, 1–2). Its proposals for reform included the creation of a federal electoral constituency, the transformation of the Senate into an indirectly elected chamber of the regions and the communities, and bringing the calendar for federal and regional elections into sync again. It was also in favour of closer links between Wallonia and Brussels, toward a federation between the two regions (4–8).

ATTITUDES TO, AND STRATEGIC USE OF, EUROPEAN INTEGRATION

The CD&V and the N-VA both expressed strong support for integration but adopted very different approaches with regard to the links between the EU dimension and further state reform. The CD&V manifesto reaffirmed the traditional pro-Europeanism of the party, voicing support for the Constitutional Treaty, more powers to the European Parliament, and a more credible foreign policy in partnership with NATO. It also called for a debate on the future of Europe and on its borders and expressed caution over the prospect of Turkey's membership. It did not, however, make any explicit link between the deepening of integration and further reform of the Belgian state (CD&V 2007a, 60–1; 2007b, 15).

The N-VA also expressed support for integration, albeit in a more cautious way than the CD&V. The party had voted in favour of the ratification of the Constitutional Treaty (BKV 2005, 69) and its 2007 manifesto reaffirmed this stance: "De N-VA wil als Vlaams-Europese partij dat de bepalingen in het Europees Grondwettelijk-Verdrag zoveel als mogelijk worden meegenomen in het nieuwe Verdrag"[8] (N-VA 2007, 54). As a nationalist party, however, the N-VA was aware that the process of integration had the potential to erode the sovereignty the party wanted to achieve for Flanders. Accordingly, the party defined itself as critical European and advocated the preservation of a confederal Europe, with strong emphasis on the respect of minority cultures and languages, democratic decision-making, and the application of the principle of subsidiarity (N-VA 2001, 3; 2007, 54; Jambon 2009). In contrast to the CD&V, the European dimension played a crucial role in the N-VA's policy of eventual independence for Flanders, as reflected in the party's then slogan "*Nodig in Vlaanderen. Nuttig in Europa*," or "necessary in Flanders and useful in Europe," and in the key passage of the 2007 manifesto: "De N-VA wil dat Vlaanderen uiteindelijk volwaardig als lidstaat aan de Europese tafel kan zitten"[9] (N-VA 2007, 54). More broadly, the party saw integration as progressively hollowing the Belgian state of its key functions, thus opening the way for Flanders to gain additional powers and eventually acquire independent statehood. Gaining direct access to EU decision-making was a key objective in this strategy. It also saw the EU context as providing the political and economic guarantees necessary to create majority support for independence in Flanders. The N-VA was aware, however, that unilateral secession might not lead to automatic EU membership for Flanders, and its objective was a negotiated process whereby the Belgian state would cease to exist and would be replaced by a Flemish and a Walloon successor states, each of them continuing as members of the EU (N-VA 2001, 3; Jambon 2009).

The VB was very critical of the direction of European integration, as the EU was seen to be in the process of building an undemocratic superstate. The Constitutional Treaty had to be rejected precisely on the ground that it would constitutionalize such a superstate.[10] The party was also critical of the immigration policy being pursued by the EU as well as the opening of the accession negotiations with Turkey, in the name of a European Europe. In contrast to this undemocratic superstate, the VB called for a confederal and intergovernmental union of sovereign nations that would respect the specificity and the right to self-determination of each nation (VB 2007, 5; also Adamson and Johns 2008). Despite this negative attitude, the party placed the acquisition of Flemish statehood within the context of the EU and cited the necessity of having direct access to European decision-making as one of the reasons why independence was preferable to autonomy within a federal Belgium (VB 2007, 5).

The Flemish liberals too maintained their traditional strong support for further integration. The party voted in favour of the ratification of the Constitutional Treaty and its leader, Verhofstadt, published a book in late 2005 (Verhofstadt 2005) in which he argued that a federal Europe was the only way forward after the collapse of the Constitutional Treaty. The 2007 manifesto called for a stronger Europe and advocated the total replacement of unanimity with majority voting, the establishment of a European diplomatic service and the creation of a European army. It did not, however, make any connections between European integration and further state reform in Belgium (O-VLD 2007, 83–5).

The SP.A, which had also voted in favour of ratification of the Constitutional Treaty (BKV 2005, 69), maintained its stance of critical support but did not devote much attention to the EU in its campaign. The relevant section of the party's manifesto confined itself to observing that the process of integration was in crisis due to the growing disconnection between the European leaders and the citizens. It criticized the liberalizing agenda of the European Commission and called for the EU to become more than just a free market, through the development of genuinely common social and environmental policies and a security and defence policy autonomous from NATO. It did not link the European context and the question of domestic state reform (SP.A 2007b, 19–24).

In a similar vein to the Flemish socialists, the PS also took a stance of critical support, in favour of further integration but critical of the direction that the EU had taken. It lamented the fact that a growing gulf had opened between the integration process and the people, arguing that not only had the EU failed to preserve the social protection systems of its member states but it had also contributed to their erosion to an extent. A renewed effort to build a genuine social Europe was necessary but, in the context of an increasingly heterogeneous Union, this could only be led by an avant-garde of committed states. The new treaty to be negotiated should incorporate as much as possible the provisions of the Constitutional Treaty, and a strengthening of the EP should be prominent among them. The party did not make any links, though, between integration and a reform of the Belgian state (PS 2007, 289–302).

The MR too called for a relaunch of integration around a new *Projet pour l'Europe*, based on the implementation of as many provisions as possible of the Constitutional Treaty. At the same time, the Francophone liberals also advocated a deepening of economic coordination within the eurozone, in the direction of an economic government for the bloc (MR 2007, G1). It did not link Europe and state reform. The CDH was the most pro-integration of the Francophone parties, calling for an institutional renewal of the Union and its reconnection with the people, going in the direction of a democratic and federal Europe. Like the other two parties, the CDH was in favour of implementing as much as possible the provisions of the CT but it went further than them in advocating the direct election of the president of the Commission. To close the gap between the elites and the masses, the party called for the building of a genuine European public sphere, notably through the creation of transnational parties and a strengthening of the role of the EU's Economic and Social Council. It did not link, however, integration and domestic reform (CDH 2007, 231–2). In a similar vein, Ecolo called in the short term for a new treaty in the spirit of the Constitutional Treaty but adopted through a different ratification process and in the medium term for the creation of a federal Europe possessing genuine political sovereignty. It also supported a strengthening of the social dimension and of the common foreign and security policy (ECO 2007b, 1–12). No links were made between Europe and state reform (ECO 2007a,b).

ELECTION OUTCOME

The election results painted a different picture, as it had been the case for some time, north and south of the linguistic divide. Among the Flemish parties, they marked a clear success for the alliance between the CD&V and the N-VA and an equally clear defeat for the two outgoing governing parties, the O-VLD and, especially so, the SP.A. The CD&V/N-VA cartel won close to 30 percent of the vote in Flanders and took thirty seats in the Chamber of Representatives, compared to twenty-one seats for the CD&V and one for the N-VA standing separately in the previous election. By contrast, the liberals obtained eighteen seats, down seven, and the socialists fourteen seats, down nine. The VB was broadly stable, losing one seat to a total of seventeen, although on a marginally higher share of the vote. Given that each member of the CD&V–N-VA cartel adopted a different strategy vis-à-vis the Europe-state restructuring link, exploitation of the European dimension was not meaningfully associated with electoral success on this occasion.

The Francophone socialist party also suffered a major defeat, losing seven percentage points in voter support in Wallonia and over three in Brussels, and only securing twenty seats in the lower house, down five on 2003. Although the Francophone liberals of the MR had to surrender one seat, they managed to increase their share of the vote in both Wallonia and Brussels, and became for the first time in many years, the largest party in the south of the country. The main winner among the Francophone parties was Ecolo, which managed to increase its share of the vote by nearly two-thirds and double its tally of seats to eight. The post-Christian democrat CDH increased its seats to ten, up two, on a slightly higher share of the vote (Blaise et al. 2007; Pilet and Van Haute 2008).

The victory of the CD&V/N-VA alliance, which had made further state reform a key plank of its campaign, gave greater salience to the question of state restructuring in the negotiations on government formation in the wake of the election. The united front put forward by the Francophone parties in rejecting it, though, meant that the margin for compromise was much smaller than in the previous critical junctures, thus raising the spectre of a confrontational stalemate (Pilet and Van Haute 2008, 550). Negotiations proved very difficult indeed and the country had to experience its longest-ever government-formation crisis (Van Aelst and Louwerse 2014). Short-lived governments led by Verhofstadt, Yves Leterme, and Herman Van Rompuy followed each other from autumn 2007 to spring 2010, when an early election was called. Negotiations on state reform continued throughout this period but failed to reach an agreement able to command widespread enough support (Govaert 2009; 2012b).

The June 2010 Federal Election

PARTIES

With a notable exception and a minor one, the party landscape on the eve of the 2010 election both in the north and in the south of Belgium remained the same as in 2007. The major exception was the breaking up of the alliance between the CD&V and the N-VA. Due to divergences with the Christian democrats on the conduct of the negotiations on state reform, the N-VA declined to join the Leterme

I government formed in March 2008 and decided to terminate the cartel at its congress later that year (Govaert 2009, 44–6). The party stood alone and performed strongly in the 2009 regional election, winning 13 percent of the vote and sixteen seats in the Flemish parliament (Brack and Pilet 2010, 553). The minor change was the dissolution of the cartel between the Flemish socialists and Spirit, also in 2008, and the subsequent merger of the latter with the green party in 2009 (DS 2009).

POSITION ON STATE RESTRUCTURING

In the wake of the government crisis and the tensions among parties over the reform of the state, the latter featured prominently in the campaign for the 2010 election (Blaise et al. 2010, 16–17). The Flemish parties clustered around three broad positions: the CD&V and the O-VLD put forward a confederalist position, advocating a further deepening of Flanders's autonomy, but rejected secessionism; the N-VA and the VB called for the independence of Flanders, to be achieved gradually for the former and immediately for the latter; while the SP.A defended the federal status quo. The CD&V argued that a further reform of the state was necessary to ensure the prosperity of all Belgians: "Onze finaliteit blijft het confederaal model met het zwaartepunt van de bevoegdheden bij de deelstaten. De vijf resoluties van het Vlaams Parlement blijven ons referentiekader"[11] (CD&V 2010, 3, also 43), while rejecting independence: "We willen het land grondig hervormen, niet splitsen"[12] (43). The party called in particular for the devolution of greater socioeconomic powers to the regions, notably as regards the labour market, and the splitting of the BHV district (42–3). In a similar vein, the O-VLD argued that a thorough state reform was necessary in order to tackle the challenges the country was facing. The liberals called for "Een confederaal model, waarbij het zwaartepunt van de bevoegdheden bij de deelstaten ligt"[13] (O-VLD 2010, 29) and firmly rejected secession: "Separatisme en een onafhankelijk Vlaanderen: neen, dank u"[14] (34). The party stressed the need to devolve competences over healthcare to the communities/regions and to make the latter fiscally autonomous by 2020 (29–35).

The N-VA also presented a further reform of the state as essential because, in a nutshell, "De Belgische structuren werken immers niet meer"[15] (N-VA 2010, 6) and, again, committed itself not to join a government unless such a reform figured in the latter's program. It called for a shift to a confederal structure in the short term – one in which the federated states had control over all powers and financial resources, some of which they would then delegate to the confederal level (64–70) – but did not hide its advocacy of independence as the party's long term constitutional goal. The rationale for such a policy was presented as two-fold. First, in the context of European integration and globalization, the federal state had become outdated. Second, Flanders and Wallonia had increasingly grown apart in terms of interests and public policy preferences, turning the country into "the sum of two democracies" and making agreement at the federal level virtually impossible to achieve (5–6).

The VB, as usual, opened its manifesto with a commitment to Flanders's independence, under the headline *Project Vlaamse Staat*, or The Flemish State Project (VB 2010, 3). Its discourse was uncompromising, labelling Belgium a failed state (in English) and arguing: "Het is dus zaak om België snel te beëindigen"[16] (VB 2010, 48) and "dat in plaats van veel energie te investeren in staatshervormingen en confederalisme, Vlaanderen veeleer zou investeren in het actief voorbereiden van de Vlaamse Onafhankelijkheid en van een Ordelijke Opdeling van België"[17] (7). Pending the achievement of independence, however, the party called for a return to the five resolutions of the Flemish parliament as the starting point for any negotiations after the election (3).

The SP.A was the only large Flemish party not campaigning for a major change in Flanders's constitutional status. It supported a reform of the state that would strengthen governments at all levels and improve cooperation between them. In the name of a "social state reform," it called for "meer middelen voor de federale overheid die garant staat voor een degelijke sociale bescherming en meer bevoegdheden voor de gemeenschappen en gewesten om beter te kunnen investeren in mensen, kennis en duurzame ontwikkeling"[18] (SP.A 2010, 40). The party also supported a refinancing of Brussels, a key demand of the Francophones, a negotiated division of the BHV district, and the replacement of the Senate with a joint assembly of community and regional representatives (40–1).

In stark contrast to their Flemish counterparts, but broadly in line with their 2007 positions, the Francophone parties clustered together in defending the federal state and the rights of the Francophones. The PS argued that "il est dès lors impératif de stabiliser l'Etat fédéral"[19] (PS 2010, 145), calling for the regions to be given the means to operate more autonomously and more effectively but for the federal government to retain control over key social and economic policies (146). The party also supported a strengthening of the Brussels region and of its financing as well as its enlargement if the rights of the Francophones living in the Flemish periphery of the capital could no longer be guaranteed (ibid.). The MR also accepted that the structure of the state might need to evolve but argued that a new reform could only be justified if it improved citizens' lives and the overall functioning of the state. The party advocated closer links between Wallonia and Brussels, leading to the emergence of a federation between the two regions, and rejected the division of the BHV district unless the Brussels region were enlarged (MR 2010, 128–31). From a similar perspective, the CDH called for a reform that would bring an end to the institutional conflict, based on the following guidelines: the maintenance of a strong system of social security at the federal level, the rejection of fiscal competition between the regions, respect for the principle that the transfer of competences ought to be matched by corresponding resources, and protection of the rights of Francophones (CDH 2010, 3, also 6–10). Ecolo put considerable emphasis on state reform in its program. The opening section of its manifesto pleaded for a modernization of the federal state, guided by the principles of loyal cooperation between levels of government and of interregional as well as interpersonal solidarity (ECO 2010, 3, also 5). The party supported the idea of a federal constituency[20] and of transforming the Senate into a chamber representing the communities and the regions (4–5). Like the other Francophone parties, it advocated a strengthening of the Brussels region, closer links between the latter and Wallonia, and the protection of the rights of Francophones in the Flemish periphery of Brussels and beyond (6–9).

ATTITUDES TO, AND STRATEGIC USE OF, EUROPEAN INTEGRATION

Attitudes to integration and to the EU remained broadly positive across the board but with some significant differences between the mainstream Flemish parties on the one hand and their nationalist counterparts on the other, as well as between the two sides of the linguistic border. All parties, save the VB, had voted in favour of ratification of the Lisbon Treaty in the federal Chamber of Representatives (BKV 2008, esp. 87). The mainstream Flemish parties were still strong supporters of integration but had toned down their enthusiasm for a United States of Europe. The CD&V voiced support for "een sterk Europa met efficiënte instellingen"[21] (CD&V 2010, 64), in the context of which the stability and growth pact would be strengthened and closer cooperation in the fields of justice, asylum, and migration could be put in place. The liberals emphasized the economic side of integration, arguing that "We moeten openstaan voor nauwere economische samenwerking om de economische basis van de euro te vrijwaren"[22] (O-VLD 2010, 60), while the socialists were still critical of the weakness of the social dimension of integration, stressing that "Een meer evenwichtige verdeling tussen de drie pijlers van de EU2020-strategie is nodig, met prioriteit voor directe investeringen in de sociale pijler."[23] (SP.A 2010, 37, also 38).

The two Flemish nationalist parties had both abandoned the ideal of a *Europa der volkeren* as an alternative model of integration but had different attitudes toward the EU. The N-VA self-defined as a "pro-Europese partij in het Europese integratieproject" (N-VA 2010, 9), advocating a stronger and more united Europe, with a strengthened role for the European Commission in the socioeconomic sphere. Its vision, though, was for the EU to retain a confederal nature rather than evolve into a United States of Europe (Jambon 2009). The VB's discourse was more critical, and defended an intergovernmental EU, in which member states cooperate with each other instead of transferring their sovereignty to the EU: "Het Vlaams Belang wil: geen federaal Europa, maar de EU als intergouvernementele statenbond waarvan Vlaanderen als soevereine staat volwaardig lid is"[24] (VB 2010, 44). As already mentioned, the VB was the only party that had not supported ratification of the Lisbon Treaty.

The Francophone parties, on the other hand, maintained their strong support for further integration along federalist lines. The PS, not surprisingly, stressed the need for a genuine social dimension: "Pour le PS, la création d'une Europe sociale et solidaire reste l'objectif premier"[25] (PS 2010, 156). The party called for a European investment strategy funded by a levy on financial transactions, the harmonization of corporate taxation, a strengthening of cohesion policy, as well as a more unified foreign policy (156–9). The MR devoted a substantial section of its manifesto to the EU, whose central message was that "Le MR est convaincu qu'une Europe plus intégrée est la solution aux problèmes présents et à venir"[26] (MR 2010, 161). The proposals put forward included an effective economic government for the eurozone, an increase in the EU budget, a completion of the internal market, and a genuinely common defence policy (162–73). The CDH's manifesto was much more concise but no less integrationist, calling for a "Europe fédérale forte qui rassemble les citoyens européens au-delà des frontières et des langues au sein d'une Union européenne"[27] (CDH 2010, 38). Ecolo also retained a federalist approach, advocating "une optique résolument fédéraliste de l'Union européenne"[28] (ECO 2010, 177). In a similar vein to the socialists, the greens supported a European economic government, fiscal harmonization, stricter regulation of finance, and an investment strategy supported by an increased EU budget (177–8).

In contrast to the broad consensus existing vis-à-vis European integration, parties diverged sharply as regards the connection between the latter and domestic state restructuring. The mainstream Flemish parties and all the Francophone parties made no links between the two. The VB stressed that an independent Flanders would be a member state of the European Union but did not significantly exploit the European dimension to bolster the case for independence (VB 2010, 6–7, 47–8). A passage of its manifesto even stated: "Vlaanderen mag niet aanvaarden dat de EU ooit beslist over de opportuniteit van Vlaamse Onafhankelijkheid"[29] (43). The N-VA, by contrast, played the European card to the full, making the changing context of an integrating Europe the cornerstone of its strategy and the key reason for Flanders to become, after a transitional confederal phase, an independent member state of the EU. It manifesto argued that "België biedt immers niet de schaalvoordelen die Europa ons wel kan bieden ... Wat Vlaanderen niet op zichzelf kan oplossen, kan België ook niet. De Europese integratie maakt dit proces dus mogelijk"[30] (N-VA 2010, 5) and claimed that "Vlaanderen als lidstaat van de Europese Unie biedt het beste perspectief om een doeltreffend en democratisch zelfbestuur te organiseren in een snel veranderende wereld"[31] (9, more broadly 5–10, 64–70). Access to EU decision-making was central to the party's vision: "Vlaanderen moet de bevoegdheid krijgen zichzelf te vertegenwoordigen aan de Europese tafel voor zijn eigen bevoegdheden"[32] (10).

ELECTION OUTCOME

In line with established patterns, the results of the election were vastly different north and south of the language border. The Flemish results were dominated by the triumph of the N-VA, which won nearly 28 percent of the vote and twenty-seven seats in the Chamber of Representatives. This was only slightly less than what was obtained in 2007 by the CD&V/N-VA cartel and a dramatic surge compared to 2003 – the previous election in which the N-VA stood alone – when the party scored less than five percent of the vote and gained a single seat. The CD&V and the VB paid the highest price for the N-VA's advance. The Christian democrats, with a share of 17 percent and seventeen seats, recorded their worst ever result while the far-right party lost a third of its support and had to surrender five seats. The liberals and, to a lesser extent, the socialists declined further to a total of thirteen seats each in the lower house, down five and one, respectively, on the previous election. Strategic exploitation of the European dimension was thus strongly associated with electoral success for the N-VA.

There was also a clear winner, albeit one of a very different complexion, on the Francophone side: the PS. The party recovered strongly from its defeat in the previous election, winning 38 percent of the vote in Wallonia and 27 in Brussels, and securing twenty-six seats, up six on 2007. All the other parties lost ground, most notably the liberals, who surrendered five seats to a total of eighteen, but also the CDH, down one to nine, and Ecolo, which managed to hold on to its tally of seats but saw its vote share being marginally eroded (Blaise et al. 2010; Abts et al. 2012).

In spite of their differences, the two sets of results had one element in common: the rallying of voters around the party that was perceived as embodying the respective community's interests on the crucial question of state reform. This was particularly the case in Flanders, where state reform was the most important issue for the N-VA voters, 63 percent of whom wanted further devolution of powers to the communities/regions and 17 percent the division of Belgium into two independent states (Swyngedouw and Abts 2011, 16–20). Moreover, there is evidence that the N-VA's campaign was particularly successful in attracting new voters to the party (25).

A fundamental change had thus taken place in how positions on state restructuring on the two sides of the linguistic border aligned. In the previous critical junctures there was a broad convergence between Flemings and Francophones on the desirability of state reform, with disagreements between them confined to the details of its design and execution. By 2010, though, such a convergence had disappeared, making it much more difficult to achieve positive sum reform packages. In the wake of the election, this was further compounded by the fact that the two leading players – the N-VA and the PS – were also very far from each other on the left-right spectrum. In sum, if the outcome of the election further reinforced the salience and the urgency of state restructuring, it also made it exceptionally arduous to achieve.

The Sixth Reform of the State

The highly fragmented and polarized party constellation bequeathed by the election made the government formation negotiations exceedingly difficult. Over a year after the election the country was still without a government, breaking the record set in the previous parliament. Needless to say, the fundamental stumbling block was the question of state reform. The prospect of a partition of Belgium, brought to the fore by the N-VA's success, was widely debated and hanged like a sword of Damocles over the negotiations. Only in October 2011 could an agreement be reached by eight parties – the CD&V, the O-VLD, the SP.A, and Groen! (so excluding the N-VA) on the Flemish side and the PS, the MR, the CDH, and Ecolo on the Francophone side – thus clearing the way for a new government, led by the PS's Elio Di Rupo, to take office in December 2011 (Govaert 2012a).

The agreement, known as the sixth reform of the Belgian state, was a carefully crafted compromise between the key demands of the two communities. The Flemish side obtained the division of the BHV electoral district, the devolution of family policy to the communities and of competences in the economic and employment fields to the regions, and greater fiscal autonomy for both. The Francophones obtained a strengthening of the Brussels region, receiving more resources through a reform of the finance law as well as constitutive autonomy, judicial safeguards for the Francophones living in Flanders, and the retention of social security at the federal level. The reform package also included the transformation of the Senate into an indirectly elected assembly.[33]

The reform clearly fell short of the N-VA's vision of a radical transformation, which explains the party's refusal to endorse it. Although Belgian politics, given the dualistic nature of the country, had long followed a confederal logic, the functioning of the state after this sixth round of reform kept its federal character, with the federal level of government retaining a prominent role. Nonetheless the reform still marked an important further step in the process of restructuring of the Belgian state set in motion in 1970, which has been characterized by a continual shift of power away from the centre and toward the communities and the regions. Moreover, the consolidation of the N-VA as Flanders's quasi-*Volkspartei* in the 2014 election (Swyngedouw and Abts 2011, 12) signals that a large section of the Flemish community is still unsatisfied with the current constitutional settlement, thus making further reforms in the future likely.

Summary

This latest critical juncture of state restructuring in Belgium conformed very closely to the bottom-up dynamic. In a manner reminiscent of the first juncture in the 1960s, the dramatic rise of the N-VA acted as the crucial catalyst that made reform ultimately inevitable. The fact that the N-VA put forward an independentist position gave additional sharpness and urgency to its challenge. In line with the magnitude of the challenge, the reform enacted was of considerable constitutional significance, moving Belgium one step closer to a confederal order. In line with expectations, the European dimension was at the heart of the N-VA's vision of an independent future for Flanders and the party exploited it intensely in the 2010 campaign. By contrast, the other parties – the VB included – once again largely failed to link Europe and state restructuring. The different strategies adopted by the N-VA and the VB vis-à-vis such a link is particularly instructive and confirms the important role played by attitudes in shaping rhetorical strategies. The opposite electoral trajectories of the two parties suggests that the N-VA's Europeanization strategy was the more successful one, at least on this occasion.

7.3 UK: DEEPENING DEVOLUTION AND SCOTLAND'S BID FOR INDEPENDENCE

In 1999 the former Welsh Secretary and mastermind of devolution to Wales, Ron Davies, described devolution as "a process not an event" (BBC 1999). And so indeed it has proven. Leaving aside the case of Northern Ireland, where devolution restored, on a different basis, the autonomy status in place between 1921 and 1972, three aspects of such a process are noteworthy. The first is the failed attempt to expand devolution beyond Scotland and Wales to regional bodies in England. The second is the deepening of the devolution of powers to Wales to acquire some of those already granted to Scotland. The third, and most important, is the evolution of the Scottish devolution settlement itself, fuelled by the rise of the SNP and the 2014 independence referendum, which culminated in the Scotland Act 2016. After briefly summarizing the first two developments, the remainder of this section will focus on the evolution of the Scottish devolution settlement.

After creating regional development agencies in its first term in office from 1997–2001 (NA 2014a), the Labour Party committed itself in its 2001 manifesto to establishing directly elected regional governments in those regions in which public support for them, to be ascertained by holding referendums, existed (LAB 2001, 34–5). In spring 2003 the Regional Assemblies (Preparations) Act 2003 was passed (UKP 2003), laying down the legal framework for the creation of directly elected regional assemblies, followed in July by the Draft Regional Assemblies Bill (UKG 2004), outlining the functioning and the powers of the proposed assemblies. The latter would have related to the promotion of economic and social development, mainly in the form of democratic supervision of the regional development agencies already in operation. On the belief that popular support for such assemblies was stronger in the north, the government planned to hold referendums in Northeast England, Northwest England, and Yorkshire and the Humber. In the first referendum held in the northeast in November 2004, however, 78 percent of voters rejected the proposals. Following such an overwhelming defeat, the government shelved its plans for further referendums and effectively abandoned its attempt to create regional governments in England (Sandford 2009). The regional development agencies themselves were then abolished by the Cameron government in 2010 (Sandford 2013).

Developments in Wales were initially spurred by dissatisfaction with the single corporate body structure of the National Assembly for Wales, meaning the absence of a clear separation between the assembly and the executive. In 2002 the Assembly passed a resolution calling for a separation between the two and established a commission, known as the Richard Commission, to examine the powers and the electoral arrangements for the Assembly (NAW 2014; NA 2014b). In its report released in March 2004, the commission recommended the separation called for by the Assembly as well as the granting to it of derived lawmaking powers in some areas (NA 2014b). The Labour government endorsed some of these proposals in its *Better Governance for Wales* white paper issued in June 2005 (UKG 2005) and turned them into law in the Government of Wales Act 2006. The Act created a separate Welsh Government,[34] allowed the central parliament to give lawmaking powers to the Assembly on a case-by-case basis through devolution orders, and provided for a future granting of primary lawmaking powers subject to approval in a referendum (UKP 2006).

Following the 2007 regional election, in which the Labour Party fell short of an overall majority, the coalition agreement between the latter and Plaid Cymru included a commitment to holding such a referendum within the subsequent assembly term (BBC 2007). The referendum was held on 3 March 2011 and resulted in 63 percent of voters approving the granting of primary legislative powers to the Welsh assembly in all its areas of competence (Wyn Jones and Scully 2012). Following the acquisition of these powers, the British government established in October 2011 the Commission on Devolution in Wales, better known as the Silk Commission after its chairman, to review the financing arrangements for the Welsh Assembly in the first instance and the overall devolution settlement subsequently. The commission issued a first report, on fiscal matters, in November 2012, and a second report, on the overall powers of the Assembly, in March 2014. The first report recommended the devolution of some taxes, such as stamp duty on property purchases, amounting to about a quarter of its budget and the possibility of varying income tax, subject to a referendum (CDW 2012). The second report recommended further devolution of powers to the Assembly – including over policing, energy projects, and the water industry – and a shift to a residual powers model whereby all matters not expressly reserved for the central government would fall under the competences of the Assembly (CDW 2014). The British government endorsed most of the proposals put forward and turned them into law in the Wales Act 2014 (UKP 2014).

In a nutshell, the evolution of Welsh devolution has been characterized by a drive to bring it into line with the Scottish settlement, thus removing asymmetry between the constitutional status of the two regions and widening the percentage of the UK population living under strong regional government. Looking into the future,

Welsh First Minister Carwyn Jones has called for a federal arrangement for the UK (Jones 2012) while PC supports an independent Wales in a confederal arrangement with the other nations of the British Isles (PC 2011, 3, 14–18; Wood 2014).

In Scotland, devolution suffered some teething problems in its early years – notably concerning the new parliament building – and a degree of disillusionment took hold among the population (Boon and Curtice 2003; Bromley and Curtice 2003). The SNP went through a difficult period, performing poorly in the 2001 general election and in the 2003 regional election, in which it lost eight seats compared to 1999, leading to the resignation of it leader and the return of Alex Salmond at the head of the party in 2004 (Bromley 2006, 197–9). The Labour Party, however, also declined in popularity in the course of the 2003–07 Scottish parliament, making the 2007 election a closely fought contest.

The 2007 Scottish Parliament Election, the Calman Commission, and the Scotland Act 2012

POSITIONS ON STATE RESTRUCTURING

Under the renewed Salmond leadership, the SNP focused its campaign on presenting itself as a party ready for office, to offer a credible alternative to the electorate after eight years of Labour-Liberal Democrat coalitions. It did, however, maintain its commitment to secession and promised to issue a white paper on independence as a preparation for holding a referendum within the new parliamentary term (SNP 2007, 15). Its manifesto argued: "The 300-year old Union is no longer fit for purpose ... Independence is the natural state for nations like our own ... With independence Scotland will be free to flourish and grow" (7). The Labour Party defended the devolution settlement as offering Scotland the best of both worlds – profiting from the strong UK economy while enjoying autonomy in the devolved matters – and committed itself to making the Scottish parliament more efficient in its operation and more responsive vis-à-vis the citizens (LAB-S 2007, 97–8). The Liberal Democrats called for the devolution of additional powers to the Scottish parliament – in areas such as electoral laws, energy, and transport – as well as the introduction of a system of fiscal federalism granting Scotland extensive tax-raising powers (LD-S 2007, 86). The Conservatives focused their campaign on offering an alternative program of government and did not address the question of Scotland's constitutional status (CON-S 2007).

ATTITUDES TO, AND STRATEGIC USE OF,
EUROPEAN INTEGRATION

None of the parties articulated a position on integration, nor did they link Europe and Scotland's constitutional status. The SNP only committed itself to strengthening Scotland's voice in the EU and streamlining the implementation of EU law in Scotland (SNP 2007, 16), while Labour confined itself to remarking that Scotland enjoyed strong influence in EU decision-making via the political weight of the UK government and its direct membership of the body representing regions with lawmaking powers (LAB-S 2007, 101–2). The Liberal Democrats called for Scotland do be more involved in EU policymaking (LD-S 2007, 87). The Conservatives did not include Europe in their manifesto (CON-S 2007).

ELECTION OUTCOME AND ITS AFTERMATH

The election results saw the SNP making major advances, gaining twenty seats to a total of forty-seven. The Labour Party was the main loser, down four seats to a total of forty-six. The Liberal Democrats and Conservatives were each down one seat. The SNP garnered its highest ever share of the vote – breaking the record set in October 1974 – and had for the first time the largest representation in the Scottish parliament (Curtice et al. 2009; Johns et al. 2010). This major nationalist advance was not matched, however, by a corresponding rise in support for independence, which remained broadly stable (Ashfold 2014, 1–3).

Following an attempt to create a majority coalition with the Lib Dems, the SNP went on to form a single party minority government led by Salmond as first minister, whose program included initiating a national conversation on independence (SG 2013a). The Labour Party, later supported by the other two main statewide parties, reacted by establishing a commission charged with examining possible changes to the devolution settlement enshrined in the Scotland Act 1998. The commission, known as the Calman Commission after its chairman, issued a first report in December 2008 and a final report in June 2009, which recommended the granting of wider taxation powers to the Scottish parliament (CoSC 2014). The Conservative-Liberal Democrat coalition government that took office at the

UK level in May 2010 endorsed the bulk of the commission's proposals and introduced a bill to parliament to turn them into law in November 2010, which became the Scotland Act 2012. Under the latter's terms, Scotland gained the power to vary income tax by 10 percent, control over other taxes such as stamp duty and landfill tax, some borrowing powers, and some additional lawmaking competences (UKP 2012). Although of considerable constitutional significance on its own merits, by the time it entered into force the Act had already been effectively overtaken by events in the wake of the dramatic results of the 2011 Scottish parliament election.

The 2011 Scottish Parliament Election, the 2014 Referendum, and the Scotland Act 2016

POSITIONS ON STATE RESTRUCTURING

The 2011 election marked a crucial turning point in Scottish politics. Although the SNP focused its campaign on its record in government, it also renewed its call for Scotland to achieve independence, subject to endorsement by the electorate in a referendum. The party argued that it would provide the best constitutional framework for the country to reach its ambitions while transforming its relationship with the rest of the UK into a "partnership of equals" (SNP 2011, 28). In the short term the SNP promised to put pressure on the UK government to improve the provisions of the Scotland Bill, calling for a financing model allowing Scotland to keep all revenues raised within its borders and transferring a set amount to the central treasury to cover its share of UK-wide services (ibid.). The Labour Party supported further devolution of powers as set out in its Scotland Bill, notably with regard to additional tax-raising and borrowing powers (LAB-S 2011, 17). Neither the Liberal Democrats nor the Conservatives called for any changes to the region's constitutional status (LD-S 2011; CON-S 2011).

ATTITUDES TO, AND STRATEGIC USE OF,
EUROPEAN INTEGRATION

None of the parties formulated a policy on European integration in their manifestos (SNP 2011, 29; LAB-S 2011; LD-S 2011; CON-S 2011).[35] More widely, the SNP had cooled its attitudes toward the EU and had voted against ratification of the Lisbon Treaty in the House of Commons (Hansard 2008; Massetti 2009, 521). From a

UK-wide perspective, the Labour Party had also cooled down but retained a cautiously positive stance whereas the Conservatives had become mostly critical, leaving the Liberal Democrats as the only party still broadly pro-EU (Budge et al. 2007, 166–9; Kavanagh and Cowley 2010, 45–95). Labour and the Liberal Democrats had supported ratification of the Lisbon Treaty while the Conservatives had voted against (Hansard 2008). None of the statewide parties made any connections between the European dimension and Scotland's constitutional status (CON-S 2011; LAB-S 2011; LD-S 2011). The SNP made use of it to stress the continuity it would bring in the transition to independence: "as members of the EU there will continue to be open borders, shared rights, free trade and extensive cooperation" (SNP 2011, 28).

ELECTION OUTCOME

The election was a triumph for the SNP. Against the expectations of almost all observers and the mechanics of the electoral system, which make it difficult for a party to achieve an absolute majority, the SNP won sixty-nine seats, up twenty-three on the previous election and more than double its 2003 tally. This was at the expense primarily of the Liberal Democrats, whose representation in parliament collapsed from seventeen to five seats, but also of the Labour Party, down seven seats to thirty-seven. The Conservatives also lost, down five seats to a total of fifteen (Scully 2013; Carman et al. 2014). As in the previous election, though, this major surge in electoral support for the SNP was not matched by a corresponding increase in public support for independence, which remained broadly in line with recent trends (Ashfold 2014, 1–3).

To the 2014 Referendum and the Scotland Act 2016

Nonetheless, the SNP was able for the first time to form a single-party majority government committed to secession. The party's plan to hold a referendum on independence, however, faced a legal obstacle as Scotland's constitutional status was a matter reserved for Westminster. A referendum could therefore only be held with the latter's agreement. After negotiations with the UK government, the so-called Edinburgh Agreement was reached in October 2012 and given legal form in February 2013 (UKG-SG 2012; UKP 2013). Although the SNP had originally wanted to hold a two-question referendum, under the terms of the agreement there would be only one question – on whether voters wanted independence or not – approved by the Electoral Commission. In November 2013 it was announced that the referendum would be held on 18 September 2014 on the question "Should Scotland be an independent country?" UK, EU, and Commonwealth citizens resident in Scotland would constitute the electorate.

Shortly afterward the Scottish government published its independence prospectus *Scotland's Future – Your Guide to an Independent Scotland* (SG 2013a,b). The government presented independence as giving Scotland the ability to fully control the decisions affecting its future, particularly so in the fields of economic and social policy and revenues from natural resources (2013b, 2). According to the document's preface, attributed to the first minister, independence would also bring direct access to EU decision-making: "we will be able to represent Scotland at the top tables of Europe as a constructive member state and stand up for vital Scottish interests" (2013b, 6). Two umbrella organizations were set up to fight the campaign, bringing together the main parties and grassroots organizations: Yes Scotland, led by the SNP and the Green Party, supporting a Yes vote, and Better Together, including the three main statewide parties, calling for a No vote. The most debated issues in the campaign were the economic aspects, especially the currency union regime proposed, the future of welfare services such as the NHS, the question of the removal of nuclear weapons from their current Scottish base, and Scotland's ability to remain within the EU (Dardanelli and Mitchell 2014, 92–100).

On the latter question, the Scottish government proposed to negotiate an amendment to the EU treaties, on the basis of art. 48 of the Treaty on European Union (TEU), within the eighteen-month period it identified as the transition phase to independence, should Scots vote Yes in the 18 September referendum (SG 2013a, 220–2). However, it was not clear whether all matters could be successfully negotiated within that time scale – particularly when it comes to the opt-outs the UK was granted in very different circumstances – given the need to secure the agreement of the other member states.

The use of article 48 as the legal basis of the process was itself far from uncontroversial. Some observers argued that Scotland would have had to apply for membership under article 49 TEU, which governs the entry of new members, implying that it would have found itself, however temporarily, outside the EU upon independence. The legal analysis conducted by the UK government saw article 49 as the only viable option (UKG 2014, 62–3). The former presidents of the European Council, Herman Van Rompuy, and of the European Commission, José Manuel Barroso, also made public statements to the same effect (UKG 2014, 62; BBC 2014a). In the final stages of the campaign, Mr Cameron argued that an independent Scotland would find itself outside the EU and would have to join a queue to re-enter (Dickie 2014). Spain, widely suspected of being the most hostile to EU membership for an independent Scotland, promised "not to interfere" in the process but signalled it would expect it to follow article 49 (Buck and Dickie 2014; Garea 2014).

Effectively expelling Scotland upon independence, however, would have been hugely problematic and most analysts concluded that a negotiated solution enabling Scotland to remain within the EU was the most likely scenario (Edward 2013; Connolly 2013; Gounin 2013; Tierney 2013; Douglas-Scott 2014; ScP 2014). Moreover, the Conservative Party's promise to hold a UK-wide referendum on EU membership by 2017 offered an additional rhetorical weapon to the SNP, to the effect that independence would be the only way of securing Scotland's continuing membership of the EU (BBC 2014b). Opinion survey evidence indicates that voters believed the SNP strategy was viable: asked whether an independent Scotland would be allowed to be part of the EU, 63 percent thought it would definitely, or probably, be allowed to do so. The percentage of those so thinking increased to 86 percent among those intending to vote Yes in the referendum and was higher than 50 percent across those who voted SNP, Labour, and Liberal Democrats in the 2011 election (ICM 2014).

As mentioned above, the major surge in support for the SNP between 2007 and 2011 was not matched by a corresponding increase in support for independence and this was still by and large true at the start of the referendum campaign. Initial poll findings on the question to be asked in the referendum gave only around 30 percent Yes against 50 percent No and 20 percent undecided (WST 2014). Support for Yes, though, grew considerably in the course of the campaign reaching a majority in one poll two weeks before the referendum date (BBC 2014c). Although a pro-independence business organization was formed, the vast majority of businesses, the larger ones in particular, opposed it, often outspokenly so (Rigby et al. 2014). According to the CBI, 90 percent of the business community was against (Gordon and Jenkins 2014). Uncertainty over the currency regime and the size of monetary reserves an independent Scotland would need loomed especially large in their opposition (Fleming 2014).

Although, as seen above, the UK government refused to approve a two-question referendum in the wake of the 2011 Scottish election, all three main statewide parties offered the devolution of more powers to Scotland, chiefly in the fiscal and welfare areas, if voters rejected independence (BBC 2014d). Prior to the referendum campaign, opinion polls had indicated that the so-called "devo max" option would have been voters' first choice in a three-way contest with independence and the status quo (Riddoch 2012). In the event Scots rejected independence in the referendum by 55 percent to 45 percent on a record high turnout of 85 percent (BBC 2014e). In the wake of the referendum, the UK government appointed a cross-party commission to give shape to the pledge of more powers for Scotland (Parker et al., 2014). The Smith Commission, after its chairperson, reported in November 2014 recommending the devolution to Scotland of increased fiscal powers – including full control over income tax – and wider competences in the economic and social policy fields (SC 2014). These recommendations were by and large implemented in the Scotland Act 2016, which also made Scotland's devolved institutions permanent (UKP 2016).

Summary

Like the previous ones, this latest juncture of the process of state restructuring in the UK conformed closely to the bottom-up model. The challenge brought about by growing support for the SNP and culminating in the independence referendum of September 2014 triggered a quasi-unanimous promise by the statewide parties to devolve further lawmaking and fiscal powers, leading to the Scotland Act 2016. Even more clearly than in the previous critical junctures, the SNP's secession threat was the key factor in the process. As well as being deepened, the constitutional transformation of the UK state was also widened – in terms of the percentage of the population living under strong regional government – by the increase in the powers of the Welsh Assembly, a process in which Plaid Cymru played a significant role. The Welsh regional-nationalist party was instrumental in securing the Labour Party's commitment to further devolution when the latter become dependent on the former after failing to secure a majority in the 2003 election.

In stark contrast, the top-down attempt to create weak regional governments in the English regions failed after the negative result of the 2004 referendum in Northeast England. While the European dimension did not feature prominently in the Scottish elections of 2007 and 2011, it returned to centre stage in the runup to the referendum. Continued membership of the EU for an independent Scotland was a crucial element in the SNP's case for secession and became one of the foci of debate in the campaign. Plans for a UK-wide referendum on EU membership lent additional weight to the SNP argument. While the unionist parties also exploited the European dimension to counter the appeal of secession, they did so less intensively and, public opinion data suggest, less successfully than the Yes campaign.

7.4 SPAIN: THE REFORM OF THE REGIONAL STATUTES OF AUTONOMY AND THE CATALAN CHALLENGE

Brief Historical Overview

The formation of the Spanish state is often traced back to 1469, when the crowns of Castile and Aragon were united. This is, however, misleading as no unified polity emerged from the dynastic union, each of the realms retaining its own institutions. It was a situation akin to that of the 1603–1707 union of the crowns of England and Scotland, which Koenigsberger (1975, 12) and Elliott (1992) have termed "composite monarchies." By the time Charles I abdicated in the mid-sixteenth century, Spain was still a geographical expression, with a clear separation between the lands of the Crown of Aragon, on the one hand, and those of the Crown of Castile on the other (Elliott 1963b, 65–74; Linz 1973, 38–40, 97; Lynch 1981, 209). The Crown of Aragon itself was a confederal union of the Kingdom of Aragon, the Principality of Catalonia, the Kingdom of Valencia, and the Kingdom of Majorca, each with its own parliament and government endowed with extensive powers (Bisson 1986/2000; Davies 2011, 151–227). Although the Crown of Castile was more centralized, it also included territories, such as the northeastern Basque provinces, enjoying particular rights and freedoms, known as *fueros*, notably as regarded taxation (Irigoin and Grafe 2008, 177). The kingdoms incorporated by Castile in the course of its medieval expansion also retained a formal existence, although without institutions of their own. It was only in the first half of the seventeenth century, under the rule of King Philip IV and Prime Minister Olivares, that the monarchy attempted to bring its various possessions into a more unified polity. This led to discontent in the lands of the Crown of Aragon, including a large-scale revolt in Catalonia that degenerated into a war pitching Castilian troops against Franco-Catalan forces at the end of which the Catalan territory north of the Pyrenees had to be surrendered to France (Elliott 1963a; Linz 1973, 42–8).

The extinction of the Spanish line of the House of Habsburg in 1700 led to the War of the Spanish Succession, in which the Kingdom of Castile was loyal to the Bourbon King Philip V while the realms of the Crown of Aragon supported the Austrian Habsburg Archduke Charles. The war ended with the capitulation of Barcelona on 11 September 1714. The victorious Philip V then proceeded to reorganize his possessions into a more centralized, genuine Kingdom of Spain. With the Nueva Planta decrees of 1716 the Crown of Aragon was extinguished, the self-government institutions of its realms abolished,[36] and the official use of the Catalan language banned, although the Basque provinces and Navarre, which had supported Philip V in the war, were allowed to keep their *fueros* (Payne 1973, 351–7; Díez Medrano 1995, 34–5). In the course of the eighteenth century a two-tier system of territorial administration emerged, with the introduction of *intendencias* and the acquisition of a more political role by the *capitanías generales*, which had their origin as military districts. The former, numbering thirty-two at the end of the century, can be seen as precursors of the provinces created in the nineteenth century, while the latter, fourteen in total, prefigured the modern regions (García-Gallo de Diego 1979; Esdaile 2002/2003, 40). When Napoleonic France invaded Spain in 1808, provincial *juntas* were formed to organize resistance, which later came together to create a supreme central *junta* in an embryonic federation (Carr 1982, 80, 89–92). Going against that, the Napoleonic puppet state headed by Joseph I planned to introduce a system of uniform prefectures modelled on the French *départements*, but the reform was not implemented, while Catalonia was annexed by France and divided into four *départements* (Sahlins 1989, 202). Resistance against the invader stoked Spanish patriotism and sowed the seeds for the emergence of Spanish nationalism in the course of the century.

The nineteenth century witnessed a continual struggle between liberals and conservatives, each of them further divided into moderate and radicals, in which the centralization/autonomy question featured prominently. Liberals wanted to build a modern national state with a uniform structure of territorial administration while conservatives defended the traditional liberties and privileges (Linz 1973, 54; Esteban 1981, 11–16; Cuchillo 1993, 211). Following attempts in 1812 and 1822, a territorial reform in 1833 created forty-nine provinces, which are by and large the ones still in existence today. Each province was governed by a *diputación* or provincial assembly and government. The Basque provinces and Navarre were given the status of province but retained their traditional *fueros*. In the course of the century, economic development became more uneven across regions, with Catalonia and the Basque provinces – Biscay in particular[37] – enjoying rapid industrialization while the rest of the country remained largely rural and mired in widespread poverty. A cultural renaissance and revival of the vernacular language in Catalonia, spurred by Romanticism, rekindled a regional consciousness and lay the ground for the later emergence of political *Catalanisme*. The modernizing and centralizing drive, coupled with the disruption brought about by economic change, triggered a reaction known as Carlism,[38] which provoked two civil wars, the Carlist Wars. Carlism was particularly strong in the Basque provinces, caused, among other factors, by a strong defence of the provinces' traditional *fueros* (Díez Medrano 1995, 56–78).[39] When the second Carlist war ended in defeat for the Carlist forces in 1876, the *fueros* were abolished, although two years later a fiscal arrangement known as *concierto*, restoring some of the old privileges, was agreed (70). In the 1890s Basque nationalist ideas started to be formulated by Sabino Arana, who in 1895 founded the Partido Nacionalista Vasco/ Euzko Alderdi Jeltzalea (PNV/EAJ), or Basque Nationalist Party.

Over the same period, federal and republican ideas started to get considerable support in Catalonia, notably in the first general election held under universal male suffrage in January 1869. The federal republic established in 1873 under the leadership of the Catalan Francesc Pi i Margall, however, was plagued by instability and short-lived, collapsing within less than two years (Hennessy 1962; Linz 1973, 64). Catalanism started to acquire a more political character in the 1880s. Centre Catalá was set up in 1882, a memorandum of grievances, *Memorial de Greuges*, was addressed to the king in 1885, and a project for a regional statute of autonomy, known as the *Bases de Manresa*, drafted in 1892. Catalanism had two different strands, one progressive and republican and the other conservative and monarchical (Balcells [1991] 1996, 35–54; Conversi 1997, 17–30; Caminal 1998, 27). In the last two decades of the nineteenth century both strands oscillated between a tendency to assume a leading role in Spain (Rossinyol 1974, 311–26; Ucelay da Cal 2003) and the desire for autonomy for Catalonia. Spain's defeat in the 1898 war with the USA, resulting in the loss of its last remaining colonies, was widely perceived, notably in Catalonia, as the nadir of the country's decline from its former great power status. The crisis of the Spanish state and the concomitant emergence of regional nationalism in Catalonia as well as in the Basque provinces gave birth to an enduring controversy over whether Spain was a mononational or a multinational state (Linz 1973, 33–8).[40]

In 1901 a Catalan regionalist party, the conservative Lliga Regionalista, won the election in Barcelona and established itself as the dominant political voice of Catalanism. In 1914 the Lliga obtained the creation of the Mancomunitat, a federation of the four Catalan provinces, which, although its powers did not exceed those of the *diputaciones*, was the first recognition of Catalonia's identity as a regional entity since 1714 (Rossinyol 1974, 336–45; Balcells [1991] 1996, 67–82). In 1919, the Mancomunitat put forward a draft statute of autonomy but, following the Primo de Rivera coup d'état in 1923, the Mancomunitat itself was disbanded two years later (Balcells 2010). The repression of Catalonia's aspirations under the Primo de Rivera dictatorship radicalized many on the progressive wing of Catalan nationalism and pushed them toward an independentist position. The most prominent organization among them was Estat Catalá, founded by Francesc Maciá in 1922, which merged with other left-wing parties to form Esquerra Republicana de Catalunya (ERC), or Catalan Republican Left, in March 1931. At the fall of the monarchy in April 1931, Maciá, the leader of ERC, which had triumphed in the local election in Catalonia, declared a Catalan republic within an Iberian federation (Maciá [1931] 2006).[41] Following negotiations with republican leaders in Madrid, however, Maciá renounced independence and agreed to an autonomy status for Catalonia within a republican Spain (Rossinyol 1974, 360–2). A statute of autonomy was approved by a large majority in a regional referendum in August 1931 and entered into force the following year (Caminal 1998, 40). Although constrained by the constitution adopted in December 1931, the statute established regional institutions, given the historical name of Generalitat, and granted them wide-ranging competences over matters such as culture and education, law and order, civil law, healthcare, broadcasting, and public works (Rossinyol 1974, 362–9; Tornos Mas 2007, 191–9).

A statute of autonomy was also drafted for the three Basque provinces and Navarre in spring 1931 but was rejected by the Constituent Assembly on grounds of incompatibility with the constitution that was in the process of being drafted. A second draft statute for the Basque provinces only went to a referendum in 1933 but failed to obtain a majority vote in Álava, where support for Basque nationalism was weak. A third draft was approved in 1936 but failed to be ratified due to the outbreak of the civil war in July. A statute of autonomy was also approved by referendum in June 1936 in Galicia but, like the Basque one, failed to be implemented. Autonomy projects were debated in other regions too, such as Andalusia (Lacomba 2006, 177–80) and Aragon but came to nothing.

With the onset of the Franco dictatorship, the Generalitat of Catalonia was abolished (although it was kept alive in exile) and the official use of Catalan was banned (Balcells [1991] 1996, 125–34). The *conciertos* of Biscay and Guipúzcoa were also abolished and the official use of Basque banned. In Álava and Navarre, however, which had sided with the nationalists in the war, the *conciertos* were maintained and the use of Basque was more tolerated (Linz 1973, 75). Thus, not even under Franco was a fully uniform structure of territorial administration in place. Resistance to the regime turned violent in the Basque provinces in the late 1960s, when the armed secessionist organization Euskadi Ta Askatasuna (ETA), or Basque Homeland and Freedom, started a campaign of bombings and assassinations that would only end in the 2010s (Conversi 1997, 98–104).

Following Franco's death in late 1975, decentralization was widely seen by Spain's political forces and civil society as being an essential element of democratization. Catalan society mobilized in favour of a restoration of the 1932 statute of autonomy and, coordinated by the civil society platform Assemblea de Catalunya, mass demonstrations in support of it were held in the course of 1976. Following the first democratic election in June 1977 the elected representatives from Catalonia joined in an Assemblea de Parlamentaris, demanding the re-establishment of the Generalitat and the return of its president in exile, Josep Tarradellas. In the wake of another massive demonstration on 11 September (Conversi 1997, 142),[42] the government accepted and passed a decree-law later that month, provisionally restoring the Generalitat. In the Basque provinces, the Francoist decree that had abolished the *conciertos* of Biscay and Guipúzcoa was repealed in October 1976. Basque representatives gathered in an assembly in the wake of the 1977 election to prepare the restoration of autonomy, and in January 1978 a provisional regional government, the Consejo General Vasco, was established. Provisional autonomy regimes soon followed in other regions for a total of fourteen by the end of 1978 (Aja 2003, 61–2). The democratic constitution in force since December 1978, provided for regional autonomy in the form of the creation of autonomous communities (ACs), initially distinguished into a strong form, intended for Catalonia, the Basque provinces, and Galicia, and a weak form for the other regions. Between 1979 and 1983, seventeen such ACs were created, covering the entire state territory, with Andalusia, the Canary Islands, Navarre, and Valencia eventually acquiring the strong form as well. Since the first regional elections in 1980, regional-nationalist parties won office in Catalonia and the Basque Country, as the region was by then called, but statewide parties prevailed elsewhere (Gunther and Montero 2009, 71–96).

A reform in 1992 largely did away with the difference between strong and weak autonomy, thus making the system more symmetrical, although some important differences remained (Aja 2003, 169–206). In its wake, the former weak regions, but also the Canaries, reformed their statute of autonomy to enshrine their new status. The leading nationalist parties in Catalonia, the Basque Country, and Galicia reacted to this uniformization of autonomy by issuing the Declaration of Barcelona in July 1998, calling for an official recognition of Spain's multinational character and the consequent need for a special status for the regions where minority nations live (Aja 2003, 90–3). The perceived unsympathetic attitude of the 2000–04 government led by José Maria Aznar, which enjoyed a majority in parliament and was thus not dependent on the support of the regional-nationalist parties, unlike its two predecessors, spurred demands for a strengthening of autonomy in the Basque Country and Catalonia (Colino 2009, 266).

Basque Premier Juan José Ibarretxe presented a proposal for a radical reform of the region's statute of autonomy in 2003, known as the Ibarretxe Plan, which would have given sovereignty to the region and establish a confederal link with the rest of the country. The Basque parliament approved it by a narrow majority in December 2004, but it was rejected as unconstitutional by the state parliament in February 2005 (Keating and Bray 2006). If the Basque reform remained stillborn and had no significant effect on the system, the reform of Catalonia's statute and its ramifications have presented a major challenge to the country's constitutional order and its territorial integrity. The following sections analyze the process and the role the European dimension played within it.

The Reform of Catalonia's Statute and the 2006 Referendum

Preparations for a reform of the statute started in the Catalan parliament in 2000 and gathered momentum after the November 2003 regional election (Tornos Mas 2007, 103–5). The election marked a turning point in Catalonia's post-Franco politics as a coalition of three left-wing parties managed to evict the conservative regional-nationalist Convergència i Unió (CiU) party federation from office for the first time since 1980. The coalition was formed by the Partit dels Socialistes de Catalunya (PS-C), a regional party affiliated with the statewide Partido Socialista Obrero Español (PSOE), which won forty-two seats (against fifty-two in the previous election in 1999), the left-wing regional-nationalist Esquerra Republicana de Catalunya, with twenty-three seats (plus eleven on 1999), and the far-left regional party Iniciativa per Catalunya Verds (ICV), with nine seats (up six on 1999). CiU retained the largest number of seats, forty-six, but lost ten compared to the previous election, while the statewide and conservative Partido Popular (PP-C) gained three seats to a total of fifteen. The electoral success of ERC, advocating secession, and of ICV, with a regional-nationalist position, added salience to the reform of the statute and the coalition agreement between the three parties included a commitment to its implementation (PS-C et al. 2003, 3). The socialist victory in the 2004 general election injected further impetus into the process (Tornos Mas 2007, 104).[43]

PARTY POSITIONS IN THE DRAFTING PROCESS

In January 2005, a committee charged with the drafting of the new statute was set up in the Catalan parliament. Its starting point was a report produced by the government-run think tank Institut d'Estudis

Autonòmics, which was given the remit of proposing a text that would maximize Catalonia's autonomy within the limits imposed by the constitution. The demand for Catalonia to have a voice in EU affairs was an important element in the remit and was shared by the CiU opposition.[44] ICV went further than the other parties in stressing the importance of the European context to the reform (ICV 2003, 4). The parliamentary committee approved a first draft in July 2005, with the support of the PS-C, ERC, and ICV, the opposition of the PP-C, and the abstention of CiU. The latter advocated a more ambitious extension of competences and the inclusion of a fiscal agreement – similar to those enjoyed by the Basque Country and Navarre – that would fundamentally change Catalonia's fiscal relations with the state (CiU 2003; Tornos Mas 2007, 111). After negotiations among the parties a final draft was approved by parliament in September 2005 by 120 votes to 15. The PP-C was the only party to vote against, on the grounds that the draft was highly likely to be unconstitutional and that it was a purely political exercise, which would not address the real concerns of the citizens. At the opposite end of the spectrum, ERC did not hide the fact that for them it was just an intermediate step toward the party's final goal: an independent state (Tornos Mas 2007, 121). The most significant innovations of the draft statute were as follows: 1) the definition of Catalonia as a nation and the concomitant claim of its right to self-government and to a special constitutional status by virtue of its historical rights; 2) an expansion of its competences – mainly in the areas of education, economic activity, immigration, and infrastructure – as well as their entrenchment through a more detailed definitions of functions and roles; 3) the creation of an embryonic Catalan judiciary; 4) the setting up of channels for Catalonia's participation in Spain's European affairs; 5) the reform of the financing system; 6) establishing the Generalitat as the general agent of the state in Catalonia so that it would exercise the latter's competences via delegation as well as its own; 7) reintroduction of the *vegueries* as a tier of government between the Generalitat and the municipalities[45] (Tornos Mas 2007, 120, 437–520).

NEGOTIATIONS WITH MADRID

The draft statute then passed to the central parliament for approval, which started to debate it in November 2005. Although Prime Minister José Rodríguez Zapatero was positive, there were reservations within the ranks of his own socialist party as well as very strong opposition from the PP. The definition of Catalonia as a nation, a term the constitution reserves for Spain as a whole, was particularly controversial, while amendments were also put forward in relation to the proposed division of competences and the financing system. The PP's opposition was radical and all-encompassing, rejecting the draft in its totality as incompatible with the constitution. Given the strength of the opposition the document raised, crucially within the PSOE itself, the margin for a compromise that would be acceptable to both sides appeared very thin. At a meeting between Mr Zapatero and CiU's leader Artur Mas in January 2006, however, an agreement was found, albeit without the involvement of the three parties in the Catalan governing coalition (Barbeta 2006a). Thus, although it opened the way to the approval of the statute, it did so at the price of dividing the Catalan parties, with significant effects on the referendum outcome and subsequent developments.

Following detailed analysis in a working group, a revised draft was presented in March. This contained a number of significant changes compared to the draft approved by the Catalan parliament the year before. The most important included: a) references to Catalonia as a nation were eliminated and the region was referred to as a *nacionalidad*, in line with the distinction drawn in the constitution between *nación*, reserved for Spain as a whole, and *nacionalidad*, applied to regions possessing traits such as a distinct language, traditional institutions etc.; b) a modification of the division of competences, notably concerning shared competences; c) a curtailment of the provisions concerning the involvement of the Generalitat in EU and external affairs and a reaffirmation of the state's competence in these fields; d) a rejection of the proposed bilateral model of fiscal relations between the region and the state (Tornos Mas 2007, 125–39). While CiU defended the revised draft as the best that could be achieved in the circumstances, ERC was very critical, especially with regard to the financing system and the refusal to recognize Catalonia as a nation. Announcing its opposition in the parliamentary committee, its representative signalled that such a refusal would leave independence as the only alternative: "quizás lo que hoy no quieren reconoscer como nación mañana deberán hacerlo como Estado"[46] (quoted in Tornos Mas 2007, 152). The final draft was then approved by the lower house by 189 votes to 154, those of the PP-C and ERC, on 30 March, and by the Senate on 10 May (Barbeta 2006b,c).

REFERENDUM

The statute was then put to a referendum on 18 June 2006. The campaign took place in an atmosphere of fatigue and disillusionment among the electorate that had built up for several months. The previous February a mass demonstration was held in Barcelona in the name of "Som una nació i tenim el dret de decidir"[47] (Bracero 2006a). CiU, the PS-C, and ICV campaigned in favour of ratification while ERC and the PP-C, albeit for opposite reasons, called for a No vote. CiU and the PS-C ran a largely coordinated campaign aimed at mobilizing voters and obtaining the largest possible support for the statute (Quadrado 2006). CiU tried to capitalize on the desire for a new framework, under the slogan "1979 o Futur?" It stressed the national recognition of Catalonia, the new system of financing, and the expanded competences. It also mentioned the new external relations framework and the enhanced involvement in EU affairs but did not appeal to the European dimension to strengthen the case for a Yes vote (CiU 2006). The PS-C sought to exploit the unpopularity of the PP in Catalonia, by presenting the choice in partisan terms, with the slogan "Sí: guanya Catalunya – No: guanya el PP"[48] (PS-C 2006; Ellakuría 2006). The socialists stressed the advances the statute would bring in terms of rights and quality of democracy, as well as a new financing system. They also emphasized that it would allow Catalonia to have a greater say in EU affairs but, like CiU, they did not exploit Europe to bolster support for the new statute (PS-C 2006). In a similar vein, ICV also emphasized the strengthening of citizen rights, especially social rights, the new statute would bring as well as recognition of Catalonia's national character and a greater equality between Catalan and Castilian (ICV 2006a). The party also played to its supporters' traditional foes by trying to convey the message that it was the conservative and reactionary forces of Spanish society that opposed the statute (ICV 2006b). Although, as seen above, the party had stressed the European dimension at the time of the drafting of the statute, it decided not to exploit it in the referendum campaign (2006a,b).

Under pressure from its rank-and-file (Bracero and Aroca 2006; Bracero 2006b), ERC campaigned for a No vote, under the slogan: "Ara toca No – Catalunya mereix més,"[49] hoping that a rejection of the statute as curtailed by the state parliament would lend public support to its call for new negotiations with Madrid on the implementation of the original version approved by the Catalan parliament

(ERC 2006). The party argued that the statute put to the vote would not recognize Catalonia as a nation and would not address the *espoli fiscal*, or fiscal plunder, it was suffering. Accepting it would also mean endorsing the Mas-Zapatero pact struck behind the back of the Catalan parliament (ERC 2006). The republicans, however, called for a No vote on the grounds that their own independentist policy – within which, as discussed below, the European dimension played a crucial role – was superior to the statute and did not appeal to Europe to bolster their case for rejection.

In line with the stance it had adopted throughout the process of revision of the statute, the PP-C also called for a No vote. It argued that the statute was unconstitutional, and because it effectively amounted to a constitutional amendment by stealth, all Spaniards had the right to take a decision on it. It singled out in particular the new financing system, deemed to go against the principle of solidarity and to threaten the functioning of the fiscal system as a whole, and the judicial aspects, which would violate the principle of citizens' equality before the law. From its conservative viewpoint, it also attacked the statute as being interventionist and illiberal, arguing that it would damage the economy by fragmenting the regulatory framework. It did not exploit the European dimension (PP-C 2006).

On a turnout of 49 percent, 74 percent of voters approved it against 21 percent who rejected it. While the actual result was thus strongly positive, the low turnout clearly indicated the people's reservations and ambivalence toward the new statute, and the divisions among parties, notably between the two regional-nationalist parties. No sooner had the new statute entered into force in August 2006 than it was targeted by multiple challenges on grounds of unconstitutionality before the Constitutional Court (Brunet 2006; Tornos Mas 2007, 161). As we will see in the following section, the court's ruling would then have a major impact on the politics of self-government in Catalonia and reverberate across the country.

The Constitutional Court Ruling and the November 2010 Election

ERC's decision to campaign for a No vote in the referendum triggered a crisis within the three-party governing coalition as Generalitat President Pasqual Maragall expelled the republican ministers from the government and was forced to promise an early election in autumn. The election, held on 1 November, saw ICV performing best, with a gain of three seats to a total of twelve, while its coalition partners the PS-C, down five seats to thirty-seven, and ERC, down two to twenty-one, suffered losses. CiU made a modest advance, up two seats to a total of forty-eight, while the PP-C lost one seat (Pallarés and Muñoz 2008). With the new statute approved, albeit reluctantly, in the referendum and the ruling of the Constitutional Court pending, the election results were primarily driven by factors other than the constitutional question and were essentially directionless where the latter was concerned.[50] Following the election, a new three-party left-wing coalition government was formed, headed by José Montilla, who was committed to implementing the new statute, also in cooperation with CiU and the PP-C (Noguer 2006).

The Constitutional Court announced its ruling on 28 June 2010 and published it on 9 July. The ruling found fourteen articles to be partially or totally unconstitutional and a further twenty-three to be compatible with the constitution only if interpreted as prescribed by the Court. Additionally, the Court ruled that the preamble has no legal standing. The ruling affected the following key provisions of the statute: 1) the definition of Catalonia as a nation contained in the preamble would not have any legal effect and the adjective "national" employed elsewhere had to be understood as related to Catalonia as a *nacionalidad* rather than as a *nación*; 2) the Catalan language could not be given priority over Castilian by the Catalan public administration; 3) no Catalan judicial body could be created; 4) there would not be a link between the sum paid in taxes by Catalonia and the amount of state investment in the region; 5) Catalonia's autonomy could not be considered as being legally grounded in any historical right; 6) the creation of the *vegueries* could not entail the abolition of the provinces (TC 2010). The amendments imposed by the Constitutional Court thus compounded those made in the state parliament, to leave the final version of the statute a pale reflection of the one approved by the Catalan parliament in 2005. The Court's decision was greeted with an immediate condemnation by the Catalan governing coalition and CiU (Noguer 2010; Piñol 2010) and by a mobilization of civil society. On 10 July, more than a million people demonstrated in Barcelona against the ruling, under the slogan "Som una nació. Nosaltres decidim"[51] (Barbeta 2010).

POSITIONS ON STATE RESTRUCTURING

The ruling of the Constitutional Court determined that in the November 2010 election, in contrast to the previous one, the constitutional question was at the heart of the campaign. CiU stressed Catalonia's national character and the right to self-determination flowing from such a character (CiU 2010, 81–2). From that premise it demanded a new financing arrangement for the region: "Situem com una de les primeres prioritats d'aquest dret a decidir la gestió plena dels nostres recursos econòmics a través d'un model de finançament propi, com ho és el concert econòmic"[52] (CiU 2010, 82). More generally, the party called for Catalonia to acquire greater self-governing capacity and, with a clear reference to the PS-C, argued that only a party not in a position of dependence vis-à-vis statewide political forces would be able to deliver it. The nationalist federation also committed itself to implementing the new statute as much as possible, notably concerning competences and investments, with a view to establishing a more and more bilateral relationship with the central government (82–3).

Since the early 1990s, ERC had adopted a secessionist position, calling for Catalonia to become an independent state within the EU (Baras and Matas Dalmases 1998, 208; Argelaguet et al. 2004, 14, 21; Castro 2011, 59–66). In the course of the negotiations on the new statute, the republicans had made it clear that they considered it only a transitory step and that their constitutional goal was still an independent state: in the words of the party's leader: "de l'Estatut a l'Estat"[53] (Carod 2003). Its 2010 manifesto, whose opening section was headlined "Cap a l'Estat propi,"[54] reaffirmed such a position: "si Esquerra disposa algun dia de la meitat més un dels diputats del Parlament de Catalunya proclamarà la independència"[55] (ERC 2010, 9). In the meantime, the party would work to stoke the emerging social movement in favour of independence and seek a majority in parliament for calling a referendum on it (ERC 2010, 9).

The PS-C committed itself to implementing the new *Estatut* as much as possible, in the spirit of the vote of the Catalan parliament and people as well as, echoing CiU, to working toward a new financing mechanism that would reduce Catalonia's fiscal deficit. Alongside that, however, the party also reiterated its call for Spain to become a genuine federal state that would fully recognize Catalonia's national status (PS-C 2010, 48–9).

ICV also called for a political and judicial strategy that would lead to as full an implementation as possible of the new statute in the short term as well as for a constitutional reform that would transform the country into a federal and explicitly multinational state in the medium term. It went further than the socialists, however, in calling for such a reform to include the right to self-determination. Were this to be rejected by the Spanish state, the party supported the exercise of Catalonia's right to decide, that is the holding of a referendum in which the people would be asked to choose between the constitutional status quo, statehood within a Spanish federation, and independence (ICV 2010, 221–2; more widely 221–43). The party preferred the second option, labelled later in the document as "un Estat propi en una Espanya federal plurinacional i una Europa unida"[56] (239). ICV called for a federal Europe of the Peoples in which Catalonia would find full recognition as a sovereign nation (esp. 222, 241–2).

In contrast to the other main parties, the PP-C ignored the whole question of the *Estatut* and the ruling of the Constitutional Tribunal in its campaign and focused on the economic crisis instead, thus implicitly endorsing the status quo (PP-C 2010).

ATTITUDES TO, AND STRATEGIC USE OF,
EUROPEAN INTEGRATION

There was broad support for European integration across the political spectrum, although the two regional-nationalist parties – CiU and, especially, ERC – were less positive about the direction the EU had taken since the Constitutional Treaty. The former was divided over the Constitutional Treaty and supported the Lisbon Treaty without enthusiasm while the latter called for a No vote in the referendum on the Constitutional Treaty and voted against ratification of the Lisbon Treaty (Roig 2005; Massetti 2009, 521; LV 2008).

CiU did not pay much attention to Europe in its manifesto, confining itself to seeking greater recognition for, and a stronger presence of, Catalonia and its language within the EU. The underlying attitude remained positive but with less enthusiasm for a federal Europe than in the past (CiU 2010, 89–92). In relation to state restructuring, the manifesto placed Catalonia within a European context but did not use it to support its demands for a new financing arrangement and for a recognition of the region's national status (81–3, 89).

Despite its critical attitude toward the "constitutional" evolution of the EU, ERC retained a stronger commitment to further integration, calling for "una Europa supraestatal més forta, amb un nivell de govern europeu, amb millors institucions i més marge de maniobra respecte els interessos dels estats membres"[57] (ERC 2010, 191). ERC also reaffirmed its commitment for Catalonia to achieve independence as an EU member state and acknowledged the importance of building international support for it but did not exploit the European dimension further to bolster its policy (ERC 2010, 7–11, 189–94).

The PS-C displayed a strongly pro-European outlook, expressing support for "reforçar la construcció política comunitària, conscients que en el marc de la situació sòcioeconòmica actual i futura, necessitem més Europa que mai"[58] (PS-C 2010, 67). The party also committed itself to making European policy a central aspect of domestic policy in Catalonia, to Europeanizing the Catalan administration, and to increasing awareness of integration among the general population (65). Despite its strongly pro-European stance, the PS-C largely aligned itself with the other parties in failing to appeal to Europe to support its policy on Catalonia's constitutional status (48–9, 65).

ICV was even more outspoken in its support for integration, calling for efforts toward a federal Europe to be at the heart of the Catalan government's external action in the next parliament (ICV 2010, 269–70). Echoing the PS-C, it called for a greater participation of Catalonia in the EU decision-making processes as well as greater awareness of integration within the region (269–71). As already seen, ICV called for Catalonia to achieve a national status within a federal Spain and a federal Europe – specifically a Europe of the Peoples – and acknowledged the possibility for it of becoming a member state of the European Union but, like ERC, did not attempt to exploit the European dimension further to lend greater weight to its proposals (222–3, 241–2).

Although the PP-C remained broadly supportive of integration, it did not address it in its manifesto and made no connections between the European dimension and Catalonia's status (PP-C 2010).

Interestingly, in a move anticipating those later adopted by the wider independentist movement, Solidaritat Catalana per la Independència (SI), or Catalan Solidarity for Independence, a startup secessionist party led by the former president of Barcelona F.C., Joan

Laporta, put the European dimension at the heart of its campaign, under the slogan *Catalunya proper Estat d'Europa*.⁵⁹

ELECTION OUTCOME

The election results handed a major success to CiU and a severe blow to the *tripartit*, the three-party left-wing coalition that had governed Catalonia since 2003. The regional-nationalist conservative federation won sixty-two seats, up fourteen on the previous election and its fourth best tally ever. The heaviest defeat among the outgoing governing parties was suffered by ERC, which lost over half of its parliamentary representation, down eleven to ten seats, followed by the PS-C, down nine to a total of twenty-eight, and ICV, which won ten seats, two fewer than in 2006. The PP-C performed strongly, gaining four seats to a total of eighteen. The main drivers of these results appear to have been the electorate's shift to the right and, particularly so, a desire for a change of government after seven years of the *tripartit* (Rico 2012, 225–7).

Their significance in terms of the constitutional question, on the other hand, was largely muted, as the similar stances taken by CiU and the PS-C were rewarded very differently and the results of the other parties virtually cancelled each other out. The secessionist ERC suffered a major defeat but the ICV, with its strong defence of the right to decide, successfully limited its losses and the SI startup managed to secure four seats, while at the opposite end of the spectrum of constitutional positions, the PP-C also did well. The defeat – or limited success in SI's case – of the parties that had exploited Europe in relation to state restructuring meant that it was not associated with electoral success on this occasion. The overall picture painted by the electoral results was thus one of mainstream endorsement for a pragmatic response to the ruling of the Constitutional Court, focused on a new financing arrangement, with a moderate degree of polarization at the more radical ends of the spectrum.

Economic Crisis, Mass Mobilization, and the November 2012 Election

The convergence of four main factors in the 2010–12 period produced an escalation in the dispute between Catalonia and the Spanish state and brought the demand for independence to the fore. The first factor was the change of government at the state level in the wake of the November 2011 general election. The election produced a landslide victory for the PP and the worst ever defeat for the PSOE, the largest ever swing to the right in the post-Franco era (Chari 2013). Given that the PP had traditionally been more hostile than the PSOE toward Catalonia's demands, its triumph in the election did not bode well for the Catalan government's hopes of securing a more favourable financial arrangement.

The salience of the latter was sharpened by the deepening of the eurozone's economic and financial crisis in the first half of 2012, which affected Spain deeply. The Spanish regions found themselves on the frontline of the crisis, given their links to troubled banks and the size of their debt, none more so than Catalonia, which had the largest debt burden of all (Johnson et al. 2012). In July 2012 Catalonia found itself unable to meet its financial obligations and was forced to ask for a bailout by the central government (Barbeta 2012a), thus taking its long-standing complaint of being victim of an *espoli fiscal* to a dramatic new level.

Over the same period a grassroots mobilization in favour of independence was gathering strength and culminated in a mass demonstration in September 2012. Among the most prominent manifestations of this mobilization was the holding of unofficial independence referendums by many towns between 2009 and 2011 (Muñoz and Guinjoan 2013). The secessionist citizen association Assemblea Nacional Catalana (ANC), or Catalan National Assembly, founded in March 2012, organized a giant demonstration demanding independence on Catalonia's national day, 11 September, under the slogan *Catalunya, nou Estat d'Europa*,[60] in which an estimated 1.5 million people took part (Pi 2012a). Prior to the demonstration, the ANC's president, Carme Forcadell, predicted: "El 12 de setembre, el Govern haurà de començar a treballar per la independència de Catalunya"[61] (Ara 2012). The last, and most important, factor was the Catalan government's failure to reach an agreement with the central government on a more favourable financing arrangement for the region. At a crucial meeting with the Spanish prime minister, Mariano Rajoy, on 20 September all the Catalan premier, Artur Mas, could obtain was a clear rejection of his proposals on the grounds that they would be in breach of the constitution (Barbeta 2012b). In the context of the deep economic crisis and under pressure from the street, such clear rejection effectively spelled the end of the pragmatic path the Catalan government had trodden since the ruling of the Constitutional Court and the 2010 election.

With a view to riding the wave of popular mobilization and capitalizing on the central government's refusal to negotiate, the Catalan premier reacted by calling an early regional election for the following November. In a speech announcing his decision on 25 September, Mas repeatedly made references to the demands coming from civil society: "En moments exceptionals, decisions exceptionals … La veu del carrer, al ser massiva i potent, s'ha de traslladar a les urnes"[62] (PdC 2012a, 3; also Barbeta 2012c). Two days later, a resolution calling on the Catalan government to hold a referendum on self-determination within the next parliamentary term was approved by the parliament by eighty-four votes to twenty-one. The resolution was initiated by the leaders of the CiU and ERC parliamentary groups and was supported also by ICV and a few others secessionist representatives, while the PS-C abstained and the PP-C voted against (Barbeta 2012d). It was the first time that the two regional-nationalist parties, very distant from each other on the left-right spectrum, led a joint initiative on a national issue and the first time CiU abandoned its traditionally moderate constitutional stance and openly, if still somewhat ambiguously, embraced a secessionist course.

POSITIONS ON STATE RESTRUCTURING

In this context, the campaign for the November 2012 snap election was, even more so than the previous one, focused on the constitutional question, although the economic crisis also loomed large (Martí 2013, 509). The question of whether an independent Catalonia could remain within the EU featured prominently in the campaign (Pi 2012b). CiU placed its policy on the so-called *transició nacional*, or national transition, at the forefront of its manifesto and for the first time openly campaigned in favour of Catalonia's statehood: "És l'hora que Catalunya inicïi el rumb cap a l'estat propi"[63] (CiU 2012, 9). The manifesto argued that this was so because "Després de més de trenta anys de democràcia, s'ha constatat que l'encaix de Catalunya a l'Estat espanyol resulta de viabilitat molt difícil. Se'ns han tancat les portes, i per tant, és hora d'iniciar el nostre propi camí"[64] (ibid.). In the name of Catalonia being a national community and of the principles of democracy, the party federation called for the Catalan people to be given the opportunity to exercise their right to self-determination and committed itself to doing so in the next parliamentary term (ibid.; more widely, 10–13). With a view to laying the ground for Catalonia to become independent, CiU promised to develop a series of institutions needed to make statehood viable, *in primis* a Catalan fiscal revenue agency (14–15).

ERC married its secessionist position to a strong defence of social rights: "la independència del nostre país és imprescindible per continuar existint com a nació, per protegir els drets socials de la ciutadania, per desenvolupar tot el nostre potencial com a país i per garantir la continuïtat de l'estat del benestar"[65] (ERC 2012, 4). To achieve such an objective, the party committed itself to "celebrar, durant el 2014, un referèndum sobre la independència de Catalunya, per esdevenir un nou Estat en el si de la Unió Europea"[66] (ibid.; more widely 6–10).

The PS-C argued that the secessionist path, on which CiU and ERC had embarked, and the PP's refusal to revisit the constitutional architecture born out of the 1978 constitution were both leading into a cul-de-sac and presented its proposals for a federal reform of the state as the right middle way between them: "L'alternativa federalista és l'única capaç d'articular un sistema institucional equilibrat, en el qual Catalunya formi part d'Espanya sense renunciar gens a la seva identitat i als seus projectes col·lectius"[67] (PS-C 2012, 5). According to the party, a successful federal reform would rest on four Rs: recognition, rules, revenues, and representation. These referred to the recognition of Catalonia as a nation, a clearer division of competences between the federal government and the constituent governments, a fairer fiscal revenues system, and a reform of the Senate to turn it into a genuine federal body. It also argued that such a reform would have to be approved by the Catalan people in a referendum (6–10).

In contrast to the other parties, ICV emphasized the issues related to the economic crisis over those of a constitutional nature. It acknowledged that different constitutional positions coexisted within its members and its electorate, and focused on Catalonia's right to decide its preferred constitutional status, whatever that might turn out to be, on the basis of its sovereignty as a nation (ICV 2012, 131, also 133–5). The Edinburgh Agreement between the Scottish and the British governments, mentioned above, was pointed out as a model to follow (132). The thread running through the party's constitutional policy was the acquisition of sovereignty and statehood: "hem reivindicat des de fa temps la construcció d'un Estat propi, que pot establir, a partir de la pròpia sobirania, una relació de caràcter federal, confederal o ser present directament en l'àmbit europeu, depenent de la voluntat de pacte de l'Estat i de la lliure decisió de la ciutadania de Catalunya"[68] (134).

The PP-C mounted a strong defence of Catalonia within Spain: "Tenemos la posibilidad de decir alto y claro, con nuestro voto, que queremos seguir conviviendo con el resto de España"[69] (PP-C 2012, 5). Its only departure from the constitutional status quo was the promise to seek a more advantageous financing arrangement for Catalonia (6, 8).

ATTITUDES TO, AND STRATEGIC USE OF, EUROPEAN INTEGRATION

CiU returned to a strong pro-integration outlook. It argued that Catalonia had to show it had a lot to offer to the building of Europe in order to be accepted as a new EU member state: "estem disposats a cedir part de la nostra sobirania per a la construcció d'una Europa més forta políticament i econòmicament, una Europa que es vagi transformant en un veritable espai federal"[70] (CiU 2012, 16). The document emphasized Catalonia's European character and stressed that its national transition would take place in the context of Europe: "volem tenir un estat propi en el marc d'Europa"[71] (13). Moreover, it went further to argue that the EU context was a *conditio sine qua non* for such a transition: "La nostra transició nacional cap a un estat propi passa necessàriament per continuar formant part d'Europa"[72] (15). In a very similar vein, the ERC also expressed strong support for integration and made clear Catalonia would achieve independence firmly within the context of European integration:

> ERC defensa una Catalunya integrada i compromesa amb Europa ... Catalunya sempre ha estat favorable a un enfortiment politic de la Unió i de les seves institucions ... Per aixo creiem fermament en una Catalunya independent integrada a Europa. Perque Catalunya ha contribuit a aquesta Unio Europea i perque Catalunya es Europa i els catalans som ciutadans europeus. Com Escòcia, Catalunya aspira a esdevenir un Estat més d'aquesta Unió i formar part de la fraternitat europea. Per això optem per un creixement de la Unió Europea des de dins de la mateixa Unió.[73] (ERC 2012, 4–5, also 6–10.)

The PS-C reaffirmed its strong support for integration, calling for the achievement of a federal Europe together with a strengthening of its democratic character (PS-C 2012, 10–11). It also argued that the model of shared sovereignty it advocated for Spain was in line with that operating within the EU: "Vivim temps de sobiranies compartides. Creiem en un projecte de sobirania compartida entre Catalunya i Espanya, i evidentment també amb Europa, perquè som i ens sentim europeus i perquè tenim clar que els reptes de Catalunya i Espanya i la seva solució es troben avui a Europa "[74] (5).

ICV maintained its position in favour of a federal Europe while at the same time calling for a concerted effort at the European level to fight austerity policies (ICV 2012, 147–8). It did not make strong links between European integration and constitutional reform in Spain, confining itself to calling for an internal federalism linked also to federalism at the European level (132).

The PP-C did not formulate a European policy in its manifesto but appealed to the European dimension to undermine the lure of independence: "Es un grave error querer romper con el resto de España, porque esta ruptura conllevaría romper con la Unión Europea y, a la vez, una fractura social en Cataluña"[75] (PP-C 2012, 5).

ELECTION OUTCOME

The main winner of the election was ERC, which more than doubled its tally of seats to twenty-one, thus regaining the representation it had in the 2006–10 parliament and the status of third largest party. The biggest loser was CiU, which only won fifty seats, twelve fewer than in the 2010 election but the results also marked a defeat for the PS-C, which lost eight seats to a total of twenty, its worst-ever results. ICV and, to a lesser extent, the PP-C gained some ground, increasing their representation in parliament by three and one seats, respectively. The fiercely anti-independence Ciutadans (Cs), also performed strongly, tripling its number of seats (Martí 2013, 512–14; Rico and Liñeira 2014, 265–8).

The election results seem to have been driven by a combination of polarization on the constitutional question, on the one hand, and a rejection of austerity policies and mainstream parties, on the other hand. Thus, CiU, recent convert to the independentist cause and blamed for austerity policies, was punished severely alongside the constitutionally middle-of-the-road and still blamed for the economic crisis PS-C, while the left-wing sovereigntist ERC and ICV were rewarded and so were the strongly anti-secessionist and outsiders PP-C and Ciutadans. The effect was to strengthen the call for a referendum on self-determination and to place CiU in a position of relative dependence vis-à-vis the parties most vocally championing it, ERC and ICV. Given the contrasting fortunes of CiU and ERC, exploitation of the European dimension was associated both with success and with defeat in this election. It is possible that voters rewarded ERC's long-standing commitment to independence while punishing CiU's for its late-in-the-day conversion as well as for its economic policy in the context of the crisis (see also Rico and Liñeira 2014, 268–72).

The November 2014 "Referendum" and the September 2015 Election

The political constellation produced by the 2012 election soon bore fruits. Privileging their national loyalties over their ideological ones, CiU and ERC reached an unprecedented agreement whereby the republicans would offer external support to a CiU government in exchange for the latter's commitment to hold a referendum on independence in the course of 2014 (Barbeta 2012e). In January 2013 the Parliament of Catalonia approved by eighty-five votes to forty-one the *Declaració de sobirania i del dret a decidir del poble de Catalunya*, or Declaration of Sovereignty and of the Right to Decide of the People of Catalonia (PdC 2012b), which was later ruled unconstitutional by the Constitutional Court (Fabra 2014). Further impetus to the secessionist drive, however, was given once again by the mobilization of civil society. On Catalonia's national day in September 2013, the ANC organized a giant human chain covering the length of Catalonia from north to south, dubbed the *Via Catalana cap a l'independència,* or the Catalan Way to Independence, in which an estimated 1.6 million people took part (Barbeta 2012f). In December 2013 the Catalan government announced the date of the referendum, 9 November 2014, and that the electorate would be asked two questions: first, whether Catalonia should be a state and, second, whether that state should be independent (GdC 2013). A proposal to hold such referendum with the blessing of the central government, thus in conformity with the constitution, was rejected by a large majority in the Spanish parliament in April 2014 (Barbeta 2014a). Added impetus to the secessionist drive was given by the

May 2014 European election in which ERC came up top in Catalonia, with 23.7 percent of the vote, ahead of CiU, with a share of 21.8 percent, while the PS-C sank again to its worst ever score in a European election (Barbeta 2014b). Another massive rally in favour of the referendum was held in Barcelona on 11 September 2014 (Noguer and Ríos 2014).

The Catalan regional-nationalist parties' drive for independence has been closely mirrored – and, as seen above, significantly influenced – by profound changes in public attitudes. Support for independence has grown dramatically, from less than 20 percent in 2003 to close to 50 percent ten years later (Guibernau 2013, 386; Serrano 2013, esp. 525–7). From being traditionally – in the post-Franco era – the third constitutional preference, after autonomous community and being a constituent unit of a Spanish federal state, independent statehood is now by a wide margin the preferred choice. According to the autumn 2014 survey conducted by the Catalan government-run Centre d'Estudis d'Opinió, 45 percent of respondents supported independence, 23 percent the status quo, and 20 percent the status of constituent unit of a federal state. Among CiU and ERC voters, support for independence reached 75 percent and 88 percent, respectively. Not surprisingly, the majority of those favouring independence stated that they had adopted such a position in recent years, and this is particularly the case among the CiU electorate. On the two questions the Catalonia government planned to put to a referendum in November 2014, 58 percent would have voted Yes to the first question – whether Catalan should be a state – and 82 percent of those intending to vote Yes to the first question would have also voted Yes on the second one – whether such a Catalan state should be independent. Fully 92 percent of ERC voters and 74 percent of CiU voters, as well as a plurality of 36 percent among ICV voters, would have voted Yes on both questions (CEO 2014: 39–43). On the question of whether an independent Catalonia would find itself outside the EU, 45 percent thought it quite or very likely versus 38 percent thinking it quite or very unlikely. Among the regional-nationalist electorate, however, opinions were very different: 52 percent of CiU voters and 62 percent of ERC voters judged it quite or very unlikely (53–4), thus showing that the Europeanization strategies chosen by the two parties were successful within their own electorate.

In the event, the Constitutional Court suspended Catalonia's law laying the legal ground for the referendum, in response to which the

Catalan government decided to hold a consultative vote in its stead. On the original date intended, 9 November, 80 percent of around two million participants voted Yes to an independent state (Pérez and Ríos 2014). In January 2015, the Catalan premier, Mas, announced the calling of an early regional election for the following September, with the intention of turning it into a plebiscite on independence (Gil del Olmo and Ríos 2015).

PARTIES

The Catalan party system experienced far-reaching changes between the 2012 and the 2015 elections. The most dramatic was the breakup of the long-standing CiU party federation, which had been hitherto the dominant political force in Catalonia, over the issue of independence. Determined to maintain its leadership of the secessionist drive, threatened by the rise of ERC, Convergència Democràtica de Catalunya (CDC) decided to ally itself with the latter in a broad-based electoral cartel dubbed Junts pel Sí (JxS), or Together for a Yes, whereas Unió Democràtica de Catalunya (UDC) eventually decided to fight the election as a standalone party. The second change was the forming of a left alliance between ICV and the statewide startup movement Podemos under the banner Catalunya Sí Que Es Pot (CSQEP), or Catalonia Yes We Can. On the far left as well as on the radical secessionist end of the political spectrum, rising support turned Candidatura d'Unitat Popular (CUP), or Popular Unity Candidacy, into a serious contender for the first time. Lastly, Ciutadans (Cs) firmly established itself as a centre-right and anti-secessionist party (Martí and Cetrà 2016, 109–11).

POSITIONS ON STATE RESTRUCTURING

Given the stated objective of treating the election as a referendum on independence, the question of Catalonia's constitutional status was at the heart of the campaign more than ever before. Not surprisingly, Junts pel Sí called explicitly for secession. As an independent state, its manifesto argued, Catalonia would be better able to restore prosperity and safeguard its social model, on the grounds that it would have full autonomy to make its own policy and fiscal choices, it would enjoy greater resources for public services and investment, and would be able to borrow on international financial markets (JxS 2015, 21–5). From a very different perspective, CUP saw independence as part of a radical program of freeing Catalonia from the political and economic order enshrined in the 1978 constitution in order to build a truly democratic, non-capitalist, and non-patriarchal society (CUP 2015, 3–6). CSQEP did not embrace independence, but it argued that the constitutional status quo was no longer viable and called for Catalonia to move from being an autonomous community to being a "sovereign political subject," with the right to freely decide its constitutional future (CSQEP 2015, esp. 208–10). In a similar vein, the PS-C argued that the "state of autonomies" had run its course and advocated holding a referendum on a federal constitutional reform. Key elements of such a reform would be a new system of fiscal federalism, a territorialization of the judicial system, and enhanced representation for the constituent units in the upper house (PS-C 2015, 26–7). Ciutadans attacked the divisiveness of secessionist nationalism and called for greater unity within Catalonia and between Catalonia and the rest of Spain. It argued that a German-style cooperative federalism was the best institutional architecture for a diverse society such as Spain. The state of autonomies thus needed to be reformed in particular as regards clarity of responsibilities, fiscal transfers, uniformity of public services, cooperation between levels of government, and local – as opposed to regional – autonomy (Cs 2015, 7–13). The PP-C also attacked secessionism for its divisiveness and for having hijacked the Catalan government over the last few years, diverting efforts away from pressing social and economic challenges. In contrast to Ciutadans, however, it did not put forward proposals for a reform of the state of autonomies (PP-C 2015, esp. 3–7, 21–4).

ATTITUDES TO, AND STRATEGIC USE OF, EUROPEAN INTEGRATION

Junts pel Sí followed in the footsteps of CiU's and ERC's previous campaigns in putting forward a strongly positive attitude toward the EU. A key passage read: "la pertinença a la Unió i a l'euro és cabdal per garantir la continuïtat i la millora de la prosperitat assolida"[76] (JxS 2015, 11). Looking forward, the manifesto argued that an independent Catalonia "Des de la seva nova condició d'Estat membre de la Unió Europea, promourà un model d'Europa federal que afavoreixi una integració creixent"[77] (111). JxS placed Catalonia's independence firmly in the context of the EU (esp. 33–5, 51, 110) but was more defensive and less assured in exploiting it than CiU and ERC had been previously. The third section of its manifesto, devoted to outlining the vision of an independent Catalonia, was headlined "Catalunya, nou Estat d'Europa" (54). In the opening section, though, the manifesto felt compelled to defend secession against the accusation that it would threaten Catalonia's membership of the EU: "contràriament al que alguns volen fer creure, aquesta pertinença no està amenaçada per la independència"[78] (11). The main way in which the manifesto strategically exploited the European dimension was in arguing that Catalonia would be able to leverage its desire to retain membership of the EU to gain international support for its secessionist drive and an external safeguard against possible political tensions generated by such a drive (34).

In sharp contrast, CUP rejected the EU on the ground that it "només serveix per garantir els privilegis del capital i que no representa els interessos de les classes populars europees"[79] and advocated alternative forms of international relations for the peoples of Europe and the Mediterranean (CUP 2015, 13). CSQEP displayed markedly different attitudes toward integration and toward the current EU. On the one hand, it advocated a strengthening of Catalonia as an international actor committed to a united and federal Europe (CSQEP 2015, 228). On the other hand, it called for an end to austerity and for a refoundation of Europe along democratic principles, as regarded in particular the governance of the eurozone (17–18, 21, 66–7, 224–6). The coalition linked the European dimension and state restructuring in Spain to argue that the latter would grant Catalonia a special status through which it would enjoy direct representation in the EU institutions, notably the European Council (210, 228). The PS-C was strongly positive toward integration, calling for a federal and social Europe. This would be based on a federal economic government, a common treasury, the issuing of eurobonds, an expansion of the EU budget, a reform of the ECB, as well as a stronger role for the European Parliament (PS-C 2015, 24). Ciutadans also had a strongly pro-EU stance: "Necessitem més Europa, més unitat política, econòmica i financera dins de la Unió Europea" (Cs 2015, 3). From that perspective, it exploited Europe to attack the independentist parties, arguing that secession would leave Catalonia outside the EU and the eurozone, and this would take a heavy economic toll on the newborn state (2–5). The PP-C did not take a position on integration in its manifesto but used the European dimension to attack the secessionist parties. It did so in two ways. First, it argued that a strong PP would be the best guarantee that the secessionists would not succeed in separating Catalonia from Spain and from Europe (PP-C 2015, 22). Second, it also stressed the fact that the PP was the largest party not only in Spain but also, via its membership of the European People's Party, EU-wide, and was thus in a position to leverage its international connection against the prospect of Catalonia's secession (7, 22–3).

ELECTION OUTCOME

The Junts pel Sí came first by a large margin, securing 40 percent of the vote and sixty-two seats in the Catalan parliament. Put into context, though, the result was actually a blow for the joint list. Compared to the scores achieved separately by CiU and ERC in 2012, the two parties lost five percentage points and nine seats. Moreover, and most importantly, they fell short of gaining the absolute majority needed to put into place their secessionist agenda. The CUP achieved a significant success, gaining over 8 percent of the vote and ten seats, its first ever representation in the regional parliament. The most spectacular gains were made by Ciutadans, up ten percentage points and sixteen seats on the previous election and the second-best performance by far. The other three lists all lost votes and seats. The PS-C lost two percentage points in electoral support and only managed to retain sixteen seats, its worst ever tally. CSQEP shed one percentage point in the vote share and two seats, while the biggest loser was the PP-C, which had to surrender over four percentage points in support and eight seats compared to 2012 (Martí and Cetrà 2016, 113–16; Orriols and Rodon, 2016, 370–1).

The significance of these results for the politics of independence and state restructuring was a complex one. On the one hand, they marked a setback for the mainstream secessionist agenda, given Junts pel Sí's failure to gain a majority, either of seats or votes. While a numerical secessionist majority could be achieved by an alliance with the CUP, this would be at the price of uniting parties far apart on the left-right spectrum. The predicament was a particularly painful one for the once solidly conservative CDC, who had already paid a high price for its secessionist course and alliance with ERC. Moreover, the secessionist option as a whole, measured in terms of support for JxS and the CUP, had failed to attract a majority of the votes. Taking into account the positions defended by CSQEP and the PS-C, on the other hand, it is clear that the Catalan voters had still expressed a strong demand for a significant change in Catalonia's constitutional status, thus keeping the issue of state restructuring firmly on the agenda. This, though, was in a context of growing polarization on the centre-periphery dimension, as indicated by the fact that intransigent opposition to regional nationalism and state restructuring – no longer defended solely by the PP-C but also by Ciutadans – made significant advances as well. In the end, an agreement between JxS and the CUP allowed for the formation of a Catalan government – at the price of Mas stepping down – committed to taking its secessionist agenda forward (see also Martí and Cetrà 2016, 116–18; Orriols and Rodon 2016, 371–7).

Summary

Twenty-five years after the first post-Franco statutes of autonomy were approved, their revision in the 2000–10s marked a critical juncture in the evolution of the state structure known as the *estado de las autonomías*. Although the outcome of this juncture is still uncertain at the time of writing, it clearly has the potential to change the constitutional nature of the Spanish state significantly, given the severity of Catalonia's independentist challenge.

The unfolding of the process has followed a bottom-up dynamic, driven by the demand for greater autonomy coming from the regions and, Catalonia *in primis*, with regional-nationalist parties playing a central role within it. Catalonia's demand for self-government has undergone a profound transformation in the course of the juncture, from having long been considered a prominent example of non-independentist nationalism (e.g., Diez Medrano 1995, 3–8) to a markedly secessionist stance. As in the other countries analyzed, political parties have been the dominant actors in the process, shaping its direction and tempo. The role of CiU has been particularly noteworthy, as its conversion to the independentist cause from 2012 onward marked a key turning point in Catalonia's relations with the rest of Spain. Less eye-catching but important over the long term was the delayed effect of ERC's own conversion to independence in the late 1980s–early 1990s. Although for a long time it did not seem to have fundamentally changed the party's fortunes, it eventually allowed it to reap the benefits of the shift toward independence within civil society and effectively be in a position to dictate the policy of the Catalan government. Grassroots mobilization in favour of independence played a crucial role and was arguably instrumental in fostering a strategic change of direction on the part of CiU. Parties and civil society organization thus appear to have influenced each other in a process of radicalization over Catalonia's constitutional status (Crameri 2015).

As expected, the European dimension featured prominently in this juncture of state restructuring in Spain. At a more pedestrian level, adapting Catalonia's statute of autonomy – like those of the other regions – to the realities of Spain's EU membership was one of the rationales for undertaking the revision in the first place. More profoundly, though, the parties involved in the process exploited Europe strategically so as better to pursue their objectives and so did civil society organizations. The most intense use of the European dimension was made by parties focusing their campaign on independence – i.e., CiU and ERC – while the PP-C and Ciutadans made some negative use of it to counter the lure of secession. Likewise, the European dimension was at the heart of the independentist demonstration of September 2012, as reflected in the slogan *nou estat d'Europa*. The spokesperson of CiU, Francesc Homs, admitted in October 2012 that continuity within the EU was the cornerstone of the Catalan government's independentist drive (García 2012). The 2015 election campaign, though, showed the secessionist parties more cautious and defensive and at the same time parties such as Ciutadans being more assertive in strategically linking the European dimension to independence. This could be a signal that the idea of independence in Europe might have been weakened in the last few years by the hard light thrown on the question of whether a secessionist region would be able to transition seamlessly to the status of member state, and that statewide parties, especially newer ones, might be more willing to exploit the European dimension than in the past.

On the whole, though, public opinion data show that the strategy of regional-nationalist parties resonated with the electorate at large and with their own voters in particular, who came to see independence as their preferred constitutional status and believed that independence would likely take place within the European Union. By contrast, whenever independence was away from the limelight, strategic linkages between Europe and domestic reform correspondingly faded away. In the early 1970s, Linz (1973, 106) doubted that sufficient support for secession could be mustered in Catalonia in the foreseeable future, citing the economic costs of leaving the protected

Spanish market as a key obstacle. In this respect, we can see how Spain's membership of a European Union with a single market and a single currency helped transform attitudes to independence in Catalonia among the elites and the mass public to the point of becoming their first choice.

7.5 GENERAL SUMMARY

The three critical junctures analyzed in this chapter provide powerful illustrations of the bottom-up dynamic of state restructuring and of the influence the European dimension can have within it. In the three cases, regional-nationalist parties were the central actors driving the process and their policy of independence was a key factor leading to actual or potential change in the constitutional structure of their respective countries. These parties all campaigned on a platform of independence in Europe, and public support for the latter increased markedly in Scotland and Catalonia, though to a lesser extent in Flanders. Thus, the European dimension was prominent in all three cases through its being exploited by the regional-nationalist parties in relation to their pursuit of independence. While some negative – in the statistical sense – use of Europe could be observed, occasionally of a significant extent, positive linkage on the part of statewide parties was once again conspicuous by its weakness. The regional-nationalist discourse on independence in Europe continued to be focused on aspects such as continuity in the economic environment and access to EU decision-making, showing that, somewhat surprisingly, the eurozone crisis and the concomitant decline in public support for integration appear to have had little effect.

8

European Integration and State Restructuring: A Realist Bargain Approach

Bringing together the findings of the preceding chapters, this chapter presents the results of synoptic comparative analyses of *how* European integration influences state restructuring and the *extent to which* it does so. The analyses of *how*, performed on the basis of a QCA methodology, provide strong empirical support for the conceptual and theoretical claims the book puts forward. A macroanalysis of the thirteen critical junctures underscores the existence of two distinct forms of state restructuring – bottom up and top down – and the fact that Europeanization is present in the former but not in the latter. A micro-analysis of 127 party observations at election and referendum times confirms these results further, by showing that positive – in the statistical sense – exploitation of the European dimension in relation to state restructuring is almost exclusively carried out by regional parties with a radical constitutional position and favourable attitudes to integration as well as operating at a time of high integration. There is thus consistent evidence that European integration influences state restructuring as theorized by the realist bargain model: primarily through the agency of regional-nationalist parties in bottom-up dynamics of reform. Although less conclusively so, the evidence reviewed in relation to the *to what extent* question also suggests that such an influence has likely been significant, albeit in a punctuated manner. These findings call for a reassessment of how we view the connections between the process of European integration and the changing structure of Western European states.

8.1 SYNOPTIC COMPARATIVE ANALYSES OF "HOW"

Two QCA analyses have been performed to answer the *how* question: a macro-analysis with the thirteen critical junctures as cases and a micro-analysis with 127 party-election/referendum observations as cases. For each of them, necessity and sufficiency tests have been carried out with *fsQCA2.5*, a recently developed software specifically designed to perform QCA analysis (Ragin et al. 2006). The necessity test is performed in a single step. The sufficiency test proceeds in two steps. *fsQCA2.5* first organizes conditions and outcome into a truth table matching each configuration of conditions to the outcome. It then performs a so-called minimization operation to produce complex, parsimonious, and intermediate solutions. Such solutions are configurations of conditions that, through their consistent association with the outcome, can be seen as being sufficient to produce the latter (Ragin 2008, 124–44). Intermediate solutions "strike a balance between parsimony and complexity, based on the substantive and theoretical knowledge of the investigator" (175) and are thus the most informative.[1]

Macro csQCA Analysis

The macro-analysis is performed with the crisp-set variant of QCA (csQCA), a procedure in which conditions and outcomes are dichotomized into membership, coded as 1, or non-membership, coded as 0. For this analysis, the cases are the thirteen critical junctures identified in chapter 1 (table A9). The outcome is the degree of Europeanization of party campaigns at each critical juncture (MaO, *europ*), based on the findings presented in chapters 3–7. Six conditions have been included in the analysis: the constitutional significance of the reforms (MaC1, *consig*), the role played by regional parties (MaC2, *regpar*), the size of the country (MaC3, *size*), whether the country is in the centre or the periphery of the EU (MaC4, *cenpar*), the level of integration (MaC5, *integ*), and the country's prevailing attitudes to the EU (MaC6, *atteu*). Section A1 details the coding of the outcome and the conditions and table A10 presents the data matrix.

The first two conditions are intended to test the core proposition of the realist bargain model, i.e., that Europeanization is only present in bottom-up critical junctures, in which the reforms involved are of high constitutional significance and regional parties play an important role. The third and the fourth conditions test the connection between general country characteristics – i.e., which do not change across critical junctures – and the Europeanization of state restructuring. The realist bargain model does not formulate theoretical expectations as to the link between either size or centre-periphery location and Europeanization, so they are included as control conditions. Both could plausibly operate in either direction. In other words, Europeanization could be stronger in large countries – where regional autonomy tends to be higher – or, conversely, in smaller countries, which may be more likely to be open to the European influence. Likewise, Europeanization may be higher in countries located at the core of the EU, where the connection with the European dimension may be felt more strongly, or in those located in the periphery, where Europe may have a higher salience. The last two conditions, by contrast, are hypothesized to be positively associated with Europeanization, as the mechanisms postulated by the theoretical model are more likely to be at work when integration is higher and when a country's general attitude to integration is positive. In line with the macro-hypotheses 1–3 introduced in chapter 2, I expect MaC1 and MaC2 to be individually necessary and jointly sufficient for Europeanization to occur.

The results of the necessity test reported in table A11 indicate that two conditions are necessary – as pointed out by consistency scores of 1 – for Europeanization to occur: a) a high constitutional significance of the reforms at stake (MaC1=1) and b) regional parties playing an important role (MaC2=1). The results of the sufficiency test reported in table A12 and section A2 produce an intermediate solution consisting of four different causal paths leading to the outcome, thus showing that Europeanization occurs in countries characterized by a variety of conditions.[2] All the causal paths, however, include *consig* (MaC1) and *regpar* (MaC2), and the parsimonious solution indicates that those two conditions by themselves are sufficient to produce the outcome in all cases, the other ones being superfluous. High constitutional significance and an important role played by regional parties – which table A11 shows are always present together – are thus both necessary and sufficient for Europeanization to occur, as hypothesized. Although at a high level of aggregation, these results provide clear support to the conceptualizations and theorizations advanced in chapters 1 and 2. First, the fact that MaC1 and MaC2 are always present together validates the conceptual construct of the bottom-up form of state restructuring, of which they are the key properties. Second, the fact that the outcome occurs only when they are present signals that Europeanization only occurs when state restructuring takes a bottom-up form.

Micro fsQCA Analysis

To further validate the results obtained by the macro csQCA analysis, a micro fuzzy-set QCA (fsQCA) analysis has been performed. The fuzzy-set variant of QCA is centred on the notion of degrees of membership in categories – sets – which are coded on a scale from 0 to 1. The scale employed here is a six-value one that includes the following scores: 0; 0.17; 033, 0.67, 0.83; 1. This variant of QCA allows for a more fine-grained measurement of conditions and outcomes. For this analysis, the cases are the 127 party-election/referendum observations detailed in chapters 3–7 and reported in table A13. The two outcomes of the analysis are the *intensity* with which parties linked the European dimension and state restructuring (MiO1, *europ-i*) and the *direction* of the linkage made (MiO2, *europ-d*), i.e., whether it was used in favour or against state restructuring. Seven conditions have been included in the analysis[3]: whether a party is a statewide or a regional party (MiC1, *partyp*); the party's status within the party system (MiC2, *syssta*); its left-right position (MiC3, *leri*), its constitutional position (MiC4, *cospos*), the level of European integration (MiC5, *integ*), the party's attitudes to integration (MiC6, *attint*), and its attitudes to the EU (MiC7, *atteu*). Section A3 lists the party codes; section A4 outlines the six-value scales employed to code the outcome and the conditions; section A5 details the coding of the outcome and the conditions for each case and the sources on which it is based; and table A13 presents the data matrix.

The results of the necessity test reported in table A17 show that one condition is necessary – as indicated by a consistency score of 1 – and three others are almost always necessary – as indicated by consistency scores above 0.9 – for a party to engage in strategic use of Europe to support state restructuring (i.e., MiO2=1): a) having a radical constitutional position (*cospos*); b) being a regional party (*partyp*); c) being active at a time of high integration (*integ*); and d) having a positive attitude to integration (*attint*). The results of the sufficiency test reported in table A18 and section A6[4] – based on a frequency threshold of 1 and a consistency threshold of 0.85 – produce an intermediate solution consisting of three different causal paths leading to the outcome. The solution has an a overall consistency of 0.835714 and a coverage of 0.700180, meaning that it is sufficient to produce strategic use of Europe by a political party 83 percent of the time and that such configuration of conditions covers 70 percent of the cases. The presence of three causal paths shows that parties' decision to exploit the European dimension in relation to state restructuring is determined in complex ways through the interaction of several conditions.[5] The four conditions identified as necessary or almost always necessary (*partyp*, *cospos*, *integ*, *attint*), however, are present in each of the causal paths, i.e., they are shown to be both necessary and, in conjunction with other factors, sufficient most of the time to produce the outcome.

The crucial role played by these factors can be appreciated further from the data displayed in tables A14, A15, and A16, which reproduce excerpts from table A13. The first table shows that all cases of intense exploitation of the European dimension are of regional parties with a radical constitutional position and positive attitudes to integration, and operating at a time of high integration. Tables A15 and A16, by contrast, show that statewide parties' positive use of Europe has been very weak, despite generally favourable attitudes to both integration and the EU, and almost overshadowed by the occurrence of negative use.

Going back to the micro-hypotheses introduced in chapter 2 – leaving aside for the time being MicroH1, which has not been tested directly through this QCA analysis – we can see that they are all empirically supported. The results of the micro-analysis thus reinforce the picture painted by the macro-analysis and further substantiate the realist bargain model.

8.2 THE ARGUMENT RESTATED I: TWO FORMS OF STATE RESTRUCTURING

In light of the evidence reviewed in the preceding chapters and of the synoptic comparative analyses reported above, we can say that the conceptual distinction between the bottom-up and the top-down form of state restructuring finds empirical validation. The two forms consistently differ in terms of actor configuration, dynamic, and constitutional significance, and these differences have profound implications for understanding the phenomenon of state restructuring and for assessing the influence of the European dimension on it. As conceptualized in chapter 1, the top-down form emerges out of competition among statewide parties only, is enacted to improve the functioning of the state, and does not change the latter's constitutional nature. The reforms in Italy in the 1960s, in France in the 1980s, and in Denmark in the 2000s closely conform to this model.

Bottom-up state restructuring, by contrast, emerges out of competition between one or more regional (typically regional-nationalist) parties and their statewide rivals, is enacted in response to the challenge posed by the former to the latter in terms of electoral support and the territorial integrity of the state, and transforms the constitutional nature of the state. The reforms enacted in Belgium (in several rounds since 1970), Italy (in the 1990s–2000s), the UK (in the 1990s and the 2010s, after a failed attempt in the 1970s), and Spain (in the 1970s–80s and, potentially, in the 2010s) provide clear illustration of this second form. In all these cases, a regionalist challenge was at the heart of the process, the reforms were enacted by statewide parties to address the challenge, and they have entailed significant constitutional change. The experience of Italy illustrates the connection between regionalist challenges and strong state restructuring particularly well. The absence of a bottom-up demand for autonomy led to a delayed and weak implementation of the ordinary regions in the 1960s and 1970s. After the rise of the Lega Nord prompted a major strengthening of regional autonomy, under the terms of the 2001 constitutional reforms, the subsequent decline of the party has gone hand in hand, again, with an atrophying of the spirit embodied in the reforms, whose provisions have only patchily been implemented, notably as regards fiscal federalism (see, e.g., Brunazzo 2010; Ricolfi 2012; Antonini 2013; Massetti and Toubeau 2013; Baldini and Baldi 2014).

8.3 THE ARGUMENT RESTATED II: INTEGRATION INFLUENCES RESTRUCTURING VIA A REALIST BARGAIN PROCESS

Likewise, the evidence reviewed in the preceding chapters and the results of the QCA analyses delineate a clear pattern of how European integration influences state restructuring. None of the critical junctures conforming to the top-down model experienced Europeanization while all those conforming to the bottom-up model did so, to a greater or lesser extent. The strategic device of exploiting the European dimension – to a significant extent – to bolster the case for state restructuring has exclusively been employed by regional-nationalist parties, while statewide parties have made very little positive use of Europe or have actually used it in a negative direction.

Regional-Nationalist Parties' Reaction to the EU Context

As documented by a substantial literature and expected theoretically by the realist bargain model, regional-nationalist parties have reacted to the opportunities, incentives, and constraints generated by the EU context by manoeuvring on the constitutional spectrum and on that of attitudes to integration and to the EU. Four trajectories can be identified.[6] The first is exemplified by the SNP. Always committed to independence for Scotland, the SNP reversed its hostility to the EU in the 1980s and adopted a policy of independence in Europe centred on a positive exploitation of the opportunities and incentives offered by the EU context. The second trajectory is that of parties – including CiU, ERC, PC, and VU/N-VA – which have shifted, at different points in time, from demanding autonomy to adopting an independence in Europe position similar to the SNP's. For all of them the shift from an autonomist to a secessionist position has coincided with the adoption of a strategic focus on Europe. If, in the SNP's case, the European dimension has primarily been seen as facilitating the pursuit of a pre-existent objective, i.e., as an *opportunity*, in the case of the other four parties the EU can be seen as having generated *incentives* for them to change their policy. These five parties have all behaved as the realist bargain theory expected them to.

Two other parties, however, have followed a different trajectory. The VB, which has had a secessionist position since its birth, has moved from a pro-integration to a progressively more Eurosceptic position and largely failed to exploit the European dimension to boost support for itself and for Flanders's independence. This could be explained by the fact that the party decided to campaign primarily on an extreme-right platform, as opposed to one of radical nationalism (Govaert 1992, 24). Indeed, many scholars classify it as an extreme-right rather than as a regional-nationalist one (e.g., Deschouwer 2009, 88–90). The last trajectory is that of the LN. Initially the party moved in the same direction as the four parties following the second trajectory discussed above, that isized shifted from a federalist to an independentist position and placed the latter in a European frame. However, it has subsequently returned to an autonomist stance and has become increasingly critical of the EU (Chari et al. 2004; Giordano 2004; Quaglia 2008, 67–9; Massetti 2009, 521) amid a general rightward shift. As in the case of the VB, this could be explained by the decision to compete primarily on the left-right spectrum rather than the centre-periphery one. An additional factor setting the case of the LN apart from that of the other parties is that the latter all operate in regions with a long-established identity as a stateless nation whereas the LN's secessionist move was predicated on its attempt to forge a separate national identity for Northern Italians, which has had very little success. We can say that the LN was never a genuine regional-nationalist party but rather a party that tried and failed to become one. With the above caveats about the VB and the LN, we can thus see that the regional-nationalist parties analyzed in this book have behaved remarkably in line with the theoretical expectations of the realist bargain model. Thus, MicroH1 is also validated.

Properties of the European Dimension Exploited

As expected, regional-nationalist parties have exploited the European dimension selectively, stressing the elements they considered advantageous and ignoring or downplaying the others. Their rhetorical strategies focused on three properties in particular. At the most general level, they have linked their demands to Europe to make them appear modern and progressive rather than inward- and backward-looking, a charge often levelled at minority nationalism. The underlying argument has been that European integration is transforming the state system of the nineteenth century and the first half of the twentieth century, in which stateless nations found themselves trapped, and thus opened opportunities for the latter to acquire self-government within a new European political order. The rhetorical appeal to Europe was thus intended to give a powerful external legitimation to their demands for autonomy or independence. The second aspect of the European dimension regional-nationalist parties have consistently exploited is that economic integration – in the form of a customs union initially, of a single market later, and of a monetary union most recently – progressively removed most of the economic costs of independence for a small country by guaranteeing market access and regulatory – as well as, within the eurozone, monetary – continuity. Lastly, parties have stressed the importance of gaining access to the top table of EU decision-making – that of the European Council and of the Council of the EU – which is a prerogative of the member states. As discussed in chapter 2, the regions of federal member states do not have an effective channel of representation to the EU and can only gain access to the Council if they represent their respective state as a whole. In contrast, the principle of subsidiarity, which generated considerable hopes among those favouring the decentralization of power in the early 1990s (e.g., Scott et al. 1994), has been used to a more limited extent than one might have expected. Because the most intense exploitation of the European dimension has been made in connection with independence, however, this is not surprising as subsidiarity provides support for devolution within an existing state rather than for acquiring separate statehood.

The statewide parties that opposed state restructuring have been equally selective, and their use of Europe has been a mirror image of that made by the regional-nationalists. At a general level, they have appealed to Europe to argue that smaller political units and separation are against the tide of history as represented by the movement toward an ever closer union among the European countries. More specifically, they have tried to counter the appeal of the notion of getting a seat at the top table by arguing that smaller countries have less weight in EU decision-making, hence stateless nations such as Scotland or Catalonia can be more influential if they operate within the heavyweights UK or Spain rather than as independent states. To counter the appeal of independence in Europe, in particular, they have exploited the fact that there are no clear legal provisions for the creation of new member states within the EU to argue that a seceding region would find itself outside the Union and face the potential veto of one or more existing members in trying to regain access.

Use of "Europe" Over Time

In aggregate terms, the linkage between European integration and state restructuring has grown significantly over time, with a particular sharp discontinuity between the period after the Single European Act and the one before. Although, as we have seen in chapters 3 and 4, some parties deployed the linkage already in the 1960s, table A14 shows that intense use of Europe is a post-1985 phenomenon. The deepening of economic integration and the growing importance of EU decision-making since then are likely to be the key factors accounting for this growth. Such growth has not been a linear product of integration, though, as a closer look at Belgium and the UK – the two cases that offer the best opportunity to compare like with like over time – shows. While in Belgium the Europeanization of state restructuring was highest at T5, in the UK it peaked at T4 and subsequently remained at a high but slightly lower level. If we include the case of Spain too, the pattern that emerges is that regional-nationalist parties put the greatest emphasis on Europe the first time they campaigned on an independence in Europe ticket – e.g., the SNP, PC, and ERC in the early 1990s and the N-VA and CiU in the 2010s – and subsequently maintained the policy but placed less emphasis on it. The second reason why the intensity with which Europe is linked with state restructuring fluctuates over time rather than rising in line with integration is that it is heavily dependent on the salience of state restructuring at a given point in time and a party's decision to prioritize it in its campaigning.

The foci of parties' strategic use of Europe have remained broadly – and, perhaps, surprisingly – consistent over time, thus indicating that the specific features of each of the five periods I have identified have been less consequential than the broad nature of the process of European integration as such. Remarkably, the unprecedented degree of politicization of Europe in the most recent period does not appear to have led to a significant change in the way parties exploit the European dimension in connection with state restructuring. The most visible change appears to be the decline of the appeal of the Europe of the Regions notion. As we have seen in chapters 3 and 4, this exerted a powerful attraction on regional-nationalist parties for a long time up to the 1990s. They hoped that self-government for their stateless nations could be achieved in the context of a soft deconstruction of the existing state order set in motion by integration. Once it became clear, however, that the Europe of the Regions scenario would remain a distant dream, parties reoriented their strategies in the direction of achieving traditional statehood for their regions. Paradoxically, the realization that a Europe of the Regions was not a realistic objective took place after the EU institutions appeared to endorse a mild version of it.

Back to the Literature

How does this realist bargain account speak to the existing literature? Three main points should be emphasized. First, it demonstrates that the early contributions to this literature, dating from the mid-1970s, were correct in predicting that integration and state restructuring would be increasingly linked. Birch (1978) was arguably the most foresighted among these scholars, as the institutional incentives to independence in Europe he identified have indeed been proven to be central to the regional-nationalist parties' exploitation of the European dimension. Second, the account lends support to the economic integration-political disintegration thesis (e.g., Meadwell and Martin 1996; Alesina and Spolaore 1997) but also shows that the latter needs to be adapted and specified to apply satisfactorily to the EU context. It is important to acknowledge that the EU also places constraints on political fragmentation and that the crucial variable in determining the actual impact of the European dimension on state restructuring is how political parties strategically exploit the links between the two. Parties' choices, in turn, are shaped by their attitudes to integration and to the EU, thus showing that their decisions are determined by more than a mere calculus of the economic costs and benefits of independence. Third, it challenges two claims central to the multilevel governance literature: a) that the EU empowers the regions primarily through the effects of its cohesion policy (e.g., Marks 1993; Marks et al. 1996); and b) that the links between the EU and the regions have all but erased the traditional boundary between domestic and international politics (e.g., Hooghe and Marks 2001, 78; Piattoni 2010, 250). Cohesion policy has played only a marginal role in the cases of bottom-up state restructuring – where it has been overshadowed by much more powerful factors – and no role at all in the top-down ones, where Europeanization has been absent in the first place. By implication, this also invalidates the claims made by Hix and Goetz (2000) and Bartolini (2005), reviewed in the introduction, to the effect that EU policies have had a decentralizing effect at the domestic level. Likewise, the fact that the Europe-state restructuring linkage has been closely associated with secessionism and independence in Europe demonstrates that the European context only exercises significant influence when the politics of state restructuring ceases to be entirely domestic and acquires an international dimension. In other words, it points to the "realist" nature of the process, as defined in chapter 2, as opposed to a purported demise of the domestic/international dichotomy.

8.4 TO WHAT EXTENT DOES EUROPEAN INTEGRATION INFLUENCE STATE RESTRUCTURING?

Having seen how European integration influences state restructuring, we can now turn to the subsidiary question the book seeks to address: to what extent does it do so? As discussed in chapter 2, this question can only be answered in a more speculative and tentative manner as we do not have a robust way of isolating the influence of integration from that of many other factors. That said, it is worthwhile to review the evidence that has a bearing on this question to see to what extent it sheds light on it. In order to do so, we can disaggregate the question into three distinct subquestions. The first is whether the regional-nationalist parties that have strategically exploited Europe have benefited electorally from doing so and have thus been more successful than those who have not. The second is whether mass support for independence has grown as a result of such parties' playing the European card. In other words whether it has grown more significantly in the regions that have experienced more intense Europeanization compared to those in which parties have made little use of Europe. The third is whether state restructuring itself has gone further in the countries that have experienced more Europeanization compared to those that have not.

Have Regional-Nationalist Parties Benefited?

As seen in the preceding chapters, the short term electoral impact of playing the European card has often been mixed. Taking a longer term perspective, the electoral trajectories of the regional-nationalist parties analyzed in the book can be placed into three groups. The first, including the SNP, the N-VA, and ERC, is made up of those that have gained strength over time and become the first party in their region. All of them have exploited Europe considerably and this is likely to have contributed to their success. In the second group we can find CiU in Catalonia and PC in Wales, who have broadly maintained their status, a prominent one for the former and a more subordinate one for the latter. Although these parties have also played the European card, the latter much more than the former, it does not seem to have significantly affected their fortunes. In the case of CiU, this might also have been due to the fact that it has been competing against ERC, which has a longer and more consistent record of using Europe. The third group is made up of those who rose to prominence but subsequently declined or ceased to exist altogether: the RW and the VB in Belgium and the LN in Italy. The effective demise of the RW took place already by the late 1970s, so its experience is of limited interest from a longitudinal perspective. As we have already seen, the VB and the LN, which both moved from a pro- to an anti-integration stance and largely ceased to exploit the European dimension to bolster their autonomy demands, have lost electoral support, the former especially so. The pattern defined by these trajectories is thus that the three successful parties have played the European card intensely whereas the two unsuccessful ones have failed to do so and two other parties have not derived significant electoral benefits from it. In other words, using Europe appears to have been necessary, though not sufficient, for a regional-nationalist party to be successful.

Has Mass Support for Independence Increased?

To what extent has the electoral success of Europe-exploiting regional-nationalist parties been matched by an increase in mass support for independence itself? The two have been closely related in Scotland and Catalonia but less so in Flanders, while Northern Italy presents a contrasted picture. In Scotland, the rise of the SNP since 2007 has been accompanied, though not initially, by a concomitant rise is support for independence, culminating in the 45 percent scored by the Yes side in the 2014 referendum. As seen in chapter 7, support for independence has grown even more dramatically in Catalonia, outstripping the growth in electoral support for ERC. This has taken place in the context of a pro-secession mobilization at the grassroots level and the embrace of independence by the traditionally moderate CiU. In Flanders, however, support for independence has not grown proportionally to the rise of the N-VA. As seen in chapter 7, while there is strong demand for greater autonomy for the region, independence remains a minority preference, even among N-VA voters themselves (Swyngedouw and Abts 2011, 16–20; Abts et al. 2014, 219–45). While doing justice to the question of why this has been so is beyond the scope of the book, it is worth mentioning two prominent reasons that are likely to have a bearing on it. First, given that Flanders is the demographic and economic senior partner in Belgium's binational federation, if it wants greater autonomy it is in a strong position to obtain it. Second, the intractable question of what would happen to Brussels were Belgium to be partitioned (e.g., Bruxant 2010), makes it difficult, even for nationalists, to prefer an independent Flanders to a looser Belgian confederation. In Northern Italy, although we do not have good data, there is some indication that support for independence might have also grown, particularly in Veneto (e.g., Diamanti 2014), despite the Lega Nord's abandonment of its secessionist position and its increasing focus on left-right – as opposed to centre-periphery – issues. A complicating factor at play in this case is the uncertainty as to which territorial unit should/ would aim for independence. On the one hand, the Lega Nord's effort in building identification with Padania in the 1990s largely failed to create a distinct national identity in the North. On the other hand, in the region where secessionist sentiments appear to be strongest, Veneto, the emphasis is increasingly on the region rather than on Padania but no political party has so far articulated it effectively. Moreover, such sentiments appear to be rooted in a deep disillusion with the Italian state more than in the emergence of a separate national identification, either with Padania or with Veneto (Diamanti 2014). Although the pattern is not univocal, we can thus say that, on the whole, support for independence has increased in the regions in which "Europe-exploiting" regional-nationalist parties have been most successful.

Has State Restructuring Deepened?

Lastly, how do the two preceding aspects relate to the end question itself: has state restructuring gone farther because of European integration? The most clear-cut case is that of the UK, where the SNP has been a pioneer in playing the European card, grown to become the largest party in Scotland, boosted mass support for independence significantly, and, as a result, succeeded in forcing a profound transformation of the constitutional architecture of the state. In many ways Belgium's experience has been similar, in that the N-VA has also exploited Europe intensely, become the largest Flemish party, and succeeded in triggering further reform of the Belgian state, even in the absence of a major increase in support for independence among the electorate. Spain has the potential to follow in the footsteps of the UK and Belgium, but the outcome is still uncertain. ERC and, more recently, CiU/CDC have embraced independence in Europe, the former has succeeded in overtaking the traditionally more cautious CiU as Catalonia's largest party, and mass support for independence has grown dramatically. Although this has pushed state restructuring high on the Spanish political agenda, it is unclear whether reforms able to accommodate Catalonia's demands will eventually be put in place. Italy's trajectory has been the most divergent. As already mentioned, the ambitions embodied in the 2001 reform have only partially been fulfilled. This has taken place against the backdrop of the LN switching back from an independentist to an autonomist position, failing to generate a nationalist movement in the northern part of the country, adopting an increasingly Eurosceptic stance, prioritizing left-right issues, and losing electoral support.

In sum, what emerges from this brief analysis of the *to what extent* question is that regional-nationalist parties that have exploited the European dimension significantly have been more successful than those who have failed to do so, that mass support for independence has increased in most of the regions where parties have played the European card, and that reforms have also gone farthest – or have the potential to do so – in the countries where the politics of state restructuring has witnessed the most significant Europeanization. While, as pointed out above, we cannot measure the exact magnitude of the influence of European integration on strong state restructuring, the evidence is consistent with the hypothesis that the former has had a significant, albeit punctuated, positive – in the statistical sense – influence on the latter. We can thus say that the hypothesis passes a hoop test, as set out in chapter 2.

8.5 SUMMARY

This chapter has complemented the analysis conducted in chapters 3–7 by presenting the results of synoptic comparative analyses of *how* and the *extent to which* European integration influences state restructuring. The findings substantiate a realist bargain account of the connections between the two phenomena. There are two distinct forms of state restructuring, and European integration has a discernible influence only where and when restructuring follows a bottom-up dynamic. This is because the bulk of the positive strategic linkage between the two has been made by regional-nationalist parties, which are absent in top-down processes. Such linkage has been centred on the notion of independence in Europe and has focused in particular on economic integration as a facilitator of independence and the advantages of direct access to EU decision-making. On the whole, regional-nationalist parties that have played the European card have been more successful than those who have not done so, and restructuring has gone farther in those states that have experienced the most intense Europeanization of the politics of state reform. Although punctuated – i.e., dependent on the agency of regional-nationalist parties in bottom-up dynamics – the influence of European integration on state restructuring thus emerges as a significant and positive – in the statistical sense – one.

A limitation of the analysis presented in this book is that time and space constraints have prevented me from tracing the detailed decision-making processes that have led statewide parties to enact restructuring, i.e., from exploring at the micro level a key stage of the causal mechanism theorized. There is thus considerable scope for further research along these lines. While studying these processes would face considerable difficulties, especially in terms of access to decision-makers, it would also shed much light on the micro-mechanisms connecting European integration and state restructuring and would thus be well worth pursuing. Covell (1982) is an early example of the insights to be gained from this kind of micro-level analysis. The conclusions, below, remark on the implications of these findings for our understanding of the evolution of the state in the context of European integration.

Conclusions

The picture painted by the preceding chapters is thus a highly contrasted one. Instead of the widespread emergence of a regime of multilevel governance we find a sharply differentiated pattern. European integration has had a punctuated influence on the evolution of state structures rather than a uniform effect. Its influence has been considerable in some cases but virtually absent in others. In assessing the causal connections between European integration and state restructuring we thus need to account for these contrasts. Likewise, the intrastate/interstate boundary has not faded away; it is still highly relevant and is most clearly perforated only when prospects of secession or state dissolution naturally bring the international dimension into the domestic sphere.

As we have seen, the agency of regional-nationalist parties is the principal transmission belt through which Europe influences state restructuring. In turn, such parties have a significant presence only in areas of long-standing minority nationalism, whose roots typically predate the onset of integration. This implies that European integration's strong influence on the evolution of state structures is dependent on pre-existing regional nationalism. In other words, integration facilitates the flourishing of regional nationalism but does not create it. The case of Italy illustrates this well. The influence of European integration on state restructuring in Italy in the 1990s–early 2000s was closely linked to the Lega Nord's attempt to foster a separate national identity in the north of the country. Once it became clear that the attempt had failed and the party refocused itself on left-right issues, state restructuring and the European dimension were also quickly displaced from the political agenda. As seen in chapter 3, Europe was also notably absent from the first critical juncture of state reform in the 1960s–70s. Given that regional nationalism has deep roots in some Western European countries only and is unlikely to establish itself in the others, the implication is that integration can have a very uneven effect on the evolution of state structures across Europe.

If the Europeanization of state restructuring has been very uneven, as the realist bargain model expects, it has nonetheless been significant in the countries where the mechanisms highlighted in this book have been at work. The case of Belgium, of course, looms large here. A country at the heart of European integration in many respects, it is also the one that has transformed itself the most profoundly since 1950. Already twenty years ago, Newman (1995, 66) argued that "the Belgian state is a shell of its former self" and the process of restructuring has deepened further since. As Birch (1978) predicted almost forty years ago, European integration has the potential to be a "game changer" for regional-nationalist parties because it appears to offer the context within which independent statehood for stateless nations becomes both desirable and viable. Whether by pursuing independence as a sincere strategic goal or as a tactical move to secure autonomy as a second best, regional-nationalist parties have been able to reap considerable rewards from their exploitation of the European dimension. They have also benefited from the fact that their argument – i.e., that Europe facilitates independence – has resonated more with voters than the opposite argument – that state fragmentation runs counter to European integration – put forward by their statewide competitors.

While the argument that Europe makes independence viable for stateless nations has resonated with the electorate in several cases, secessions and state dissolutions remain very difficult in high-income, established democracies. The economic and political viability of small states is certainly enhanced in the context of the European Union compared to other areas of the world. This should be understood, however, primarily with regard to the *long-term* viability of such states. Even within the EU, the *short-term* costs of secession, especially transition and uncertainty costs, remain sufficiently high to deter a significant number of voters who might otherwise favour independent statehood for their region. The 2014 independence referendum in Scotland provided a clear illustration of this.

Worldwide, the number of states has increased and their average size has decreased throughout the nineteentth and twentieth centuries. If this has broadly gone hand in hand with the expansion of international trade, as Alesina and Spolaore (2003) have argued, it has also been closely linked to the spread of nationalism and democracy (Wimmer and Feinstein, 2010). Once democratization is achieved, it is likely that the effect of trade on the number and size of states may be less significant, which would explain why no secessions from established democracies have ever taken place (Dion 1996).

Moreover, as remarked in chapter 2, if the European Union context can be seen to facilitate transitions to independence, through both economic and political mechanisms, it also places a significant constraint in the shape of the lack of an accepted legal procedure for the internal creation of new member states. If the prevailing interpretation, as seen in chapter 7, is that a seceding region would be able to remain within the EU if it so wished, a substantial body of opinion argues that it would find itself outside the Union and would have to apply for membership, thus being subject to the potential veto of the rump state from which it seceded and/or of other states. Even if the former interpretation is indeed the correct one, a successful transition to independent membership would in any case be dependent on the positive outcome of complex negotiations and the goodwill of the other member states. It seems clear that while negotiated secessions and state dissolutions would be possible within the EU, unilateral ones would be extremely difficult, if not impossible, to achieve (see also Closa 2016).

If the strategy of independence in Europe has been a rewarding one for several regional-nationalist parties, its ability to deliver the ultimate goal has not been tested. Until it is, the credibility of the strategy is likely to be sustained and regional-nationalist parties can thus be expected to continue to benefit from it. If one of the regions with strong support for independence does manage to secede, however, the strategy would face its ultimate test and, depending on the outcome of that test, it might see its credibility destroyed. While secessions remain very difficult, it is not inconceivable that the test might come sooner or later. In light of the dramatic surge in support for the SNP in the wake of the 2014 referendum in Scotland and the continuing secessionist mobilization in Catalonia, either region may soon face such a test. The future viability of the strategy – and, consequently, the principal channel through which European integration affects state restructuring – thus depends crucially on whether it will be put to its ultimate test.

As things stand, regional nationalism is thus emboldened by European integration but at the same time it still faces significant obstacles in reaching its ultimate objective of independent statehood. The tension between these two forces produces the particular state restructuring dynamic that we have seen unfolding in several cases analyzed in this book. As minority nationalism is strengthened in the regions in which it already had deep roots, unitary states face mounting pressures, articulated by the regional-nationalist parties, to restructure themselves into federal or partially federal states. Once this first step is achieved, though, the pressure continues in the direction of forms of confederalism that would effectively grant one or more regions internal sovereignty within the existing state borders. This can be clearly seen in Belgium and the UK as well as, though facing much greater resistance, in Spain.

The preceding discussion points to what we can call the triple paradox of European integration and state restructuring. The first, and most obvious, paradox is that integration is driven by an ethos of ever closer union, but at the same time it generates incentives and opportunities that, under certain conditions, have a disaggregating effect. The outcome, however, is not a wholesale reshaping of the existing state system, as early advocates of a Europe of the Regions hoped, but highly uneven internal restructuring. The second paradox is that the strong form of state restructuring – i.e., the one most affected by European integration – leads to the emergence of con/federal constitutional orders that are more difficult to represent effectively in Brussels than the previous unitary states, on the grounds that only state governments have a stake in the key institutions of EU decision-making (e.g., Jeffery 1996; Bomberg and Peterson 1998; Hopkins 2002, 196). The problem is exacerbated in cases of asymmetrical restructuring (Dardanelli 2005a, 159) – e.g., the type leading to a partially federal constitutional order, as defined in chapter 1– so that the more asymmetrical the internal order, the more difficult it is to represent its variety of interests at the EU level. The third paradox is that integration and Europeanization are meant to make its member states more alike and more closely linked to each other but the state restructuring dynamics they facilitate actually lead to increasingly divergent constitutional orders. Because higher constitutionally diversity among its member states makes the effective functioning of the EU more difficult, this has significant consequences for European integration itself.

Brexit has thrown a sharp light on some of these tensions and paradoxes and added an extra dimension of complexity. On one side, the rising British Euroscepticism, heavily concentrated in England, has been fuelled, among other factors, by the perceived threat that the ultimate destination of European integration is the demise of the European national states as we know them. Regional-nationalists' embrace of Europe and the EU's own region-friendly policies have fed into these perceptions. On the other side, the marked variation in voting patterns in the referendum between England and Scotland has confirmed the different way the European Union is seen in a stateless nation such as Scotland. The SNP's threat that a UK's withdrawal from the EU rejected by Scotland would justify a new attempt at independence is, and will likely remain, an important issue in the governing of the UK post-Brexit and may eventually lead to a breakup of the state. Yet, an independent, and EU-member state, Scotland would face multiple challenges in managing its relations with an out-of-the-EU rump UK, which would remain its largest market and closest partner in so many respects. Thus Scotland's independence faces at the same time renewed urgency in the eyes of many and even more formidable political and economic obstacles than in 2014. On a wider scale, and highly simplifying the range of possible scenarios we can foresee, Brexit may signal the beginning of a process of reversal of integration or even of unravelling of the Union. If so, the dynamics investigated in this book would gradually cease to operate. Conversely, though, it may spur the remaining twenty-seven EU countries to deepen integration further. Were that to happen, the paradoxes of integration described above would be exacerbated further.

The connections between European integration and state restructuring are thus complex and multifaceted and their ramifications far-reaching, and more so than ever before in the post-Brexit world. McAllister's (1975, 196) remark "Thus the impact of the 'Community dimension' upon State structures is highly complex, full of paradox and irony" has been proven prescient indeed. In this book I have attempted to shed light on the nexus by analyzing these connections across space and over time. I hope the book deepens our understanding of the evolution of state structures in the context of European integration.

APPENDIX

Table A1
Typologies of State Structures

	Rokkan and Urwin (1982)	Elazar (1987)	Keating (1998a)	Lijphart (1999)	Keman (2001)	Svenden (2006)	Watts (2008)	Dardanelli (2017)
Austria	Mech. Feder.	Federation	Federalism	Federal and Cent.	Federal (0.05)	Federal	Federation	Federal (14)
Belgium	Unitary	Union	Federalism	Federal and Dec.	Federal (0.41)	Federal	Federation	Federal (14)
Denmark	Unitary	Federacy*	–	Unitary and Dec.	Unitary (-0.25)	Unitary dec.	Federacy*	Unitary with SA (7,17)
Finland	Unitary	Federacy**	Funct. reg.	Unitary and Dec.	Unitary (-0.96)	Unitary dec.	Federacy**	Unitary with SA (6, 17)
France	Unitary	–	Weak reg.	Unitary and Cent.	Unitary (-1.23)	Unitary dec.	–	Unitary (10)
Germany	Mech. Feder.	Federation	Federalism	Federal and Dec.	Federal (1.56)	Federal	Federation	Federal (15)
Ireland	Unitary	–	–	Unitary and Cent.	Unitary (-1.02)	–	–	Unitary (7)
Italy	Unitary	Union	Weak reg.	Unitary and Cent.	Federal (0.21)	Unitary dec.	Dec. union	Federal (15/16)
Netherlands	Union	CD unit. state	Funct. reg.	Semi-federal	Unitary (-0.74)	–	Dec. union	Unitary (10)
Norway	Unitary	–	–	Unitary and Dec.	Unitary (-0.26)	Unitary dec.	–	Unitary (12)
Portugal	Unitary	Federacy***	Funct. reg.	Unitary and Cent.	Unitary (-0.98)	Unitary cent.	Federacy***	Unitary with SA (0, 15)
Spain	Union	Union	Strong reg.	Semi-federal	Unitary (-0.23)	Regionalized	Federation	Federal (14/15)
Sweden	Unitary	–	Func.l reg.	Unitary and dec.	Unitary (-0.89)	Unitary dec.	–	Unitary (12)
Switzerland	Org. feder.	Federation	Federalism	Federal and dec.	Federal (1.72)	Federal	Federation	Federal (18)
UK	Union	Union	Funt.l reg.	Unitary and cent.	Unitary (-1.00)	Regionalized	Dec. union	Partially federal (10, 14, 12)

Note: *relative to the Faroes and Greenland; **relative to Åland; ***relative to Azores and Madeira.

Table A2
Typology of State Restructuring

A	*Strong – change of kind between categories*

A1.1	Unitary to federal: creation of strong regional governments or strengthening of existing regional governments covering the entire state population to a RAI-RSF score ≥13	A1.2	Federal to unitary: abolition or weakening of strong regional governments covering the entire state population to a RAI-RSF score <13
A2.1	Unitary to partially federal: creation of strong regional governments or strengthening of existing regional governments covering more than 10% but less than 100% of the state population to a RAI-RSF score ≥13	A2.2	Partially federal to unitary: abolition or weakening of strong regional governments covering more than 10% but less than 100% of the state population to a RAI-RSF score <13
A3.1	Unitary to unitary with SA: creation of strong regional governments or strengthening of existing regional governments covering less than 10% of the state population to a RAI-RSF score ≥13	A3.2	Unitary with SA to unitary: abolition or weakening of strong regional governments covering less than 10% of the state population to a RAI-RSF score <13
A4.1	Unitary with SA to federal: extension of strong regional governments to entire state population.	A4.2	Federal to unitary with SA: abolition or weakening of strong regional governments to a RAI-RSF score <13, covering more than 90% but less than 100% of the state population
A5.1	Unitary with SA to partially federal: extension of strong regional governments to more than 10% but less than 100% of the state population	A5.2	Partially federal to unitary with SA: abolition or weakening of strong regional government to a RAI-RSF score <13 covering more than 90% but less than 100% of the state population
A6.1	Partially federal to federal: extension of strong regional governments to entire state population	A6.2	Federal to partially federal: abolition or weakening of strong regional government to a RAI-RSF score <13 covering up to 90% of the state population

Table A2
Typology of State Restructuring (*continued*)

B	Weak – *change of degree within categories*		
B1.1	Introduction of macro-local governments	B1.2	Abolition of macro-local governments
B2.1	Introduction of weak regional governments (RAI-RSF score <13)	B2.2	Abolition of weak regional governments (RAI-RSF score <13)
B3.1	Replacement of macro-local governments with more autonomous but still weak regional governments (RAI-RSF score <13)	B3.2	Replacement of weak regional governments (RAI-RSF score <13) with macro-local governments with lower autonomy
B4.1	Replacement of weak regional governments (RAI-RSF score <13) with more autonomous macro-local governments	B4.2	Replacement of macro-local government with regional government with lower autonomy
B5.1	Increase in the autonomy of macro-local governments	B5.2	Decrease in the autonomy of macro-local governments
B6.1	Replacement of existing tier of macro-local governments with new tier of macro-local governments with higher autonomy	B6.2	Replacement of existing tier of macro-local governments with new tier of macro-local governments with lower autonomy
B7.1	Increase in the autonomy of weak regional governments, to a RAI-RSF score <13	B7.2	Decrease in the autonomy of weak regional governments (RAI-RSF score <13)
B8.1	Replacement of existing tier of weak regional governments with new tier of regional governments with higher but still weak autonomy (RAI-RSF score <13)	B8.2	Replacement of existing tier of weak regional governments (RAI-RSF score <13) with new tier of regional governments with lower autonomy
B9.1	Increase in the autonomy of regional governments in federal and (for regions already possessing an autonomy RAI-RSF score ≥13) partially federal or unitary with special autonomy states	B9.2	Decrease in the autonomy of regional governments in federal and (for regions already possessing an autonomy RAI-RSF score ≥13) partially federal or unitary with special autonomy states, to a RAI-RSF score ≥13
B10.1	Strong autonomy (RAI-RSF score ≥13) granted to more but not all regions in a partially federal state	B10.2	Some but not all regions in a partially federal state lose strong autonomy (RAI-RSF score ≥13)

Table A3
State Restructuring in Western Europe, 1950–2017

	State structures, 1950	Restructuring	State structures, 2017
Austria	Federal (15)	Weakening of the autonomy of strong regional governments: B9.2	Federal (14)
Belgium	Unitary (10)	Introduction of strong regional governments and formal transformation into a federal state: A1.1	Federal (14)
Denmark	Unitary with SA (6, 17)	Strengthening of traditional macro-local governments followed by replacement of the latter with regional governments with lower autonomy: (B5.1 > B4.2) > B3.1	Unitary with SA (7, 17)
Finland	Unitary with SA (1, 17)	Replacement of traditional macro-local units with new macro-local units with higher autonomy: B6.1	Unitary with SA (6, 17)
France	Unitary (7)	Strengthening of the traditional macro-local governments and introduction of regional governments with low autonomy: B2.1, B5.1	Unitary (10)
Germany	Federal (17)	Weakening of the autonomy of strong regional governments: B9.2	Federal (15)
Ireland	Unitary (7)	Introduction of weak regional governments: B2.1	Unitary (7)
Italy	Partially federal (8, 12)	Extension of strong regional government to the entire country: A6.1	Federal (15/16)
Netherlands	Unitary (8)	Strengthening of traditional macro-local governments: B5.1	Unitary (10)
Norway	Unitary (5)	Strengthening of traditional macro-local governments: B5.1	Unitary (12)
Portugal	Unitary (2)	Abolition of traditional macro-local governments and introduction of strong regional government for Azores and Madeira: B1.2, A3.1	Unitary with SA (0, 15)
Spain	Unitary (3)	Introduction of strong regional governments: A1.1	Federal (14/15)
Sweden	Unitary (12)	No change	Unitary (12)
Switzerland	Federal (18)	No change	Federal (18)
UK	Unitary with SA (10)	Extension of strong regional government to Scotland and Wales: A5.1	Partially federal (10, 14, 9, 12)

Table A4
Critical Junctures of State Restructuring

	Critical junctures
Belgium	BE1 (1968–70), BE2 (1978–80), BE3 (1987–89), BE4 (1991–93), BE5 (1999–2001), BE6 (2007–11)
Denmark	DK1 (1966–67), DK2 (2001–05)
France	FR1 (1981–82)
Italy	IT1 (1963–70, IT2 (1992–2001)
Spain	ES1 (1977–83), ES2 (2006–17)
UK	UK1 (1974–79), UK2 (1992–97), UK3 (2007–16)

Table A5
Dynamics of State Restructuring

	Bottom up	Top down
Regional demands for self-government	Present	Absent
Party competition	Regional and statewide parties	Statewide parties only
Objective	Holding state together	Improving administration
Extent of restructuring	Strong	Weak

Table A6
Critical Junctures by Type of Dynamic

		Bottom up	Top down
1	BE1	√	
2	BE2	√	
3	BE3	√	
4	BE4	√	
5	BE5	√	
6	BE6	√	
7	DK1		√
8	DK2		√
9	FR1		√
10	IT1		√
11	IT2	√	
12	ES1	√	
13	ES2	√	
14	UK1	√	
15	UK2	√	
16	UK3	√	
Total	16	12	4

Table A7
Stylized Features of the EU by Time Period

	T1 (1952–72)	T2 (1973–84)	T3 (1985–93)	T4 (1994–04)	T5 (2005–17)
Focus of integration	• Customs union • Negative integration • CAP	• Economic crisis • Enlargement adaptation • EMS • Shift to direct EP election	• Single market • Regional policy • Social Europe	• Monetary union • Failure of social Europe	• Euro crisis • High politicization • Brexit
Level of integration	Low	Low	Medium	High	Very high
Territorial scope	6	9–10	10–12	15	25–28
Institutional set-up	• Commission activism but Council fightback • Unanimity	• Council dominant • Unanimity	• Commission strong • QMV • EP starting to assert itself	• Weakening of Commission • Rise of EP	• European Council-EP bi-pole • German leadership

Table A8
Critical Junctures of State Restructuring and EU Membership

	Before EU membership	Since EU membership
Belgium	–	BE1, BE2, BE3, BE4, BE5, BE6
Denmark	DK1	DK2
France	–	FR1
Italy	–	IT1, IT2
Spain	ES1	ES2
UK	–	UK1, UK2, UK3

Table A9
Critical Junctures of State Restructuring by EU Time Period

	T1 (1952–72)	T2 (1973–84)	T3 (1985–93)	T4 (1994–2004)	T5 (2005–17)
Belgium	BE1	BE2	BE3, BE4	(BE5)	BE6
Denmark	[DK1]	–	–	DK2	–
France	–	FR1	–	–	–
Italy	IT1	–	–	IT2	–
Spain	–	[ES1]	–	–	ES2
UK	–	UK1	–	UK2	UK3
	2	3	2	3	3

SECTION A1 – MACRO CSQCA OUTCOME AND CONDITION CODES

Outcome

O: Degree of Europeanization (*europ*):
0=no significant Europeanization; 1=at least some Europeanization. IT1, FR1, DK2 are coded 0; BE1, BE2, BE3, BE4, BE6, ES2, IT2, UK1, UK2, UK3 are coded 1.

Conditions

C1: Constitutional significance (*consig*):
0=restructuring does not change the constitutional nature of the state; 1=restructuring changes the constitutional nature of the state. IT1, FR1, DK2 are coded 0; BE1, BE2, BE3, BE4, BE6, ES2, IT2, UK1, UK2, UK3 are coded 1.

C2: Regional parties (*regpar*):
0=regional parties played no significant part; 1=regional parties played a significant part. IT1, FR1, DK2 are coded 0; BE1, BE2, BE3, BE4, BE6, ES2, IT2, UK1, UK2, UK3 are coded 1.

C3: Size (*size*):
0=small state (population below 30m); 1=large state (population above 30m). BE1, BE2, BE3, BE4, BE6, DK2 are coded 0; FR1, IT1, IT2, ES2, UK1, UK2, UK3 are coded 1.

C4: Centre-periphery (*cenper*):
0=the state is not in the EU core (joined later); 1=the state is in the EU core (founding member). DK2, ES2, UK1, UK2, UK3 are coded 0; BE1, BE2, BE3, BE4, BE6, FR1, IT1, IT2 are coded 1.

C5: Integration (*integ*):
0=low level of integration (before the Single European Act); 1=high level of integration (after the Single European Act). BE1, BE2, FR1, IT1, UK1 are coded 0; BE3, BE4, BE6, DK2, ES2, IT2, UK2, UK3 are coded 1.

C6: Attitudes to the EU (*atteu*):
0=the state has an overall sceptical attitude to the EU; 1=the state has an overall positive attitudes to the EU. DK2, UK1, UK2, UK3 are coded 0; BE1, BE2, BE3, BE4, BE6, FR1, IT1, IT2, ES2 are coded 1.

Table A10
Macro csQCA Scores

CJ	C1 consig	C2 regpar	C3 size	C4 cenper	C5 integ	C6 atteu	O europ
BE1	1	1	0	1	0	1	1
BE2	1	1	0	1	0	1	1
BE3	1	1	0	1	1	1	1
BE4	1	1	0	1	1	1	1
BE6	1	1	0	1	1	1	1
DK2	0	0	0	0	1	0	0
ES2	1	1	1	0	1	1	1
FR1	0	0	1	1	0	1	0
IT1	0	0	1	1	0	1	0
IT2	1	1	1	1	1	1	1
UK1	1	1	1	0	0	0	1
UK2	1	1	1	0	1	0	1
UK3	1	1	1	0	1	0	1

Table A11
Macro csQCA Necessity

Conditions tested	Consistency
consig	**1.000000**
~consig	0.000000
regpar	**1.000000**
~regpar	0.000000
size	0.500000
~size	0.500000
cenper	0.600000
~cenper	0.400000
integ	0.700000
~integ	0.300000
atteu	0.700000
~atteu	0.300000

Note: necessary conditions shown in bold.

Table A12
Macro csQCA Sufficiency Truth Table

C1	C2	C3	C4	C5	C6	O1	Raw const.	No	Cases
1	1	0	1	1	1	1	1	3	BE3, BE4, BE6
1	1	1	0	1	1	1	1	1	ES2
1	1	0	1	0	1	1	1	2	BE1, BE2
1	1	1	0	1	0	1	1	2	UK2, UK3
1	1	1	1	1	1	1	1	1	IT2
1	1	1	0	0	0	1	1	1	UK1
0	0	1	1	0	1	0	0	2	FR1, IT1
0	0	0	0	1	0	0	0	1	DK2

SECTION A2 – MACRO CSQCA SUFFICIENCY, FSQCA2.5 OUTPUT

****
TRUTH TABLE ANALYSIS
****

File: F:/Data/2 csQCA macro data v3.1.csv
Model: europ = f(consig, regpar, size, cenper, integ, atteu)

Rows: 8

Algorithm: Quine-McCluskey
  True: 1

— COMPLEX SOLUTION —
frequency cutoff: 1.000000
consistency cutoff: 1.000000

	raw coverage	unique coverage	consistency
consig*regpar*size*~cenper*~atteu	0.300000	0.300000	1.000000
consig*regpar*~size*cenper*atteu	0.500000	0.500000	1.000000
consig*regpar*size*integ*atteu	0.200000	0.200000	1.000000

solution coverage: 1.000000
solution consistency: 1.000000

****
TRUTH TABLE ANALYSIS
****

File: F:/Data/2 csQCA macro data v3.1.csv
Model: europ = f(consig, regpar, size, cenper, integ, atteu)

Rows: 8

Algorithm: Quine-McCluskey
  True: 1-L

— PARSIMONIOUS SOLUTION —
frequency cutoff: 1.000000
consistency cutoff: 1.000000

	raw coverage	unique coverage	consistency
consig	1.000000	0.000000	1.000000
regpar	1.000000	0.000000	1.000000

solution coverage: 1.000000
solution consistency: 1.000000

****
TRUTH TABLE ANALYSIS
****

File: F:/Data/2 csQCA macro data v3.1.csv

Model: europ = f(atteu, integ, cenper, size, regpar, consig)

Rows: 16

Algorithm: Quine-McCluskey
True: 1
0 Matrix: oL
Don't Care: -

— INTERMEDIATE SOLUTION —
frequency cutoff: 1.000000
consistency cutoff: 1.000000
Assumptions:
atteu (present)
integ (present)
regpar (present)
consig (present)

	raw coverage	unique coverage	consistency
~cenper*size*regpar*consig	0.400000	0.300000	1.000000
atteu*cenper*~size*regpar*consig	0.500000	0.200000	1.000000
atteu*integ*cenper*regpar*consig	0.400000	0.000000	1.000000
atteu*integ*size*regpar*consig	0.200000	0.000000	1.000000

solution coverage: 1.000000
solution consistency: 1.000000

SECTION A3 — MICRO FSQCA PARTY CODES

T1

Italy (IT1): Democrazia Cristiana (DC63), Partito Comunista Italiano (PCI63), Partito Socialista Italiano (PSI63).

Belgium (BE1): Parti socialiste belge/Belgische Socialistische Partij (PSB68), Parti de la Liberté et du Progrès/Partij voor Vrijheid en Vooruitgang (PLP68), Christelijke Volkspartij (CVP68), Volksunie (VU68), Parti social-chrétien (PSC68), Rassemblement wallon (RW68).

T2

Belgium (BE2): Christelijke Volkspartij (CVP78), Socialistische Partij (SP78), Partij voor Vrijheid en Vooruitgang (PVV78), Volksunie (VU78), Parti socialiste

(PS78), Parti social-chrétien (PSC78), Parti des réformes et de la libérté 'de Wallonie (PRLW78), Rassemblement wallon (RW78).

UK (UK1): Conservative Party (CON-S79, CON-W 79), Labour Party (LAB-S79, LAB-W79), Scottish National Party (SNP79), Plaid Cymru (PC79).

France (FR1): Parti socialiste (PSF81), Parti communiste français (PCF81), Rassemblement pour la République (RPR81), Union pour la démocratie française (UDF81).

T3

Belgium (BE3, BE4): Christelijke Volkspartij (CVP87, CVP91), Socialistische Partij (SP87, SP91), Partij voor Vrijheid en Vooruitgang (PVV87, PVV91), Volksunie (VU87, VU91), Vlaams Blok (VB87, VB91), Parti socialiste (PS87, PS91, Parti réformateur libéral (PRL87, PRL91), Parti social chrétien (PSC87, PSC91).

T4

UK (UK2): Conservative Party (CON-S92, CON-W92, CON-S97, CON-W97), Labour Party (LAB-S92, LAB-W92, LAB-S97, LAB-W97), Scottish National Party (SNP92, SNP97), Plaid Cymru (PC92, PC97).

Italy (IT2): Democrazia Cristiana (DC92), Partito Democratico della Sinistra (PDS92, PDS94), Partito Socialista Italiano (PSI92), Lega Nord (LN92, LN94, LN96), Partito Popolare Italiano (PPI94), Forza Italia (FI94, FI96), L'Ulivo (UL96).

Denmark (DK2): Socialdemokraterne (DSD01, DSD05), Venstre (DV01, DV05), Det Konservative Folkeparti (DKF01, DKF05), Socialistik Folkeparti (SF01, SF05), Dansk Folkeparti (DF01, DF05), Det Radikale Venstre (DRV01, DRV05).

T5

Belgium (BE6): Christen-Democratisch & Vlaams (CD&V07, CD&V10), Open Vlaamse Liberalen en Democraten (O-VLD07, O-VLD10), Socialisten en Progressieven – Anders (SP.A07, SP.A10), Nieuw-Vlaamse Alliantie (N-VA07, N-VA10), Vlaams Belang (VB07, VB10), Parti socialiste (PS07, PS10), Mouvement réformateur (MR07, MR10), Centre démocrate humaniste (CDH07, CDH10), Ecolo (ECO07, ECO10).

UK (UK3): Conservative Party (CON-S07, CON-S11), Labour Party (LAB-S07, LAB-S11), Liberal Democrats (LD-S07, LD-S11), Scottish National Party (SNP07, SNP11), Yes Scotland (YS14), Better Together (BT14).

Spain (ES2): Convergència i Unió (CiU06, CiU10, CiU12),* Partit dels Socialistes de Catalunya (PS-C06, PS-C10, PS-C12, PS-C15), Esquerra Republicana de Catalunya (ERC06, ERC10, ERC12), Iniciativa per Catalunya Verds (ICV06, ICV10, ICV12), Partido Popular de Cataluña (PP-C06, PP-C10, PP-C12, PP-C15), Junts pel Sí (JxS15), Catalunya Sí Que Es Pot (CSQEP15), Candidatura d'Unitat Popular (CUP15), Ciutadans (Cs15).

SECTION A4 – MICRO FSQCA OUTCOME AND CONDITION CODES

Outcomes

O1: Use of Europe – intensity (*europ-i*):
0=no use of the European dimension in relation to state reform; 0.17=some marginal use; 0.33=moderate use; 0.67=significant use; 0.83=intense use; 1=European dimension 'placed at centre stage.'

O2: Use of Europe – direction (*europ-d*):
0=European dimension used against state reform; 0.5=mixed use; 1=European dimension used in favour of state reform.

Conditions

C1: Party type (*partyp*):
0=centralized statewide party; 0.17=decentralized statewide party; 0.33=autonomous branch of statewide party; 0.67=regional party with significant statewide links; 0.83=regional party with weak statewide links (including parties operating in several regions but not statewide); 1=regional party.

C2: Party system status (*syssta*):
0=virtually no chances of gaining office at either state or regional level; 0.17=very unlikely to gain office; 0.33=unlikely to gain office; 0.67=likely to gain office; 0.83=very likely to gain office; 1=virtually certain to gain office.

C3: Left-right position (*leri*):
0=far left; 0.17=left; 0.33=centre-left; 0.67=centre-right; 0.83=right; 1=far right.

C4: Constitutional position (*cospos*):
0=no increase or reduction in regional autonomy; 0.17=minor increase in regional autonomy; 0.33=moderate increase in regional autonomy; 0.67=significant increase in regional autonomy; 0.83=major increase in regional autonomy; 1=independence.

* For the sake of tractability, the CiU is treated here as a single party, although it was formally a federation of two distinct parties (Baras and Matas Dalmases 1998, 162–9).

C5: Depth of integration (*integ*):
0=no integration; 0.17=Paris and Rome treaties, completion of customs union; 0.33=EMS and direct election of the EP; 0.67=Single European Act; 0.83=Maastricht treaty; 1=Lisbon treaty.

C6: Attitudes to integration (*attint*):
0=total rejection of integration; 0.17=strong opposition to integration; 0.33=mostly critical of integration; 0.67=supportive of integration with some reservations; 0.83=strong support for integration; 1=enthusiastic support for integration.

C7: Attitudes to the EU (*atteu*):
0=support for withdrawal from the EU; 0.17=opposition to ratification of a treaty; 0.33=mostly critical; 0.67=mostly positive with some reservations; 0.83=strongly positive; 1=enthusiastic.

SECTION A5 – MICRO FSQCA CODING AND SOURCES*

O1 intensity (europ-i) and O2 direction (europ-d) of 'Use of Europe'

T1

IT1: DC63, PCI63 and PSI63 made no connections between European integration and the implementation of the regions (section 3.2) so they are all coded 0 for intensity and '-' for direction.

---

* The manifestos for the Belgian general elections of 1968, 1978, 1987, and 1991; the French presidential and parliamentary elections of 1981; the Danish general elections of 2001 and 2005, and the Italian general elections of 1992, 1994, and 1996 were collected by the Manifesto Research Group (Budge et al. 2001) and supplied by GESIS, (www.gesis.org/en/services/). The manifestos were made available in electronic form through a joint effort between the Zentralarchiv für Empirische. Sozialforschung (ZA), Wissenschaftszentrum Berlin (WZB), the Vrije Universiteit Amsterdam (VU), and the Party Manifestoes Project. MS Word transcription were made available by Paul Pennings and Hans Keman, Vrije Universiteit Amsterdam, Comparative Electronic Manifestos Project, in cooperation with the Social Science Research Centre Berlin (Andrea Volkens, Hans-Dieter Klingemann) the Zentralarchiv für empirische Sozialforschung, GESIS, Universität zu Köln, and the Manifesto Research Group (chairman: Ian Budge). Financed by the Netherlands Organization for Scientific Research (NWO project 480-42-005). The manifestos for the Belgian general elections of 2007 and 2010; the Italian general election of 1963, the Catalan regional elections of 2010 and 2012 and the Catalan referendum of 2006; the UK general elections of 1992 and 1997; the Scottish and Welsh referendums of 1979, the Scottish referendum of 2014 and the Scottish regional elections of 2007 and 2011; and the other documents were collected/accessed by the author.

BE1: CVP68, PSC68, and PSB68 made no connections between the European dimension and state reform. PLP68 made some use of Europe to undermine calls for the federalization of Belgium. The RW placed its call for Wallonia's autonomy within a European context but did not significantly exploit the latter to strengthen its demand. The VU made moderate use of the European dimension to buttress its case for federalism (section 3.3). CVP68, PSC68 and PSB68 are coded 0, PLP68 and RW68 are coded 0.17, and VU68 is coded 0.33 for intensity. As for direction, PLP68 is coded 0, RW68 and VU68 are coded 1, and CVP68, PSC68, and PSB68 are coded '-'.

T2

UK1: in Scotland, the SNP placed independence in a European context but did not exploit the latter in its campaign, nor did the Labour Party. The No campaign run jointly by the Conservatives and the business organizations made some limited use of the European dimension to undermine the rationale for devolution (section 4.2). SNP79 is coded 0.17 for intensity and 1 for direction, LAB-S79 is coded 0 for intensity and '-' for direction, CON-S79 is coded 0.17 for intensity and 0 for direction. In Wales, neither Labour nor the Conservatives linked Europe and devolution while PC placed its support for self-government for Wales in a European dimension. CON-W79 and LAB-W79 are coded 0 for intensity and '-' for direction, PC79 is coded 0.33 for intensity and 1 for direction.

BE2: RW78 placed its demands for Wallonia's autonomy in a European context but did not explicitly used the latter to support such demands. All the other parties made no links between the development of regionalization and Europe (section 4.3). RW78 is coded 0.17 for intensity and 1 for direction. CVP78, SP78, PVV78, VU78, PS78, PSC78, PRLW78 are coded 0 for intensity and '-' for direction.

FR1: None of the parties made links between European integration and decentralization (section 4.4) so PSF81, PCF81, RPR81, UDF81 are all coded 0 for intensity and '-' for direction.

T3

BE3: the CVP and, to a greater extent, the VU made a positive connectiom between European integration and federalization. PS87, PRL87, PSC87 made some modest links between the European and the regional level while SP87 and PVV 87 failed to do so (section 5.2). CVP87 and VU87 are coded 0.33 and 0.67, respectively, for intensity and 1 for direction. PS87, PRL87 and PSC87 are coded 0.17 for intensity and 1 for direction while SP87 and PVV87 are coded 0 for intensity and '-' for direction.

BE4: CVP91, PSC91, PS91, PVV91, PRL91 made no connections between Europe and state reform. VB91 placed Flanders's independence within the EU context but made little effort to exploit the latter, ECO91 made some links between Europe and state reform, the SP made moderate use of Europe to strenghten its federalist position while the VU exploited the European dimension considerably (section 5.2). VB91 and ECO91 are coded 0.17, SP91 is coded 0.33, and VU91 is coded 0.67, respectively, for intensity, and 1 for direction, the other parties are all coded 0 for intensity and '-' for direction.

T4

UK2: in the 1992 general election campaign, the Conservatives made considerable use of the European dimension to attack the case for a Scottish parliament but did not do so with regard to a Welsh assembly. Labour placed its support for devolution in a European dimension but did not exploit the latter to bolster support for it. Both the SNP and PC ran a heavily Europeanized campaign (section 6.2). CON-S92 is coded 0.67 for intensity and 0 for direction; CON-W92 is coded 0 for intensity and '-' for direction, LAB-S92 and LAB-W92 are coded 0.17 for intensity and 1 for direction, while SNP92 and PC92 are coded 1 for both intensity and direction. In the 1997 general election campaign, the Conservatives continued to exploit Europe to undermine support for a Scottish parliament, although to a lesser extent than in 1992, and neglected again to do so in relation to a Welsh assembly. The Labour Party maintained a European framework for its devolution policy but largely failed to exploit it in the campaign. Europe was heavily exploited, in contrast, by PC and, though to a lesser extent than in the previous election, the SNP (section 6.2). CON-S97 is coded 0.33 for intensity and 0 for direction; CON-W97 is coded 0 for intensity and '-' for direction, LAB-S97 and LAB-W97 are coded 0.17 for intensity and 1 for direction; SNP97 is coded 0.67 for intensity and 1 for direction and PC97 is coded 1 for both intensity and direction.

IT2: in the 1992 general election campaign, the DC made some modest appeals to Europe to undermine the case for further devolution while the LN placed its call for federalism in a European dimension (section 6.3). The PDS and the PSI did not link integration and state restructuring. DC92 is coded 0.17 for intensity and 0 for direction, LN92 is coded 0.33 for intensity and 1 for direction while PDS92 and PSI92 are coded 0 for intensity and '-' for direction. In the 1994 general election campaign, none of the parties linked Europe and state reform (section 6.3). PDS94, FI94, LN94, and PPI94 are all coded 0 for intensity and '-' for direction. In the 1996 general election campaign, the OT coalition linked only very weakly the European dimension and state reform while the LN exploited Europe considerably. FI did not link the two (section 6.3). UL96 and LN96 are coded 0.17 and 0.83, respectively, for intensity and 1 for direction whereas FI96 is coded 0 for intensity and '-' for direction.

DK2: in the 2001 general election campaign, none of the parties linked Europe and state reform (section 6.4). DSD01, DV01, DKF01, SF01, DF01, DRV01 are all coded 0 for intensity and '-' for direction. The same was true for the 2005 general election campaign (section 6.4). DSD05, DV05, DKF05, SF05, DF05, DRV05 are all coded 0 for intensity and '-' for direction.

T5

BE6: in the 2007 general election campaign, CD&V07, O-VLD07, SP.A07, PS07, MR07, CDH07, ECO07 did not link Europe and state reform (section 7.2). They are all coded 0 for intensity and '-' for direction. The VB made use of the European dimension while the N-VA exploited it considerably. VB07 and N-VA07 are coded 0.33 and 0.83, respectively, for intensity and 1 for direction. A very similar situation occurred for the 2010 general election, but VB's use of Europe was weaker whereas the N-VA's was stronger (section 7.2). VB10 and N-VA10 are coded 0.17 and 1, respectively, for intensity and 1 for direction. The other parties are all coded 0 for intensity and '-' for direction.

UK3: in the campaign for the 2007 regional election in Scotland, none of the parties linked Europe and Scotland's constitutional status significantly (7.3). SNP07, LAB-S07, LD-S07, and CON-S07 are all coded 0 for intensity and '-' for direction. In the campaign for the 2011 Scottish election, all the statewide parties failed to link Europe and constitutional reform while the SNP exploited the European dimension to stress the continuity it would bring in the transition to independence (section 7.3). SNP11 is coded 0.67 for intensity and 1 for direction, the other parties are all coded 0 for intensity and '-' for direction. In the campaign for the 2014 independence referendum, the SNP-led Yes camp exploited 'Europe' significantly while the No camp bringing together the three main statewide parties did so to a lesser extent (section 7.3). YS14 is coded 0.67 for intensity and 1 for direction while BT14 is coded 0.33 for intensity and 0 for direction.

ES2: in the campaign for the 2006 referendum, the CiU and the PS-C made some use of the European dimension while ICV, ERC and the PP-C failed to do so (section 7.4). CiU06 and PS-C06 are coded 0.17 for intensity and 1 for direction. ICV06, ERC06, and PP-C06 are coded 0 for intensity and '-' for direction. In the campaign for the 2010 regional election, the CiU and the PS-C placed Catalonia within a European context but did not use it to support a change of constitutional status. ERC reaffirmed its commitment for Catalonia to achieve independence as an EU member state but did not exploit the European dimension further to bolster its policy and ICV campaigned on similar lines. The PP-C made no connections between Europe and Catalonia's constitutional status (section 7.4). CiU10 and PS-C10 are coded 0.17 for intensity and 1 for direction, ERC10 and ICV10 are coded 0.33 for intensity and 1 for direction, and PP-C10 is coded 0 for intensity and '-' for direction. In the campaign for the 2012 regional election, both CiU and ERC exploited Europe considerably, while PS-C and, even less so, ICV did so only modestly and the PP-C made some use of it to attack independence (section 7.4). CiU12 and ERC12 are coded 0.83 for intensity and 1 for direction, PS-C12 and ICV12 are coded 0.33 and 0.17, respectively, for intensity and 1 for direction and PP-C12 is coded 0.17 for intensity and 0 for direction. In the campaign for the 2015 regional election, JxS framed Catalonia's independence as a transition to a status of EU member state and leveraged the European dimension as a safeguard for the process of secession. CSQEP made moderate use of the European dimension to argue that the state reform it advocated would have granted Catalonia direct access to the EU institutions. Ciutadans and, to a lesser extent, the PP-C made a 'negative' use of the European dimension to undermine the appeal of independence. The PS-C and CUP did not link Europe and state reform (section 7.4). JxS15 is coded 0.67 for intensity and 1 for direction, CSQEP15 is coded 0.33 for intensity and 1 for direction, Cs15 is coded 0.67 for intensity and 0 for direction, PP-C is coded is coded 0.33 for intensity and 0 for direction, and PS-C15 and CUP15 are coded 0 for intensity and '-' for direction.

C1 – Party type (partyp)

T1

IT1: all parties were centralized statewide parties (Allum 1969, 207-14, 246; Leonardi and Wertman 1989, 136-45; Cotta and Verzichelli 2007, 35-66). DC63, PCI63, PSI63 are all coded 0.

BE1: the PSB and the PLP were statewide parties, the former with a more decentralized structure than the latter (Mabille and Lorwin 1977; Rudd 1988; Deschouwer 2009, 77-83). The CVP and the PSC were by 1968 separate parties only active in their respective language region but retained cooperation in government formation (Lamberts 2004; Deschouwer 2009, 75-7, 152). The VU and the RW were regional parties (Deschouwer 2009, 84-7). PLP68 is coded 0, PSB68 is coded 0.17, CVP68 and PSC68 are coded 0.67, and VU68 and RW68 are coded 1.

T2

UK1: the Scottish branches of the Conservative and Labour parties had some limited autonomy from the statewide parties while the Welsh branches had even less autonomy. The SNP and the PC were regional parties (Kellas 1984, 114-22; Tanner 2000, 276-86; Melding 2005; McAllister 2001). CON-S79 and LAB-S79 are coded 0.17, CON-W79 and LAB-W79 are coded 0, SNP79 and PC79 are coded 1.

BE2: the CVP, the SP, the PVV, the PS, the PSC, and the PRL were all regional parties maintaining cooperation with their ideological 'siblings' across the language divide in government formation. The VU and the RW were regional parties (Deschouwer 2009, 75-87, 152). CVP78, SP78, PVV78, PS78, PSC78, PRLW78 are coded 0.67, VU78 and RW78 are coded 1.

FR1: all parties were centralized statewide parties (Courtois and Peschanski 1988; Ladrech and Marlière 1999; Frears 1988; Lauber 1988) so PSF81, PCF81, RPR81, UDF81 are all coded 0.

T3

BE3: all parties maintained the categorizations listed at BE2, save the RW which was no longer active. CVP87, SP87, PVV87, PS87, PSC87, PRL87 are coded 0.67, VU78 is coded 1.

BE4: all parties had the same categorization as at BE3, save the VB which was a new regional party (Deschouwer 2009, 75–87, 152). CVP91, SP91, PVV91, PS91, PSC91, PRL91 are coded 0.67, VU91 and VB91 are coded 1.

T4

UK2: all parties maintained the categorizations listed at UK1. CON-S792, CON-S97, LAB-S92 and LAB-S97 are coded 0.17; CON-W92, CON-W97, LAB-W92 and LAB-W97 are coded 0; SNP92, SNP97, PC92, PC97 are coded 1.

IT2: the DC, the PDS – the PCI's successor – and the PSI remained centralized statewide parties. The LN was a macro-regional party, active in the Northern regions. The PPI was the successor of the DC for the 1994 election. FI was a centralized statewide party. The UL coalition was centred on the PDS and its coding is based on the latter (Cotta and Verzichelli 2007, 35–66; Diamanti 1993). DC92, PDS92, PSI92, PPI94, PDS94, FI94, FI96, UL96 are coded 0; LN92, LN94 and LN96 are coded 0.83.

DK2: all parties were centralized statewide parties (Bille 1994). DSD01, DV01, DKF01, SF01, DF01, DRV01, DSD05, DV05, DKF05, SF05, DF05, DRV05 are all coded 0.

T5

BE6: the practice of 'symmetrical' governing coalitions, which require cooperation between parties of the same ideological orientation, had come to an end so the 'traditional' parties were by then close to being regional parties while Ecolo had close links and a joint parliamentary group with the Flemish greens (Deschouwer, 2009: 152-3). The N-VA, the VU's successor, was a new regional party which ran in a cartel with the CD&V for the 2007 election (Govaert 2002; Mabille 2011, 401). CD&V07, CD&V10, O-VLD07, O-VLD10, SP.A07, SP.A10, PS07, PS10, MR07, MR10, CDH07, CDH10 and N-VA07 are coded 0.83, ECO07 and ECO10 are coded 0.67; N-VA10, VB07 and VB10 are coded 1.

UK3: the Scottish branches of the Conservative, Labour and Liberal Democratic parties increased their autonomy following devolution (Lynch and Birrell 2004;

Fabre 2011) while the SNP maintained its categorization. The YS campaigning body is coded as a regional party while the BT camp is coded as a statewide party with some autonomy. CON-S07, CON-S11, LAB-S07, LAB-S11, LD-S07, LD-S11, and BT14 are coded 0.33; SNP07, SNP11 and YS14 are coded 1.

ES2: CiU, the ERC, the JxS coalition between them, and the CUP were regional parties. The PP-C was a regional branch with little autonomy from the statewide party. Ciutadans was a recently 'nationalized' party with its roots and leadership closely linked to Catalonia. The PS-C was a regional party affiliated with the statewide PSOE. It could be categorized as either a regional party with statewide links or an autonomous branch of a statewide party, the former has been chosen here. Both ICV and CSQEP were regional parties with close links with the statewide Izquierda Unida and Podemos (Baras and Matas Dalmases 1998a; Roller and Van Houten 2003; Van Biezen 2003, 93–102; Fabre 2011; Rodriguez and Barrio 2015, 10; Orriols and Cordero 2016, 3). CiU06, CiU10, CiU12, ERC06, ERC10, ERC12, JxS15, and CUP15 are coded 1; ICV06, ICV10, ICV12 and CSQEP15 are coded 0.83; PS-C06, PS-C10, PS-C12, and PS-C15 are coded 0.67; Cs15 is coded 0.17; and PP-C06, PP-C10, PP-C12, and PP-C15 are coded 0.

C2 – Party system status (syssta)

T1

IT1: since 1948, the DC had always been the main governing party while the PCI had considered uncoalitionable and the PSI had become a partner of the DC (section 3.2). DC63 is coded 1, PSI63 is coded 0.67, and PCI63 is coded 0.

BE1: the CVP and the PSC were together the largest 'party family' and were virtually indispensable in any governing coalition. The PSB was the second largest party and a regular participant in coalitions but with a less central status in the system. The PLP was the traditional third party and had participated in fewer coalitions so had a more marginal system status. The VU and the RW were outsider parties with a radical constitutional agenda and were largely considered 'uncoalitionable' (section 3.3). CVP68 and PSC68 are coded 1, PSB68 is coded 0.83, PLP68 is coded 0.67, and VU68 and RW68 are coded 0.17.

T2

UK1: at the time of the 1979 referendums, the Conservative party had a high probability of winning the next election after the governing Labour Party had been increasingly weakened. The SNP and the PC had no chance of gaining office at central level (section 4.2). CON-S79 and CON-W79 are coded 0.83, LAB-S79 and LAB-W79 are coded 0.33, and SNP79 and PC79 are coded 0.

BE2: the CVP and the PSC as well as the PS and the SP maintained their status while the PVV and the PRL were in a slightly stronger position than the PLP at T1. The 'stigma' attached to the VU and the RW had largely disappeared and both had been briefly in government but they approached the 1978 election in a weak position, the RW especially so (section 4.3). CVP78 and PSC78 are coded 1, PS78, SP78, PVV78, and PRLW78 are coded 0.83, VU78 is coded 0.33, and RW78 is coded 0.17.

FR1: the RPR and the UDF had been in office throughout the Fifth Republic while the PSF and the PCF had been in the opposition. In the 1978 parliamentary election, though, the two alliances had approximately equal strength (section 4.4). RPR81 and UDF81 are coded 0.83 while PSF81 and PCF81 are coded 0.67.

T3

BE3: most parties maintained roughly the status they had at T2, save the two liberal parties which were weakened by the decline of the PVV (section 5.2). CVP87 and PSC87 are coded 1, PS87 and SP87 are coded 0.83, PVV87 and PRL87 are coded 0.67, and VU87 is coded 0.33.

BE4: the liberal parties strengthened their position while the VB was considered totally uncoalitionable (section 5.2). CVP91 and PSC91 are coded 1, PS91, SP91, PVV91, PRL91 are coded 0.83, VU91 is coded 0.33, and VB91 is coded 0.

T4

UK2: in the 1992 election, the incumbent Conservatives were in a slightly stronger position than the revitalized Labour Party while the SNP and the PC had the same status as at T2 (section 6.2). CON-S92 and CON-W92 are coded 0.83, LAB-S92 and LAB-W92 are coded 0.67, and SNP92 and PC92 are coded 0. In the 1997 election, the rejuvenated Labour Party was highly likely to win and the Conservatives to lose. The SNP and the PC maintained their status (section 6.2). LAB-S97 and LAB-W97 are coded 0.83, CON-S97 and CON-W97 are coded 0.33, and SNP97 and PC97 are coded 0.

IT2: in the 1992 election, the DC's status was weakened compared to T1 while that of the PDS – the PCI's successor – was stronger. The PSI had roughly maintained its status while the LN was largely considered uncoalitionable (section 6.3). DC92 is coded 0.83, PDS92 and PSI92 are coded 0.67 and LN92 is coded 0.17. In the 1994 election, the alliance between FI and the LN was more likely to win than the one led by the PDS. The PPI had little chance of success (section 6.3). FI94 and LN94 are coded 0.83, PDS94 is coded 0.67 and PPI94 is coded 0.33. In the 1996 election, the UL alliance and the one led by FI had roughly equal chances of gaining office, the standalone LN was highly unlikely to gain office (section 6.3). UL96 is coded 0.83, FI96 is coded 0.83 and LN96 is coded 0.17.

DK2: in the 2001 election the alliance formed by the DV and the DKF was slightly more likely to win than the one grouping the DSD and the DRV. The DF and the SF were unlikely to be included in a coalition (section 6.4). DV01 and DKF01 are coded 0.83, DSD01 and DRV01 are coded 0.67, DF01 and SF01 are coded 0.17. Broadly the same picture held for the 2005 election (section 6.4). DV05 and DKF05 are coded 0.83, DSD05 and DRV05 are coded 0.67, DF05 and SF05 are coded 0.17.

T5

BE6: in the 2007 general election campaign, the cartel between the CD&V and the N-VA and the PS were the dominant parties on the two sides of the linguistic divide and were almost certain to gain office. The SP.A and the two liberal parties were less likely while Ecolo was unlikely and the VB was still uncoalitionable (section 7.2). CD&V07, N-VA07 and PS07 are coded 1, O-VLD07, MR07, SP.A07, CDH07 are coded 0.67, ECO07 is coded 0.33 and VB07 is coded 0. A broadly similar picture was true for the 2010 general election campaign, save that the standalone N-VA was by then less likely to gain office (section 7.2). CD&V10, and PS10 are coded 1, O-VLD10, N-VA10, MR10, SP.A10, CDH10 are coded 0.67, ECO10 is coded 0.33 and VB10 is coded 0.

UK3: in the 2007 election, the coalition between Labour and the Liberal Democrats, on the one hand, and the SNP on the other were roughly equally likely to win office while the Conservatives were highly unlikely to do so (section 7.3). LAB-S07, LD-S07, SNP07 are coded 0.67, CON-S07 is coded 0.17. In the 2011 election, the SNP was more likely to gain office than Labour and the Liberal Democrats while the Conservatives maintained their status (section 7.3). SNP11 is coded 0.83, LAB-S11 and LD-S11 are coded 0.67 and CON-S11 are coded 0.17. The two camps in the 2014 referendum are both coded 0.5.

ES2: at the time of the 2006 referendum, a coalition formed by the PS-C, the ERC and the ICV was in office while CiU and the PP-C were in opposition. The former, though, retained a fair likelihood of winning office at the next election while the PP-C was highly unlikely to do so (section 7.4). PS-C06, ERC06 and ICV06 are coded 0.83, CiU06 is coded 0.67 and PP-C06 is coded 0.17. In the 2010 election, in contrast, CiU was likely to win and the three left-wing parties to lose, while the PP-C was in the same situation (section 7.4). CiU10 is coded 0.83, PS-C10, ERC10, ICV10 are coded 0.33, PP-C10 is coded 0.17. In the 2012 election, CiU was weaker but likely to retain office while ERC was rising and the other parties maintained their status (section 7.4). CiU12 is coded 0.83, ERC12 is coded 0.67, PS-C12 and ICV12 are coded 0.33, and PP-C12 is coded 0.17. In the 2015 election, JxS was highly likely to win office. The other parties, the CUP, the PP-C and Ciutadans especially, had a low probability of winning office (section 7.4). JxS is coded 0.83; CSQEP15 and PS-C15 are coded 0.33; and CUP15, PP-C15 and Cs15 are coded 0.17.

C3 – Left-right position (leri)

T1

IT1: the DC was a classic Christian democratic party, the PCI was a radical, communist party while the PSI was a socialist party who had just severed its links with the PCI and decided to ally itself with the DC (Allum 1969; Cotta and Verzichelli 2007, 35–66). DC63 is coded 0.67, PCI63 is coded 0 and PSI63 is coded 0.33.

BE1: the CVP and the PSC were Christian democratic parties, centrist on economic matters and culturally conservative (Hill 1969, 78–83; Dewachter 1987, 293; Lamberts 2004; Deschouwer 2009, 75–7). The VU was also predominantly Catholic and centrist (Herremans 1962, 11–14; Dewachter 1987, 300; De Winter 1998). The PSB was a pragmatic social democratic party, frequently in coalition with the Christian-democrats (Mabille and Lorwin 1977; Hill 1969, 83–8; Dewachter 1987, 293; Deschouwer 2009, 77–83). The RW brought together both liberals and socialists but its economic program was closer to the former than to the latter; it is thus best categorized as a centre-left party (Buelens and Van Dyck 1998; Delforge 2003, 4; Dewachter 1987, 300). The PLP was a centre-right liberal party, conservative on economic matters (Rudd 1988; Hill 1969, 88–90). PSB68 and RW68 are coded 0.33. CVP68, PSC68, VU68 are coded 0.67, and PLP68 is coded 0.83.

T2

UK1: the Conservatives had a rightist position combining economic liberalism and cultural conservatism (Butler and Kavanagh 1980, 60–85). The Labour Party had a mainstream socialist position (Butler and Kavanagh 1980, 47–59). The SNP and the PC had a broadly left-of-centre position (Bennie et al. 1997, 82–3; McAllister 2001, 156–84). LAB-S79 and LAB-W79 are coded 0.17, SNP79 and PC79 are coded 0.33, CON-S79 and CON-W79 are coded 0.83.

BE2: the PVV and the PRLW, and the PS and SP inherited the positions of their unified predecessors while the other parties broadly maintained their positions (Deschouwer 2009, 77–83). PS78, SP78, and RW78 are coded 0.33, CVP78, PSC78, VU78 are coded 0.67, PVV78 and PRLW78 are coded 0.83.

FR1: the PS was a mainstream socialist party, the PCF was an orthodox communist party, the UDF was a centre-right liberal party and the RPR was a conservative party (Courtois and Peschanski 1988; Ladrech and Marlière 1999;

Frears 1988; Lauber 1988) so PCF81 is coded 0, PSF81 is coded 0.17, UDF81 is coded 0.67 and RPR81 is coded 0.83.

T3

BE3: all parties maintained their position so PS87 and SP87 are coded 0.33, CVP87, PSC87, VU87 are coded 0.67, PVV87 and PRL87 are coded 0.83.

BE4: all parties maintained their positions save the VU, which moved slightly to the left (Govaert 1993, 56–7). The VB had an extreme-right position (CRISP 1992). PS91, SP91, and VU91 are coded 0.33, CVP91 and PSC91 are coded 0.67, PVV91 and PRL91 are coded 0.83, and VB91 is coded 1.

T4

UK2: all the parties maintained their position, save the Labour Party which moved to the centre (Butler and Kavanagh 1992, 43–66). LAB-S92, LAB-S97, SNP92, SNP97, PC92 and PC97 are coded 0.33; CON-S92, CON-W92, CON-S97 and CON-W97 are coded 0.83.

IT2: the DC, and its successor the PPI, and the PSI maintained their positions. The PDS had become a social-democratic party while FI was a new conservative party (Cotta and Verzichelli 2007, 35–66). The LN had a broadly centre-right position (Diamanti 1993, 69–75). DC92, PPI94, LN92, LN94 and LN96 are coded 0.67; PDS92, PSI92, PDS94, UL96 are coded 0.33, FI94 and FI96 are coded 0.83.

DK2: the SF was a left party, the DSD was a social-democratic party, the DRV was a centre-left liberal party, the DV was a centre-right liberal party, the DKF was a conservative party and the DF was a new right party (Christensen 2010; Bille 1989, 1999; Andersen and Jensen 2001; Rydgren 2004). SF01 and SF05 are coded 0.17; DSD01, DSD05, DRV01, DRV05 are coded 0.33; DV01 and DV05 are coded 0.67; while DKF01, DKF05, DF01 and DF05 are coded 0.83.

T5

BE6: all the parties broadly maintained the positions they had at T3. Ecolo was close to the position of the PS (Buelens and Deschouwer 2002). The N-VA had a rightist position, to the right of the CD&V and close to that of the O-VLD (Govaert 2002, 34–6; Swyngedouw and Abts 2011, 14–16). PS07, PS10, ECO07, ECO10, SP.A07 and SP.A10 are coded 0.33; CD&V07, CD&V10, CDH07 and CDH10 are coded 0.67; O-VLD07, O-VLD10, N-VA07, N-VA10, MR07, MR10 are coded 0.83; VB07 and VB10 are coded 1.

UK3: all the parties broadly maintained the positions they had at T4 while the Liberal Democrats were a centrist party that allied itself with the Conservatives at the state level (Clark 2012; McGarvey and Cairney 2008, 46–67). LAB-S07, LAB-S11, SNP07, SNP11 are coded 0.33, LD-S07 and LD-S11 are coded 0.67, CON-S07 and CON-S11 are coded 0.83. As both YS14 and BT14 were broad coalitions, especially the latter, they are coded 0.5.

ES2: the PS-C was a social-democratic party while the PP-C was a conservative party (Gunther and Montero 2009, 124–7; 130–2). The CiU had a moderate right-of-centre position, while the ERC, the ICV and CSQEP were to the left of the PS-C. As a coalition of CDC and ERC, JxS was positioned in the middle of the spectrum. The CUP was a far left party while Ciutadans was on the centre-right (Baras and Matas Dalmases 1998; Martí and Cetrà 2016, 109–11; Orriols and Cordero 2016, 3; Orriols and Rodon 2016, 367–70). CUP15 is coded 0; ERC06, ERC10, ERC12, ICV06, ICV10, ICV12 and CSQEP15 are coded 0.17; PS-C06, PS-C10, PS-C12, and PS-C15 are coded 0.33; JxS15 is coded 0.5; CiU06, CiU10, CiU12, and Cs15 are coded 0.67; and PP-C06, PP-C10, PP-C12, and PP-C15 are coded 0.83.

C4 – Constitutional position (cospos)

T1

IT1: both the DC and the PCI supported the implementation of the ordinary regions, but the issue had a low priority for them while it was more important for the PSI (section 3.2). DC63, PCI63 are coded 0.17, PSI63 is coded 0.33.

BE1: the CVP and the PSB supported the introduction of forms of regional autonomy but rejected federalism. The PLP and, less strongly so, the PSC defended the constitutional status quo while the VU and the RW called for Belgium to become a federal state (section 3.3). VU1 and RW1 are coded 0.67, CVP1 and PSB1 are coded 0.33, and PLP1 and PSC1 are coded 0.

T2

UK1: the Labour Party supported the creation of regional assemblies in Scotland and Wales. The Conservative party defended the status quo and rejected devolution. The SNP supported independence for Scotland while the PC advocated "full self-government" for Wales (section 4.2). LAB-S79 and LAB-W79 are coded 0.33, CON-S79 and CON-W79 are coded 0, SNP79 is coded 1 and PC79 is coded 0.83.

BE2: the CVP, the PVV, and the SP all supported a completion of state reform, the latter two calling for directly elected regional/community assemblies. The VU maintained its federalist position, calling for a Flemish state in a Belgian federal state. The PS, the PRLW, and the PSC also supported a completion of state reform, especially as regarded the implementation of the regions while the RW maintained its federalist position (section 4.3). CVP78, SP78, PVV78, PS78, PSC78, PRLW78 are coded 0.33, VU78 and RW78 are coded 0.67.

FR1: the PSF and the PCF supported the creation of directly elected regional councils while the RPR and the UDF were in favour of decentralization but stopped short of endorsing the above (section 4.4). PSF81 and PCF81 are coded 0.33 while RPR81 and UDF81 are coded 0.17.

T3

BE3: all parties expressed support for a further reform in a federal direction, though with some differences of emphasis between them (section 5.2). CVP87, PVV87, PS87 and VU87 are coded 0.67 while SP87, PRL87, and PSC87 are coded 0.33.

BE4: all the traditional parties clustered together in support of a completion of the reform process with the achievement of a federal state, with only marginal differences between them. The VU shifted its position to a 'confederal' model while the VB wanted Flanders to become an independent republic (section 5.2). CVP91, PVV91, SP91, PS91, PRL91, and PSC91 are coded 0.33, VU91 is coded 0.67, and VB91 is coded 1.

T4

UK2: in both the 1992 and the 1997 elections, the Labour Party was committed to establishing a Scottish parliament and a Welsh assembly, the Conservative party defended the status quo while the SNP and PC supported independence (section 6.2). CON-S92 and CON-S97 are coded 0, LAB-S92 and LAB-S97 are coded 0.67, and SNP92, SNP97, PC92 and PC97 are coded 1.

IT2: in the 1992 election, the PDS, the PSI and, to a lesser extent, the DC supported a general strengthening of the autonomy of the ordinary regions. The LN called for a more radical federal reform, centred on the creation of three 'macro-regions' (section 6.3). DC92 is coded 0.17, PDS92 and PSI92 are coded 0.33 and LN92 is coded 0.83. In the 1994 election, the PDS and the PPI maintained their previous position while FI endorsed a strong form of fiscal federalism and the LN moderated its position to converge on that of FI (section 6.3). PPI94 is coded 0.17, PDS94 is coded 0.33 while FI94 and LN94 are coded 0.67. In the 1996 election, the UL alliance called for a federal reform, FI toned down its support for fiscal federalism whereas the LN radicalized its discourse in a 'confederal' direction (section 6.3). UL96 is coded 0.67, FI96 is coded 0.33 and LN96 is coded 0.83.

DK2: as the reform did not entail an increase in regional autonomy, party positions have been coded on the basis of how distant they were from the status quo. In the 2001 election, the DKF and the DF were in favour of abolishing the counties while the DV, the DSD, the DRV and the SF supported the status quo (section 6.4). DSD01, DV01, DRV01 and SF01 are coded 0, DKF01 and DF01 are coded 0.67. In the 2005 election the DV had switched to supporting the reform – a compromise between the status quo and the stance of the DKF and the DF – while the other parties maintained their position (section 6.4). DSD05, DRV05, SF05 are coded 0; DV05 is coded 0.33; DKF05 and DF05 are coded 0.67.

T5

BE6: in the 2007 general election campaign, the SP.A supported only a moderate strengthening of the regions, the CD&V and, to a lesser extent, the O-VLD called for further reform in a confederal direction, the N-VA for confederalism in the short term and independence later, and the VB for independence immediately. All the Francophone parties defended the status quo (section 7.2). PS07, MR07, CDH07, ECO07 are coded 0; SP.A07 is coded 01.7; O-VLD is coded 0.33; CD&V07 is coded 0.67, N-VA07 is coded 0.83 and VB07 is coded 1. In the 2010 general election campaign, the CD&V and the O-VLD put forward a 'confederalist' position, the N-VA and the VB called for independence – to be achieved gradually for the former and immediately for the latter – while the SP.A and the French-speaking parties defended the federal status quo (section 7.2). PS10, MR10, CDH10, ECO10 and SP.A10 are coded 0; CD&V10 and O-VLD10 are coded 0.67, N-VA10 and VB10 are coded 1.

UK3: in the 2007 election, the Conservatives and the Labour Party defended the status quo, the Liberal Democrats called for the devolution of some additional powers and the SNP maintained its call for independence (section 7.3). CON-S07 and LAB-S07 are coded 0, LD-S07 are coded 0.17, and SNP07 is coded 1. In the 2011 election, the Conservatives and the Liberal Democrats supported the status quo, the Labour Party called for a deepening of devolution and the SNP stuck with independence (section 8.3). CON-S11 and LD-S11 are coded 0, LAB-S11 is coded 0.33, and SNP11 is coded 1. In the 2014 referendum, the Yes side supported independence while the No side supported a 'devo max' option (section 7.3). YS14 is coded 1 while BT14 is coded 0.67.

ES2: in the campaign for the 2006 referendum, CiU, the PS-C and ICV supported a Yes vote while ERC and the PP-C called for a No vote for opposite reasons (section 7.4). CiU06, PS-C06 and ICV06 are coded 0.67, ERC06 is coded 1 and PP-C06 is coded 0. In the campaign for the 2010 regional election, CiU vowed to implement as much as possible the new *Estatut* and sought a new financing system for the region, the PS-C also committed itself to implementing the *Estatut* and reiterated its call for a federal reform of the state and the ICV was broadly on the same line but with a more radical position. ERC reaffirmed its commitment for Catalonia to achieve independence while the PP-C defended the status quo (section 7.4). CiU10 and PS-C10 are coded 0.67, ICV10 is coded 0.83, ERC10 is coded 1 and PP-C10 is coded 0. In the campaign for the 2012 regional election, all parties maintained their position save CiU, which moved close to supporting independence (section 7.4). PS-C12 is coded 0.67, CiU12 and ICV12 are coded 0.83, ERC12 is coded 1 and PP-C12 is coded 0. In the campaign for the 2015 election, JxS and CUP supported independence, CSQEP called for Catalonia to acquire 'sovereignty,' the PS-C restated its support for a federal reform, while Ciutadans supported more modest reforms and the PP-C defended the status quo (section 7.4). JxS15 and CUP15 are coded 1, CSQEP15 is coded 0.83, PS-C15 is coded 0.67, Cs15 is coded 0.17, and PP-C15 is coded 0.

C5 – Depth of integration (integ)

T1

At T1 what is now the European Union (European Communities at the time) was governed by the Paris and Rome treaties and had recently completed a customs union (section 3.1). All parties are coded 0.17.

T2

At T2 integration in what is now the European Union (European Communities at the time) had deepened with the creation of the European Monetary System and the direct election of the European Parliament (section 4.1). All parties are coded 0.33.

T3

At T3 integration had deepened considerably with the adoption of the Single European Act and the single market program (section 5.1). All parties are coded 0.67.

T4

At T4 the European Union had come formally into being in the wake of the adoption of the Maastricht Treaty and integration was further deepened by the Amsterdam and Nice treaties as well as by the completion of the single market program (section 6.1). All parties are coded 0.83.

T5

At T5 integration in the European Union had deepened further with the coming into force of the Lisbon Treaty (section 7.1). All parties are coded 1.

C6 – Attitudes to integration (attint)

T1

IT1: the DC was strongly in favour of integration, the PCI was hostile, and the PSI had an intermediate position between the two (section 3.2). DC63 is coded 1, PCI63 is coded 0.33, and PSI63 is coded 0.67.

BE1: all parties were strongly in favour of European integration (section 3.3). CVP68, PSC68, PSB68, PLP68, VU68, and RW68 are all coded 1.

T2

UK1: the Conservative party and Plaid Cymru were broadly supportive of integration whereas the Labour Party and the SNP were largely hostile (section 4.2). CON-S79, CON-W79, PC79 are coded 0.67, LAB-S79, LAB-W79, and SNP79 are coded 0.17.

BE2: all parties maintained their strong support (section 4.3). CVP78, PVV78, SP78, VU78, PS78, PRLW78, PSC78, and RW78 are all coded 1.

FR1: the PSF was in favour of integration and of a strengthening of the EU institutions, while the RPR and the UDF supported integration from a intergovernmental perspective and the PCF was hostile (section 4.4). PSF81 is coded 0.83, RPR81 and UDF81 are coded 0.67, PCF81 is coded 0.33.

T3

BE3: all parties maintained strong support for integration (section 5.2). CVP87, PVV87, SP87, VU87, PS87, PRL87 and PSC87 are all coded 1.

BE4: the traditional parties continued to be strong supporters of integration but the two Flemish nationalist parties started to express some reservations (section 5.2). CVP91, PVV91, SP91, PS91, PRL91, and PSC91 are all coded 1, VU91 is coded 0.83, and VB91 is coded 0.67.

T4

UK2: the Conservatives were increasingly cautious on integration, especially in the 1997 election, whereas the Labour Party had become supportive and the SNP adopted a pragmatic pro-integration position. PC was strongly supportive in 1992 and only slightly less so in 1997 (section 6.2). CON-S92, CON-W92, LAB-S92, LAB-W92, LAB-S97, LAB-W97, SNP92 and SNP97 are coded 0.67, CON-S97 and CON-W97 are coded 0.33, while PC92 is coded 1 and PC97 is coded 0.83.

IT2: all statewide parties were strong supporters of integration in the 1992 election while the LN also in favour but less strongly so (section 6.3). DC92, PDS92, PSI92 are all coded 1, LN92 is coded 0.83. In the 1994 election, the PDS, the PPI and the LN maintained their positions while the FI displayed a cautious pro-integration stance (section 6.3). PDS94 and PPI94 are coded 1, LN94 is coded 0.83 and FI94 is coded 0.67. In the 1996 election, the UL followed the position taken by the PDS in the previous election while the LN and FI also maintained their positions (section 6.3). UL96 is coded 1, LN96 is coded 0.83, FI96 is coded 0.67.

DK2: at the time of the 2001 and 2005 elections, the DKF, the DRV and the DV were the most supportive of integration, the DSD and, especially, the SF less so while the DF was hostile (section 6.4). DKF01, DKF05, DRV01, DRV05, DV01, DV05 are coded 0.83, DSD01 and DSD05 are coded 0.67, SF01 and SF05 are coded 0.33, and DF01 and DF05 are coded 0.17.

T5

BE6: in the 2007 election, all parties save the N-VA and the VB maintained strong support for integration. The N-VA was more cautious while the VB had become markedly critical (section 7.2). CD&V07, O-VLD07, SP.A07, PS07, MR07, CDH07 and ECO07 are coded 1, N-VA07 is coded 0.83 and VB07 is coded 0.33. In the 2010, parties broadly maintained their positions but the mainstream Flemish parties put forward a more cautious approach (section 7.2). PS07, MR07, CDH07, ECO10 are coded 1; CD&V07, O-VLD07, SP.A07, and N-VA07 are coded 0.83 and VB07 is coded 0.33.

UK3: throughout the period, the Conservatives had become mostly critical of integration whereas the Labour Party, the Liberal Democrats and the SNP retained a positive approach (section 7.3). CON-S07 and CON-S11 are coded 0.33, LAB-S07, LAB-S11, LD-S07, SNP07, SNP11, YS14 are coded 0.67. As the Better Together group brought together parties with different attitudes to integration, BT14 is coded 0.5.

ES2: at the time of the 2006 referendum and of the 2010 regional election, CiU, the ERC, and the PP-C were solid supporters of integration while the PS-C and the ICV were even more strongly committed (section 7.4). CiU06, CiU10, ERC06, ERC10, PP-C06 and PP-C10 are coded 0.83, PS-C06, PS-C10, ICV06, ICV10 are coded 1. In the campaign for the 2012 regional election, CiU and ERC returned to strong support for integration, while the other parties maintained their positions (section 7.4). CiU12, ERC12, PS-C12, ICV12 are coded 1, PP-C12 is coded 0.83. In the campaign for the 2015 regional election, JxS, the PS-C, and CSQEP advocated a federal Europe. Ciutadans was in favour of greater integration but fell short of supporting a federal Europe while the PP-C did not take a position but was generally supportive. The CUP did not take a position on integration either but advocated withdrawal from the EU (section 7.4). JxS15, PS-C15, and CSQEP15 are coded 1; Cs15 and PP-C15 are coded 0.83; and CUP15 is coded 0.

C7 – Attitudes to the EU (atteu)

T1

IT1: the DC identified integration with the EU whereas the PCI and the PSI were more critical of the existing EU than of the idea of integration itself (section 3.2). DC63 is coded 1, PCI63 is coded 0.17, and PSI63 is coded 0.33.

BE1: the mainstream parties all identified integration with the EU whereas the VU and the RW supported alternative forms of integration (section 3.3). CVP68,

PSC68, PSB68, PLP68 are coded 1, RW68 is coded 0.67, and VU68 is coded 0.33.

T2

UK1: both the Conservatives and Labour identified integration with the EU, while the SNP supported withdrawal and the PC also had a negative stance (section 4.2). CON-S79 and CON-W79 are coded 0.67, LAB-S79, LAB-W79, PC79 are coded 0.17, and SNP79 is coded 0..

BE2: the Christian democrat and liberal parties were strongly supportive, the socialist parties – especially the Flemish one – were marginally more critical while the VU and the RW maintained their alternative visions (section 4.3). CVP78, PVV78, PRLW78, PSC78 are coded 1, PS78 is coded 0.83, SP78 and RW78 are coded 0.67, and VU78 is coded 0.33.

FR1: all parties identified integration with the EU but the RPR and the UDF are more positive toward the latter than toward the former while the reverse was true for the PCF (section 4.4). RPR81, UDF81, and PSF81 are coded 0.83, PCF81 is coded 0.17.

T3

BE3: all parties, saved the two socialist ones, were as supportive of the EU as they were of integration. The PS and the SP were critical of the weakness of the social dimension. The VU had toned down its support for an alternative form of integration (section 5.2). CVP87, PVV87, PRL87, PSC87 are coded 1, PS87, SP87, VU87 are coded 0.83.

BE4: the traditional parties maintained the position they had at the time of the previous election and supported ratification of the Maastricht Treaty whereas the VU and the VB were critical and voted against ratification (section 5.2). CVP91, PVV91, PSC91, PRL91 are coded 1, PS91 is coded 0.83, SP91 is coded 0.67, and VU91 and VB91 are coded 0.17.

T4

UK2: for most parties attitudes to the EU were aligned with attitudes to integration save for PC, which was slightly less positive on the EU than it was on integration in 1992 (section 6.2). CON-S92, CON-W92, LAB-S92, LAB-W92, LAB-S97, LAB-W97, SNP92 and SNP97 are coded 0.67, PC92 and PC97 are coded 0.83, and CON-S97 and CON-W97 are coded 0.33.

IT2: attitudes to the EU were in line with attitudes to integration for all parties (section 6.3). DC92, PPI94, PDS92, PDS94, PSI92, UL96 are all coded 1; LN92, LN94 and LN96 are coded 0.83; FI94 and FI96 are coded 0.67.

DK2: attitudes to the EU were in line with attitudes to integration for all parties (section 6.4). DKF01, DKF05, DRV01, DRV05, DV01, DV05 are coded 0.83, DSD01 and DSD05 are coded 0.67, SF01 and SF05 are coded 0.33, and DF01 and DF05 are coded 0.17.

T5

BE6: in the 2007 election, the Christian democratic and liberal parties and, to a lesser extent, the N-VA and Ecolo were strongly in favour, the two socialist parties were critical supporters, and the VB was negative. The latter was the only one rejecting ratification of the Constitutional Treaty (section 7.2). CD&V07, O-VLD07, MR07, and CDH07 are coded 1, N-VA07 and ECO07 are coded 0.83, SP.A07 and PS07 are coded 0.67 and VB07 is coded 0.17. Positions were broadly the same in the 2010 election, although the socialist parties were marginally less critical and all, save the VB, supported ratification of the Lisbon treaty (section 7.2). CD&V10, O-VLD10, MR10, CDH10 are coded 1, N-VA10, PS10, SP.A10, ECO10 are coded 0.83, and VB10 is coded 0.17.

UK3: the Labour Party supported ratification of the Lisbon treaty while the Conservatives and the SNP voted against. In the 2014 referendum campaign, the YS camp was positive toward the EU while the BT camp housed different attitudes (section 7.3). LAB-S07 and LAB-S11 are coded 0.67, CON-S07, CON-S11, SNP07 and SNP11 are coded 0.17, while YS14 is coded 0.67 and BT14 is coded.

ES2: in the campaigns for the 2006 referendum and the 2010 regional election, attitudes to the EU were in line with attitudes to integration for the PS-C and the PP-C and both parties supported ratification of the CT and of the Lisbon Treaty; CiU was divided over the CT and reluctantly supported Lisbon; ICV called for a No vote on the first and abstained on the second while ERC also called for a No to the CT and voted against Lisbon (section 7.4). PS-C06 is coded 1, PP-C06 is coded 0.83, CiU06 is coded 0.67, and ERC06 and ICV06 are coded 0.17. PS-C10 is coded 1, PP-C10 is coded 0.83, CiU10 is coded 0.67, ICV10 is coded 0.33 and ERC10 is coded 0.17. In the campaign for the 2012 regional election CiU and ERC were more positive toward the EU while ICV was critical of austerity policies (section 8.4). PS-C12 is coded 1, PP-C12 and CiU12 are coded 0.83, ERC12 is coded 0.67 and ICV12 is coded 0.33. In the campaign for the 2015 regional election, attitudes to the EU were in line with attitudes to integration for all parties save CSQEP and, to a lesser extent, the PS-C. CSQEP was strongly critical of the policies enacted by the EU in the context of the euro-crisis and advocated a radical policy change. The PS-C echoed some of these criticisms but was more moderate in its opposition and less radical in demanding reform (section 7.4). JxS15 is coded 1, Cs15 and PP-C15 are coded 0.83, PS-C15 is coded 0.67, CSQEP15 is coded 0.33, and CUP15 is coded 0.

Table A1.3
Micro fsQCA Scores

Timepoint	Critical juncture	Election/ Referendum	Party	C1 partyp	C2 syssta	C3 leri	C4 cospos	C5 integ	C6 attint	C7 atteu	O1 europ-i	O2 europ-d
T1	IT1	1963	DC63	0	1	0.67	0.17	0.17	1	1	0	–
T1	IT1	1963	PCI63	0	0	0	0.17	0.17	0.33	0.17	0	–
T1	IT1	1963	PSI63	0	0.67	0.33	0.33	0.17	0.67	0.33	0	–
T1	BE1	1968	PSB68	0.17	0.83	0.33	0.33	0.17	1	1	0	–
T1	BE1	1968	PLP68	0	0.67	0.83	0	0.17	1	1	0.17	0
T1	BE1	1968	CVP68	0.67	1	0.67	0.33	0.17	1	1	0	–
T1	BE1	1968	VU68	1	0.17	0.67	0.67	0.17	1	0.33	0.33	1
T1	BE1	1968	PSC68	0.67	1	0.67	0	0.17	1	1	0	–
T1	BE1	1968	RW68	1	0.17	0.33	0.67	0.17	1	0.67	0.17	1
T2	BE2	1978	CVP78	0.67	1	0.67	0.33	0.33	1	1	0	–
T2	BE2	1978	SP78	0.67	0.83	0.33	0.33	0.33	1	0.67	0	–
T2	BE2	1978	PVV78	0.67	0.83	0.83	0.33	0.33	1	1	0	–
T2	BE2	1978	VU78	1	0.33	0.67	0.67	0.33	1	0.33	0	–
T2	BE2	1978	PSB78	0.67	0.83	0.33	0.33	0.33	1	0.83	0	–
T2	BE2	1978	PSC78	0.67	1	0.67	0.33	0.33	1	1	0	–
T2	BE2	1978	PRLW78	0.67	0.83	0.83	0.33	0.33	1	1	0	–
T2	BE2	1978	RW78	1	0.17	0.33	0.67	0.33	1	0.67	0.17	1
T2	UK1	1979	CON-S79	0.17	0.83	0.83	0	0.33	0.67	0.67	0.17	0
T2	UK1	1979	LAB-S79	0.17	0.33	0.17	0.33	0.33	0.17	0.17	0	–
T2	UK1	1979	SNP79	1	0	0.33	1	0.33	0.17	0	0.17	1
T2	UK1	1979	CON-W79	0	0.83	0.83	0	0.33	0.67	0.67	0	–
T2	UK1	1979	LAB-W79	0	0.33	0.17	0.33	0.33	0.17	0.17	0	–

Table A13
Micro fsQCA Scores (continued)

Timepoint	Critical juncture	Election/ Referendum	Party	C1 partyp	C2 syssta	C3 leri	C4 cospos	C5 integ	C6 attint	C7 atteu	O1 europ-i	O2 europ-d
T2	UK1	1979	PC79	1	0	0.33	0.83	0.33	0.67	0.17	0.33	1
T2	FR1	1981	PSF81	0	0.67	0.17	0.33	0.33	0.83	0.83	0	–
T2	FR1	1981	PCF81	0	0.67	0	0.33	0.33	0.33	0.17	0	–
T2	FR1	1981	RPR81	0	0.83	0.83	0.17	0.33	0.67	0.83	0	–
T2	FR1	1981	UDF81	0	0.83	0.67	0.17	0.33	0.67	0.83	0	–
T3	BE3	1987	CVP87	0.67	1	0.67	0.67	0.67	1	1	0.17	1
T3	BE3	1987	SP87	0.67	0.83	0.33	0.33	0.67	1	0.83	0	–
T3	BE3	1987	PVV87	0.67	0.67	0.83	0.67	0.67	1	1	0	–
T3	BE3	1987	VU87	1	0.33	0.67	0.67	0.67	1	0.83	0.67	1
T3	BE3	1987	PS87	0.67	0.83	0.33	0.67	0.67	1	0.83	0.17	1
T3	BE3	1987	PRL87	0.67	0.67	0.83	0.33	0.67	1	1	0.17	1
T3	BE3	1987	PSC87	0.67	1	0.67	0.33	0.67	1	1	0.17	1
T3	BE4	1991	CVP91	0.67	1	0.67	0.33	0.67	1	1	0	–
T3	BE4	1991	SP91	0.67	0.83	0.33	0.33	0.67	1	0.67	0.33	1
T3	BE4	1991	PVV91	0.67	0.83	0.83	0.33	0.67	1	1	0	–
T3	BE4	1991	VU91	1	0.33	0.33	0.67	0.67	0.83	0.17	0.67	1
T3	BE4	1991	VB91	1	0	1	1	0.67	0.67	0.17	0.17	1
T3	BE4	1991	PS91	0.67	0.83	0.33	0.33	0.67	1	0.83	0	–
T3	BE4	1991	PRL91	0.67	0.83	0.83	0.33	0.67	1	1	0	–
T3	BE4	1991	PSC91	0.67	1	0.67	0.33	0.67	1	1	0	–
T3	BE4	1991	ECO91	0.67	0.17	0.17	0.33	0.67	1	0.17	0.17	1
T4	UK2	1992	CON-S92	0.17	0.83	0.83	0	0.83	0.67	0.67	0.67	0

T4	UK2	1992	LAB-S92	0.17	0.67	0.33	0.67	0.83	0.67	0.67	0.17	1
T4	UK2	1992	SNP92	1	0	0.33	1	0.83	0.67	0.67	1	1
T4	UK2	1992	CON-W92	0	0.83	0.83	0	0.83	0.67	0.67	0	—
T4	UK2	1992	LAB-W92	0	0.67	0.33	0.33	0.83	0.67	0.67	0.17	1
T4	UK2	1992	PC92	1	0	0.33	1	0.83	1	0.83	1	1
T4	UK2	1997	CON-S97	0.17	0.33	0.83	0	0.83	0.33	0.33	0.33	0
T4	UK2	1997	LAB-S97	0.17	0.83	0.33	0.67	0.83	0.67	0.67	0.17	1
T4	UK2	1997	SNP97	1	0	0.33	1	0.83	0.67	0.67	0.67	1
T4	UK2	1997	CON-W97	0	0.83	0.83	0	0.83	0.33	0.33	0	—
T4	UK2	1997	LAB-W97	0	0.67	0.33	0.33	0.83	0.67	0.67	0.17	1
T4	UK2	1997	PC97	1	0	0.33	1	0.83	0.83	0.83	1	1
T4	IT2	1992	DC92	0	0.83	0.67	0.17	0.83	1	1	0.17	0
T4	IT2	1992	PDS92	0	0.67	0.33	0.33	0.83	1	1	0	—
T4	IT2	1992	PSI92	0	0.67	0.33	0.33	0.83	1	1	0	—
T4	IT2	1992	LN92	0.83	0.17	0.67	0.83	0.83	0.83	0.83	0	—
T4	IT2	1994	PDS94	0	0.67	0.33	0.33	0.83	1	1	0	—
T4	IT2	1994	FI94	0	0.83	0.83	0.67	0.83	0.67	0.67	0	—
T4	IT2	1994	LN94	0.83	0.83	0.67	0.67	0.83	0.83	0.83	0	—
T4	IT2	1994	PPI94	0	0.33	0.67	0.17	0.83	1	1	0	—
T4	IT2	1996	UL96	0	0.83	0.33	0.67	0.83	1	1	0	—
T4	IT2	1996	FI96	0	0.83	0.83	0.33	0.83	1	1	0.17	1
T4	IT2	1996	LN96	0.83	0.17	0.67	0.83	0.83	0.67	0.67	0	—
T4	DK2	2001	DSD01	0	0.67	0.33	0	0.83	0.83	0.83	0.83	1
T4	DK2	2001	DV01	0	0.83	0.67	0	0.83	0.67	0.67	0	—
T4	DK2	2001	DKF01	0	0.83	0.83	0.67	0.83	0.83	0.83	0	—

Table A13
Micro fsQCA Scores (continued)

Timepoint	Critical juncture	Election/ Referendum	Party	C1 partyp	C2 syssta	C3 leri	C4 cospos	C5 integ	C6 attint	C7 atteu	O1 europ-i	O2 europ-d
T4	DK2	2001	SF01	0	0.17	0.17	0	0.83	0.33	0.33	0	–
T4	DK2	2001	DF01	0	0.17	0.83	0.67	0.83	0.17	0.17	0	–
T4	DK2	2001	DRV01	0	0.67	0.33	0	0.83	0.83	0.83	0	–
T4	DK2	2005	DSD05	0	0.67	0.33	0	0.83	0.67	0.67	0	–
T4	DK2	2005	DV05	0	0.83	0.67	0.33	0.83	0.83	0.83	0	–
T4	DK2	2005	DKF05	0	0.83	0.83	0.67	0.83	0.83	0.83	0	–
T4	DK2	2005	SF05	0	0.17	0.17	0	0.83	0.33	0.33	0	–
T4	DK2	2005	DF05	0	0.17	0.83	0.67	0.83	0.17	0.17	0	–
T4	DK2	2005	DRV05	0	0.67	0.33	0	0.83	0.83	0.83	0	–
T5	BE6	2007	CD&V07	0.83	1	0.67	0.67	1	1	1	0	–
T5	BE6	2007	O-VLD07	0.83	0.67	0.83	0.33	1	1	1	0	–
T5	BE6	2007	SP.A07	0.83	0.67	0.33	0.17	1	1	0.67	0	–
T5	BE6	2007	N-VA07	0.83	1	0.83	0.83	1	0.83	0.83	0.83	1
T5	BE6	2007	VB07	1	0	1	1	1	0.33	0.17	0.33	1
T5	BE6	2007	PS07	0.83	1	0.33	0	1	1	0.67	0	–
T5	BE6	2007	MR07	0.83	0.67	0.83	0	1	1	1	0	–
T5	BE6	2007	CDH07	0.83	0.67	0.67	0	1	1	1	0	–
T5	BE6	2007	ECO07	0.67	0.33	0.33	0	1	1	0.83	0	–
T5	BE6	2010	CD&V10	0.83	1	0.67	0.67	1	0.83	1	0	–
T5	BE6	2010	O-VLD10	0.83	0.67	0.83	0.67	1	0.83	1	0	–
T5	BE6	2010	SP.A10	0.83	0.67	0.33	0	1	0.83	0.83	0	–
T5	BE6	2010	N-VA10	1	0.67	0.83	1	1	0.83	0.83	1	1

T5	BE6	2010	VB10	1	0	1	1	1	0.33	0.17	0.17	1
T5	BE6	2010	PS10	0.83	1	0.33	0	1	1	0.83	0	–
T5	BE6	2010	MR10	0.83	0.67	0.83	0	1	1	1	0	–
T5	BE6	2010	CDH10	0.83	0.67	0.67	0	1	1	1	0	–
T5	BE6	2010	ECO10	0.67	0.33	0.33	0	1	1	0.83	0	1
T5	ES2	2006	CiU06	1	0.67	0.67	0.67	1	0.83	0.67	0.17	1
T5	ES2	2006	PS-C06	0.67	0.83	0.33	0.67	1	1	1	0.17	1
T5	ES2	2006	ERC06	1	0.83	0.17	1	1	0.83	0.17	0	–
T5	ES2	2006	ICV06	0.83	0.83	0.17	0.67	1	1	0.17	0	–
T5	ES2	2006	PP-C06	0	0.17	0.83	0	1	0.83	0.83	0	–
T5	ES2	2010	CiU10	1	0.83	0.67	0.67	1	0.83	0.67	0.17	1
T5	ES2	2010	PS-C10	0.67	0.33	0.33	0.67	1	1	1	0.17	1
T5	ES2	2010	ERC10	1	0.33	0.17	1	1	0.83	0.17	0.33	1
T5	ES2	2010	ICV10	0.83	0.33	0.17	0.83	1	1	0.33	0.33	1
T5	ES2	2010	PP-C10	0	0.17	0.83	0	1	0.83	0.83	0	–
T5	ES2	2012	CiU12	1	0.83	0.67	0.83	1	1	0.83	0.83	1
T5	ES2	2012	PS-C12	0.67	0.33	0.33	0.67	1	1	1	0.33	1
T5	ES2	2012	ERC12	1	0.67	0.17	1	1	1	0.67	0.83	1
T5	ES2	2012	ICV12	0.83	0.33	0.17	0.83	1	1	0.33	0.17	1
T5	ES2	2012	PP-C12	0	0.17	0.83	0	1	0.83	0.83	0.17	1
T5	ES2	2015	JxS15	1	0.83	0.5	1	1	1	1	0.67	0
T5	ES2	2015	CUP15	1	0.17	0	1	1	0	0	0	1
T5	ES2	2015	PS-C15	0.67	0.33	0.33	0.67	1	1	0.67	0	–
T5	ES2	2015	CSQEP15	0.83	0.33	0.17	0.83	1	1	0.33	0.33	1
T5	ES2	2015	Cs15	0.17	0.17	0.67	0.17	1	0.83	0.83	0.67	0
T5	ES2	2015	PP-C15	0	0.17	0.83	0	1	0.83	0.83	0.33	0

Table A13
Micro fsQCA Scores (*continued*)

Timepoint	Critical juncture	Election/ Referendum	Party	C1 partyp	C2 syssta	C3 leri	C4 cospos	C5 integ	C6 attint	C7 atteu	O1 europ-i	O2 europ-d
T5	UK3	2007	CON-S07	0.33	0.17	0.83	0	1	0.33	0.17	0	–
T5	UK3	2007	LAB-S07	0.33	0.67	0.33	0	1	0.67	0.67	0	–
T5	UK3	2007	LD-S07	0.33	0.67	0.67	0.17	1	0.67	0.67	0	–
T5	UK3	2007	SNP07	1	0.67	0.33	1	1	0.67	0.67	0	–
T5	UK3	2011	CON-S11	0.33	0.17	0.83	0	1	0.33	0.17	0	–
T5	UK3	2011	LAB-S11	0.33	0.67	0.33	0.33	1	0.67	0.67	0	–
T5	UK3	2011	LD-S11	0.33	0.67	0.67	0	1	0.67	0.67	0	–
T5	UK3	2011	SNP11	1	0.83	0.33	1	1	0.67	0.17	0.67	1
T5	UK3	2014	YS14	1	0.5	0.5	1	1	0.67	0.67	0.67	1
T5	UK3	2014	BT14	0.33	0.5	0.5	0.67	1	0.5	0.5	0.33	0

Table A14
Intense 'Positive' Use of Europe ($O_1 > 0.5$; $O_2 = 1$)

Timepoint	Critical juncture	Election/ Referendum	Party	C1 partyp	C2 syssta	C3 leri	C4 cospos	C5 integ	C6 attint	C7 atten	O1 europ-i	O2 europ-d
T3	BE3	1987	VU87	1	0.33	0.67	0.67	0.67	1	0.83	0.67	1
T3	BE4	1991	VU91	1	0.33	0.33	0.67	0.67	0.83	0.17	0.67	1
T4	UK2	1992	SNP92	1	0	0.33	1	0.83	0.67	0.67	1	1
T4	UK2	1992	PC92	1	0	0.33	1	0.83	1	0.83	1	1
T4	UK2	1997	PC97	1	0	0.33	1	0.83	0.83	0.83	1	1
T4	IT2	1996	LN96	0.83	0.17	0.67	0.83	0.83	0.83	0.83	0.83	1
T5	BE6	2007	N-VA07	0.83	1	0.83	0.83	1	0.83	0.83	0.83	1
T5	BE6	2010	N-VA10	1	0.67	0.83	1	1	0.83	0.83	1	1
T5	UK3	2011	SNP11	1	0.83	0.33	1	1	0.67	0.17	0.67	1
T5	UK3	2014	YS14	1	0.5	0.5	1	1	0.67	0.67	0.67	1
T5	ES2	2012	CiU12	1	0.83	0.67	0.83	1	1	0.83	0.83	1
T5	ES2	2012	ERC12	1	0.67	0.17	1	1	1	0.67	0.83	1
T5	ES2	2015	JxS15	1	0.83	0.5	1	1	1	1	0.67	1

Table A15
Statewide Parties' 'Positive' Use of Europe (O2=1)

Timepoint	Critical juncture	Election/ Referendum	Party	C1 partyp	C2 syssta	C3 leri	C4 cospos	C5 integ	C6 attint	C7 atteu	O1 europ-i	O2 europ-d
T3	BE3	1987	CVP87	0.67	1	0.67	0.67	0.67	1	1	0.17	1
T3	BE3	1987	PS87	0.67	0.83	0.33	0.67	0.67	1	0.83	0.17	1
T3	BE3	1987	PRL87	0.67	0.67	0.83	0.33	0.67	1	1	0.17	1
T3	BE3	1987	PSC87	0.67	1	0.67	0.33	0.67	1	1	0.17	1
T3	BE4	1991	SP91	0.67	0.83	0.33	0.33	0.67	1	0.67	0.33	1
T3	BE4	1991	ECO91	0.67	0.17	0.17	0.33	0.67	1	0.17	0.17	1
T4	UK2	1992	LAB-S92	0.17	0.67	0.33	0.67	0.83	0.67	0.67	0.17	1
T4	UK2	1992	LAB-W92	0	0.67	0.33	0.33	0.83	0.67	0.67	0.17	1
T4	UK2	1997	LAB-S97	0.17	0.83	0.33	0.67	0.83	0.67	0.67	0.17	1
T4	UK2	1997	LAB-W97	0	0.67	0.33	0.33	0.83	0.67	0.67	0.17	1
T4	IT2	1996	UL96	0	0.83	0.33	0.67	0.83	1	1	0.17	1
T5	ES2	2006	PS-C06	0.67	0.83	0.33	0.67	1	1	1	0.17	1
T5	ES2	2010	PS-C10	0.67	0.33	0.33	0.67	1	1	1	0.17	1
T5	ES2	2012	PS-C12	0.67	0.33	0.33	0.67	1	1	1	0.33	1

Table A16
Statewide Parties' 'Negative' Use of Europe (O2=0)

Timepoint	Critical juncture	Election/ Referendum	Party	C1 partyp	C2 syssta	C3 leri	C4 cospos	C5 integ	C6 attint	C7 atteu	O1 europ-i	O2 europ-d
T1	BE1	1968	PLP68	0	0.67	0.83	0	0.17	1	1	0.17	0
T2	UK1	1979	CON-S79	0.17	0.83	0.83	0	0.33	0.67	0.67	0.17	0
T4	UK2	1992	CON-S92	0.17	0.83	0.83	0	0.83	0.67	0.67	0.67	0
T4	UK2	1997	CON-S97	0.17	0.33	0.83	0	0.83	0.33	0.33	0.33	0
T4	IT2	1992	DC92	0	0.83	0.67	0.17	0.83	1	1	0.17	0
T5	UK3	2014	BT14	0.33	0.5	0.5	0.67	1	0.5	0.5	0.33	0
T5	ES2	2012	PP-C12	0	0.17	0.83	0	1	0.83	0.83	0.17	0
T5	ES2	2015	Cs15	0.17	0.17	0.67	0.17	1	0.83	0.83	0.67	0
T5	ES2	2015	PP-C15	0	0.17	0.83	0	1	0.83	0.83	0.33	0

Table A17
Micro fsQCA Necessity

Conditions tested	Consistency
partyp	**0.969479**
~partyp	0.212448
syssta	0.591263
~syssta	0.751047
leri	0.710951
~leri	0.721125
cospos	**1.000000**
~cospos	0.332735
integ	**0.959904**
~integ	0.292041
attint	**0.959904**
~attint	0.251346
atteu	0.841412
~atteu	0.491323

Note: necessary conditions shown in bold.

Table A18
Micro fsQCA Sufficiency Truth Table for *europ-i* Outcome (O1)

C1	C2	C3	C4	C5	C6	C7	O1	Raw const.	No	Cases
1	0	1	1	1	1	1	1	0.923628	2	VU87, LN96
1	1	0	1	1	1	0	1	0.915493	1	SNP11
1	0	0	1	1	1	1	1	0.86178	6	SNP92, PC92, SNP97, PC97, [PS-C10], [PS-C12]
1	0	1	1	1	1	0	1	0.857558	1	VB91
1	0	1	1	0	1	0	0	0.811927	1	VU68
1	0	0	1	0	1	0	0	0.804296	1	PC79
1	0	0	0	1	1	0	0	0.79703	1	ECO91
1	1	0	1	1	1	1	0	0.774194	3	PS87, PS-C06, [ERC12]
1	0	0	1	0	0	0	0	0.771689	1	SNP79
1	1	1	1	1	1	1	0	0.762887	6	CVP87, [N-VA07], [N-VA10], CiU06, CiU10, [CiU12]
1	0	0	1	0	1	1	0	0.76247	2	RW68, RW78
1	1	0	0	1	1	1	0	0.757475	1	SP91
1	0	0	1	1	1	0	0	0.756395	5	[VU91], ERC10, ICV10, ICV12, CSQEP15
1	0	1	1	1	0	0	0	0.752665	2	VB07, VB10
1	1	1	0	1	1	1	0	0.699387	2	PRL87, PSC87
0	1	0	0	1	1	1	0	0.608919	2	LAB-W92, LAB-W97
0	1	0	1	1	1	1	0	0.575365	3	LAB-S92, LAB-S97, UL96

Note: following Vis (2011, table A2), contradictory cases – i.e., cases that display an outcome at odds with the coding of column 8 – are shown in square brackets. Only actually occurring configurations are included; the full table is available from the author upon request.

SECTION A6 – MICRO FSQCA SUFFICIENCY, FSQCA2.5 OUTPUT

****
TRUTH TABLE ANALYSIS
****

File: F:/Data/1.1 fsQCA micro data D1 v6.csv
Model: europ-i = f(partyp, syssta, leri, cospos, integ, attint, atteu)

Rows: 17

Algorithm: Quine-McCluskey
 True: 1

--- COMPLEX SOLUTION ---
frequency cutoff: 1.000000
consistency cutoff: 0.857558

	raw coverage	unique coverage	consistency
partyp*~syssta*leri*cospos*integ*attint	0.502095	0.029324	0.865841
partyp*~syssta*cospos*integ*attint*atteu	0.602035	0.110114	0.871750
partyp*syssta*~leri*cospos*integ*attint*~atteu	0.311191	0.059246	0.915493

solution coverage: 0.700180

solution consistency: 0.835714

****
TRUTH TABLE ANALYSIS
****

File: F:/Data/1.1 fsQCA micro data D1 v6.csv
Model: europ-i = f(partyp, syssta, leri, cospos, integ, attint, atteu)

Rows: 17

Algorithm: Quine-McCluskey
 True: 1-L

--- PARSIMONIOUS SOLUTION ---
frequency cutoff: 1.000000
consistency cutoff: 0.857558

	raw coverage	unique coverage	consistency
syssta*~atteu	0.331538	0.029922	0.812317
~syssta*integ*atteu	0.632555	0.110114	0.843575
leri*integ*attint*~atteu	0.402753	-0.000000	0.790834
~syssta*leri*integ*attint	0.532615	-0.000000	0.833333

solution coverage: 0.730700

solution consistency: 0.797518

****

TRUTH TABLE ANALYSIS

****

File: F:/Data/1.1 fsQCA micro data D1 v6.csv
Model: europ-i = f(atteu, attint, integ, cospos, leri, syssta, partyp)

Rows: 5

Algorithm: Quine-McCluskey
    True: 1
  0 Matrix: 0L
Don't Care: -

— INTERMEDIATE SOLUTION —
frequency cutoff: 1.000000
consistency cutoff: 0.857558
Assumptions:
attint (present)
integ (present)
cospos (present)
~syssta (absent)
partyp (present)

	raw coverage	unique coverage	consistency
atteu*attint*integ*cospos*~syssta*partyp	0.602035	0.110114	0.871750
attint*integ*cospos*leri*~syssta*partyp	0.502095	0.029324	0.865841
~atteu*attint*integ*cospos*~leri*syssta*partyp	0.311191	0.059246	0.915493

solution coverage: 0.700180

solution consistency: 0.835714

Table A19
Micro fsQCA Sufficiency, membership in Solution Paths and Outcome

	Path 1[a]	Path 2[b]	Path 3[c]	Outcome
VU68	0.17	0.17	0.17	0.33
RW68	0.17	0.17	0.17	0.17
RW78	0.33	0.33	0.17	0.17
SNP79	0	0.17	0	0.17
PC79	0.17	0.33	0	0.33
CVP87	0	0	0	0.17
VU87	**0.67**	**0.67**	**0.17**	**0.67**
PS87	0.17	0.17	0.17	0.17
PRL87	0.33	0.33	0	0.17
PSC87	0	0	0	0.17
SP91	0.17	0.17	0.33	0.33
VU91	*0.17*	*0.33*	*0.33*	*0.67*
VB91	*0.17*	*0.67*	*0*	*0.17*
ECO91	0.17	0.17	0.17	0.17
LAB-S92	0.17	0.17	0.17	0.17
LAB-W92	0	0	0	0.17
SNP92	**0.67**	**0.33**	**0**	**1**
PC92	**0.83**	**0.33**	**0**	**1**
LAB-S97	0.17	0.17	0.17	0.17
LAB-W97	0	0	0	0.17
SNP97	**0.67**	**0.33**	**0**	**0.67**
PC97	**0.83**	**0.33**	**0**	**1**
UL96	0	0	0	0.17
LN96	**0.83**	**0.67**	**0.17**	**0.83**
N-VA07	*0*	*0*	*0.17*	*0.83*
VB07	0.17	0.33	0	0.33
N-VA10	*0.33*	*0.33*	*0.17*	*1*
VB10	0.17	0.33	0	0.17
SNP11	**0.17**	**0.17**	**0.67**	**0.67**
CiU06	0.33	0.33	0.33	0.17
PS-C06	0.17	0.17	0	0.17
CiU10	0.17	0.17	0.33	0.17
PS-C10	0.67	0.33	0	0.17
ERC10	0.17	0.17	0.33	0.33
ICV10	0.33	0.17	0.33	0.33
CiU12	*0.17*	*0.17*	*0.17*	*0.83*
PS-C12	0.67	0.33	0	0.33
ERC12	0.33	0.33	0.33	0.83
ICV12	0.33	0.17	0.33	0.17
CSQEP15	0.33	0.17	0.33	0.33

Note: cases with membership in at least one of the paths as well as in the outcome shown in bold; cases with membership in the outcome but not in any of the paths shown in italics.

[a] partyp*~syssta*cospos*integ*attint*atteu;

[b] partyp*~syssta*leri*cospos*integ*attint*;

[c] partyp*syssta*~leri*cospos*integ*attint*~atteu

Appendix

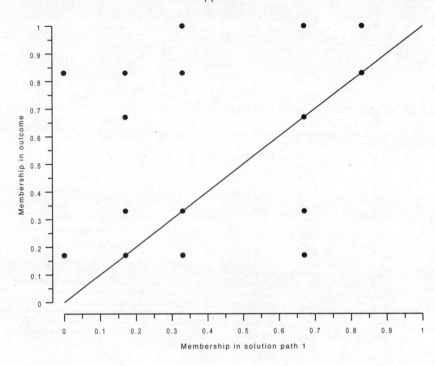

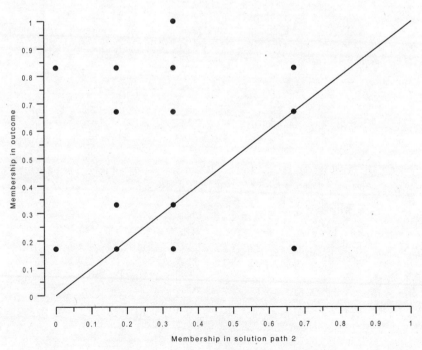

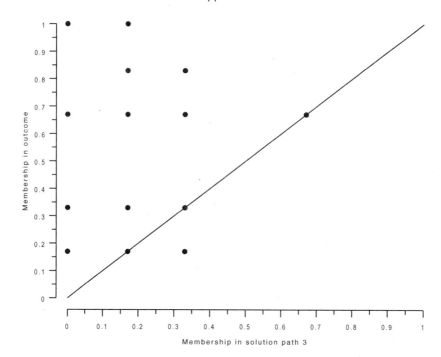

Notes

INTRODUCTION

1 For the sake of concision, the terms European Union and EU are used also to refer to its predecessor organizations.
2 Meaning that the seceding region would remain within the European Union as an additional member state.
3 Here and elsewhere I use the term "Europe" as a shorter synonym for European Union and European integration. I do not mean to imply that the EU is coterminous with Europe in the wider sense of the word.

CHAPTER ONE

1 The term "structure" has previously been employed with this meaning both in the academic literature and in public policy. For the former, see, for instance, Aubert (1978, 74) and McRae (1986, 23), while a prominent example of the latter is the Danish reform of the mid-2000s, which was officially called *Strukturreformen*, or structural reform – see chapter 6.
2 On the relationship between conceptualization and measurement, see Goertz (2006, esp. 27–67).
3 On the distinction between differences of degree and of kind, see, among others, Goertz (2006, 5).
4 Somewhat surprisingly, he did not offer a concise definition of a federation. The closest is "modern federalism is based on the linkage of federated or constituent states, which come together to form a larger state" (Elazar 1987, 40).
5 He also presents (Keating 1998a, 118) another classification around five categories – federal states, fully regionalized states, partly regionalized states, administrative regionalization, indirectly elected regions – in which some countries feature in more than one category at the same time.

6 The problems generated by combining the self-rule and share rule dimensions to measure regional autonomy, hence decentralization, are illustrated by a comparison of the 2010 RAI scores for Germany and Switzerland. Germany scores 37 on the total RAI versus Switzerland's 26.5 (Hooghe et al. 2016, Appendix – Country Scores). On this measure, then, Germany should be considered much *more* decentralized than Switzerland is. Yet, this is difficult to reconcile with the general consensus among scholars that Germany is a more centralized federal state than Switzerland (e.g., Abromeit 1992; Klatt 1999; McKay 2001; Braun 2003; Vatter 2007a,b).

7 As detailed in the main text, the autonomy of the traditional macro-local units of government is never higher than 12 on the RAI-RSF while that of regional governments in the traditional federal states is never lower than 14 (Hooghe et al. 2016, Appendix). A RAI-RSF score of 13 thus emerges as an empirical threshold between weak and strong regional government and, by extension, between unitary and federal structures. This can be treated as a systematized concept, as defined by Adcock and Collier (2001, 531).

8 Borrowing from US constitutional terminology (Van Dyke 1992; Statham 2002), I distinguish between incorporated and unincorporated territories. The former are territories that are constitutionally an integral part of the state, whereas the latter are under the sovereignty of the state but are not constitutionally considered an integral part of it. If the areas enjoying special autonomy are non-incorporated, i.e., they are considered to be separate from the main constitutional body of the state, they are best described as federacies (Elazar 1987, 54–7; Watts 2008, 10).

9 This category also includes the union state identified by Rokkan and Urwin (1982, 11). Departing from Hooghe et al.'s (2016) conceptualization, but in line with established scholarly practice (e.g., Heinelt and Bertrana 2011), I categorize counties, provinces, *départements*, etc. as the upper tier of local government – rather than the lower tier of regional government – and I label it macro-local.

10 By Western Europe, I mean Austria (AT), Belgium (BE), Denmark (DK), Finland (FI), France (FR), Germany (DE), Ireland (IR), Italy (IT), The Netherlands (NL), Norway (NO), Portugal (PT), Spain (ES), Sweden (SE), Switzerland (CH), and the United Kingdom (UK). The mini-states (population below 1m) Iceland, Luxembourg, and Malta, and the micro-states (population below 100,000) Andorra, Liechtenstein, Monaco, San Marino, and Vatican are not included.

11 With about 0.9 percent of the population (SD 2012, 8).

12 A similar level of autonomy has also been granted to Greenland, whose population is roughly the size of the Faroes (Hooghe et al. 2016, 364–8; SD 2012, 8).

13 With about 0.5 percent of the population (StaFi 2013).

14 This score somewhat underestimates their autonomy compared with that of the provinces (e.g., Weibel 1971; Adorni and Francia 1998), hence I consider

them borderline strong regional governments and I treat Italy in 1950 as a partially federal state. The combined population of the four regions was about 14 percent of Italy's total in 1952 (ISTAT 2016).
15 With 4.85 percent of the population (INE 2013).
16 The provinces of Álava and Navarre had retained a special fiscal regime and scored 7.
17 Like in the case of the Italian special status regions, the RAI-RSF arguably underestimates the de facto autonomy of Northern Ireland under the 1922–72 home rule regime, mainly due to the tutelage by central government (e.g., Birrell and Murie 1980; Buckland 1981). I classify it as a strong regional government. Northern Ireland had around 2.7 percent of the UK population in 1950 (NIC 2011).
18 Which had been suspended between 1972 and 1999.
19 Where the traditional counties have been abolished. The combined population of Scotland, Wales, and Northern Ireland was about 16 percent of the UK total in 2011 (ONS 2012).
20 As the RAI-RSF scores are based on 2010 data, they underestimate the autonomy of the Welsh Assembly, which was boosted significantly after a referendum in March 2011. I classify it a strong regional government.
21 In a similar vein, although Finland falls in the same category as Denmark and France, its restructuring is arguably less consequential as it has brought a more modest change in the way the state functions.
22 Although it failed, I consider this a critical juncture and I include it in the analysis because reform was realistically possible. This is on the basis of the rationale Mahoney and Goertz (2004) call "the possibility principle"; see also Capoccia and Kelemen (2007, 352).
23 A reorganization of the regions took effect in 2016, reducing their number to thirteen in metropolitan France and expanding their competences. It did not, however, fundamentally change their constitutional status.
24 The notions of "top down" and "bottom up" have been employed in the literature on state restructuring before, both implicitly (e.g., Sharpe 1993, 3–26) and explicitly (e.g., Keating 1998a, esp. 47–61; Parks and Elcock 2000: 97–101; John 2001, 112–22), but with a different meaning and specification from those given to them here.
25 I use the term regionalist to refer to parties that operate only in one or a few regions of the state and have as their main objective the acquisition or preservation of autonomy for their region/s. A subset of them, the regional-nationalist parties, are marked, in addition, by a conceptualization of their region/s as a nation distinct from the majority nation that inhabit the state. The distinction between regionalism and regional nationalism goes back at least to Loughlin (1985, 232). I prefer the term "regional-nationalist" to that of "ethno-nationalist," used by some authors, because the former is more neutral. The "ethnic" assumption of the latter is clearly unwarranted in many cases and is thus a misleading label.

26 On the centrality of self-determination in nationalism, see among others Miller (2006, 530). On the distinction between secessionist and autonomist nationalism, see Lluch (2012).

CHAPTER TWO

1. Based on this conceptualization, I use the terms "Europe," "the European dimension," and "European integration" interchangeably with "European Union" and "EU."
2. This is broadly based on an approach informed by bounded rationality and institutionalism, on which, see, among others, Scharpf (1997).
3. I use "granting" rather than "devolving" because, while in most cases the powers granted to regional governments were indeed devolved from those exercised by the state government, in some cases – notably Denmark's – such powers were previously exercised by lower, macro-local units of government.
4. I use the term "independence" to refer to sovereign statehood and the term "autonomy" to refer to a self-governing regime within an existing sovereign state. I conceptualize the former as a dichotomy and the latter as a continuum. Hence, either a political unit has sovereign statehood or it does not, while there are degrees of autonomy.
5. Secession, defined as the act of separating from an existing state to form a new one, implies that the rump state (i.e., the former state minus the region/s that have seceded) becomes the successor state and thus inherits the international benefits and obligations of the former state. In case of dissolution, in contrast, the former state ceases to exist and no state acts as a successor state.
6. Previous research has shown that attitudes to European integration as an idea, as opposed to the existing EU, are particularly important, see Elias (2009) and Dardanelli (2014).
7. On the concept of bounded rationality and the role of imperfect information, see Kato (1996, 574–5) and Shepsle (1989, 140). On the crucial role of perceptions, see North (1995, 17), Enelow and Hinich (1984, esp. 207), and Kato (1996, 580–1).
8. On the methodological problems Europeanization research faces, see, among others, Haverland (2006).
9. In many cases the origins of the process of state restructuring can also be traced back to before 1950, but these are outside the scope of the book.
10. For bicameral parliaments, I consider the lower house only.
11. On the centrality of rhetoric in politics, see, among others, Arendt (1959, 3, 26–7), Edelman (1964, esp. 114), Laitin (1977, 158–61), Riker (1996), Breuning and Ishiyama (1998), Schimmelfennig (2003, 194–238), and Alonso (2012, 35–9).
12. The manifestos for the Belgian general elections of 1968, 1978, and 1991 and the Italian general election of 1992 were collected by the Manifesto Research Group (Budge et al. 2001) and supplied by GESIS (www.gesis.org/en/services/). The manifestos were made available in electronic form through a joint effort

between the Zentralarchiv für Empirische Sozialforschung (ZA), Wissenschaftszentrum Berlin (WZB), the Vrije Universiteit Amsterdam (VU), and the Party Manifestoes Project. MS Word transcription were made available by Paul Pennings and Hans Keman, Vrije Universiteit Amsterdam, Comparative Electronic Manifestos Project, in cooperation with the Social Science Reserach Centre Berlin (Andrea Volkens, Hans-Dieter Klingemann), the Zentralarchiv für empirische Sozialforschung, GESIS, Universität zu Köln, and the Manifesto Research Group (chairman: Ian Budge). Financed by the Netherlands Organization for Scientific Research (NWO project 480-42-005). The other documents were collected/accessed by the author.

13 In QCA terminology, conditions and outcomes are the equivalent of independent and dependent variables, respectively, in regression analysis.

CHAPTER THREE

1 In the early 1970s the budget was around 0.50 percent of the EU GDP and over 70 percent was allocated to the agricultural policy (Wallace 1980, 40).
2 I use the name European Parliament also to refer to the institution under its previous names, from the Common Assembly of the ECSC onward.
3 Under the terms of the Treaty of Paris, for instance, Belgium had one member of the Commission against two for Germany, and ten members of the EP against eighteen for Germany.
4 Even the kingdom established in 1861 was still incomplete. Italy only achieved full unification at the end of World War I, when, save for small border adjustments after World War II, it acquired more or less the territory it encompasses today. For a concise overview of Italy's history, see Duggan (1994).
5 On the different trajectories of unification of Italy and Germany and on the impact these had on the structuring of the state born of such process in the two cases, see Ziblatt (2006).
6 Due to space limitations, it is not possible here to give a full account of the factors that led to the choice of a unitary versus a federal structure. Ziblatt (2006) offers the best analysis currently available.
7 Including female suffrage, which would only be introduced in 1946.
8 "Hitherto in Italian history no other regionalist proposal had been formulated so clearly and explicitly."
9 "Opposed to all forms of federative organization of the state."
10 "Once the communist and the socialist parties had been excluded from the government, the regions offered to the left new opportunities for political action."
11 The pre-constitution statutes were converted into constitutional laws. The last special region, Friuli-Julian Venetia, was set up in 1963 once a border dispute with Yugoslavia had been settled.
12 The PSDI was a social-democratic party that had broken away from the PSI in 1947, the PLI was a liberal-conservative party, while the PRI was a liberal-radical party.
13 "conditions of more secure democratic stability."

14 "the most important reform of the democratic state."
15 "we want the regions, but in a situation of political stability in order to prevent unsettling actions by the PCI."
16 "The regions are not for today, they are for the future, when the PSI will have taken bold, historic decisions."
17 "from the regions and from the law on land holding."
18 "For a democratization of the state."'
19 "the urgent implementation of the normal-statute regions and the full development of local autonomy."
20 "fragmentation of the country."
21 "an objective to be pursued with all efforts."
22 "all the limitations and the dangers, economic and political, of a pro-European policy and a process of economic integration trapped within the constraints and the political-military platform of the Common Market."
23 "cage inside which Italy is forced to follow the direction set by the most reactionary international groups."
24 "an avant-garde role in the democratic movement for [European] unity."
25 All seats refer to the Chamber of Deputies, the lower house of parliament.
26 "In the context of the full implementation of the Constitution, the creation of the ordinary-statute regions takes particular importance. The parties are in agreement that the implementing laws, including the electoral law, be among the first actions of the government."
27 Similar bodies, the Commissions de développement économique régional, had been set up in France earlier the same year, see Hansen (1968, 83).
28 The decline in the number of those with no opinion was largely compensated by an increase in those responding "neither good nor harm" and "as much good as harm."
29 Rotelli (1967, 349) observed that in the constitutional assembly too the question of planning had no influence on the debate on the regions.
30 The most comprehensive account of Belgium's history before the twentieth century is in Pirenne (1948–52a-d). Kossman (1978) covers in detail the period 1780–1940, while Dumont (1977) offers a one-volume narrative history from the origins.
31 This was a new meaning of the term Flanders, see Zolberg (1974, 182) and Murphy (1988, 7). On the history of the Flemish movement see Wils (1992; 2009).
32 On this see Destatte (1997).
33 Although the Flemish catholic prime minister De Decker had perhaps been the first to suggest federalism for Belgium, in 1856 (Delforge 1999, 273).
34 On the VU, see Herremans (1962b,c) and De Winter (1998). On the RW, see Buelens and Van Dyck (1998) and Delforge (2003).
35 The crisis concerned the forced transfer to Wallonia of the French-language section of the University of Louvain (Goffart 1969; Coombes and Norton-Taylor 1968, 63).

36 "The fundamental objective of the RW is to stop the Flemish nationalist tide and to check its desire to dominate the Belgian state."
37 As a young professor at Leuven in the 1930s, he helped set up the weekly *Nieuw Vlaanderen*, which advocated federalism and corporatism, see Herremans (1962a, 6), Kossman (1978, 642), and Gérard-Libois (1987, 4).
38 "intends to maintain the national cohesion of public and private entities and is an opponent of federalism."
39 On the connections between federalization of Belgium and European federalism within the wider Flemish movement, see also Herremans (1961b, 10, 14–15; 1962b, 5) and CRISP (1965, 230).
40 "In the long term, with the other regions of Europe."
41 "Faster European integration on the basis of regions."
42 "The law of the regions rather than the law of the states."
43 Where the community party Front démocratique des francophones (FDF) almost doubled its share of the vote (Fraeys 1969, 288).
44 "The state must revise its organization."
45 "'But this Belgium must at the same time be more regional and more European." The second time he said, "Dit meer regionaal België moet terzfelder tijd meer Europees zijn" (BKV 1968, 5).
46 "The unitary state, as the laws still govern it in its structures and operation, has been overtaken by the events. The communities and the regions must take their place in the renovated structures of the state, better adapted to the specific conditions of the country."
47 To use the terminology of Dewachter et al. (1977, 250).
48 Both the liberals and the VU softened their positions over the period of the negotiations and tactically converged on the emerging compromise, see PLP (1970a,b) and VU (1970a, 4; 1970c, 3) respectively.
49 This interepretation was already widespread among contemporary observers, see for instance, Irving (1979, 251).

CHAPTER FOUR

1 Originally "of Great Britain and Ireland" and, following the secession of most of Ireland, "of Great Britain and Northern Ireland." Brief overviews of the process are offered by Bulpitt ([1983] 2008, 73–97) and McLean and McMillan (2005, 1–11). A concise single-volume history of the British Isles is Davies (1999).
2 Scotland and England had already been in a dynastic union since 1603.
3 The text is reproduced in Davies (1999, 1139–40).
4 In the remainder of this brief account, I focus on developments concerning Scotland and Wales, leaving aside the evolution of the Irish question.
5 The PC's vote share in the October 1974 election was slightly below that achieved by the party in 1970, but its tally of three MPs was the largest the party had ever had.

6 The party had already published a white paper in September 1974, i.e., before the election, outlining the principles of its devolution policy, see Bogdanor (1999, 178).
7 On this, see, among others, McLean and McMillan (2005, 168, 205) and Mitchell (2009, 151–6). Explaining Labour's decision to offer devolution for Wales is beyond the scope of this book, but it could be seen as being dictated by a logic of appropriateness rather than a logic of instrumentality. On the difference between the two logics, see, among others, Hall and Taylor (1996).
8 At the time of the election, the Walloon party was called Parti des réformes et de la liberté de Wallonie (PRLW).
9 "a Flemish state within a Belgian federal state."
10 "the institutional condition for economic recovery: integral federalism."
11 This also implied the creation of the province of Flemish Brabant and the splitting of the Brussels-Halle-Vilvoorde electoral district, see Menu (1994b, 280).
12 "a flourishing Flemish region in a modern Belgium."
13 "We will not take a nationalist turn."
14 "a real solution to the dispute between the communities can only come from a deepening of regionalization."
15 "the central government is overburdened with problems that would be better dealt with at the level of the regions and the communities."
16 "The PRLW wants to structure Belgium in simple and effective way, without additional expenditures and by bringing government closer to the citizen."
17 "faster construction of Europe."
18 "For a European Wallonia."
19 "a strong Europe, politically united, economically strong, and socially progressive."
20 "political self-rule for the Flemish state."
21 "a confederal Europe of cultural nations."
22 Seats refer to the Chamber of Representatives, the lower house of parliament.
23 *Pays* were subdivisions of the *provinces*, see Bazoche (2008, 16–18).
24 First pointed out by Tocqueville ([1856] 1967, esp. 98); for a recent detailed analysis, see Mannoni (1994–96).
25 "Local elected representatives should have the power to decide in all fields touching upon the life of citizens."
26 "the construction of collective facilities."
27 A search in the archive of *Le Monde*, covering the period 10 April–10 May 1981, also failed to retrieve programmatic statements on regionalization by Giscard d'Estaing.
28 "A real regional reform ... giving regional governments full responsibility for public infrastructure as well as significant competences in the field of support to small and medium size enterprises, education and employment, urban planning, and culture."
29 "A strong France in an independent Europe."
30 "A strong and effective Europe."

31 "The sovereignty and the democratic authority of the states."
32 "European integration must be deepened."
33 "foster the economic, social, sanitary, cultural, and scientific development of the region and the planned use of its territory."

CHAPTER FIVE

1 For an overview of the Brussels question in Belgian politics prior to the 1988 reform, see De Ridder and Fraga (1986).
2 For a brief summary of the Fourons dispute, see Deschouwer (2009, 52–3); for an in-depth treatment see CRISP (1979; 1983).
3 This section draws on Deschouwer (1999, 93–7).
4 A green party, Agalev, started to gain support but, only achieving 6.1 per cent of the vote in 1985, was still far from threatening the position of the more established parties.
5 A green party, Ecolo, also emerged in Wallonia but, as in Flanders, was still much smaller than the traditional parties – scoring 6.2 per cent in 1985.
6 "The autumn 1987 electoral campaign was dominated by topics related to the dispute between the two communities."
7 "The 1980 state reform was a first important step in this direction. It now needs to be deepened and completed."
8 "a fully fledged federal state in which the Flemish community would be granted extensive autonomy."
9 "the largest possible transfer of power to the Flemish community while preserving the [country's] economic and monetary union and a reversible, transparent, and purely complementary national solidarity."
10 "the general principle is that political institutions should adapt to the demand for more autonomy."
11 "The unfinished 1980 state reform should be deepened in order to arrive at a workable federal model, which is a condition for the survival of the Belgian polity to which we are attached."
12 "Thorough reform, leading to the greatest possible autonomy [for the communities]."
13 "The question should not be, what powers are devolved to the communities. It is the communities who should decide what to leave to the national government and how the financing is to be arranged after negotiations between them."
14 "a coherent, clear, simple, and balanced reform of Belgium: integral federalism."
15 "Like it or not, integral federalism is now the only way of remedying the ever more serious dysfunctions of the Belgian state, which may lead to its breakup or its complete 'Flemishization.'."
16 "a unifying form of federalism, which favours greater autonomy for the regions and the communities as well as the introduction of mechanisms strengthening the central state."

17 "We consider the national powers as a temporary transitional arrangement until European integration is achieved and the communities operate directly within the European context."
18 "it is of high importance that Flanders gets a direct representation in the European institutions."
19 "A unique opportunity for Flanders, as it is located at the heart of Europe."
20 "These new Flanders and Belgium thus go towards a European future." It also claimed that its advocacy of subsidiarity was rooted in its commitment to federalism and European integration (CVP 1987, 11).
21 "Our federalist ideal fits fully within the process of European integration."
22 "It could also be a harbinger of how nations would live together in the Europe of the future."
23 "The Flemish socialists strive for an open and progressive Europe in a federal perspective."
24 "Market integration would only widen the gap between rich and poor in Europe."
25 "Flanders and Belgium can only play a role in the world within a European Community based on liberal principles: free movement of persons, goods, services, and capital."
26 "flanking measures are necessary if the single market is not to exacerbate social and regional disparities."
27 "a strong and united Europe is essential. The liberals have always been at the forefront of the struggle for European unification."
28 "European integration should acknowledge the regional dimension. The notion of a Europe of the Regions addresses the will of the citizens and their demand for effectiveness and realism."
29 "the PSC is attached to the continuation of European integration."
30 "the PSC is opposed to a confederal model whereby the Belgian state is emptied of substance pending the emergence of a Europe of the Regions."
31 See also VLD (1992, 2), where the issue of fiscal responsibility is stressed.
32 "an independent Flanders in a federal Belgium and a federal Europe."
33 "Flanders must thus become a geographically small but strong independent state in Europe, with Brussels as capital."
34 Although, as seen above, the VLD's founding manifesto did place Flanders and a federal Belgium firmly in a European context.
35 "A federated state of a confederation which currently is still Belgian but will be European."
36 "less Belgium, more Flanders, and more Europe."
37 "This is thus the new European order. In this order Belgium is redundant."
38 "A link must exist between the creation of the economic and monetary union and progress in the field of fiscal and social harmonization."
39 "for regions and communities to be fully involved in the European decision-making process."
40 It would subsequently vote against the ratification of the treaty in parliament (Deschouwer and Van Assche 2008, 79).

41 As already mentioned, the PVV underwent a profound transformation in the wake of the election, adopting the new name Vlaamse Liberalen en Democraten (VLD) in 1992 and emphasizing its Flemish character.
42 Such a law has not been passed so residual powers still remain with the central state.

CHAPTER SIX

1 Formally, Trentino and South Tyrol are autonomous provinces within the region of Trentino-South Tyrol, but their status is comparable to that of the special statute regions; see, among others, King (1987, 333–4).
2 "The development of the regional institutions is one of the DC's priority objectives for the next parliament."
3 "All matters not reserved to state legislation should be conferred to the regions, so that ours would become a quasi-federal state."
4 "A truly political regionalism, approaching federalism."
5 "The federalism that will unite Europe would not divide Italy."
6 "Strong regionalism, inspired by federalism ... which is very different from a mere decentralization of the state as well as from a divisive confederation of republics."
7 "The European option is a paramount and irreversible choice for Italy ... Italy can only pursue economic and social modernization within the process of European unity."
8 "A federal project for a strong Europe."
9 "The Northern League is clearly in favour of a united Europe. Only a united Europe would be able to address the problems and the challenges of the future decades."
10 Which also signed an agreement with the far-left PRC whereby the two would not directly compete in the single-member constituencies.
11 "The Northern League considers Europe the primary framework for its political actions."
12 On how important the fear of exclusion was in shaping Italy's attitudes toward EMU, see Dyson and Featherstone (1996, esp. 273–4, 280, 288).
13 "It is vital to avoid Padania's exclusion from the institutionalization of a 'hard core' to which it is intimately linked."
14 This was the first time the Italian electorate was called to vote on a constitutional amendment.
15 Although the new regional presidents would soon be referred to as *governatori*, or governors, the system introduced by the reform was not fully presidential in that the president is not elected separately from the assembly and needs the latter's confidence to stay in office (Baldi 2006, 114–15).
16 Several boundary changes in the course of the nineteenth and twentieth centuries had led to an increase in the number of counties from 18 to 24 by 1970 (DCB 2014).

17 "It makes no sense for a small country such as Denmark to have three levels of government. The counties must therefore be abolished."
18 "the county tier and its tax-raising power is inappropriate and unnecessary. Three tax-raising tiers of government hinder the dynamic development of the public administration."
19 "The Danish People's Party is an opponent of the European Union and we fight all attempts at creating a European federal state."
20 The opt-outs cover the euro as well as aspects of justice and home affairs, and security and defence policy, see Kelstrup (2013) for an overview and Adler-Nissen (2013), Marcussen (2013), and Wivel (2013) for details.
21 Between 1993 and 1996, the governing coalition also included two other parties.
22 "The government has no plans to change the municipal structure." However, there is evidence that he himself, a former county mayor, was in favour of the reform, see Bundgaard and Vrangbæk (2007, 501).
23 Although he was understood to be personally sympathetic to the case for reform, his attempt was probably dictated by concerns about party unity, see Bundgaard and Vrangbæk (2007, 501).
24 On the composition and work of the commission, see Bundgaard and Vrangbæk (2007, 503–8) and Christiansen and Klitgaard (2008, 79–105).
25 "The largest and most important reform of the public sector for many years."

CHAPTER SEVEN

1 The EU enlarged further to Romania and Bulgaria in 2007, and Croatia in 2013.
2 "Fundamentally, the CD&V wants a clear, transparent state organization of which the core lies with the regions, in terms of both competences and resources. ... So the CD&V clearly chooses a further confederal evolution in which the competences of the federal government are defined clearly and all other competences belong to the regions."
3 "that Flanders has its own socioeconomic, fiscal, and financial policies, tailor-made for the Flemings."
4 As the BHV district straddled the boundary between monolingual Flanders and bilingual Brussels, the Flemish parties had long demanded its division, see, among others, Brassinne (2005).
5 "The final goal of the N-VA is Flanders as an independent state in a democratic Europe."
6 "The VB is the only party that directly and resolutely chooses Flemish independence."
7 "Open VLD is against separatism."
8 "As a Flemish-European party, the N-VA wants the provisions of the European Constitutional Treaty integrated as much as possible into the new treaty."
9 "The N-VA wishes that Flanders eventually becomes a fully fledged member state negotiating at the European table."

10 The party had voted against the ratification of the treaty in parliament (BKV 2005, 69).
11 "Our goal remains a confederal model, in which the bulk of the competences lies with the federated states. The five resolutions of the Flemish Parliament remain our point of reference."
12 "We want to reform the country thoroughly, not to split it."
13 "A confederal model, in which the bulk of the competences lies with the federated states.'
14 "Separatism and an independent Flanders: no, thank you."
15 "The Belgian structures no longer work."
16 "It is therefore important to put an end to Belgium quickly."
17 "Instead of investing much energy in state reforms and confederalism, Flanders should rather invest in the active preparation of Flemish Independence and an Orderly Division of Belgium."
18 "more resources for the federal government, which guarantees adequate social protection, and more competences for the communities and regions to better invest in people, knowledge, and sustainable development."
19 "It is essential to stablize the federal state."
20 That is a constituency for the election of the federal parliament spanning the entire country and in which both Dutch and French speakers would be elected.
21 "A strong Europe with efficient institutions."
22 "We must be open to closer economic cooperation to safeguard the economic basis of the euro."
23 "A more balanced distribution between the three pillars of the EU 2020 strategy is needed, with priority for direct investment in the social pillar."
24 "Vlaams Belang wants: no federal Europe, but an EU as an intergovernmental confederation, of which Flanders as a sovereign state, is a full member."
25 "For the PS, the creation of a social and solidaristic Europe remain the first objective."
26 "The MR is convinced that a more integrated Europe is the solution to the problems of today and tomorrow."
27 "A strong federal Europe, which brings together the European citizens across borders and languages in a European Union."
28 "A resolutely federal outlook on the European Union."
29 "Flanders would not accept that the EU ever decided on the appropriateness of Flemish Independence."
30 "Belgium, indeed, does not offer the economies of scale that Europe is able to offer ... What Flanders cannot resolve by itself, cannot be resolved by Belgium. European integration makes this process possible."
31 "Flanders as a member state of the European Union offers the best prospects for effective and democratic self-government in a rapidly changing world."
32 "Flanders needs to obtain the competence to represent itself at the European table for its own competences."
33 For an early, primarily legal, assessment, see Sautois and Uyttendaele (2013).
34 Known as the Welsh Assembly Government until 2011, see BBC (2011).

35 As EU policy is a matter reserved for Westminster, it is not suprising that parties did not formally address it in their manifesto for the regional elections.
36 Catalonia, however, was able to retain its distinct civil law system.
37 The three Basque provinces are Álava (Araba in Basque), Biscay (Vizcaya in Spanish and Bizkaia in Basque), and Guipúzcoa (Gipuzkoa in Basque).
38 After Carlos, a pretender to the throne drawing support from traditionalists (Carr 1982, 184–5).
39 These were mainly to do to with a privileged tax regime and exemption from military service and custom duties (Carr 1982, 63).
40 For a broader discussion of the idea of Spain in the nineteenth century, see Álvarez Junco (2001).
41 An independent Catalan state had twice been declared previously, in 1641 (Elliott 1963a, 521–2) and 1873 (Carr 1982, 331).
42 In the late nineteenth century, 11 September, commemorating the fall of Barcelona in 1714, was adopted as the national day of Catalonia.
43 For an overview of the statewide Spanish party system, see Ramiro and Morales (2010).
44 See PS-C et al. (2003, 12–15), PS-C (2003, 12), ICV (2003, 29), and CiU (2003, 46).
45 *Vegueries* were the upper tier of local government before 1716.
46 "Those who do not want to recognize us as a nation today will have to do so as a state tomorrow."
47 "We are a nation, and we have the right to decide."
48 "Yes: Catalonia wins; No: the PP wins."
49 "Now it's no, Catalonia deserves more."
50 For this reason, I have not analyzed them here.
51 "We are a nation. We decide."
52 "Within this right to decide, we set as a priority the complete management of our economic resources, through an autonomous financing model such as the *concierto* [enjoyed by the Basque Country]."
53 "From the statute to the state."
54 ""Toward our own state."
55 "If one day ERC controls a majority of the members of the Parliament of Catalonia, it would declare independence."
56 "our own state in a federal and multinational Spain and a united Europe."
57 "a stronger supranational Europe, with a European level of government, better institutions, and a greater margin for manoeuvre vis-à-vis the interests of the member states."
58 "strengthening the building of a political Europe, conscious that in the context of today's and tomorrow's socioeconomic situation we need more Europe than ever."
59 "Catalonia, Europe's next state," see DDD (2010).
60 "Catalonia, a new European state."
61 "On 12 September the government will have to start working for Catalonia's independence."

62 "In exceptional times, exceptional decisions … the voice of the street, massive and powerful, should be transferred to the ballot box."
63 "It is time for Catalonia to set off on the path to its own state."
64 "After more than thirty years of democracy, we have found that it is very difficult for Catalonia to fit in the Spanish state. Doors have been shut, and therefore it is time for us to set off on our own path."
65 "the independence of our country is essential if we are to continue to exist as a nation, to protect our social rights, to develop our potential as a country, and to guarantee the continuity of our welfare state."
66 "calling, in the course of 2014, a referendum on the independence of Catalonia, to become a new state within the European Union."
67 "The federalist alternative is the only one able to deliver a balanced institutional system, within which Catalonia would remain a part of Spain but without renouncing its identity and its collective pursuits."
68 "We have long called for the acquisition of our own state, which can, on the basis of its sovereignty, establish a federal or confederal relation [with the rest of Spain] or be present directly in the European context, depending on the willingness to negotiate on the part of the State and the free decision of the citizens of Catalonia."
69 "With our vote, we have the opportunity to say loud and clear that we want to continue to live together with the rest of Spain."
70 "we are prepared to sacrify part of our sovereignty for the sake of building an economically and politically stronger Europe, a Europe set to become a genuine federal entity."
71 "We want to have our own state in Europe."
72 "Our national transition is necessarily dependent on continuing to be part of 'Europe.'"
73 "ERC defends a Catalonia integrated with, and committed to, Europe … Catalonia has always been in favour of a political strengthening of the Union and of its institutions … We therefore firmly believe in an independent Catalonia integrated with Europe. Because Catalonia has contributed to this European Union and because Catalonia is Europe and the Catalans are European citizens. Like Scotland, Catalonia aspires to become an additional member state of this Union and join the European brotherhood. We therefore believe in an 'internal enlargement' of the European Union."
74 "We live in times of shared sovereignty. We believe in a project of shared sovereignty between Catalonia and Spain and of course also with Europe, because we are and we feel European and because it is clear to us that the challenges facing Catalonia and Spain and the solutions to them are to be found in Europe."
75 "It is a serious mistake to want to break away from Spain, because it would entail breaking away from the European Union too, as well as creating a social divide in Catalonia."
76 "Membership of the Union and of the euro is crucial to ensure the preservation and enhancement of the prosperity we have acquired."

77 "From its new status as a member state of the European Union, [Catalonia] will promote a federal model for Europe, favouring growing integration."
78 "contrary to what some would have us believe, membership [of the EU] is not threatened by independence."
79 "it only guarantees privileges for capital and does not represent the interests of the European working classes."

CHAPTER EIGHT

1 Complex solutions exclude all so-called logical remainders, i.e., configurations of conditions that lack empirical cases; parsimonious solutions include all logical remainders; while intermediate solutions only include those logical remainders that are consistent with the theoretical expectations of the researcher (Ragin 2008, 173–5).
2 The sign "~" indicates the absence of a condition.
3 The selection of conditions is based on Dardanelli (2014, 218–20). The condition "regional economic status" has not been included because is not relevant to the analysis conducted here, given that many observations concern statewide parties in general elections.
4 The sufficiency test has been performed on the cases displaying positive use (i.e., $MiO2=1$).
5 These results confirm the findings of Dardanelli (2014), whose analysis was based on a different set of cases.
6 As the RW ceased to be a significant political force by the late 1970s, its subsequent trajectory cannot meaningfully be compared with that of the other regional-nationalist parties.

References

Abromeit, Heidrun. 1992. *Der verkappte Einheitsstaat.* Opladen: Leske und Budrich.
Abts, Koen, Dmitriy Poznyak, and Marc Swyngedouw. 2012. "The Federal Elections in Belgium, June 2010." *Electoral Studies* 31 (2): 448–52.
Abts, Koen, Marc Swyngedouw, Jaak Billiet, and Bart Meuleman. 2014. *Vlaanderen Kiest.* Leuven: Lannoo Campus.
Adamson, Kevin, and Robert Johns. 2008. "The Vlaams Blok, Its Electorate and the Ideological Rearticulation of 'Europe.'" *Journal of Political Ideologies* 13 (2): 133–56.
Adcock, Robert, and David Collier. 2001. "Measurement Validity: A Shared Standard for Qualitative and Quantitative Research." *American Political Science Review* 95 (3): 529–45.
Adler-Nissen, Rebecca. 2013. "Justice and Home Affairs – Denmark as an Active Differential European." In *Denmark and the European Union*, edited by Lee Miles and Anders Wivel, 65–79. Abingdon: Routledge.
Adorni, Daniela and Enrico Francia. 1998. "Autonomie Locali." In *Guida all'Italia contemporanea – Vol. II Istituzioni politiche e forme di governo*, edited by Massimo Firpo, Nicola Tranfaglia, and Pier Giorgio Zunino, 165–247. Milan: Garzanti.
Agnew, John. 2002. *Place and Politics in Modern Italy.* Chicago, IL: University of Chicago Press.
– 1997. "The Dramaturgy of Horizons: Geographical Scale in the 'Reconstruction of Italy' by the New Italian Political Parties, 1992–95." *Political Geography* 16 (2): 99–121.
Agranoff, Bob (ed.). 1999. *Accommodating Diversity: Asymmetry in Federal States.* Baden-Baden: Nomos.
Aja, Eliseo. 2003. *El Estado autonómico – Federalismo y hechos diferenciales,* second ed. Madrid: Alianza.
Alesina, Alberto and Enrico Spolaore. 2003. *The Size of Nations.* Cambridge, MA: MIT Press.

– 1997. "On the Number and Size of Nations." *The Quarterly Journal of Economics* 112 (4): 1027–56.
Alesina, Alberto, Enrico Spolaore, and Romain Wacziarg. 2000. "Economic Integration and Political Disintegration." *The American Economic Review* 90 (5): 1276–96.
Allen, David. 2005. "Cohesion and the Structural Funds – Competing Pressures for Reform?" In *Policy-Making in the European Union*, fifth ed., edited by Helen Wallace, William Wallace, and Mark Pollack, 213–41. Oxford: Oxford University Press.
Allievi, Stefano. 1992. *Le parole della Lega – Il movimento politico che vuole un'altra Italia*. Milan: Garzanti.
Allum, Percy. 1969. "Italy." In *European Political Parties*, edited by Stanley Henig and John Pinder, 193–255. London: Allen and Unwin.
Alonso, Sonia. 2012. *Challenging the State: Devolution and the Battle for Partisan Credibility*. Oxford: Oxford University Press.
Alter, Karen. 2002. *Establishing the Supremacy of European Law*. Oxford: Oxford University Press.
Álvarez Junco, José. 2001. *Mater Dolorosa – La idea de España en el siglo XIX*. Madrid: Taurus.
Amat, Francesc and Albert Falcó-Gimeno. 2014. "The Legislative Dynamics of Political Decentralization in Parliamentary Democracies." *Comparative Political Studies* 47 (6): 820–50.
Amoretti, Ugo. 2002. "Italy Decentralizes." *Journal of Democracy* 13 (2): 126–40.
Andersen, Jørgen Goul. 2003. "The General Election of Denmark, November 2001." *Electoral Studies* 22 (1): 186–93.
– 2006. "The Parliamentary Election in Denmark, February 2005." *Electoral Studies* 22 (1): 186–93.
Andersen, Jørgen Goul, and Jan Bendix Jensen. 2001. "The Danish *Venstre*: Liberal, Agrarian or Centrist? In *From Farmyard to City Square?" The Electoral Adaptation of the Nordic Agrarian Parties*, edited by David Arter, 96–131. Aldershot: Ashgate.
Andersen, Vibeke Normann. 2010. "Denmark." In *Changing Government Relations in Europe – From Localism to Intergovernmentalism*, edited by Mike Goldsmith and Edward Page, 47–67. Abingdon: Routledge.
Anderson, James. 1991. "Skeptical Reflections on a Europe of Regions: Britain, Germany, and the ERDF." *Journal of Public Policy* 10 (4): 417–47.
Anderson, James, and James Goodman. 1995. "Regions, States and the European Union: Modernist Reaction or Postmodern Adaptation?" *Review of International Political Economy* 2 (4): 600–31.
Antonini, Luca. 2013. *Federalismo all'italiana – Dietro le quinte della grande incompiuta*. Venice: Marsilio.
Apel, Emmanuel. 1998. *European Monetary Integration 1958–2002*. London: Routledge.
Ara. 2012. Carme Forcadell, presidenta de l'ANC: "El 12 de setembre, el Govern haurà de començar a treballar per la independència de Catalunya."

Ara.cat, www.ara.cat/especials/onzesetembre2012/Carme_Forcadell-ANC_0_763723714.html.
Arendt, Hannah. 1959. *The Human Condition*. Chicago, IL: University of Chicago Press.
Argelaguet, Jordi, Margarita Gómez-Reino Cachafeiro, and Romain Pasquier. 2004. "L'Esquerra Republicana de Catalunya – La troisième force de l'espace politique catalan." *Pôle Sud* 20: 9–24.
Arzaghi, Mohammed, and Vernon Henderson. 2005. "Why Countries Are Fiscally Decentralizing." *Journal of Public Economics* 89 (7): 1157–89.
Ashfold, Tom. 2014. *Polling Data on the Scottish Independence Referendum*. Library Note LLN 2014/027. London: The House of Lords.
Ashford, Nigel. 1980. "The European Economic Community." In *Conservative Party Politics*, edited by Zig Layton-Henry, 95–125. London: Macmillan.
Aubert, Jean-François. 1978. *Exposé des institutions politiques de la Suisse à partir de quelques affaires controversées*. Lausanne: Payot.
Aylott, Nicholas. 1999. "Paradoxes and Opportunism: The Danish Election of March 1998." *Government and Opposition* 34 (1): 59–77.
Bache, Ian, and Rachel Jones. 2000. "Has EU Regional Policy Empowered the Regions?" *Regional and Federal Studies* 10 (3): 1–20.
Baker, David, Andrew Gamble, Nick Randall, and David Seawright. 2008. "Euroscepticism in the British Party System: A Source of Fascination, Perplexity, and Sometimes Frustration." In *Opposing Europe?*, edited by Paul Taggart and Aleks Szczerbiak, 93–116. Oxford: Oxford University Press.
Balcells, Albert. 2010. *El projecte d'autonomia de la Mancomunitat de Catalunya del 1919 i el seu context històric*. Barcelona: Parlament de Catalunya.
– [1991] 1996. *Catalan Nationalism – Past and Present*. New York, NY: St Martin's Press.
Baldersheim, Harald, and Anne Lise Fimreite. 2006. "Norwegian Centre-Periphery Relations in Flux: Abolition or Reconstruction of Regional Governance." *West European Politics* 28 (4): 764–80.
Baldersheim, Harald, and Lawrence Rose. 2010. "The Staying Power of the Norwegian Periphery." In *Territorial Choice – The Politics of Boundaries and Borders*, edited by Harald Baldersheim and Richard Rose, 80–100. Basingstoke: Palgrave Macmillan.
Baldi, Brunetta. 2006. *Regioni e federalismo – L'Italia e l'Europa*. Bologna: CLUEB.
Baldini, Gianfranco, and Brunetta Baldi. 2014. "Decentralization in Italy and the Troubles of Federalization." *Regional and Federal Studies* 24 (1): 87–108.
Baras, Montserrat, and Jordi Matas Dalmases. 1998. "Els partits polítics i el sistema de partits." In *El sistema polític de Catalunya*, edited by Miquel Caminal Badia and Jordi Matas Dalmases, 161–90. Barcelona: Tecnos.
Barbeta, Jordi. 2014a. "El diàlogo no encuentra vía." *La Vanguardia*, 9 April.
– 2014b. "Majoria sobiranista amb 'sorpasso' d'ERC." *La Vanguardia*, 26 May.

- 2012a. "Catalunya pide rescate y pacto fiscal." *La Vanguardia*, 25 July.
- 2012b. "Se ha perdido una oportunidad histórica." *La Vanguardia*, 21 September.
- 2012c. "Mas convoca elecciones y abre el proceso de autodeterminación." *La Vanguardia*, 26 September.
- 2012d. "El Parlament expresa la necesidad de que Catalunya haga su propio camino." *La Vanguardia*, 28 September.
- 2012e. "Mas y Junqueras pactan estabilidad y la convocatoria de la consulta en el 2014." *La Vanguardia*, 19 December.
- 2012f. "Mobilització sense precedents per la independència de Catalunya." *La Vanguardia*, 12 September.
- 2010. "Catalunya no se rinde." *La Vanguardia*, 11 July.
- 2006a. "Zapatero y Mas pactan el Estatut." *La Vanguardia*, 22 January.
- 2006b. "El Congreso aprueba el Estatut y cunde la idea de que España empieza a cambiar." *La Vanguardia*, 31 March.
- 2006c. "España aprueba el Estatut de Catalunya." *La Vanguardia*, 11 May.

Bartolini, Stefano. 2005. *Restructuring Europe*. Oxford: Oxford University Press.

Baskaran, Thushyanthan. 2010. "Supranational Integration and National Reorganization: On the Maastricht Treaty's Impact on Fiscal Decentralization in EU Countries." *Constitutional Political Economy* 21 (4): 309–35.

Bassanini, Franco. 1970. *L'attuazione dell'ordinamento regionale*. Florence: La Nuova Italia.

Bazoche, Maud. 2008. *Département ou région? Les réformes territoriales de Fénelon à Jacques Attali*. Paris: L'Harmattan.

BBC. 2014a. "Extremely Difficult for Scotland to Join EU-Barroso." *BBC News*, 16 February, www.bbc.co.uk/news/uk-politics-26215579.
- 2014b. "Scottish Independence: Scotland 'Committed' to EU, Says Salmond." *BBC News*, 29 April, www.bbc.co.uk/news/uk-scotland-scotland-politics-27180301.
- 2014c. "Scottish Independence: Vote 'Will Go to the Wire.'" *BBC News*, 7 September, www.bbc.co.uk/news/uk-scotland-29096458.
- 2014d. "Scottish Independence: Cameron, Miliband and Clegg Sign 'No' Vote Pledge." *BBC News*, 16 September, www.bbc.co.uk/news/uk-scotland-scotland-politics-29213418.
- 2014e. "Scottish Referendum: Scotland Votes 'No' to Independence." *BBC News*, 19 September, www.bbc.co.uk/news/uk-scotland-29270441.
- 2011. "Carwyn Jones Unveils Three New Faces in Welsh Cabinet." *BBC News*, 13 May, www.bbc.co.uk/news/uk-wales-politics-13389400.
- 2007. "Labour Agrees Historic Coalition." *BBC News*, 6 July, news.bbc.co.uk/1/hi/wales/6275036.stm.
- 1999. "UK Politics – Ron Davies' Fightback Begins." *BBC News*, 4 February, news.bbc.co.uk/1/hi/uk_politics/272015.stm.

Beirich, Heidim and Dwayne Woods. 2000. "Globalisation, Workers and the Northern League." *West European Politics* 23 (1): 130–43.

Bell, David, and Byron Criddle. 1984. *The French Socialist Party – Resurgence and Victory*. Oxford: Clarendon Press.
Bennie, Lynn, Jack Brand, and James Mitchell. 1997. *How Scotland Votes*. Manchester: Manchester University Press.
Benoit, Kenneth, and Michael Laver. 2006. *Party Policy in Modern Democracies*. London: Routledge.
Berlucchi, Maria Chiara. 1997. "Quale secessione in Italia?" *Rivista italiana di scienza politica* 27 (2): 345–72.
Besserman, Lawrence. 1996. "The Challenge of Periodization: Old Paradigms and New Perspectives." In *The Challenge of Periodization – Old Paradigms and New Perspectives*, edited by Lawrence Besserman, 3–27. New York, NY: Garland.
Besson, Jean, and Geneviève Bibes. 1993. "Né maggioranza né opposizione: le elezioni politiche del 5 e 6 aprile 1992." In *Politica in Italia – I fatti dell'anno e le interpretazioni – Edizione 1993*, edited by Stephen Hellman and Gianfranco Pasquino, 57–82. Bologna: Il Mulino.
Bille, Lars. 1999. "The Danish Social Democratic Party." In *Social Democratic Parties in the European Union*, edited by Robert Ladrech and Philippe Marlière, 43–55. Basingstoke: Macmillan.
– 1994. "Denmark: The Decline of the Membership Party?" In *How Parties Organize: Change and Adaptation in Party Organizations in Western Democracies*, edited by Richard Katz and Peter Mair, 134–57. London: Sage.
– 1989. "Denmark: The Oscillating Party System." *West European Politics* 12 (4): 42–58.
Bindseil, Ulrich, and Cordula Handtke. 1997. "The Power Distribution in Decision Making among EU Member States." *European Journal of Political Economy* 13 (1): 171–85.
Biorcio, Roberto. 1999. "La Lega Nord e la transizione italiana." *Rivista italiana di scienza politica* 29 (1): 55–87.
– 1997. *La Padania promessa – La storia, le idee e la logica d'azione della Lega Nord*. Milan: Il Saggiatore.
Birch, Anthony. 1978. "Minority Nationalist Movements and Theories of Political Integration." *World Politics* 30 (3): 325–44.
Birrell, Derek and Alan Murie. 1980. *Policy and Government in Northern Ireland – Lessons of Devolution*. Dublin: Gill and Macmillan.
Bisson, Thomas. [1986] 2000. *The Medieval Crown of Aragon*. Oxford: Clarendon Press.
Biugan, Ketil. 1999. "The 1998 Danish Parliamentary Election: Social Democrats Muddle Through to Victory." *West European Politics* 22 (1): 172–8.
BKV. 2008. Integraal Verslag, Plenumvergadering, 10-04-2008, Namiddag. *Belgische Kamer van Volksvertegenwoordigers*. Available at www.dekamer.be [accessed 23 August 2011].
– 2005. Integraal Verslag, met vertaald beknopt verslag van de toespraken. Plenumvergadering, 19-05-2005, Avond. *Belgische Kamer van de Volksvertengenwoordigers*. Available at www.dekamer.be [accessed 23 August 2011].

- 1968. Parlementaire Handelingen, Vergadering van dinsdag 25 juni 1968. *Belgische Kamer van Volksvertegenwoordigers*. Available at www.dekamer.be [accessed 23 August 2011].
Blaise, Pierre, Vincent de Coorebyter, and Jean Faniel. 2010. Les résultats des élections fédérales du 13 juin 2010. *Courrier hebdomadaire* 2082–3. Brussels: CRISP.
- 2007. Les résultats des élections fédérales du 10 juin 2007. *Courrier hebdomadaire* 1964–5. Brussels: CRISP.
Blom-Hansen, Jens. 2010. "Municipal Amalgamations and Common Pool Problems: The Danish Local Government Reform in 2007." *Scandinavian Political Studies* 33 (1): 51–73.
Bochel, John, David Denver, and Allan Macartney. 1981. "The Background to the Referendum." In *The Referendum Experience: Scotland 1979*, edited by John Bochel, David Denver, and Allan Macartney, 1–11. Aberdeen: Aberdeen University Press.
Bogdanor, Vernon. 1999. *Devolution in the United Kingdom*. Oxford: Oxford University Press.
- 1980. "Devolution." In *Conservative Party Politics*, edited by Zig Layton-Henry, 75–94. London: Macmillan.
Bolton, Patrick, and Gerard Roland. 1997. "The Breakup of Nations: A Political Economy Analysis." *Quarterly Journal of Economics* 112 (4): 1057–90.
Bomberg, Elizabeth, and John Peterson. 1998. "European Union Decision Making: The Role of Sub-national Authorities." *Political Studies* 46 (2): 219–35.
Boon, Martin, and John Curtice. 2003. *Scottish Elections Research*. London: The Electoral Commission, available at www.electoralcommission.org.uk/__data/assets/electoral_commission_pdf_file/0014/16106/ICMScottishElectionsreportfinal_9921-8023__E__N__S__W__.pdf.
Börzel, Tanja. 2005. "Europeanization: How the European Union Interacts with Its Member States." In *The Member States of the European Union*, edited by Simon Bulmer and Christian Lequesne, 45–69. Oxford: Oxford University Press.
- 2002. *States and Regions in the European Union – Institutional Adaptation in Germany and Spain*. Cambridge: Cambridge University Press.
Bossi, Umberto, and Daniele Vimercati. 1992. *Vento dal Nord – La mia Lega, la mia vita*. Milan: Sperling & Kupfer.
Bound, Joy, and Kevin Featherstone. 1982. "The French Left and the European Community." In *Contemporary French Political Parties*, edited by David Bell. 165–89. London: Croom Helm.
Bourricaud, François. 1977. "The Right in France since 1945" *Comparative Politics* 10 (1): 5–34.
Bracero, Francesc. 2006a. "Carod cree que la manifestación muestra que "España tiene un problema" con Catalunya." *La Vanguardia*, 20 February.

- 2006b. "Las bases de Esquerra instan a la cúpula a cambiar el voto nulo por el no en el referéndum." *La Vanguardia*, 3 May.
Bracero, Francesc, and Jaume Aroca. 2006. "La direction de ERC se decanta por el no al Estatut espoleada por la reacción de sus bases." *La Vanguardia*, 26 January.
Brack, Nathalie, and Jean-Benoît Pilet. 2010. "One Country, Two Party Systems? The 2009 Belgian Regional Elections." *Regional and Federal Studies* 20 (4–5): 549–59.
Brancati, Dawn. 2014. "Another Great Illusion: The Advancement of Separatism through Economic Integration." *Political Science Research and Methods* 2 (1): 69–95.
- 2006. "Decentralization: Fueling the Fire or Dampening the Flames of Ethnic Conflict and Secessionism?" *International Organization* 60 (3): 651–85.
Brand, Jack. 1978. *The National Movement in Scotland*. London: Routledge and Kegan Paul.
Brand, Jack, and James Mitchell. 1994. *General Election in Scotland, 1992* [computer file]. Colchester, Essex: UK Data Archive [distributor], March 1994. SN: 3171, dx.doi.org/10.5255/UKDA-SN-3171-1.
Brassinne de la Buissière, Jacques. 2005. "Les négociations communautaires sous le gouvernement Verhofstadt II : forum institutionnel et Bruxelles-Hal-Vilvorde."*Courrier hebdomadaire* 1903–4. Brussels: CRISP
- 1999. "Wallonia and the Reform of the State." In *L'idée fédéraliste dans les Etats-nations*, edited by Philippe Destatte, 307–29. Brussels: Presses interuniversitaires européennes
- 1997. "La Constitution flamande – Essai de constitution pour la Flandre (1996)." *Courrier hebdomadaire* 1569–70. Brussels: CRISP.
Braun, Daniela, and Markus Tausendpfund. 2014. "The Impact of the Euro Crisis on Citizens' Support for the European Union." *Journal of European Integration* 36 (3): 231–45.
Braun, Dietmar. 2003. "Dezentraler und unitarischer Föderalismus – Die Schweiz und Deutschland in Vergleich." *Schweizerische Zeitschrift für Politikwissenschaft* 9 (1): 57–89
Breuning, Marijke and John Ishiyama. 1998. "The Rhetoric of Nationalism: Rhetorical Strategies of the Volksunie and Vlaams Blok in Belgium, 1991–1995." *Political Communication* 15 (1): 5–26.
Bromley, Catherine. 2006. "Devolution and Electoral Politics in Scotland." In *Devolution and Electoral Politics*, edited by Dan Hough and Charlie Jeffery. 192–213. Manchester: Manchester University Press
Bromley, Catherine, and John Curtice. 2003. "Devolution: Scorecard and Prospects." In *Devolution – Scottish Answers to Scottish Questions?*, edited by Catherine Bromley, John Curtice, Kerstin Hinds, and Alison Park, 7–29. Edinburgh: Edinburgh University Press.
Brunazzo, Marco. 2010. "Italian Regionalism: A Semi-Federation Is Taking Shape – Or Is It?" In *Territorial Choice – The Politics of Boundaries and*

Borders, edited by Harald Baldersheim and Lawrence Rose, 180–97. Basingstoke: Palgrave Macmillan.

Brunet, José María. 2006. "El PP lleva al Constitucional más de la mitad de los artículos del Estatut." *La Vanguardia*, 1 August.

Bruxant, Martin. 2010. "Ne pas changer de nationalité, c'est capital." *La Libre*, 23 October.

Buck, Tobias, and Mure Dickie. 2014. "Spain Promises Non-interference on Scotland." *Financial Times*, 2 February.

Buckland, Patrick. 1981. *A History of Northern Ireland*. Dublin: Gill and Macmillan.

Budge, Ian, Hans-Dieter Klingemann, Andrea Volkens, Judith Bara, and Eric Tanenbaum. 2001. *Mapping Policy Preferences – Estimates for Parties, Electors, and Governments 1945–1998*. Oxford: Oxford University Press.

Budge, Ian, David Mackay, John Bartle, and Ken Newton. 2007. *The New British Politics*, fourth ed. Harlow: Pearson.

Buelens, Jo, and Kris Deschouwer. 2002. "Belgium." *Environmental Politics* 11 (1): 112–32.

Buelens, Jo, and Ruth Van Dyck. 1998. "Regionalist Parties in French-Speaking Belgium." In *Regionalist Parties in Western Europe*, edited by Lieven de Winter and Huri Türsan, 51–69. London: Routledge.

Bull, Martin. 1996. "The Italian Christian Democrats." In *Political Parties and the European Union*, edited by John Gaffney, 139–54. London: Routledge.

Bull, Martin and James Newell. 1995. "Italy Changes Course? The 1994 Elections and the Victory of the Right." *Parliamentary Affairs* 48 (1): 72–99.

– 1993. "Italian Politics and the 1992 Elections: From 'Stable Instability' to Instability and Change." *Parliamentary Affairs* 46 (2): 203–27.

Bulpitt, Jim. [1983] 2008. *Territory and Power in the United Kingdom*. Colchester: ECPR Press.

Bundgaard, Ulrik, and Karsten Vrangbæk. 2007. "Reform by Coincidence? Explaining the Policy Process of Structural Reform in Denmark." *Scandinavian Political Studies* 30 (4): 491–520.

Burnham, Peter. 2009. "State." In *The Concise Oxford Dictionary of Politics*, third ed., edited by Iain McLean and Alistair McMillan. Oxford: Oxford University Press.

Butler, David, and Dennis Kavanagh. 1997. *The British General Election of 1997*. Basingstoke: Macmillan.

– 1992. *The British General Election of 1992*. London: Macmillan.

– 1988. *The British General Election of 1987*. Basingstoke: Macmillan.

– 1980. *The British General Election of 1979*. London: Macmillan.

– 1975. *The British General Election of October 1974*. London: Macmillan.

Byrd, Peter. 1978. "The Labour Party and the Trade Unions." In *Divided Loyalties*, edited by Martin Kolinsky, 130–57. Manchester: Manchester University Press.

Cameron, David. 2014. "David Cameron: The EU Is Not Working and We Will Change It." *Sunday Telegraph*, 16 March.

Caminal Badia, Miquel. 1998. "Catalanisme i autogovern." In *El sistema polític de Catalunya*, edited by Miquel Caminal Badia and Jordi Matas Dalmases, 25–53. Barcelona: Tecnos.
Capoccia, Giovanni, and Daniel Kelemen. 2007. "The Study of Critical Junctures: Theory, Narrative and Counterfactuals in Historical Institutionalism." *World Politics* 59 (3): 341–69
Caramani, Daniele. 2004. *The Nationalization of Politics – The Formation of National Electorates and Party Systems in Western Europe*. Cambridge: Cambridge University Press.
Carman, Christopher, Robert Johns, and James Mitchell. 2014. *More Scottish than British: The 2011 Scottish Parliament Election*. Basingstoke: Palgrave Macmillan.
Carod i Rovira, Josep. 2003. "De l'Estatut a l'Estat." *Avui*, 9 April.
Carr, Raymond. 1982. *Spain, 1808–1975*, second ed. Oxford: Clarendon Press.
Castro, Carles. 2011. *Retrato electoral de Catalunya*. Barcelona: Episteme.
CD&V. 2010. *Noit Opgeven – Verkiezingsprogramma CD&V 2010*. Manifesto for the 2010 federal election. Available at http://verkiezingen.cdenv.be/ [accessed 23 August 2010].
– 2007a. *Samen Werken Werkt*. Full manifesto for the 2007 federal election. Brussels: Christen-Democratisch en Vlaams.
– 2007b. *Als het aan ons ligt Samen Werken aan Morgen*. Summary of manifesto for the 2007 federal election. Brussels: Christen-Democratisch en Vlaams.
CDH. 2010. *Un pacte pour sortir les Belges de la crise*. Manifesto for the 2010 federal election. Available at www.lecdh.be/sites/default/files/100519_Programme_synthetique_JM_o.pdf [accessed 23 August 2010].
– 2007. *C'est l'heure h*. Summary manifesto for the 2007 federal election. Brussels: Centre démocrate humaniste.
CdS. 1992a. "Forlani e Craxi: fuoco su La Malfa." *Corriere della Sera*, 18 March.
– 1992b. "Bossi sul Carroccio punta al 13 per cento." *Corriere della Sera*, 4 April.
– 1992c. "La battaglia del 50 per cento. I Quattro: o con noi o il caos." *Corriere della Sera*, 5 April.
CDW. 2014. Empowerment and Responsibility: Legislative Powers to Strengthen Wales. *Commission on Devolution in Wales*, available at commissionondevolutioninwales.independent.gov.uk/files/2014/03/Empowerment-Responsibility-Legislative-Powers-to-strengthen-Wales.pdf [accessed 4 September 2014].
– 2012. Empowerment and Responsibility: Financial Powers to Strenghten Wales. *Commission on Devolution in Wales*, available at commissionondevolutioninwales.independent.gov.uk/files/2013/01/English-WEB-main-report1.pdf [accessed 4 September 2014].
Cento Bull, Anna, and Mark Gilbert. 2001. *The Lega Nord and the Northern Question in Italian Politics*. Basingstoke: Palgrave.

CEO. 2014. *Baròmetre d'Opinió Política 32, 1a onada 2014, Dossier de premsa*. Centre d'Estudis d'Opinió, Generalitat de Catalunya, ceo.gencat.cat/ceop/AppJava/pages/index.html [accessed 25 August 2014].

Chalmers, Adam William. 2013. "Regional Authority, Transnational Lobbying and the Allocation of Structural Funds in the European Union." *Journal of Common Market Studies* 51 (5): 815–31.

Chapman, Brian. 1955. *The Prefects and Provincial France*. London: George Allen & Unwin.

Chari, Raj. 2013. "The Parliamentary Election in Spain, November 2011." *Electoral Studies* 32 (2): 377–80.

Chari, Raj, Suvi Iltanen, and Sylvia Kritzinger. 2004. "Examining and Explaining the Northern League's 'U-Turn' from Europe." *Government and Opposition* 39 (3): 423–50.

Cheshire, Paul. 1995. "European Integration and Regional Responses." In *The Regions and the New Europe*, edited by Martin Rhodes, 27–52. Manchester: Manchester University Press.

Christensen, Dag Arne. 2010. "The Danish Socialist People's Party: Still Waiting after All These Years." In *Left Parties in National Governments*, edited by Jonathan Olsen, 121–37. Basingstoke: Palgrave.

Christensen, Jørgen Grønnegård. 2000. "The Dynamics of Decentralization and Recentralization." *Public Administration* 78 (2): 389–408.

Christiansen, Peter Munk, and Michael Baggesen Klitgaard. 2008. *Den utænkelige reform – Strukturreformens tilblivelse, 2002–2005*. Odense: Syddansk Universitetsforlag.

Christiansen, Thomas. 1996. "Second Thoughts on Europe's "Third Level": The European Union's Committee of the Regions." *Publius* 26 (1): 93–116.

CiU. 2003. "Bases per a nou Estatut Nacional de Catalunya," April. Estatut de Catalunya 2006, Box 1. CEDOC, Universitat Autònoma de Barcelona.

– 2006. "Felicitats pel nou Estatut!" leaflet. CiU file. Estatut de Catalunya 2006, Box 4. CEDOC, Universitat Autònoma de Barcelona.

– 2010. *Programa de govern, projecte de país*. Manifesto for the 2010 regional election. Available at www.ciu.cat/programes.php [accessed 15 March 2011].

– 2012. *Catalunya 2020*. Manifesto for the 2012 regional election. Available at www.ciu.cat/programes.php [accessed 2 November 2012].

Clark, Alistair. 2012. *Political Parties in the UK*. Basingstoke: Palgrave Macmillan.

Closa, Carlos. 2016. "Secession from a Member State and EU Membership: The View from the Union." *European Constitutional Law Review* 12 (2): 240–64.

Cole, Alistair. 1999. "The French Socialists." In *Political Parties and the European Union*, edited by John Gaffney, 71–85. London: Routledge

Colino, César. 2009. "Constitutional Change without Constitutional Reform: Spanish Federalism and the Revision of Catalonia's Statute of Autonomy." *Publius* 39 (2): 262–88.

Collier, David. 2011. "Understanding Process Tracing." *PS Political Science and Politics* 44 (4): 823–30.
– 1993. "The Comparative Method." In *Political Science: The State of the Discipline* II, edited by Ada Finifter, 105–19. Washington, DC: American Political Science Association.
Collier, David, Jody LaPorte, and Jason Seawright. 2012. "Putting Typologies to Work: Concept-Formation, Measurement, and Analytic Rigor." *Political Research Quarterly* 65 (1): 217–32.
Collier, Ruth Berins, and David Collier. 1991. *Shaping the Political Arena – Critical Junctures, the Labor Movement, and Regime Dynamics in Latin America*. Princeton, NJ: Princeton University Press.
CON-S. 2011. *Common Sense for Scotland*. Manifesto for the 2011 regional election. Edinburgh: Scottish Conservative and Unionist Party.
– 2007. *Scottish Conservative Manifesto*. Manifesto for the 2007 regional election. Edinburgh: Scottish Conservative and Unionist Party.
– 1997. *Fighting for Scotland*. Scottish manifesto for the 1997 general election. Edinburgh: Scottish Conservative and Unionist Party.
– 1992. *The Best Future for Scotland*. Scottish manifesto for the 1992 general election. Edinburgh: Scottish Conservative and Unionist Party.
– 1979. Conservative Manifesto for Scotland. Edinburgh: Scottish Conservative and Unionist Party.
CON-W. 1997. *Opportunity and Prosperity for Wales*. Welsh manifesto for the 1997 general election. Cardiff: Welsh Conservative Party.
– 1992. *The Best Future for Wales*. Welsh manifesto for the 1992 general election. Cardiff: Welsh Conservative Party.
– 1979. Conservative Manifesto for Wales. Cardiff: Welsh Conservative Party.
Connolly, Christopher. 2013. "Independence in Europe: Secession, Sovereignty, and the European Union." *Duke Journal of Comparative and International Law* 24 (1): 51–105.
Conti, Nicolò, and Luca Verzichelli. 2005. "La dimensione europea del discorso politico in Italia: un'analisi diacronica delle preferenze partitiche (1950–2001)." In *L'Europa in Italia*, edited by Maurizio Cotta, Pierangelo Isernia and Luca Verzichelli, 61–116. Bologna: Il Mulino.
Conversi, Daniele. 1997. *The Basques, the Catalans and Spain*. London: Hurst.
Coombes, David, and Richard Norton-Taylor. 1968. "Renewal in Belgian Politics: The Election of March 1968." *Parliamentary Affairs* 22 (1): 62–72.
Coosemans, Thierry. 2007. "Les programmes des partis francophones pour les elections fédérales du 10 juin 2007." *Courrier hebdomadaire* 1950–1. Brussels: CRISP.
CoSC. 2014. *Commission on Scottish Devolution*, www.commissiononscottishdevolution.org.uk/ [accessed 25 August 2014].
Costa-i-Font, Joan, and Scott Greer. 2013. "Territory and Health: Perspectives from Economics and Political Science." In *Federalism and Decentralization in European Health and Social Care*, edited by Joan Costa-i-Font and Scott Greer, 13–45. Basingstoke: Palgrave.

Cotta, Maurizio, and Luca Verzichelli. 2007. *Political Institutions in Italy*. Oxford: Oxford University Press.

Courtois, Stéphane, and Denis Peschanski. 1988. "From Decline to Marginalization: The PCF Breaks with French Society." In *Communist Parties in Western Europe*, edited by Michael Waller and Michael Fenema, 47–68. Oxford: Blackwell.

Covell, Maureen. 1985. "Possibly Necessary but Not Necessarily Possible: Revision of the Constitution in Belgium." In *The Politics of Constitutional Change in Industrial Nations*, edited by Keith Banting and Richard Simeon, 71–94. London: Macmillan.

– 1982. "Agreeing to Disagree: Elite Bargaining and the Revision of the Belgian Constitution." *Canadian Journal of Political Science* 15 (3): 451–69.

– 1981. "Ethnic Conflict and Elite Bargaining: The Case of Belgium." *West European Politics* 4 (3): 197–218.

Craig, Fred. 1990. *British General Election Manifestos*. Aldershot: Parliamentary Research Services.

Crameri, Kathryn. 2015. "Political Power and Civil Counterpower: The Complex Dynamics of the Catalan Independence Movement." *Nationalism and Ethnic Politics* 21 (1): 104–20.

CRISP. 1983. "Les origines de la querelle fouronnaise." *Courrier hebdomadaire* 1019. Brussels: CRISP.

– 1979. "Le problème des Fourons de 1962 à nos jours." *Courrier hebdomadaire* 859. Brussels: CRISP.

– 1975. *La Belgique dans la Communauté européenne*. Dossier no. 8. Brussels: CRISP.

– 1973. "L'evolution recente de la Volksunie II." *Courrier hebdomadaire* 606. Brussels: CRISP.

– 1969a. *La Belgique dans le Marché Commun*. Dossier no. 1. Brussels: CRISP.

– 1969b. "Les trois grands partis politiques belges et l'integration européenne." *Courrier hebdomadaire* 433. Brussels: CRISP.

– 1968. "Les elections legislatives du 31 mars 1968." *Courrier hebdomadaire* 402. Brussels: CRISP.

– 1967. "Le Parti Wallon." *Courrier hebdomadaire* 367. Brussels: CRISP.

– 1966. "La Volksunie II." *Courrier hebdomadaire* 345. Brussels: CRISP.

– 1965. "Le Vlaams Aktie Komitee (VAK)." *Courrier hebdomadaire* 278. Brussels: CRISP.

– 1964. "Le congrès de Malines de la Volksunie." *Courrier hebdomadaire* 230. Brussels: CRISP.

– 1961. "Les partis politiques non traditionnels." *Courrier hebdomadaire* 101. Brussels: CRISP.

– 1959. "Les congrès wallons." *Courrier hebdomadaire* 22. Brussels: CRISP.

Cs. 2015. *Un projecte per la convivència*. Manifesto for the 2015 regional election. Available at www.ciudadanos-cs.org/statico/pdf/programas/programa-2015autonomicas-cat.pdf [accessed 10 Decemebr 2016].

CSQEP. 2015. *Catalunya Sí Que Es Pot – El programa de la gent.* Manifesto for the 2015 regional election. Available at catalunyasiqueespot.cat/wp-content/uploads/2015/09/CATSIQUESPOT_programa_10-Definitiu-2015-9-11.pdf [accessed 10 December 2016].

Cuchillo, Montserrat. 1993. "The Autonomous Communities as the Spanish Meso." In *The Rise of Meso Governments in Europe,* edited by Laurence Sharpe, 210–46. London: Sage.

CUP. 2015. *Programa polític – Per a les eleccions al Parlament de Catalunya del 27 de setembre de 2015.* Manifesto for the 2015 regional election. Available at cup.cat/sites/default/files/programa_de_la_cup_crida_constituent_27s.pdf [accessed 10 December 2016].

Curtice, John. 1999. "Is Scotland a Nation and Wales Not? Why the Two Referendum Results Were so Different." In *Scotland and Wales: Nations Again?,* edited by Bridget Taylor and Katarina Thomson, 119–47. Cardiff: University of Wales Press.

Curtice, John, David McCrone, Nicola McEwen, Michael Marsh, and Rachel Ormston. 2009. *Revolution or Evolution? The 2007 Scottish Elections.* Edinburgh: Edinburgh University Press.

CVP. 1991. *Goed leven in Flanders ook morgen.* Manifesto for the 1991 election. Collected by the Manifesto Research Group and available from GESIS, Cologne.

– 1987. *Zeg met radikaal Ja voor houvast – CVP De Goeie Weg.* Manifesto for the 1987 election. Collected by the Manifesto Research Group and available from GESIS, Cologne.

– 1978. *Er is een uitweg met de C.V.P.* Manifesto for the 1978 election. Collected by the Manifesto Research Group and available from GESIS, Cologne.

– 1968. *De CVP doet het.* Manifesto for the 1968 election. Collected by the Manifesto Research Group and available from GESIS, Cologne.

D'Angelo Bigelli, Maria Grazia. 1971. *Pietro Nenni – Dalle barricate a Palazzo Madama.* Milan: Mursia.

Daniels, Philip. 1998. "From Hostility to 'Constructive Engagement': The Europeanization of the Labour Party." *West European Politics* 21 (1): 72–96.

Dardanelli, Paolo. 2014. "European Integration, Party Strategies, and State Restructuring: A Comparative Analysis." *European Political Science Review* 6 (2): 213–36.

– 2005a. *Between Two Unions: Europeanisation and Scottish Devolution.* Manchester: Manchester University Press.

– 2005b. "Democratic Deficit or the Europeanization of Secession? Explaining the Devolution Referendums in Scotland." *Political Studies* 53 (2): 320–42.

– 2003. "Ideology and Rationality: The Europeanization of the Scottish National Party." *Österreichische Zeitschrift für Politikwissenschaft* 32 (3): 271–84.

Dardanelli, Paolo, and James Mitchell. 2014. "An Independent Scotland? The Scottish National Party's Bid for Independence and its Prospects." *The International Spectator* 49 (3): 88–105.

Davies, Norman. 2011. *Vanished Kingdoms – The History of Half-Forgotten Europe*. London: Allen Lane.
– 1999. *The Isles – A History*. Oxford: Oxford University Press.
DC. 1992. *Un programma per l'Italia verso l'Europa*. Manifesto for the 1992 election. Collected by the Manifesto Research Group and available from GESIS, Cologne.
– [1963] 1968. "Programma elettorale della Democrazia Cristiana per la IV Legislatura [Manifesto for the 1963 election]." In *Atti e documenti della Democrazia Cristiana*, vol. 2, edited by Andrea Damilano, 1473–519. Rome: Cinque Lune.
DC, PSI, PSDI and PRI. 1963. *Accordo politico programmatico per il governo di centro-sinistra tra DC, PSI, PSDI e PRI*, November 1963, London School of Economics Archive JF2 (45)/B4.
DCB. 2014. Amternes Administration 1660–1970. *Dansk Center for Byhistorie*, dendigitalebyport.byhistorie.dk/kommuner/artikel.aspx?artikel=amter.xml.
DDD. 2010. *Catalunya proper estat d'Europa: Joan Laporta cap de llista per Barcelona*. Solidaritat Catalana per la Independència. Poster for the 2010 election. Dipòsit digital de documents de la Universitat Autònoma de Barcelona, ddd.uab.cat/record/104904?ln=en.
De Bandt, Jean-Pierre. 1992. "The Belgium Federalization Process." In *Belgium and EC Membership Evaluated*, edited by M.A.G. van Meerhaeghe, 130–6. London: Pinter.
De Luca, Fausto. 1963. "Nenni indica gli obiettivi del psi in una maggioranza di centro-sinistra." *La Stampa*, 25 April.
De Ridder, Martine and Luis Ricardo Fraga. 1986. "The Brussels Issue in Belgian Politics." *West European Politics* 9 (3): 376–92.
De Ridder, Martine, Robert Peterson, and Rex Wirth. 1978. "Images of Belgian Politics: The Effects of Cleavages on the Political System." *Legislative Studies Quarterly* 3 (1): 83–108.
De Vroede, Maurits. 1975. *The Flemish Movement in Belgium*. Brussels: Flemish Cultural Council and Flemish Information Institute.
De Winter, Lieven. 2006. "Multi-level Party Competition and Coordination in Belgium." In *Devolution and Electoral Politics*, edited by Dan Hough and Charlie Jeffery, 76–95. Manchester: Manchester University Press.
– 1998. "The *Volksunie* and the Dilemma between Policy Success and Electoral Survival in Flanders." In *Regionalist Parties in Western Europe*, edited by Lieven de Winter and Huri Türsan, 28–50. London: Routledge.
De Winter, Lieven, and Pierre Baudewyns. 2009. "Belgium: Towards the Breakdown of a Nation-State in the Heart of Europe?" *Nationalism and Ethnic Politics* 15 (3–4): 280–304.
De Winter, Lieven, and Patrick Dumont. 1999. "Belgium: Party System(s) on the Eve of Disintegration?" In *Changing Party Systems in Western Europe*, edited by David Broughton and Mark Donovan, 183–206. London: Pinter.
De Winter, Lieven, and André-Paul Frognier. 1997. "L'évolution des identités politiques territoriales en Belgique durant la période 1975–1995." In *La*

réforme de l'Etat ... et après ?, edited by Serge Jaumain, 161–76. Brussels: Editions de l'Université de Bruxelles.

De Winter, Lieven, and Margarita Gomez-Reino Cachafeiro. 2002. "European Integration and Ethnoregionalist Parties." *Party Politics* 8 (4): 483–503.

Degl'Innocenti, Maurizio. 2004. *L'avvento della regione, 1970–1975 – Problemi e materiali.* Manduria: Lacaita.

Delforge, Paul. 2003. "Rassemblement wallon (1968–1976)." In *Encyclopédie du Mouvement wallon*, CD-ROM, edited by Paul Delforge, Philippe Destatte, and Micheline Libon. Namur: Institut Destrée.

– 1999. "Mouvement wallon et fédéralisme." In *L'idée fédéraliste dans les Etats-nations*, edited by Philippe Destatte, 273–303. Brussels: Presses interuniversitaires européennes.

Delruelle-Vosswinckel, N., and André-Paul Frognier. 1980. "L'opinion publique et les problèmes communautaires." *Courrier hebdomadaire* 880. Brussels: CRISP.

Delwit, Pascal. 1994. "The Belgian Socialist Party." In *Social Democratic Parties in the European Union*, edited by Robert Ladrech and Philippe Marlière, 30–42. Basingstoke: Macmillan.

Deschouwer, Kris. 2009. *The Politics of Belgium.* Basingstoke: Palgrave.

– 1999. "From Consociation to Federation: How the Belgian Parties Won." In *Party Elites in Divided Societies*, edited by Kris Deschouwer and Kurt Richard Luther, 74–107. London: Routledge

Deschouwer, Kris, and Martine Van Assche. 2008. "Hard but Hardly Relevant. Party Based Euroscepticism in Belgian Politics." In *Opposing Europe? The Comparative Party Politics of Euroscepticism. Vol. 1, Case Studies and Country Surveys*, edited by Paul Taggart and Aleks Szczerbiak, 75–92. Oxford: Oxford University Press.

Desideri, Carlo. 1995. "Italian Regions in the European Community." In *The European Union and the Regions*, edited by Barry Jones and Michael Keating, 65–87. Oxford: Clarendon Press.

Destatte, Philippe. 1999. "Some Questions Regarding the Birth of Federalist Demands in Wallonia." In *L'idée fédéraliste dans les Etats-nations*, edited by Philippe Destatte, 13–35. Brussels: Presses interuniversitaires européennes.

– 1997. *L'identité wallonne.* Charleroi: Institut Jules Destrée.

Dewachter, Wilfried. 1987. "Changes in a *Particratie:* The Belgian Party System from 1944 to 1986." In *Party Systems in Denmark, Austria, Switzerland, the Netherlands and Belgium*, edited by Hans Daalder, 285–363 London: Pinter

Dewachter, Wilfried, Edith Lismont and Guy Tegenbos. 1977. "The Effect of the Opposition Parties on the Legislative Output in a Multi-party System – The Belgian Case from 1965 to 1971." *European Journal of Political Research* 5 (3): 245–65.

DF. 2005. Danish People's Party's manifesto for the 2005 election. Collected by the Manifesto Research Group and available from GESIS, Cologne.

- 2001. *Giv danskerne en ny mulighed. Giv danmark et pusterum*. Danish People's Party's manifesto for the 2001 election. Collected by the Manifesto Research Group and available from GESIS, Cologne.
Diamanti, Ilvo. 2014. "L'indipendenza del Veneto non è uno scherzo. Bocciato lo Stato centrale, no alla politica locale." *La Repubblica*, 24 March, available at www.repubblica.it/politica/2014/03/24/news/l_indipendenza_del_veneto_non_uno_scherzo_bocciato_lo_stato_centrale_no_alla_politica_locale-81734444/ [accessed 10 December 2016].
- 1997. "The Lega Nord: From Federalism to Secession." In *Italian Politics – The Centre-Left in Power*, edited by Roberto D'Alimonte and David Nelken, 65–82. Oxford: Westview Press.
- 1996. "Il Nord senza l'Italia?" *Limes* 4 (1): 15–30.
- 1993. *La Lega – Geografia, storia e sociologia di un nuovo soggetto politico*. Rome: Donzelli.
Dickie, Mure. 2014. "Cameron Dismisses Claim That Euroscepticism Fuels Scots Yes Vote." *Financial Times*, 29 August.
Díez Medrano, Juan. 1995. *Divided Nations – Class, Politics and Nationalism in the Basque Country and Catalonia*. Ithaca, NY: Cornell University Press.
Dinan, Desmond. 2014. *Europe Recast*, second ed. Basingstoke: Palgrave Macmillan.
Dion, Stéphane. 1996. "Why Is Secession Difficult in Well-Established Democracies? Lessons from Quebec." *British Journal of Political Science* 29 (2): 269–83.
DKF. 2005. *5 gode grunde til at stemme konservativt*. Danish Conservative People's Party's manifesto for the 2005 election. Collected by the Manifesto Research Group and available from GESIS, Cologne.
- 2001. *Stem konservativt*. Danish Conservative People's Party's manifesto for the 2001 election. Collected by the Manifesto Research Group and available from GESIS, Cologne.
- 2000. *Fornuft og Fornyelse*. Danish Conservative People's Party's position paper. Copenhagen: Det Konservative Folkeparti.
Donovan, Mark. 1992. "A Party System in Transformation: The April 1992 Italian Election." *West European Politics* 15 (4): 170–7.
Douglas-Scott, Sionaidh. 2014. *How Easily Could an Independent Scotland Join the EU?* Legal Research Paper no. 46/2014, University of Oxford.
Drucker, Henry. 1976. "Partisan Implications of Devolution." Paper presented at the Tenth IPSA World Congress. Edinburgh, 16–21 August.
DRV. 2005. *Valgudtalelse*. Danish Social Liberal Party's manifesto for the 2001 election. Collected by the Manifesto Research Group and available from GESIS, Cologne.
- 2001. *Ansver for resultater – også i femtiden*. Danish Social Liberal Party's manifesto for the 2001 election. Collected by the Manifesto Research Group and available from GESIS, Cologne.
DS. 2009. SLP fuseert met Groen! *De Standaard*, 19 December, www.standaard.be/cnt/dmf20091219_022 [accessed 24 June 2012].

DSD. 2005. *Mærkesager*. Danish Social Democratic Party's manifesto for the 2005 election. Collected by the Manifesto Research Group and available from GESIS, Cologne.
– 2001. *Mennesker Først*. Danish Social Democratic Party's manifesto for the 2001 election. Collected by the Manifesto Research Group and available from GESIS, Cologne.
Duggan, Christopher. 1994. *A Concise History of Italy*. Cambridge: Cambridge University Press.
Dumont, Georges. 1977. *Histoire de la Belgique*. Paris: Hachette.
Dumont, Gérard-François. 2004. *Les régions et la régionalisation en France*. Paris: Editions Ellipses.
Dunn, James. 1974. "The Revision of the Constitution in Belgium: A Study in the Institutionalization of Ethnic Conflict." *Western Political Quarterly* 27 (1): 143–63.
Dupuis, Georges. 1974. "Préface." In Yves Mény, *Centralisation et décentralisation dans le débat politique français (1945–1969)*. Paris: Librairie générale de droit et de jurisprudence.
DV. 2005. *Valgløfter*. Venstre's manifesto for the 2005 election. Collected by the Manifesto Research Group and available from GESIS, Cologne.
– 2001. *Tid til forandring*. Venstre's manifesto for the 2001 election. Collected by the Manifesto Research Group and available from GESIS, Cologne.
Dyson, Kenneth, and Kevin Featherstone. 1996. "Italy and EMU as a 'Vincolo Esterno': Empowering the Technocrats, Transforming the State." *South European Society and Politics* 1 (2): 272–99.
ECO. 2010. *Nous restons ouvert pendant les transformations*. Manifesto for the 2010 federal election. Brussels: Écologistes Confédérés pour l'organization de luttes originales.
– 2007a. *Programme electoral d'ECOLO – Livre V Pour une société démocratique – Chapitre V.5 Institutionnel*. Manifesto for the 2007 federal election. Brussels: Écologistes Confédérés pour l'organization de luttes originales.
– 2007b. *Programme electoral d'ECOLO – Livre VI Pour une société planétaire – Chapitre VI.I Europe*. Manifesto for the 2007 federal election. Brussels: Écologistes Confédérés pour l'organization de luttes originales.
– 1991. *Programme ECOLO*. Manifesto for the 1991 general election. Collected by the Manifesto Research Group and available from GESIS, Cologne.
Economist. 2014. "Homage to Caledonia." *The Economist*, 22 February.
– 2007. "Scotland's Eurodreams." *The Economist*, 19 April.
Edelman, Murray. 1964. *The Symbolic Uses of Politics*. Urbana, IL: University of Illinois Press.
Edward, David. 2013. "EU Law and the Separation of Member States." *Fordham International Law Journal* 36 (5): 1151–68.
Elazar, Daniel. 1995. "From Statism to Federalism: A Paradigm Shift." *Publius* 25 (2): 5–18.
– 1987. *Exploring Federalism*. Tuscaloosa, AL: University of Alabama Press.

Elgie, Robert. 2003. *Political Institutions in Contemporary France*. Oxford: Oxford University Press.

Elias, Anwen. 2009. *Minority Nationalist Parties and European Integration*. Abingdon: Routledge.

Elias, Anwen, Edina Szöcsik, and Christina Isabel Zuber. 2015. "Position, Selective Emphasis and Framing: How Parties Deal with a Second Dimension in Competition." *Party Politics* 21 (6): 839–50.

Elklit, Jørgen. 1999. "The Danish March 1998 Parliamentary Election." *Electoral Studies* 18 (1): 137–42.

Ellakuría, Iñaki. 2006. "El PSC vuelve a utilizar al PP para movilizar el voto en favor del Estatut." *La Vanguardia*, 31 May.

Elliott, John. 1992. "A Europe of Composite Monarchies." *Past and Present* 137 (1): 48–71.

– 1963a. *The Revolt of the Catalans – A Study in the Decline of Spain (1598–1640)*. Cambridge: Cambridge University Press.

– 1963b. *Imperial Spain, 1469–1716*. London: Edward Arnold.

Elmelund-Prætskær, Christian, Jørgen Elklit, and Ulrik Kjaer. 2010. "The Massive Stability of the Danish Multiparty System: A Pyrrhic Victory?" In *Political Parties and Democracy – Vol. II: Europe*, edited by Kay Lawson, 121–38. Santa Barbara, CA: Praeger.

Enelow, James, and Melvin Hinich. 1984. *The Spatial Theory of Voting – An Introduction*. Cambridge: Cambridge University Press.

ERC. 2012. *Programa electoral*. Manifesto for the 2012 regional election. Barcelona: Esquerra Republicana de Catalunya.

– 2010. *Programa electoral*. Manifesto for the 2010 regional election. Barcelona: Esquerra Republicana de Catalunya.

– 2006. "Ara toca No – Catalunya mereix més" leaflet. ERC file. Estatut de Catalunya 2006, Box 4. CEDOC, Universitat Autònoma de Barcelona.

Erk, Jan, and Lawrence Anderson. 2009. "The Paradox of Federalism: Does Self-Rule Accommodate or Exacerbate Ethnic Divisions?" *Regional and Federal Studies* 19 (2): 191–202.

Esdaile, Charles. 2003. *The Peninsular War – A New History*. London: Penguin.

Esman Milton. 1977. "Scottish Nationalism, North Sea Oil, and the British Response." In *Ethnic Conflict in the Modern World*, edited by Milton Esman, 251–86. Ithaca, NY: Cornell University Press.

Esteban, Jorge de. 1981. *Las Constituciones de España*. Madrid: Taurus.

Fabra, María. 2014. "El Constitucional considera ilegal que Cataluña se declare soberana." *El Pais*, 26 March, politica.elpais.com/politica/2014/03/25/actualidad/1395768070_578313.html [accessed 18 September 2014].

Fatás, Antonio. 1997. "EMU: Countries or Regions? Lessons from the EMS Experience." *European Economic Review* 41 (3–5): 743–51.

Fearon, James, and Pieter van Houten. 2002. *The Politicization of Cultural and Economic Difference – A Return to the Theory of Regional Autonomy*

Movements. Paper presented at the Fifth Meeting of the Laboratory in Comparative Ethnic Processes, Stanford University, 10–11 May.

Feld, Werner. 1975. "Subnational Regionalism and the European Community" *Orbis* 18 (4): 1176–92.

FI. 1996. *Contratto con gli italiani: ecco il nostro impegno di governo*. Manifesto for the 1996 election, collected by the Manifesto Research Group and available from GESIS, Cologne.

– 1994. *Forza Italia*. Manifesto for the 1994 election, collected by the Manifesto Research Group and available from GESIS, Cologne.

Fitzmaurice, John. 1992. "Belgian Paradoxes: The November 1991 Election." *West European Politics* 15 (4): 178–83.

Fleming, Sam. 2014. "Scottish Currency Reserves Would Need 'Tens of Billions.'" *Financial Times*, 11 September.

Fontana, Sandro (ed.). 1973. *Il fascismo e le autonomie locali*. Bologna: Il Mulino.

Fraeys, William. 1992. "Les élections legislatives du 24 novembre 1991 – Analyze des résultats." *Res Publica* 34 (2): 131–53.

– 1988. "Les élections legislatives du 13 décembre 1987 – Analyze des résultats." *Res Publica* 30 (1): 3–24.

– 1979. "Les élections legislatives du 17 décembre 1978 – Analyze des résultats." *Res Publica* 21 (2): 309–28.

– 1969. "Les élections du 31 mars 1968." *Res Publica* 11 (1): 271–92.

Frears, John. 1988. "Liberalism in France." In *Liberal Parties in Western Europe*, edited by Emil Kirchner, 124–50. Cambridge: Cambridge University Press.

García, Luis. 2012. "El Govern admite que sin la continuidad en la UE el proceso soberanista pierde sentido." *La Vanguardia*, 25 October.

García-Gallo de Diego, Alfonso. 1979. "La Capitanía general como institución de gobierno político en España e Indias en el siglo XVIII." In *Memoria del tercer congreso venezolano de historia*. Vol. 1, 535–82. Caracas: Academia Nacional de Historia.

Garea, Fernando. 2014. "Rajoy advierte que consultas en Escocia y Cataluña provocan 'pobreza y recesión.'" *El Pais*, 17 September, politica.elpais.com/politica/2014/09/17/actualidad/1409355302_819321.html [accessed 18 September 2014].

Garmise, Shari. 1997. "The Impact of European Regional Policy on the Development of the Regional Tier in the UK." *Regional and Federal Studies* 7 (3): 1–24.

Garrett, Geoffrey and Jonathan Rodden. 2003. "Globalization and Fiscal Decentralization." In *Governance in a Global Economy*, edited by Mike Kahler and David Lake, 87–109. Princeton, NJ: Princeton University Press.

GdC. 2013. Acord per a la consulta: data i pregunta. *Generalitat de Catalunya*, 13 December, www.govern.cat/pres_gov/AppJava/govern/monografics/monografic-236550.html [accessed 25 August 2014].

George, Alexander and Andrew Bennett. 2005. *Case Studies and Theory Development in the Social Sciences*. Cambridge, MA: MIT Press.

George, Stephen, and D. Haythorne. 1996. "The British Labour Party." In *Political Parties and the European Union*, edited by John Gaffney, 110–21. London: Routledge

Gérard-Libois, J. 1987. "Gaston Eyskens. Exercices du pouvoir et traversée du désert." *Courrier hebdomadaire* 1181. Brussels: CRISP.

Gil del Olmo, Clara, and Pere Ríos. 2015. "Mas gana el pulso a ERC y convoca elecciones para el 27 de septiembre." *El País*, 15 January.

Gilbert, Mark. 2000. "The Bassanini Laws: A Half-way House in Local Government Reform." In *Italian Politics 1998 – The Return of Politics*, edited by David Hine and Salvatore Vassallo, 139–55. Oxford: Berghahn Books.

– 1995. *The Italian Revolution – The End of Politics Italian Style?* Boulder, CO: Westview.

– 1993. "Warriors of the New Pontida: The Challenge of the Lega Nord to the Italian Party System." *Political Quarterly* 64 (1): 99–106.

Ginsborg, Paul. 2003. *A History of Contemporary Italy – Society and Politics 1943–1988*. Basingstoke: Palgrave Macmillan.

Giordano, Benito. 2004. "The Politics of the Northern League and Italy's Changing Attitudes towards Europe." *Perspectives on European Politics and Society* 5 (1): 61–79.

Giscard d'Estaing, Valéry. 1981. *L'état de la France*. Paris: Fayard.

Goertz, Gary. 2006. *Social Science Concepts – A User's Guide*. Princeton, NJ: Princeton University Press.

Goffart, V. 1969. "La crise de Louvain, du 1er janvier au 31 mars 1968." *Res Publica* 11 (1): 31–76.

Gordon, Sarah, and Patrick Jenkins. 2014. "CBI Says Most Scottish Business Against Independence." *Financial Times*, 11 September.

Gounin, Yves. 2013. "Les dynamiques d'éclatements d'Etats dans l'Union européenne: casse-tête juridique, défi politique." *Politique étrangère* 78 (4): 11–22.

Govaert, Serge. 2012a. "Les négociations communautaires et la formation du gouvernement Di Rupo (juin 2010–décembre 2011)." *Courrier hebdomadaire* 2144–5. Brussels: CRISP.

– 2012b. "Les discussions communautaires sous le gouvernement Leterme II (2009–2010)." *Courrier hebdomadaire* 2126. Brussels: CRISP.

– 2009. "Les discussions communautaires sous les gouvernements Verhofstadt III, Leterme et Van Rompuy." *Courrier hebdomadaire* 2024–5. Brussels: CRISP.

– 2007. "Bruxelles-Hal-Vilvorde: du quasi-accord de 2005 à la procédure en conflit d'intérêts." *Courrier hebdomadaire* 1974. Brussels: CRISP.

– 2002. "La Volksunie – Du déclin à la disparition (1993–2001)." *Courrier hebdomadaire* 1748. Brussels: CRISP.

– 1993. "La Volksunie." *Courrier hebdomadaire* 1416–17. Brussels: CRISP.

– 1992. "Le Vlaams Blok et ses dissidences." *Courrier hebdomadaire* 1365. Brussels: CRISP.

Gravier, Jean-François. 1947. *Paris et le désert français*. Paris: Le Portulan.
Green, William. 1992. "Periodization in European and World History." *Journal of World History* 3 (1): 13–53.
Greenwood, John, and David Wilson. 1978. "The Conservative and Liberal Parties." In *Divided Loyalties*, edited by Martin Kolinsky, 158–71. Manchester: Manchester University Press.
Greer, Scott. 2009. *The Politics of European Union Health Policy*. Maidenhead: Open University Press.
– 2006. "Uninvited Europeanization: Neofunctionalism, Health Services and the EU." *Journal of European Public Policy* 13 (1): 134–52.
Grémion, Catherine. 1987. "Decentralization in France – A Historical Perspective." In *The Mitterrand Experiment*, edited by George Ross, Stanley Hoffmann, and Sylvia Malzacher, 237–47. Cambridge: Polity Press.
Guibernau, Montserrat. 2013. "Secessionism in Catalonia: After Democracy." *Ethnopolitics* 12 (4): 331–51.
Gunther, Richard, and José Ramón Montero. 2009. *The Politics of Spain*. Cambridge: Cambridge University Press.
Guyomarch Alain, Howard Machin, and Ella Ritchie. 1998. *France in the European Union*. Basingstoke: Macmillan.
Hagen, Terje, and Oddvar Kaarbøe. 2006. "The Norwegian Hospital Reform of 2002: Central Government Takes Over Ownership of Public Hospitals." *Health Policy* 76 (3): 320–33.
Hainsworth, Paul. 1981. "A Majority for the President: The French Left and the Presidential and Parliamentary Elections of 1981." *Parliamentary Affairs* 34 (4): 436–50.
Hall, Peter, and Rosemary Taylor. 1996. "Political Science and the Three New Institutionalisms." *Political Studies* 44 (5): 936–57.
Hansard. 2008. European Union (Amendment) Bill, Hansard, HC, vol. 473, column 250, 11 March 2008.
Hansen, Niles. 1968. *French Regional Planning*. Bloomington, IN: Indiana University Press.
Hansen, Tore. 1993. "Appendix: Meso Government in Denmark and Sweden." In *The Rise of Meso Governments in Europe*, edited by Laurence James Sharpe, 312–8. London: Sage.
Hassan, Gerry, and Peter Lynch. 1999. "*The Changing Politics of Scottish Labour: Culture and Values, Political Strategy and Devolution 1979–1999.*" Paper presented at the 49th PSA Annual Conference. Nottingham, 23–25 March.
Haverland, Markus. 2006. "Does the EU Cause Domestic Developments? Improving Case Selection in Europeanization Research." *West European Politics* 29 (1): 134–46.
Hayward, Jack, and Michael Watson (eds). 2009. *Planning, Politics, and Public Policy – The British, French and Italian Experience*. Cambridge: Cambridge University Press.
Heinelt, Hubert, and Xavier Bertrana (eds). 2011. *The Second Tier of Local Government in Europe*. Abingdon: Routledge.

Hennessy, Charles. 1962. *The Federal Republic in Spain – Pi y Margall and the Federal Republican Movement 1868–1874*. Oxford: Clarendon Press.

Hennig, Benjamin, Dimitris Ballas, and Danny Dorling. 2014. "European Parliament elections 2014." *Political Insight* 5 (2): 20–1.

Hepburn, Eve. 2010. *Using Europe*. Manchester: Manchester University Press.

– 2009. "Explaining Failure: the Highs and Lows of Sardinian Nationalism." *Regional and Federal Studies* 19 (4–5): 595–618.

Hermans, Theo, Louis Vos and Lode Wils (eds). 1992. *The Flemish Movement – A Documentary History 1780–1990*. London: The Athlone Press.

Herremans, Maurice-Pierre. 1962a. "Bref historique de tentative de réforme du régime unitaire en Belgique." *Courrier hebdomadaire* 135. Brussels: CRISP

– 1962b. "La Volksunie (I)." *Courrier hebdomadaire* 148. Brussels: CRISP.

– 1962c. "La Volksunie (II)." *Courrier hebdomadaire* 169. Brussels: CRISP.

– 1961a. "Le Centre Harmel." *Courrier hebdomadaire* 131. Brussels: CRISP.

– 1961b. "Le Mouvement populaire flamand (Vlaamse Volksbeweging ou VVB)." *Courrier hebdomadaire* 130. Brussels: CRISP.

Hill, Keith. 1969. "Belgium." In *European Political Parties*, edited by Stanley Henig and John Pinder, 68–96. London: Allen and Unwin.

Hix, Simon. 1999. "Dimensions and Alignments in European Union Politics: Cognitive Constraints and Partisan Responses." *European Journal of Political Research* 35 (1): 69–106.

Hix, Simon, and Klaus Goetz. 2000. "Introduction: European Integration and National Political Systems." *West European Politics* 23 (4): 1–26.

Hix, Simon, and Bjørn Høyland. 2011. *The Political System of the European Union*, third ed. Basingstoke: Palgrave.

Höbel, Alexander. 2010. *Il PCI di Luigi Longo (1964–1969)*. Naples: Edizioni Scientifiche Italiane.

Hooghe, Liesbet. 1996. "Building a Europe with the Regions: The Changing Role of the European Commission." In *Cohesion Policy and European Integration*, edited by Liesbet Hooghe, 89–126. Oxford: Oxford University Press.

Hooghe, Liesbet, and Gary Marks. 2001. *Multi-Level Governance and European Integration*. Lanham, MD: Rowman & Littlefield.

Hooghe, Liesbet, Gary Marks, Arjan H. Schakel, Sandra Chapman Osterkatz, Sara Niedzwiecki, and Sarah Shair-Rosenfield. 2016. *Measuring Regional Authority – A Postfunctionalist Theory of Governance, Vol. 1*. Oxford: Oxford University Press.

Hopkins, John. 2002. *Devolution in Context: Regional, Federal and Devolved Government in the European Union*. London: Cavendish

Hutter, Swen, and Alena Kerscher. 2014. "Politicizing Europe in Hard Times: Conflicts over Europe in France in a Long-Term Perspective, 1974–2012." *Journal of European Integration* 36 (3): 267–82.

ICM. 2014. Scotland Independence Referendum Poll 9. ICM Research, www.icmresearch.com/media-centre/polls/scottish-independence-poll-august-2014 [accessed 25 August 2014].

References

ICV. 2012. *Proposta de Programa Marc*. Manifesto for the 2012 regional election. Available at www.iniciativa.cat/icv/documents/5177 [accessed 17 July 2014].
– 2010. *Esquerra, ecologia, llibertat*. Manifesto for the 2010 regional election. Available at www.iniciativa.cat/icv/documents/2955 [accessed 15 March 2011].
– 2006a. "10 raons per dir Sí a l'Estatut" leaflet. ICV file. Estatut de Catalunya 2006, Box 4. CEDOC, Universitat Autònoma de Barcelona.
– 2006b. "A qui li molesta aquest Estatut?" leaflet. ICV file. Estatut de Catalunya 2006, Box 4. CEDOC, Universitat Autònoma de Barcelona.
– 2003. "Proposta de nou Estatut," April. ICV file. Estatut de Catalunya 2006, Box 1. CEDOC, Universitat Autònoma de Barcelona.
IdW. [2005] 2006. *Manifesto for an Independent Flanders within Europe*. English edition. Brussels: Reflection group "In de Warande."
Ignazi, Piero. 2010. "The Three Ages of Party Politics in Postwar Italy." In *Political Parties and Democracy – Vol. II: Europe*, edited by Kay Lawson, 47–70. Santa Barbara, CA: Praeger.
INE. 2013. *População residente e componentes da população*. Instituto Nacional de Estatística. Available at www.ine.pt.
Irigoin, Alejandra and Regina Grafe. 2008. "Bargaining for Absolutism: a Spanish Path to Nation-State and Empire Building." *Hispanic American Historical Review* 88 (2): 173–209.
Irving, Ronald. 1979. "The Belgian General Election of 1978: Not Quite a Non-Event." *West European Politics* 2 (2): 250–5.
ISTAT. 2016. Popolazione residente ricostruita – Anni 1952–1971. Available at dati.istat.it/Index.aspx?DataSetCode=DCIS_RICPOPRES1971 [accessed 18 October 2016].
Jaensch, Dean. 1976. "The Scottish Vote, 1974: A Realigning Party System?" *Political Studies* 24 (3): 306–19.
Jambon, Jan. 2009. N-VA leader in the Chamber of Representatives, personal interview, 28 August.
Jeffery, Charlie. 1996. "Farewell the Third Level? The German Länder and the European Policy Process." *Regional and Federal Studies* 6 (2): 56–75.
Jespersen, Knud. 2011. *A History of Denmark*, second ed. Basingstoke: Palgrave Macmillan.
John, Peter. 2001. *Local Governance in Western Europe*. London: Sage.
Johns, Robert, David Denver, James Mitchell, and Charles Pattie. 2010. *Voting for a Scottish Government – The Scottish Parliament Election of 2007*. Manchester: Manchester University Press.
Johnson, Miles, Ralph Atkins, and Claire Jones. 2012. "Catalonia Heightens Spanish Debt Fears." *Financial Times*, 28 August.
Jolly, Seth. 2007. "The Europhile Fringe? Regionalist Party Support for European Integration." *European Union Politics* 8 (1): 109–30.
Jones, Barry. 1995. "Conclusion." In *The European Union and the Regions*, edited by Barry Jones and Michael Keating, 289–96. Oxford: Clarendon Press.

Jones, Barry, and Michael Keating. 1982. "The Resolution of Internal Conflicts and External Pressures – The Labour Party's Devolution Policy." *Government and Opposition* 17 (3): 279–92.

Jones, Barry, and R.A. Wilford. 1983. "The Referendum Campaign: 8 February–1 March 1979." In *The Welsh Veto – The Wales Act 1978 and the Referendum*, edited by David Foulkes, Barry Jones, and R.A. Wilford, 118–51. Cardiff: University of Wales Press.

Jones, Carwyn. 2012. *Wales and the Future of the United Kingdom.* Speech at the 'Wales and the Changing Union' conference, available at www.clickonwales.org/2012/04/wales-and-the-future-of-the-united-kingdom/ [accessed 4 September 2014].

Jones, Peter. 1997. "Labour's Referendum Plan: Sell-out or Act of Faith?" *Scottish Affairs* 18: 1–17.

Joris, Freddy. 1998. *Les Wallons et la réforme de l'Etat – De l'Etat unitaire à l'Etat "communautaire et régional" (1890–1970)*, second ed. Charleroi: Institut Jules Destrée.

JxS. 2015. *Programa electoral.* Manifesto for the 2015 regional election. Available at juntspelsi.s3.amazonaws.com/assets/150905_Programa_electoral_v1.pdf [accessed 10 December 2016].

Kato, Junko. 1996. "Institutions and Rationality in Politics – Three Varieties of Neo-Institutionalism." *British Journal of Political Science* 26 (4): 553–82.

Kauppi, Mark. 1982. "The Decline of the Scottish National Party, 1977–81: Political and Organizational Factors." *Ethnic and Racial Studies* 5 (3): 326–48.

Kavanagh, Dennis, and Philip Cowley. 2010. *The British General Election of 2010.* Basingstoke: Palgrave Macmillan.

Keating, Michael. 2013. *Rescaling the European State – The Making of Territory and the Rise of the Meso.* Oxford: Oxford University Press.

– 2001. *Plurinational Democracy – Stateless Nations in a Post-sovereignty Era.* Oxford: Oxford University Press.

– 1998a. *The New Regionalism in Western Europe.* Cheltenham: Edward Elgar

– 1998b. "What's Wrong with Asymmetrical Government?" *Regional and Federal Studies* 8 (1): 195–218.

– 1995. "Europeanism and Regionalism." In *The European Union and the Regions*, edited by Barry Jones and Michael Keating, 1–22. Oxford: Clarendon Press.

– 1993. "The Continental Meso: Regions in the European Community." In *The Rise of Meso Government in Europe*, edited by Laurence Sharpe, 296–312. London: Sage.

Keating, Michael, and Zoe Bray. 2006. "Renegotiating Sovereignty: Basque Nationalism and the Rise and Fall of the Ibarretxe Plan." *Ethnopolitics* 5 (4): 347–64.

Kellas, James. 1991. "European Integration and the Regions" *Parliamentary Affairs* 44 (2): 226–39.

– 1984. *The Scottish Political System*, third ed. Cambridge: Cambridge University Press.

Kelstrup, Morten. 2013. "Denmark's Relation to the European Union – A History of Dualism and Pragmatism." In *Denmark and the European Union*, edited by Lee Miles and Anders Wivel, 14–29. Abingdon: Routledge.

Keman, Hans. 2001. "Federalism and Policy Performance – A Conceptual and Empirical Inquiry." In *Federalism and Political Performance*, edited by Ute Wachendorfer-Schmidt, 196–227. London: Routledge.

Kendrick, Stephen, and David McCrone. 1989. "Politics in a Cold Climate: The Conservative Decline in Scotland." *Political Studies* 37 (4): 589–603.

King, Gary, Robert Keohane, and Sidney Verba. 1994. *Designing Social Inquiry*. Princeton, NJ: Princeton University Press.

King, R.L. 1987. "Regional Government: the Italian Experience." *Environment and Planning C: Government and Politics* 5 (3): 327–46.

Kingdon, John. 1995. *Agendas, Alternatives, and Public Policies*, second ed. Harlow: Longman.

Klatt, Hartmut. 1999. "Centralizing Trends in Western German Federalism, 1949–1989." In *Recasting German Federalism*, edited by Charlie Jeffery, 40–57. London: Pinter.

Knapp, Andrew. 1994. *Gaullism since de Gaulle*. Aldershot: Dartmouth.

Knapp, Andrew, and Vincent Wright. 2001. *The Government and Politics of France*, fourth ed. London: Routledge.

Knudsen, Ann-Christina Lauring. 2008. "Euroscepticism in Denmark." In *Opposing Europe? The Comparative Party Politics of Euroscepticism*, vol. 1, edited by Aleks Szczerbiak and Paul Taggart, 152–67. Oxford: Oxford University Press.

Koenigsberger, Helmut. [1975] 1986. "Dominium Regale or Dominium Politicum et Regale – Monarchies and Parliaments in Early Modern Europe." In *Politicians and Virtuosi – Essays in Early Modern History*, edited by Helmut Koenigsberger, 1–26. London: Hambledon Press.

Kohn, Hans. 1955. *Making of the Modern French Mind*. Princeton, NJ: Van Nostrand.

Kolinsky, Martin. 1981. "The Nation-State in Western Europe: Erosion from Above and Below?" In *The Nation-State – The Formation of Modern Politics*, edited by Leonard Tirey, 82–103. Oxford: Martin Robertson.

Kossmann, Ernst. 1978. *The Low Countries 1780–1940*. Oxford: Clarendon Press.

Krogh, Simon. 2011. "Reform Politics through the Creation of Inefficient Political Institutions: The Case of the 2007 Danish Administrative Reform." *Scandinavian Political Studies* 34 (4): 307–31.

Krugman, Paul. 1993. "Lessons of Massachusetts for EMU." In *Adjustment and growth in the European monetary union*, edited by Francisco Torres and Francesco Giavazzi, 241–61. Cambridge: Cambridge University Press.

La Loggia, Enrico. 1955. *Sintesi storica della questione siciliana*. Palermo: Mori.

La Palombara, Joseph. 1966. *Italy – The Politics of Planning*. Syracuse, NY: Syracuse University Press.

LAB. 2001. *Ambitions for Britain*. Manifesto for the 2001 general election. London: The Labour Party.

LAB-S. 2011. *Fighting for What Really Matters*. Manifesto for the 2011 regional election. Glasgow: Scottish Labour Party.

– 2007. *Building Scotland*. Manifesto for the 2007 regional election. Glasgow: Scottish Labour Party.

– 1997. *Because Scotland Deserves Better*. British Labour Party's Scottish manifesto for the 1997 general election. Glasgow: Scottish Council of the Labour Party.

– 1992. *It's Time to Get Scotland Moving Again*. British Labour Party's Scottish manifesto for the 1992 general election. Glasgow: Scottish Council of the Labour Party.

– 1979. *The Better Way for Scotland*. British Labour Party's Scottish manifesto for the 1979 general election. Glasgow: Scottish Council of the Labour Party.

LAB-W. 1997. *New Labour – Because Wales Deserves Better*. British Labour Party's Welsh manifesto for the 1997 general election. Cardiff: Wales Labour Party.

– 1992. *It's Time to Get Wales Working Again*. British Labour Party's Welsh manifesto for the 1992 general election. Cardiff: Wales Labour Party.

– 1979. *The Better Way for Wales*. British Labour Party's Welsh manifesto for the 1979 general election. Cardiff: Wales Labour Party.

Lacomba, Juan Antonio. 2006. *Historia contemporánea de Andalucía – De 1800 a la actualidad*. Cordoba: Editorial Almuzara.

Ladrech, Robert. 1994. "Europeanization of Domestic Politics and Institutions: The Case of France" *Journal of Common Market Studies* 32 (1): 69–98.

Ladrech, Robert, and Philippe Marlière. 1999. "The French Socialist Party." In *Social Democratic Parties in the European Union*, edited by Robert Ladrech and Philippe Marlière, 64–78. Basingstoke: Macmillan.

Laible, Janet. 2008. *Separatism and Sovereignty in the New Europe*. New York, NY: Palgrave Macmillan.

Laitin, David. 1977. *Politics, Language, and Thought*. Chicago, IL: University of Chicago Press.

Lamberts, Emiel. 2004. "The Zenith of Christian Democracy: The Christelijke Volkspartij/Parti Social Chrétien in Belgium." In *Christian Democracy in Europe since 1945*, edited by Michael Gehler and Wolfram Kaiser, 67–84. London: Routledge.

Lamping, Wolfram. 2013. "European Union Health Care Policy." In *European Union Public Health Policy – Regional and Global Trends*, edited by Scott Greer and Paulette Kurzer, 19–35. Abingdon: Routledge.

Lane, Jan-Erik and Svante Ersson. 1999. *Politics and Society in Western Europe*, fourth ed. London: Sage.

Lane, Robert. 1991. "Scotland in Europe: An Independent Scotland in the European Community." In *Edinburgh Essays in Public Law*, edited by Wilson Finnie, C. Himsworth and N. Walker, 143–55. Edinburgh: Edinburgh University Press.

Lauber, Volkmar. 1988. "Change and Continuity in French Conservatism since 1944." In *The Transformation of Contemporary Conservatism*, edited by Brian Girvin, 33–55. London: Sage.

Law 82-213. *Loi no. 82-213 du 2 mars 1982 relative aux droits et libertés des communes, des départements et des régions*. Available at www.legifrance.gouv.fr.

LD-S. 2011. *Solutions for Scotland*. Manifesto for the 2011 regional election. Edinburgh: Scottish Liberal Democrats.

– 2007. *We Think Scotland Has a Bright Future*. Manifesto for the 2007 regional election. Edinburgh: Scottish Liberal Democrats.

LE.1980. "Interview de M. Valéry Giscard d'Estaing à l'Express." *L'Express*, 10 May.

Lecours, André. 2000. "Ethnonationalism in the West: A Theoretical Exploration." *Nationalism and Ethnic Politics* 6 (1): 103–24.

Leibfried, Stephan. 2005. "Social Policy – Left to the Judges and the Markets?" In *Policy-Making in the European Union*, fifth ed., edited by Helen Wallace, William Wallace, and Mark Pollack, 243–78. Oxford: Oxford University Press.

Lenschow, Andrea. 2005. "Environmental Policy – Contending Dynamics of Policy Change." In *Policy-Making in the European Union*, fifth ed., edited by Helen Wallace, William Wallace and Mark Pollack, 305–25. Oxford: Oxford University Press.

Leonardi, Robert, Raffaella Nanetti, and Robert Putnam. 1981. "Devolution as a Political Process: The Case of Italy." *Publius* 11 (1): 95–117.

Leonardi, Robert, and Douglas Wertman. 1989. *Italian Christian Democracy – The Politics of Dominance*. Basingstoke: Macmillan.

Levy, Roger. 1986. "The Search for a Rational Strategy: The Scottish National Party and Devolution 1974–79." *Political Studies* 34 (2): 236–48.

Lijphart, Arend. 1999. *Patterns of Democracy – Government Forms and Performance in Thirty-Six Countries*. New Haven, CT: Yale University Press.

Lindberg, Leon, and Stuart Scheingold. 1970. *Europe's Would-Be Polity – Patterns of Change in the European Community*. Englewood Cliffs, NJ: Prentice-Hall.

Linz, Juan. 1997. *Democracy, Multinationalism and Federalism*. Working paper no. 97/103. Madrid: Centro de Estudios Avanzados in Ciencias Sociales. Available at digital.march.es/ceacs-ir/es/fedora/repository/ir%3A3919.

– 1973. "Early State-Building and Late Peripheral Nationalisms against the State: The Case of Spain." In *Building States and Nations – Vol. 2, Analyses by Region*, edited by Samuel Eisenstadt and Stein Rokkan, 32–116. Beverly Hills, CA: Sage.

Lipset, Seymour Martin, and Stein Rokkan. 1967. "Cleavage Structures, Party Systems, and Voter Alignment: An Introduction." In *Party Systems and Voter Alignments – Cross-national Perspectives*, edited by Seymour Martin Lipset and Stein Rokkan, 1–64. New York, NY: Free Press.

Lluch, Jaime. 2012. "Internal Variation in Sub-State National Movements and the Moral Polity of the Nationalist." *European Political Science Review* 4 (3): 433–60.

LN. 1996. *Lega Nord – Programma elettorale*. Manifesto for the 1996 election. Collected by the Manifesto Research Group and available from GESIS, Cologne.

– 1994. *Sintesi del programma elettorale per le elezioni politiche '94*. Manifesto for the 1994 election. Collected by the Manifesto Research Group and available from GESIS, Cologne.

– 1991. "Programma della Lega Nord." *L'Europeo*, 6 December.

Loeb, N. 1969. "Les trois grands partis politiques belges et l'intégration européenne." *Courrier hebdomadaire* 433. Brussels: CRISP.

Loughlin, John. 2013. "Reconfiguring the Nation-State: Hybridity vs Uniformity." In *The Routledge Handbook of Federalism and Regionalism*, edited by John Kincaid, John Loughlin, and Wilfried Swenden, 3–18. London: Routledge.

– 1996. "'Europe of the Regions' and the Federalization of Europe." *Publius* 26 (4): 141–62.

– 1985. "Regionalism and Ethnic Nationalism in France." In *Centre-Periphery Relations in Western Europe*, edited by Yves Mény and Vincent Wright, 207–35. London: George Allen & Unwin.

LS. 1991. "DC, lo spettro delle leghe." *La Stampa*, 16 September.

– 1968. "Al Senato voto definitivo per la legge sulle regioni." *La Stampa*, 15 February.

– 1963. "La dc chiede ai socialisti scelte chiare e definitive." *La Stampa*, 19 April.

LU. 1964a. "Un serio passo avanti i comitati per la programmazione." *L'Unità*, 24 September.

– 1964b. "I comitati regionali per la programmazione." *L'Unità*, 23 September.

Luverà, Bruno. 1997. "La politica estera della Lega." *Limes* 5 (2): 87–96.

LV. 2008. "El Congreso autoriza a Zapatero a firmar el Tratado de Lisboa." *La Vanguardia*, 27 June.

Lynch, John. 1981. *Spain under the Habsburgs – Volume One: Empire and Absolutism 1516–1598*, second ed. Oxford: Basil Blackwell.

Lynch, Peter. 2002. *SNP – The History of the Scottish National Party*. Cardiff: Welsh Academic Press.

– 1996. *Minority Nationalism and European Integration*. Cardiff: University of Wales Press.

Mabille, Xavier. 2011. *Nouvelle histoire politique de la Belgique*. Brussels: CRISP.

Mabille, Xavier, and Val Lorwin. 1977. "The Belgian Socialist Party." In *Social Democratic Parties in Western Europe*, edited by William Paterson and Alastair Thomas, 389– 407. London: Croom Helm.

Macartney, Allan. 1981. "The Protagonists." In *The Referendum Experience: Scotland 1979*, Edited by John Bochel, David Denver, and Allan Macartney, 12–42. Aberdeen: Aberdeen University Press.

Machin, Howard. 1978. "All Jacobins Now? The Growing Hostility to Local Government Reform." *West European Politics* 1 (3): 133–50.

Machin, Howard, and Vincent Wright. 1977. "The French Left under the Fifth Republic – The Search for Identity in Unity" *Comparative Politics* 10 (1): 35–67.

Maciá, Francesc. [1931] 2006. "Proclamo el Estado catalán." In *Cataluña y la España plural – Discursos políticos del siglo XX*, edited by Jordi Casassas Ymbert, 85–9. Barcelona: Aurea.

Mackie, Thomas, and Richard Rose. 1974. *The International Almanac of Electoral History*. London: Macmillan.

MacMullen, Andrew. 1979. "The Belgian Election of December 1978: The Limits of Language-Community Politics?" *Parliamentary Affairs* 32 (3): 331–8.

Maes, Nelly. 2009. Former leader of VUJO [VU's youth wing], personal interview, 15 July.

Maggiorani, Mauro. 1998. *L'Europa degli altri – Comunisti italiani e integrazione europea (1957–1969)*. Rome: Carocci.

Mahoney, James. 2012. The Logic of Process Tracing Tests in the Social Sciences. *Sociological Methods and Research* 41 (4): 570–97.

Mahoney, James, and Gary Goertz. 2004. "The Possibility Principle: Choosing Negative Cases in Comparative Research." *American Political Science Review* 98 (4): 653–69.

Mahoney, James, and Dietrich Rueschmeyer. 2003. "Comparative Historical Analysis – Achievements and Agendas." In *Comparative Historical Analysis in the Social Sciences*, edited by James Mahoney and Dietrich Rueschmeyer, 3–38. Cambridge: Cambridge University Press.

Mannoni, Stefano. 1994–96. *Une et indivisible – Storia dell'accentramento amministrativo in Francia*. 2 vols. Milan: Giuffrè.

Marcussen, Martin. 2013. "Denmark and the Euro Opt-Out." In *Denmark and the European Union*, edited by Lee Miles and Anders Wivel, 47–64. Abingdon: Routledge.

Marks, Gary. 1993. "Structural Policy and Multilevel Governance in the EC." In *The State of the European Community Vol. 2*, edited by Alan Cafruny and Glenda Rosenthal, 391–410. Boulder, CO: Lynne Rienner.

Marks, Gary, Liesbet Hooghe, and Kermit Blank. 1996. "European Integration from the 1980s: State-Centric v Multi-Level Governance." *Journal of Common Market Studies* 34 (3): 341–78.

Martí, David. 2013. "The 2012 Catalan Election: The First Step towards Independence?" *Regional and Federal Studies* 23 (4): 507–16.

Martí, David, and Daniel Cetrà. 2016. "The 2015 Catalan Election: A De Facto Referendum on Independence." *Regional and Federal Studies* 26 (1): 107–19.

Martin, Jean-Clément. 1996. *Révolution et Contre-Révolution – Les rouages de l'histoire*. Rennes: Presses Universitaires de Rennes.

Martin, Steve, and Graham Pearce. 1993. "European Regional Development Strategies: Strengthening Meso-Government in the UK?" *Regional Studies* 27 (7): 681–5.

Martinsen, Dorte Sindbjerg. 2013. "Public Administration, Civil Servants and Implementation." In *Denmark and the European Union*, edited by Lee Miles and Anders Wivel, 189–203. Abingdon: Routledge.

Marx, Axel, Benoît Rihoux, and Charles Ragin. 2014. "The Origins, Development and Application of Qualitative Comparative Analysis: The First 25 Years." *European Political Science Review* 6 (1): 115–42.

Masala, Carlo. 2004. "Born for Government: The Democrazia Cristiana in Italy." In *Christian Democracy in Europe since 1945*, edited by Michael Gehler and Wolfram Kaiser, 101–17. London: Routledge.

Massetti, Emanuele. 2009. "Explaining Regionalist Party Positioning in a Multi-Dimensional Ideological Space: A Framework for Analysis." *Regional and Federal Studies* 19 (4–5): 501–31.

Massetti, Emanuele, and Simon Toubeau. 2013. "Sailing with Northern Winds: Party Politics and Federal Reforms in Italy." *West European Politics* 36 (2): 359–81.

Mayr, Walter. 2011. "The Fries Revolution: Belgium's Political Crisis Foretells EU's Future." *Spiegel Online International*, 17 March, www.spiegel.de/international/europe/the-fries-revolution-belgium-s-political-crisis-foretells-eu-s-future-a-751536.html.

Mbadinuju, Chinwoke. 1976. "Devolution: The 1975 White Paper." *Political Quarterly* 47(3): 286–96.

McAllister, Laura. 2001. *Plaid Cymru: The Emergence of a Political Party*. Bridgend: Seren.

– 2000. "Devolution and the New Context for Public Policy-Making: Lessons from the EU Structural Funds in Wales." *Public Policy and Administration* 15 (2): 38–52.

– 1998. "The Welsh Devolution Referendum: Definitely, Maybe?" *Parliamentary Affairs* 51 (2): 149–65.

McAllister, Richard. 1975. "The EEC Dimension: Intended and Unintended Consequences." In *The Failure of the State – On the Distribution of Political and Economic Power in Europe,* edited by James Cornford, 190–205. London: Croom Helm.

McCrone, David, and Bethan Lewis. 1999. "The Scottish and Welsh Referendum Campaigns." In *Scotland and Wales: Nations Again?*, edited by Bridget Taylor and Katarina Thomson, 17–39. Cardiff: University of Wales Press.

McGarry, John. 2007. "Asymmetry in Federations, Federacies and Unitary States." *Ethnopolitics* 6 (1): 105–16.

McGarvey, Neil, and Paul Cairney. 2008. *Scottish Politics – An Introduction*. Basingstoke: Palgrave Macmillan.

McKay, David. 2001. *Designing Europe – Comparative Lessons from the Federal Experience*. Oxford: Oxford University Press.

McLean, Iain, and Alistair McMillan. 2005. *State of the Union*. Oxford: Oxford University Press.

McRae, Kenneth. 1986. *Conflict and Compromise in Multilingual Societies – Belgium*. Waterloo, ON: Wilfrid Laurier University Press.

Meadwell, Hudson, and Pierre Martin. 1996. "Economic Integration and the Politics of Independence." *Nations and Nationalism* 2 (1): 67–87.

Meguid, Bonnie. 2008. *Party Competition between Unequals – Strategies and Electoral Fortunes in Western Europe*. Cambridge: Cambridge University Press.

Menu, Peter. 1994a. *Congresresoluties van de Vlaamse Politieke Partijen – 1 De Volksunie 1955–1993*. Ghent: Steunpunt Sociopolitiek Systeem.

– 1994b. *Congresresoluties van de Vlaamse Politieke Partijen – 2 De Christelijke Volkpartij 1945–1993*. Ghent: Steunpunt Sociopolitiek Systeem.

– 1994c. *Congresresoluties van de Vlaamse Politieke Partijen – 3 De (Belgische) Socialistische Partij 1945–1993*. Ghent: Steunpunt Sociopolitiek Systeem.

– 1994d. *Congresresoluties van de Vlaamse Politieke Partijen – 4 De Liberale Partij: Partij voor Vrijheid en Vooruitgang 1945–1992*. Ghent: Steunpunt Sociopolitiek Systeem.

Mény, Yves. 1974. *Centralisation et décentralisation dans le débat politique français (1945–1969)*. Paris: Librairie générale de droit et de jurisprudence.

Miller, David. 2006. "Nationalism." In *The Oxford Handbook of Political Theory*, edited by John Dryzek, Bonnie Honig and Anne Philips, 529–45. Oxford: Oxford University Press.

Mitchell, James. 2009. *Devolution in the UK*. Manchester: Manchester University Press.

– 1998a. "The Evolution of Devolution: Labour's Home Rule Strategy in Opposition." *Government and Opposition* 33 (4): 479–96.

– 1998b. "Member-State or Euro-Region? The SNP, Plaid Cymru and Europe." In *Britain For and Against Europe*, edited by David Baker and David Seawright, 108–29. Oxford: Clarendon Press.

– 1996. *Strategies for Self-Government*. Edinburgh: Polygon.

– 1990. *Conservatives and the Union – A Study of Conservative Party Attitudes to Scotland*. Edinburgh: Edinburgh University Press.

Mitchell, James, Lynn Bennie and Rob Johns. 2011. *The Scottish National Party – Transition to Power*. Oxford: Oxford University Press.

Moreno, Luis. 2001. *The Federalization of Spain*. London: Cass.

Morgan, Kenneth. 1963. *Wales in British Politics, 1868–1922*. Cardiff: University of Wales Press.

Morris, P. 1996. "The British Conservative Party." In *Political Parties and the European Union*, edited by John Gaffney, 122–38. London: Routledge.

Mosse, George. 1975. *The Nationalization of the Masses*. New York, NY: Fertig.

Mouritzen, Poul Erik. 2011. "Denmark." In *The Second Tier of Local Government in Europe*, edited by Hubert Heinelt and Xavier Bertrana, 56–72. Abingdon: Routledge.

– 2010. "The Danish Revolution in Local Government: How and Why?" In *Territorial Choice – The Politics of Boundaries and Borders*, edited by Harald Baldersheim and Lawrence Rose, 21–41. Basingstoke: Palgrave Macmillan.

Mousnier, Roland. 1980. *Les institutions de la France sous la monarchie absolue*, vol. 2. Paris: Presses universitaires de France.

– 1974. *Les institutions de la France sous la monarchie absolue*, vol. 1. Paris: Presses universitaires de France.

MR. 2010. *Programme du MR*. Manifesto for the 2010 federal election. Available at www.mr.be/media/pdf/programme-2010.pdf [accessed 23 August 2010].

– 2007. *Le programme du Mouvement réformateur*. Manifesto for the 2007 federal election. Brussels: Mouvement réformateur.

Müller, Wolfgang, and Kaare Strøm (eds). 1999. *Policy, Office, or Votes? How Political Parties in Western Europe Make Hard Decisions*. Cambridge: Cambridge University Press.

Muñoz, Jordi, and Marc Guinjoan. 2013. "Accounting for Internal Variation in Nationalist Mobilization: Unofficial Referendums for Independence in Catalonia (2009–11)." *Nations and Nationalism* 19 (1): 44–67.

Murphy, Alexander. 1988. *The Regional Dynamics of Language Differentiation in Belgium: A Study in Cultural-Political Geography*. Chicago, IL: University of Chicago.

NA. 2014a. Regional Development Agencies. *The National Archives*, www.nationalarchives.gov.uk/webarchive/regional-development-agencies.htm [accessed 4 September 2014].

– 2014b. The Richard Commission. *The National Archives*, webarchive.nationalarchives.gov.uk/20100410160947/http://www.richardcommission.gov.uk/content/template.asp?ID=/index.asp [accessed 4 September 2014].

Nandrin, Jean-Pierre. 1997. "De l'Etat unitaire à l'Etat fédéral – Bref aperçu historique de l'évolution institutionnelle de la Belgique." In *La reforme de l'Etat...et apres?*, edited by Serge Jaumain, 13–22. Brussels: Editions de l'université de Bruxelles.

Nassaux, Jean-Paul. 2002. *La réforme de l'Etat de 2001*. Complément au Dossier du CRISP no. 40 (1994). Brussels: CRISP.

NAW. 2014. The History of Welsh Devolution. *National Assembly for Wales*, www.assemblywales.org/en/abthome/role-of-assembly-how-it-works/Pages/history-welsh-devolution.aspx [accessed 4 September 2014].

Nenni, Pietro. 1963. *La battaglia socialista per la svolta a sinistra nella terza legislatura 1958–1963*. Milan: Edizioni Avanti!

Newell, James. 1996. "The Italian General Election of 21 April 1996." *Regional and Federal Studies* 6 (3): 103–11.
Newman, Saul. 1996. *Ethnoregional Conflict in Democracies – Mostly Ballots, Rarely Bullets*. Westport, CT: Greenwood Press.
– 1995. "Losing the Electoral Battles and Winning the Policy Wars: Ethnoregional Conflict in Belgium." *Nationalism and Ethnic Politics* 1 (4): 44–72.
NIC. 2011. Historic Population Trends (1841 to 2011) – Northern Ireland and the Republic of Ireland. Northern Ireland Census 2011, available at www.nisra.gov.uk/Census/Historic_Population_Trends_%281841-2011%29_NI_and_RoI.pdf.
Nielsen, François. 1980. "The Flemish Movement in Belgium after World War II: A Dynamic Analysis." *American Sociological Review* 45 (1): 76–94.
Nissen, Ove. 1991. "Key Issues in the Local Government Debate in Denmark." In *Local Government in Europe – Trends and Developments*, edited by Richard Batley and Gerry Stoker, 190–7. Basingstoke: Macmillan.
Noguer, Miquel. 2010. "Montilla, "indignado," pide a Zapatero que rehaga el pacto estatutario." *El Pais*, 29 June.
– 2006. "Montilla ofrece a la oposición un pacto para desarrollar el Estatuto catalán." *El Pais*, 25 November.
Noguer, Miquel, and Pere Ríos. 2014. "El soberanismo refuerza el pulso de Mas." *El Pais*, 11 September.
North, Douglass. 1995. "Five Propositions about Institutional Change." In *Explaining Social Institutions*, edited by Jack Knight and Itai Sened, 15–26. Ann Arbor, MI: University of Michigan Press.
N-VA. 2010. *Nu durven veranderen*. Manifesto for the 2010 federal election. Available at http://www.n-va.be/congresteksten/verkiezingsprogramma-juni-2010 [accessed 23 August 2010].
– 2007. *Voor een Sterker Vlaanderen*. Manifesto for the 2007 federal election. Brussels: Nieuw-Vlaamse Alliantie.
– 2001. *Manifest van de Nieuw-Vlaamse Alliantie*, Brussels: Nieuw-Vlaamse Alliantie, avaiable at http://www.n-va.be/files/default/nva_images/documenten/manifest.pdf [accessed 23 August 2010].
O-VLD. 2010. *Een nieuwe start*. Manifesto for the 2010 election. Brussels: Open VLD.
– 2007. *De open samenleving in de praktijk*. Manifesto for the 2007 federal election. Liberaal Archief, Ghent.
O'Neill, Kathleen. 2003. "Decentralization as an Electoral Strategy." *Comparative Political Studies* 36(9): 1068–91.
ONS. 2012. 2011 Census: Population Estimates for the United Kingdom, 27 March 2011. Office for National Statistics, available at www.ons.gov.uk/ons/dcp171778_292378.pdf.
Orriols, Lluis, and Guillermo Cordero. 2016. "The Breakdown of the Spanish Two-Party System: the Upsurge of Podemos and Ciudadanos in

the 2015 General Election." *South European Society and Politics* 21(4): 469–92.

Orriols, Lluis, and Toni Rodon. 2016. "The 2015 Catalan Election: The Independence Bid at the Polls." *South European Society and Politics* 21 (3): 359–81.

Pagano, Giuseppe. 2000. "Les résolutions du Parlement flamand pour une réforme de l'État." *Courrier hebdomadaire* 1670–1. Brussels: CRISP.

Pagano, Giuseppe, Miguel Verbeke, and Aurélien Accaputo. 2006. "Le manifeste du groupe In de Warande." *Courrier hebdomadaire* 1913–4. Brussels: CRISP.

Pallarés, Francesc, and Jordi Muñoz. 2008. "The Autonomous Elections of 1 November 2006 in Catalonia." *Regional and Federal Studies* 18 (4): 449–64.

Pansa, Giampaolo. 1963. "L'on. Moro sostiene a Milano la politica di centro-sinistra." *La Stampa*, 3 April.

Parker, George, Mure Dickie, and Alistair Gray. 2014. "Cameron Calls for Broad Constitutional Reform after Scottish Vote." *Financial Times*, 19 September.

Parks, Judith, and Howard Elcock. 2000. "Why Do Regions Demand Autonomy?" *Regional and Federal Studies* 10 (3): 87–106.

Pavone, Claudio. 1964. *Amministrazione centrale e amministrazione periferica – Da Rattazzi a Ricasoli (1859–1866)*. Milan: Giuffrè.

Payne, Stanley. 1973. *A History of Spain and Portugal*. 2 vols. Madison, WI: University of Wisconsin Press.

PC. 2011. *Ambition Is Critical – A Manifesto for a Better Wales*. Manifesto for the 2011 regional election. Cardiff: Plaid Cymru.

 – 1997. *The Best for Wales – Plaid Cymru's Programme for the New Millenium*. Manifesto for the 1997 general election. Cardiff: Plaid Cymru.

 – 1992. *Towards 2000 – Plaid Cymru's Programme for Wales in Europe*. Manifesto for the 1992 general election. Cardiff: Plaid Cymru.

 – 1979. *A Future for Wales*. Manifesto for the 1979 election. Cardiff: Plaid Cymru.

PCF. 1981. Le rapport de Georges Marchais au Comité central (12 janvier 1981). *L'Humanité*, 14 January. Collected by the Manifesto Research Group and available from GESIS, Cologne.

PCI. 1963. Il programma elettorale del P.C.I. *L'Unità*, 3 March, pp. 7–10.

PdC. 2012a. Diari de sessions del Parlament de Catalunya. IX legislatura, Quart període, Sèrie P, Número 67, 25 de setembre de 2012. Parlament de Catalunya, www.parlament.cat/activitat/dspcp/09p067.pdf.

 – 2012b. El Parlament acorda iniciar el procés per fer efectiu el dret de decidir, amb 85 vots a favor, 41 en contra i 2 abstencions. Parlament de Catalunya, www.parlament.cat/web/actualitat/noticies?p_id=129656021.

PDS. 1994. *Programma di governo del PDS – Per ricostruire un'Italia più giusta, più unita, più moderna*. Manifesto for the 1994 election. Collected by the Manifesto Research Group and available from GESIS, Cologne.

- 1992. *Costruiamo una nuova Italia – PDS opposizione che costruisce*. Manifesto for the 1992 election. Collected by the Manifesto Research Group and available from GESIS, Cologne.
Pedersen, Karina. 2005. "The 2005 Danish General Election: A Phase of Consolidation." *West European Politics* 28 (5): 1101–8.
Pérez, Fernando, and Père Ríos. 2014. "1,8 millones de personas votan por la independencia catalana en el 9-N." *El País*, 10 November.
Philipponneau, Michel. 1981. *La Grande Affaire – Décentralisation et régionalisation*. Paris: Calmann-Lévy.
Pi, Jaume. 2012a. "Masiva manifestación por la independencia de Catalunya." *La Vanguardia*, 11 September.
- 2012b. "Elecciones catalanas: El debate sobre si Catalunya estaría en la UE centra el debate a tres de 8tv." *La Vanguardia*, 21 November.
Piattoni, Simona. 2010. *The Theory of Multilevel Governance – Conceptual, Empirical and Normative Challenges*. Oxford: Oxford University Press.
Picard, Louis. 1983. "Decentralization, 'Recentralization' and 'Steering Mechanisms': Paradoxes of Local Government in Denmark." *Polity* 15 (4): 536–54.
Pieraccini, Giovanni. 2000. "Il riformismo del centro-sinistra." In *Pietro Nenni – Una vita per la democrazia e il socialismo*, edited by Giuseppe Tamburrano, 228–45. Manduria: Lacaita.
Pilet, Jean-Benoît, and Emilie Van Haute. 2008. "The Federal Elections in Belgium, June 2007." *Electoral Studies* 27 (3): 247–50.
Piñol, Angels. 2010. "CiU califica la situación de 'gravísima' y ERC augura un auge del independentismo." *El País*, 29 June.
Pirenne, Henri. [1900–32] 1948–52a. *Histoire de Belgique*, vol. 1. Brussels: La Renaissance du Livre.
- [1900–32] 1948–52b. *Histoire de Belgique*, vol. 2. Brussels: La Renaissance du Livre.
- [1900–32] 1948–52c. *Histoire de Belgique*, vol. 3. Brussels: La Renaissance du Livre.
- [1900–32] 1948–52d. *Histoire de Belgique*, vol. 4. Brussels: La Renaissance du Livre.
PLP. 1970a. Resolution sur l'autonomie culturelle, Congres national extraordinaire, Vendredi 20 et Samedi 21 mars 1970, Doc. F/4223, Liberaal Archief, Ghent.
- 1970b. Resolution sur l'organization des pouvoirs non culturels en Belgique, Congres national extraordinaire, Vendredi 20 et Samedi 21 mars 1970, Doc. F/4224, Liberaal Archief, Ghent.
- 1969. Resolutions of the national congress of 8 June 1969, Liberaal Archief, Ghent.
- 1968a. *Perspectives P.L.P.* Manifesto for the 1968 election. Collected by the Manifesto Research Group and available from GESIS, Cologne.
- 1968b. Demain Politique, no 198, 24 March 1968, Liberaal Archief, Ghent.

Pollack, Mark. 1995. "Regional Actors in an Intergovernmentalist Play: the Making and Implementation of EC Structural Policy." In *The State of the European Community Vol. 3 – Building a European Polity?*, edited by Carolyn Rhodes and Sonia Mazey, 361–90. Boulder, CO: Lynne Reinner.

PP-C. 2015. *Unidos Ganamos*. Manifesto for the 2012 regional election. Barcelona: Partido Popular de Cataluña.

– 2012. *Catalunya sí, España también*. Manifesto for the 2012 regional election. Barcelona: Partido Popular de Cataluña.

– 2010. *Solucions per a la crisi*. Manifesto for the 2010 regional election. Barcelona: Partido Popular de Cataluña.

– 2006. Anticostitucional – Estatuto de Cataluña – "Por una España sin barreras"' leaflet. PP-C file. Estatut de Catalunya 2006, Box 4. CEDOC, Universitat Autònoma de Barcelona.

PPI. 1994. *Un programma per gli italiani*. Manifesto for the 1994 election. Collected by the Manifesto Research Group and available from GESIS, Cologne.

PRC. 2014. A Fragile Rebound for EU Image on Eve of European Parliament Elections. Pew Research Center, http://www.pewglobal.org/files/2014/05/2014-05-12_Pew-Global-Attitudes-European-Union.pdf.

Price, Roger. 2005. *A Concise History of France*, second ed. Cambridge: Cambridge University Press.

Pringle, Kevin. 2000. Spokesman for Alex Salmond, SNP leader, personal interview, 4 April.

PRL. 1991. *Liberons le dynamisme*. Manifesto for the 1991 election. Collected by the Manifesto Research Group and available from GESIS, Cologne.

– 1987. *L'essentiel d'abord*. Manifesto for the 1987 election. Collected by the Manifesto Research Group and available from GESIS, Cologne.

PRLW. 1978. *Le programme du PRL*. Manifesto for the 1978 election. Collected by the Manifesto Research Group and available from GESIS, Cologne.

Pryce, Roy. 1963. "The Italian General Election 1963." *Parliamentary Affairs* 16 (3): 248–56.

PS. 2010. *Un pays stable – Des emplois durables*. Manifesto for the 2010 federal election. Available at www.ps.be/extras/lesarchives/elections2010/leprogramme/ [accessed 23 August 2010].

– 2007. *À vos côtés...* Manifesto for the 2007 federal election. Brussels: Parti socialiste.

– 1991. *L'évidence socialiste*. Manifesto for the 1991 election. Collected by the Manifesto Research Group and available from GESIS, Cologne.

– 1987. *Programme du P.S.* Manifesto for the 1987 election. Collected by the Manifesto Research Group and available from GESIS, Cologne.

– 1978. *Programme du Parti Socialiste*. Manifesto for the 1978 election. Collected by the Manifesto Research Group and available from GESIS, Cologne.

PS-C. 2015. *El nostre compromís – Solucions justes y acordades*. Manifesto for the 2015 regional election. Barcelona: Partit dels Socialistes de Catalunya.
- 2012. *L'alternativa sensata*. Manifesto for the 2012 regional election. Barcelona: Partit dels Socialistes de Catalunya.
- 2010. *Una Catalunya més forta, una societat més justa*. Manifesto for the 2010 regional election. Barcelona: Partit dels Socialistes de Catalunya.
- 2006. "Sí: Guanya Catalunya – Sí: Gana Cataluña" leaflet. PS-C file. Estatut de Catalunya 2006, Box 4. CEDOC, Universitat Autònoma de Barcelona.
- 2003. "Bases per a l'Estatut d'Autonomia de Catalunya," March. PS-C file. Estatut de Catalunya 2006, Box 1. CEDOC, Universitat Autònoma de Barcelona.

PS-C, ERC, and ICV. 2003. "Acord per a un Govern Catalanista i d'Esquerres a la Generalitat de Catalunya," December. Estatut de Catalunya 2006, Box 1. CEDOC, Universitat Autònoma de Barcelona.

PS-PSC-FDF. 1978. *Déclaration commune du P.S., du P.S.C. et du F.D.F.* Collected by the Manifesto Research Group and available from GESIS, Cologne.

PSB. 1968. *Programme P.S.B.* Manifesto for the 1968 election. Collected by the Manifesto Research Group and available from GESIS, Cologne.

PSC. 1991. *Pour qu'une société soit juste, il faut que la démocratie soit forte.* Manifesto for the 1991 election. Collected by the Manifesto Research Group and available from GESIS, Cologne.
- 1987. *Le courage des idées. Le cran de les appliquer*. Manifesto for the 1987 election. Collected by the Manifesto Research Group and available from GESIS, Cologne.
- 1978. *Aller à l'essentiel pour rendre l'avenir possible*. Manifesto for the 1978 election. Collected by the Manifesto Research Group and available from GESIS, Cologne.
- 1968. *Feu vert – Programme P.S.C.* Manifesto for the 1968 election. Collected by the Manifesto Research Group and available from GESIS, Cologne.

PSF. 1981. *110 propositions pour la France*. Manifesto for the 1981 presidential election. Collected by the Manifesto Research Group and available from GESIS, Cologne.

PSI. 1992. *Un governo per la ripresa – Argomenti socialisti*. Manifesto for the 1992 election. Collected by the Manifesto Research Group and available from GESIS, Cologne.

Putnam, Robert, Robert Leonardi, and Raffaella Nanetti. 1985. *La pianta e le radici – Il radicamento dell'istituto regionale nel sistema politico italiano*. Bologna: Il Mulino.
- 1993. *Making Democracy Work*. Princeton, NJ: Princeton University Press.

PVV. 1991. *Herstel het beleid*. Manifesto for the 1991 election. Liberaal Archief, Ghent.

- 1987. *P.V.V. Programma 13 december*. Manifesto for the 1987 election. Collected by the Manifesto Research Group and available from GESIS, Cologne.
- 1978a. *U verdient echt beter*. Manifesto for the 1978 election. Collected by the Manifesto Research Group and available from GESIS, Cologne.
- 1978b. *Wakker Worden*. Electoral brochure. Collected by the Manifesto Research Group and available from GESIS, Cologne.

Quadrado, Susana. 2006. "PSC y CiU maduran la coalición del sí al Estatut coordinando sus campañas." *La Vanguardia*, 26 April.

Quaglia, Lucia. 2008. "Euroscepticism in Italy." In *Opposing Europe?*, edited by Paul Taggart and Aleks Szczerbiak, 58–74. Oxford: Oxford University Press.

Quermonne, Jean-Louis. 1963. "Vers un régionalisme 'fonctionnel'?" *Revue française de science politique* 13 (4): 849–76.

Quévit, M., and M. Aiken. 1975. "La compétition politique au sein du système politique belge (1919–1974)." *Courrier hebdomadaire* 669–70. Brussels: CRISP.

Qvortrup, Mads. 2002. "The Emperor's New Clothes: The Danish General Election 20 November 2001." *West European Politics* 25 (2): 205–11.

Ragin, Charles. 2009. "Qualitative Comparative Analysis Using Fuzzy Sets (fsQCA)." In *Configurational Comparative Methods*, edited by Benoît Rihoux and Charles Ragin, 87–121. London: Sage.

- 2008. *Redesigning Social Inquiry*. Chicago, IL: University of Chicago Press.

Ragin, Charles, Kriss Drass, and Sean Davey. 2006. *Fuzzy-Set/Qualitative Comparative Analysis 2.0*. Department of Sociology, University of Arizona.

Ragionieri, Ernesto. 1967. "Accentramento e autonomie nella storia dell'Italia unita." In Ernesto Ragionieri, *Politica ed amministrazione nell'Italia unita*. Bari: Laterza.

Ramiro, Luis and Laura Morales. 2010. "Spanish Parties and Democracy: Weak Party-Society Linkage and Intense Party-State Symbiosis." In *Political Parties and Democracy – Vol. II: Europe*, edited by Kay Lawson, 71–95. Santa Barbara, CA: Praeger.

Rampulla, Francesco. 1997. "La legge Bassanini e le autonomie locali." *Il Politico* 62 (1): 131–42.

RCC. 1973. Royal Commission on the Constitution, 1969–1973, vol. 1, Report (Cmnd 5460). London: The Stationery Office.

Regeringen. 2004. *Det nye Danmark – En enkel offentlig sektor tæt på borgeren*. Copenhagen: Dansk Regeringen.

Renan, Ernest. [1882] 1947. "Qu'est-ce qu'une nation?" In Ernest Renan (ed.), *Oeuvres complètes* – tome I. Paris: Calmann-Levy.

Requejo, Ferran and Klaus-Jürgen Nagel (eds). 2010. *Federalism beyond Federations – Asymmetry and Processes of Resymmetrisation in Europe*. Farnham: Ashgate.

Rico, Guillem. 2012. "The 2010 Regional Election in Catalonia: A Multilevel Account in an Age of Economic Crisis." *South European Society and Politics* 17 (2): 217–38.

Rico, Guillem, and Robert Liñeira. 2014. "Bringing Secessionism into the Mainstream: The 2012 Regional Election in Catalonia." *South European Society and Politics* 19 (2): 257–80.

Ricolfi, Luca. 2012. *Il sacco del Nord*, second ed. Milan: Guerini e Associati.

Riddoch, Lesley. 2012. "Scottish People Would Have voted for 'Devo Max.' That's Why It's Not an Option." *The Guardian*, 15 October, www.theguardian.com/commentisfree/2012/oct/15/scottish-independence-devo-max-referendum [accessed 25 August 2014].

Rifflet, R. 1967. "Les groupes dirigents belges et les dimensions supranationales." *Courrier hebdomadaire* 375–6. Brussels: CRISP.

Rigby, Elisabeth, Andrea Felsted, and Daniel Thomas. 2014. "Business Finds Its Voice on Independence." *Financial Times*, 11 September.

Rihoux, Benoît, and Gisèle De Meur. 2009. "Crisp-Set Qualitative Comparative Analysis (CSQCA)." In *Configurational Comparative Methods*, edited by Benoît Rihoux and Charles Ragin, 33–68. London: Sage.

Riker, William. 1996. *The Strategy of Rhetoric*. New Haven, CT: Yale University Press.

Robson, William. 1942. *Regional Government*. London: The Fabian Society.

Rodriguez Teruel, Juan, and Astrid Barrio. 2015. "Going National: Ciudadanos from Catalonia to Spain." *South European Society and Politics* 21(4): 587–607.

Roig Madorrán, Elna. 2005. El debate para la ratificación del proyecto de Constitución Europea en Cataluña, ¿Un conflicto de Cataluña con Europa? Análisis del Real Instituto Elcano no. 6/2005. Madrid: Real Instituto Elcano, available at www.realinstitutoelcano.org/wps/portal/rielcano/contenido?WCM_GLOBAL_CONTEXT=/elcano/elcano_es/zonas_es/ari+6-2005 [accessed 25 August 2011].

Rokkan, Stein, and Derek Urwin. 1982. *Economy, Territory and Identity – Politics of the European Peripheries*. London: Sage.

Rossinyol, Jaume. 1974. *Le problème national catalan*. Paris: Mouton.

Rotelli, Ettore. 1967. *L'avvento della Regione in Italia – Dalla caduta del regime fascista alla Costituzione repubblicana (1943–1947)*. Milan: Giuffrè.

RPR. 1981. *Avec Jacques Chirac – Pour une nouvelle majorité*. Manifesto for the 1981 parliamentary election. Collected by the Manifesto Research Group and available from GESIS, Cologne.

RPR-UDF. 1981. *Un pacte et dix principes*. Manifesto for the 1981 parliamentary election. Collected by the Manifesto Research Group and available from GESIS, Cologne.

Rudd, Christopher. 1988. "The Belgian Liberal Parties: Economic Radicals and Social Conservatives." In *Liberal Parties in Western Europe*, edited by Emil Kirchner, 178– 212. Cambridge: Cambridge University Press.

Rudolph, Joseph. 1977. "Ethnonational Parties and Political Change: The Belgian and British Experience." *Polity* 9 (4): 401–26.

Ruzza, Carlo, and Oliver Schmidtke. 1993. "Roots of Success of the Lega Lombarda – Mobilization Dynamics and the Media." *West European Politics* 16 (2): 1–23.

RW. 1978. *Wallon maître chez toi*. Manifesto for the 1978 election, collected by the Manifesto Research Group and available from GESIS, Cologne.

– 1969. Congrès Général du Rassemblement Wallon. *Forces Wallonnes*, 23 March, pp. 4, 5, 8.

– 1968. Programme du Rassemblement Wallon. *Forces Wallonnes*, 16 March, p. 6.

Sahlins, Peter. 1989. *Boundaries – The Making of France and Spain in the Pyrenees*. Berkeley, CA: University of California Press.

Sakwa, Richard. 2014. *Frontline Ukraine – Crisis in the Borderlands*. London: I.B. Tauris.

Sandford, Mark. 2013. The Abolition of Regional Government. *Standard Note SN/PC/5842*. London: House of Commons Library, available at www.parliament.uk/briefing-papers/SN05842.pdf [accessed 4 September 2014].

– 2009. *The Northern Veto*. Manchester: Manchester University Press.

Sartori, Giovanni. 1970. "Concept Misformation in Comparative Politics." *American Political Science Review* 64 (4): 1033–53.

Sauger, Nicolas. 2010. "Political Parties and Democracy in France: An Ambiguous Relationship." In *Political Parties and Democracy – Vol. II: Europe,* edited by Kay Lawson, 3–26. Santa Barbara, CA: Praeger.

Sautois, Joëlle, and Marc Uyttendaele (eds). 2013. *La sixième réforme de l'État (2012–2013) – Tournant historique ou soubresaut ordinaire?* Limal: Anthemis.

Savelli, Giulio. 1992. *Che cosa vuole la Lega*. Milan: Longanesi.

Savigear, Peter. 1989. "Autonomy and the Unitary State: The Case of Corsica." In *Federalism and Nationalism,* edited by Murray Forsyth, 96–114. Leicester: Leicester University Press.

SC. 2014. Report of the Smith Commission for further devolution of powers to the Scottish Parliament. The Smith Commission, www.smith-commission.scot/wp-content/uploads/2014/11/The_Smith_Commission_Report-1.pdf.

Scharpf, Fritz. 1997. *Games Real Actors Play – Actor-Centered Institutionalism in Policy Research*. Boulder, CO: Westview Press.

– 1996. "Negative and Positive Integration in the Political Economy of European Welfare States." In *Governance in the European Union,* edited by Gary Marks, Fritz Scharpf, Philippe Schmitter and Wolfgang Streeck, 15–39. London: Sage.

Scheinman, Lawrence. 1977. "The Interfaces of Regionalism in Western Europe: Brussels and the Peripheries." In *Ethnic Conflict in the Western World*, edited by Milton Esman, 65–78. Ithaca, NY: Cornell University Press.

Schimmelfennig, Frank. 2003. *The EU, NATO and the Integration of Europe – Rules and Rhetoric*. Cambridge: Cambridge University Press.

Schmidt, Vivien. 1990. *Democratizing France – The Political and Administrative History of Decentralization*. Cambridge: Cambridge University Press.

Schneider, Carsten, and Claudius Wagemann. 2012. *Set-Theoretic Methods for the Social Sciences*. Cambridge: Cambridge University Press.

Scotsman. 1997a. "Dalyell Warns of One-Way Road to Independence." *The Scotsman*, 8 September.

– 1997b. "First Apostle of People Politics Needs Scots Seal on His Reforms." *The Scotsman*, 8 September.

– 1997c. "Cross-Party Campaign a Far Cry from Old Division." *The Scotsman*, 8 September.

– 1997d. "Tory Attack 'drags home rule debate into gutter.'" *The Scotsman*, 28 August.

– 1997e. "New Labour Opens Up to Using Umbrella." *The Scotsman*, 25 August;

– 1997f. "Set Minds and Strong Words This Time Round." *The Scotsman*, 24 August.

– 1997g. "Can They Deliver the Big Message?" *The Scotsman*, 17 August.

Scott, Andrew, John Peterson, and David Millar. 1994. "Subsidiarity: A 'Europe of the Regions' versus the British Constitution." *Journal of Common Market Studies* 32 (1): 47–68.

ScP. 2014. *Report on the Scottish Government's Proposal for an Independent Scotland: Membership of the European Union*. European and External Relations Committee, second Report, 2014 (Session 4), SP Paper 530. Edinburgh: Scottish Parliament, www.scottish.parliament.uk/S4_EuropeanandExternalRelationsCommittee/Reports/euR-14-02w.pdf.

Scroccu, Gianluca. 2012. *Alla ricerca di un socialismo possibile – Antonio Giolitti dal PCI al PSI*. Rome: Carocci.

Scully, Roger. 2013. "More Scottish than Welsh? Understanding the 2011 Devolved Elections in Scotland and Wales." *Regional and Federal Studies* 23 (5): 591–612.

SD. 2012. *Statistical Yearbook 2012*. Copenhagen: Statistics Denmark.

Seawright, David. 1999. *An Important Matter of Principle – The Decline of the Scottish Conservative and Unionist Party*. Aldershot: Ashgate.

Sechi, Salvatore. 1970. *Dopoguerra e fascismo in Sardegna – Il movimento autonomistico nella crisi dello stato liberale (1918–1926)*. Turin: Fondazione Luigi Einaudi.

Sedelmeier, Ulrich. 2005. "Eastern Enlargement – Towards a European EU?" In *Policy-Making in the European Union*, fifth ed., edited by Helen Wallace, William Wallace and Mark Pollack, 402–28. Oxford: Oxford University Press.

Selan, Valerio, and Rosita Donnini. 2009. "Regional Planning in Italy." In *Planning, Politics, and Public Policy – The British, French and Italian Experience*, edited by Jack Hayward and Michael Watson, 269–84. Cambridge: Cambridge University Press.

Serrano, Ivan. 2013. "Just a Matter of Identity? Support for Independence in Catalonia." *Regional and Federal Studies* 23 (5): 523–45.
SF. 2005. *Fordi Danmark fortjener en bedre fremtid*. Danish Socialist People's Party's manifesto for the 2005 election. Collected by the Manifesto Research Group and available from GESIS, Cologne.
– 2001. *Gi' velfærden stemme*. Danish Socialist People's Party's manifesto for the 2001 election. Collected by the Manifesto Research Group and available from GESIS, Cologne.
SG. 2013a. *Choosing Scotland's Future – A National Conversation*. The Scottish Government, www.scotland.gov.uk/Topics/constitution/a-national-conversation [accessed 25 Aug 2014].
– 2013b. *Scotland's Future – Your Guide to an Independent Scotland – A Summary*. Edinburgh: The Scottish Government.
Sharpe, Laurence James. 1993. "The European Meso: An Appraisal." In *The Rise of Meso Government in Europe*, edited by Laurence James Sharpe, 1–39. London: Sage.
– 1979. Decentralist Trends in Western Democracies: A First Appraisal. In *Decentralist Trends in Western Democracies*, edited by Laurence James Sharpe, 9–79 London: Sage
Shepsle, Kenneth. 1989. "Studying Institutions – Some Lessons from the Rational Choice Approach." *Journal of Theoretical Politics* 1 (2): 131–47.
Shields, James. 1996. "The French Gaullists." In *Political Parties and the European Union*, edited by John Gaffney. 86–109. London: Routledge.
SK. 2004. *Strukturkommissionens Betænkning. Bind 1 – Hovedbetænkningen*. Copenhagen: Indenrigs- og Sundhedsministeriet.
Smyrl, Marc. 1997. "Does European Community Regional Policy Empower the Regions?" *Governance* 10 (3): 287–309.
SNP. 2011. *Re-elect a Scottish Government Working for Scotland*. Manifesto for the 2011 regional election. Edinburgh: Scottish National Party.
– 2007. *It's Time*. Manifesto for the 2007 regional election. Edinburgh: Scottish National Party.
– 1997. *Yes We Can – Win the Best for Scotland*. Manifesto for the 1997 general election. Edinburgh: Scottish National Party.
– 1992a. *Independence in Europe – Make it happen now!* Manifesto for the 1992 general election. Edinburgh: Scottish National Party.
– 1992b. *Independence in Europe – Change Now for a Better Life*. Edinburgh: Research Department, Scottish National Party.
– 1979. *Return to nationhood – A Summary of the Ideology of Scotland's Right to Independence, the Guiding Principles of the Scottish National Party and an Outline of Its Programme for Self-Government*. West Calder: SNP Publications.
Sorens, Jason. 2009. "The Partisan Logic of Decentralization in Europe." *Regional and Federal Studies* 19 (2): 255–72.

- 2004. "Globalization, Secessionism, and Autonomy." *Electoral Studies* 23 (4): 727–52.
SP. 1991. *We zijn boven alles een sociale partij*. Manifesto for the 1991 election. Collected by the Manifesto Research Group and available from GESIS, Cologne.
- 1987. *SP-Verkiezingsmanifest*. Manifesto for the 1987 election. Collected by the Manifesto Research Group and available from GESIS, Cologne.
- 1978. *Programma Vlaamse Socialisten*. Manifesto for the 1978 election. Collected by the Manifesto Research Group and available from GESIS, Cologne.
SP.A. 2010. *We moeten weer vooruit*. Manifesto for the 2010 federal election, available at
- 2007a. *Principes voorop*. Extract from the manifesto for the 2007 federal election. Available at www.s-p-a.be/ons-programma/ [accessed 23 August 2010].
- 2007b. *De wereld is van iederen*. International section of the manifesto for the 2007 federal election. Available at tijdslijn.s-p-a.be/media/samenvatting-wereld.pdf [accessed 20 August 2009].
SP.A-Spirit. 2007. *Gemeenschappelijke programmatekst sp.a-spirit*. Manifesto for the 2007 federal election. Available at tijdslijn.s-p-a.be/media/samenvatting-wereld.pdf [accessed 20 August 2009].
Spruyt, Hendrik. 2002. "The Origins, Development, and Possible Decline of the Modern State." *Annual Review of Political Science* 5: 127–49.
SS. 1963a. "La politica di centro-sinistra nel dialogo dei capi dei partiti." *Stampa Sera*, 3 April.
- 1963b. "Discorso dell'on. Malagodi sul programma dei liberali." *Stampa Sera*, 22 April.
StaFi. 2013. *Finland in Figures 2013*. Helsinki: Statistics Finland, available at www.stat.fi/tup/suoluk/suoluk_vaesto_en.html.
Statham, Robert. 2002. *Colonial Constitutionalism – The Tyranny of United States' Offshore Territorial Policy and Relations*. Lanham, MD: Lexington Books.
Stegarescu, Dan. 2004. *Economic Integration and Fiscal Decentralization: Evidence from OECD Countries*. Discussion paper no. 04-86. Mannheim: Zentrum für Europäische Wirtschaftsforschung.
Steinmo, Sven, Kathleen Thelen and Frank Longstreth (eds). 1992. *Structuring Politics – Historical Institutionalism in Comparative Analysis*. Cambridge: Cambridge University Press.
Surridge, Paula and David McCrone. 1999. "The 1997 Scottish Referendum Vote." In *Scotland and Wales: Nations Again?*, edited by Bridget Taylor and Katarina Thomson, 41–64 Cardiff: University of Wales Press.
Sutcliffe, John. 2000. "The 1999 Reform of the Structural Funds Regulations: Multi-level Governance or Renationalization?" *Journal of European Public Policy* 7 (2): 290–309.

Swenden, Wilfried. 2006. *Federalism and Regionalism in Western Europe – A Comparative and Thematic Analysis*. Basingstoke: Palgrave.

Swyngedouw, Marc, and Koen Abts. 2011. "Les électeurs de la N-VA aux élections fédérales du 13 juin 2010." *Courrier hebdomadaire* 2125. Brussels: CRISP.

Tanner, Duncan. 2000. "Facing the New Challenge: Labour and Politics, 1970–2000." In *The Labour Party in Wales 1900–2000*, edited by Duncan Tanner, Chris Williams and Deian Hopkin, 264–93. Cardiff: University of Wales Press.

Tarlton, Charles. 1965. "Symmetry and Asymmetry as Elements of Federalism: A Theoretical Speculation." *Journal of Politics* 27 (4): 861–74.

TC. 2010. Sentencia 31/2010, de 28 de junio de 2010 (BOE núm. 172, de 16 de julio de 2010). Tribunal Constitucional. Available at www.tribunalconstitucional.es/es/jurisprudencia/paginas/Sentencia.aspx?cod=16273 [accessed 17 July 2014].

Thatcher, Margaret. 1997. "Don't wreck the heritage we all share." *The Scotsman*, 9 September.

Tierney, Stephen. 2013. "Legal Issues Surrounding the Referendum on Independence for Scotland." *European Constitutional Law Review* 9 (3): 359–90.

Times. 1997. "72 hours left to save UK, says Major." *The Times*, 29 April.

Timmermans, Arco. 1994. "Cabinet Ministers and Policy-Making in Belgium: The Impact of Coalitional Constraints." In *Cabinet Ministers and Parliamentary Government*, edited by Michael Laver and Kenneth Shepsle, 106–24. Cambridge: Cambridge University Press.

Tocqueville, Alexis de. [1856] 1967. *L'Ancien Régime et la Révolution*. Edited by J.P. Mayer. Paris: Gallimard.

Tonboe, Jens. 1991. "Centralized Economic Control in a Decentralized Welfare State: Danish Central-Local Government Relations 1970–86." In *State Restructuring and Local Power – A Comparative Perspective*, edited by Chris Pickvance and Edmond Preteceille, 18–47. London: Pinter.

Tornos Mas, Joaquín. 2007. *Los estatutos de autonomía de Cataluña*. Madrid: Iustel.

Tramontana, Carlo. 1995. *Il centro-sinistra (1962–1975) – Evoluzione costituzionale e politiche legislative*. Turin: Giappichelli.

Tréfois, Anne, and Jean Faniel. 2007a. "L'évolution des partis politiques flamands." *Courrier hebdomadaire* 1971. Brussels: CRISP.

– 2007b. "L'évolution des partis politiques francophones." *Courrier hebdomadaire* 1972. Brussels: CRISP.

Treisman, Daniel. 2002. *Defining and Measuring Decentralization: A Global Perspective*. Unpublished paper. Department of Political Science, University of California Los Angeles.

Ucelay da Cal, Enric. 2003. *El imperialismo catalán – Prat de la Riba, Cambó, D'Ors y la conquista moral de España*. Barcelona: Edhasa.

UKG. 2014. *Scotland Analysis: EU and international issues* (Cm 8765). The Secretary of State for Scotland, Her Majesty's [United Kingdom] Government. Norwich: The Stationery Office.

– 2013. *Scotland Analysis: Devolution and the Implications of Scottish Independence.* Cm 8554. Her Majesty's [United Kingdom] Government. Norwich: The Stationery Office.

– 2005. *Better Governance for Wales (Cm 6582).* Wales Office, Her Majesty's [United Kingdom] Government. Norwich: Her Majesty's Stationery Office.

– 2004. *Draft Regional Assemblies Bill (Cm 6825).* Deputy Prime Minister, Her Majesty's [United Kingdom] Government. Norwich: Her Majesty's Stationery Office.

UKG-SG. 2012. Agreement between the United Kingdom Government and the Scottish Government on a referendum on independence for Scotland. Edinburgh, 15 October, www.gov.uk/government/uploads/system/uploads/attachment_data/file/313612/scottish_referendum_agreement.pdf [accessed 25 August 2014].

UKP. 2016. *The Scotland Act 2016.* United Kingdom Parliament, available at www.legislation.gov.uk/ukpga/2016/11/pdfs/ukpga_20160011_en.pdf [accessed 30 September 2016].

– 2014. *Wales Act 2014.* United Kingdom Parliament, available at www.legislation.gov.uk/ukpga/2014/29/contents/enacted [accessed 4 September 2015].

– 2013. *The Scotland Act 1998 (Modification of Schedule 5) Order 2013.* United Kingdom Parliament, available at www.legislation.gov.uk/uksi/2013/242/pdfs/uksi_20130242_en.pdf [accessed 4 September 2014].

– 2012. *Scotland Act 2012, Chapter 11.* United Kingdom Parliament, available at www.legislation.gov.uk/ukpga/2012/11/contents/enacted [accessed 4 September 2014].

– 2006. *Government of Wales Act 2006, Chapter 32.* United Kingdom Parliament, available at www.legislation.gov.uk/ukpga/2006/32/contents [accessed 4 September 2014].

– 2003. *Regional Assemblies (Preparations) Act 2003, Chapter 10.* United Kingdom Parliament, available at www.legislation.gov.uk/ukpga/2003/10/contents [accessed 25 March 2014].

UL. 1995. *Tesi per la definizione della piattaforma programmatica dell'Ulivo.* 6 December. www.perlulivo.it/radici/vittorieelettorali/inizio/nelsegno.html.

Urwin, Derek. 1982. "Conclusion: Perspectives on Conditions of Regional Protest and Accomodation." In *The Politics of Territorial Identity – Studies in European Regionalism,* edited by Stein Rokkan and Derek Urwin, 425–36. London: Sage.

Van Aelst, Peter, and Tom Louwerse. 2014. "Parliament without Government: The Belgian Parliament and the Government Formation Processes of 2007–2011." *West European Politics* 37 (3): 475–96.

Van Dyke, Jon. 1992. "The Evolving Legal Relationships Between the United States and Its Affiliated US-Flag Islands." *University of Hawaii Law Review* 14 (2): 445–517.

Van Evera, Stephen. 1997. *Guide to Methods for Students of Political Science.* Ithaca, NY: Cornell University Press.

Van Houten, Pieter. 2003. "Globalization and Demands for Regional Autonomy in Europe." In *Governance in a Global Economy*, edited by Mike Kahler and David Lake, 110–35. Princeton, NJ: Princeton University Press.

Vatter, Adrian. 2007a. "Federalism." In *Handbook of Swiss Politics*, second ed., edited by Ulrich Klöti, Peter Knoepfel, Hanspeter Kriesi, Wolf Linder, Yannis Papadopoulos, and Pascal Sciarini, 77–99. Zurich: Neue Zürcher Zeitung Publishing.

– 2007b. "The Cantons." In *Handbook of Swiss Politics*, second ed., edited by Ulrich Klöti, Peter Knoepfel, Hanspeter Kriesi, Wolf Linder, Yannis Papadopoulos, and Pascal Sciarini, 197– 226. Zurich: Neue Zürcher Zeitung Publishing.

VB. 2010. *Vlamingen 1st – Verkiezingsprogramma 2010.* Manifesto for the 2010 federal election, available at www.vlaamsbelang.org/2010_verkiezingsprogramma/files/verkiezingsprogramma-web.pdf [accessed 23 August 2010].

– 2007. *"Toekomstplan voor Vlaandereen" – Verkiezingsprogramma 10 Juni 2007.* Manifesto for the 2007 federal election. Brussels: Vlaams Belang.

– 1991. *Uit zelfverdediging – Vlaams Blok – Eigen volk eerst.* Manifesto for the 1991 election. Collected by the Manifesto Research Group and available from GESIS, Cologne.

Verdoodt, A. 1976. "Les problèmes communautaires belges à la lumière des études d'opinion." *Courrier hebdomadaire* 742. Brussels: CRISP.

Verhofstadt, Guy. 2005. *De Verenigde Staten van Europa.* Antwerp: Uitgeverij Houtekiet.

Vis, Barbara. 2011. "Under Which Conditions Does Spending on Active Labor Market Policies Increase? An fsQCA Analysis of 53 Governments between 1985 and 2003." *European Political Science Review* 3 (2): 229–52.

VLD. 1992. *VLD Beginselverklaring.* Liberaal Archief, Ghent.

Vrangbæk, Karsten. 2010. "Structural Reform in Denmark, 2007–09: Central Reform Processes in a Decentralized Environment." *Local Government Studies* 36 (2): 205–21.

VU. 1993. *De Volksunie – Vlaamser dan ooit.* Doc. VC687, ADVN, Antwerp.

– 1991. *Verkiezigsplatform Wetgevende Verkiezingen 24 November 1991.* Manifesto for the 1991 election. Collected by the Manifesto Research Group and available from GESIS, Cologne.

– 1987. *Volksunie. Een kordate aanpak.* Manifesto for the 1987 election. Collected by the Manifesto Research Group and available from GESIS, Cologne.

– 1978. *Volksunie, Vlaams belang.* Manifesto for the 1978 election. Collected by the Manifesto Research Group and available from GESIS, Cologne, Germany.

- 1970a. Wij van den Volksunie. Doc. DA407/04, Archief Volksunie, ADVN, Antwerp.
- 1970b. Met Nederland samen Sterk in het Europa der Volken, Wij-Vlaams National 10 June 1970. Doc. VBRB14, Archief Volksunie, ADVN, Antwerp.
- 1970c. Federalistisch voorstel van de Volksunie. Doc. VBRB209, Archief Volksunie, ADVN, Antwerp.
- 1968a. Verkiezingsplatform van de Volksunie 1968. Doc. D624/AC54, Archief Volksunie, ADVN, Antwerp.
- 1968b. Een partij voor jonge dynamische mensen. Doc. D624/AC54, Archief Volksunie, ADVN, Antwerp.
- 1968c. *Waarom federalisme?* Election leaflet. Doc. DA192/11, Archief Volksunie, ADVN, Antwerp.

VUJO. 1980. *Levend Zelfbestuur.* 4th VUJO Congress, 16 November 1980, Doc. DA311/12, ADVN, Antwerp.

Wallace, Helen. 1980. *Budgetary Politics: The Finances of the European Communities.* London: Allen and Unwin.

- 1977. "The Establishment of the Regional Development Fund: Common Policy or Pork Barrel?" In *Policy-Making in the European Communities*, edited by Helen Wallace, William Wallace and Carole Webb, 137–63. Chichester: Wiley.

Walt, Stephen. 2002. "The Enduring Relevance of the Realist Tradition." In *Political Science – State of the Discipline*, edited by Ira Katznelson and Helen Milner, 197–230. New York, NY: Norton.

Watts, Ronald. 2008. *Comparing Federal Systems*, third ed. Montreal, QC: McGill-Queen's University Press.

WdE. 1968. "La Wallonie dans l'Europe." *Combat*, 14 March, p. 3.

Weber, Eugen. 1976. *Paesants into Frenchmen – The Modernization of Rural France, 1870–1914.* Stanford, CA: Stanford University Press.

Weibel, Ernest. 1971. *La création des régions autonomes à statut spécial en Italie.* Geneva: Droz.

Weiler, Joseph. 2012. "Slouching towards the Cool War; Catalonian Independence and the European Union; Roll of Honour; In This Issue; A Personal Statement." *European Journal of International Law* 23 (4): 909–13.

Wheare, Kenneth. 1946. *Federal Government.* London: Oxford University Press.

Wils, Lode. 2009. *Van de Belgische naar de Vlaamse natie – Een geschiedenis van de Vlaamse beweging.* Leuven: Acco.

- 1992. "Introduction: A Brief History of the Flemish Movement." In *The Flemish Movement – A Documentary History 1780–1990*, edited by Theo Hermans, Louis Vos and Lode Wils, 1–39. London: The Athlone Press.

Wilson, Gordon. 2000. SNP Leader 1979–1990, personal interview, 30 March.

Wilson, James, Robin Wigglesworth, and Brian Groom. 2012. "ECB 'ready to do whatever it takes.'" *Financial Times*, 26 July.

Wimmer, Andreas, and Yuval Feinstein. 2010. "The Rise of the Nation-State across the World, 1816 to 2001." *American Sociological Review* 75 (5): 764–90.

Wivel, Anders. 2013. "A Pace-Setter Out of Sync? Danish Foreign, Security and Defence Policy and the European Union." In *Denmark and the European Union*, edited by Lee Miles and Anders Wivel, 80–94. Abingdon: Routledge.

Wolfe, James. 1976. "Constitutional Devolution and Functionalist Community-Building: Inverse Trends in European Politics." *The Southern Quarterly* 14 (3): 215–29.

Wood, Leanne. 2014. *What of Wales? Putting Wales at the Heart of the Constitutional Debate in Britain*. Speech at University College London, 11 June, available at www.partyofwales.org/the-slate/2014/06/12/what-of-wales-putting-wales-at-the-heart-of-the-constitutional-debate-in-britain/?force=1 [accessed 4 September 2014].

Woods, Dwayne. 1992. "The Centre No Longer Holds: The Rise of Regional Leagues in Italian Politics." *West European Politics* 15 (2): 56–76.

Wright, Kenyon. 1997. *The People Say Yes*. Glendaruel: Argyll Publishing.

Wright, Vincent. 1979. "Regionalization under the French Fifth Republic: The Triumph of the Functional Approach." In *Decentralist Trends in Western Democracies*, edited by Laurence James Sharpe, 193–234. London: Sage.

WST. 2014. Should Scotland be an independent country? What Scotland Thinks, whatscotlandthinks.org/questions/should-scotland-be-an-independent-country-1#line.

Wyn Jones, Richard. 2009. "From Utopia to Reality: Plaid Cymru and Europe." *Nations and Nationalism* 15 (1): 129–47.

Wyn Jones, Richard, and Bethan Lewis. 1999. "The Welsh Devolution Referendum." *Politics* 19 (1): 37–46.

Wyn Jones, Richard, and Roger Scully. 2012. *Wales Says Yes – Devolution and the 2011 Welsh Referendum*. Cardiff: University of Wales Press.

Wyn Jones, Richard, and Dafydd Trystan. 1999. "The 1997 Welsh Referendum Vote." In *Scotland and Wales: Nations Again?*, edited by Bridget Taylor and Katarina Thomson, 65–93. Cardiff: University of Wales Press.

Ziblatt, Daniel. 2006. *Structuring the State – The Formation of Italy and Germany and the Puzzle of Federalism*. Princeton, NJ: Princeton University Press.

Zolberg, Aristide. 1977. "Splitting the Difference: Federalization without Federalism in Belgium." In *Ethnic Conflict in the Western World*, edited by Milton Esman, 103–42. Ithaca, NY: Cornell University Press.

– 1974. "The Making of Flemings and Walloons: Belgium: 1830–1914." *Journal of Interdisciplinary History* 5 (2): 179–235.

Index

Agalev, 317n4. *See also* Groen!
Åland Islands, 21
Alleanza Nazionale (AN), 154, 156–7
Ancram, Michael, 147
Andalusia, 211–12
Aosta Valley, 21, 59, 60, 150
Aragon, 207–8, 211; Crown of, 207–8
Arana, Sabino, 209
Austria, 20, 23, 48, 59, 134
Aznar, José Maria, 212
Azores, 22

Barcelona, 208, 210, 218; Barcelona F.C., 221
Barre, Raymond, 104
Barroso, José Manuel, 205
Basque Country, 212–14; Álava, 210–11, 311n16; Basque language, 211; Basque provinces, 207–12, 322n37, 322n39; Biscay, 209, 211–12; Consejo General Vasco, 212; Guipúzcoa, 211–12; independence of, 211, 213; 1933 referendum, 211. *See also* Euskadi Ta Askatasuna

Bassanini, Franco, 161
Belgium, 9, 20, 23–4, 37, 47, 49, 55, 68–82, 92–101, 110–11, 114–31, 176, 179–97, 242, 246, 248–51, 254, 256, 314n33; Court of Cassation, 181; Dutch language, 68–70, 78–9, 95, 114–16, 182, 184, 192; Egmont pact, 92–3, 98; French language, 68–70, 78–9, 95, 114–16, 182–4, 192, 196; German-speaking community, 79, 179; Leuven crisis, 70, 73, 314n35; St Michael's agreement, 130; Stuyvenberg agreement, 92, 98; United Belgian States, 68; Voeren/Fourons dispute, 114, 317n2. *See also* Brussels, Flanders, Wallonia
Benelux, 133
Berlingske Tidende, 169
Berlusconi, Silvio, 154, 156
Blair, Tony, 143
Bretton Woods system, 83
Brussels, 69, 71–2, 77–9, 94–5, 99–100, 114, 116–19, 122, 125, 129, 131, 140–1, 179–80, 182–5, 189, 191–2, 195–6, 250, 317n1;

Brussel-Halle-Vilvoorde/ Bruxelles-Hal-Vilvorde (BHV), 183–5, 190–2, 196, 316n11, 320n4
Bulgaria, 320n1

Cameron, David, 205
Campaign for a Scottish Assembly, 136
Canary Islands, 212
Candidatura d'Unitat Popular (CUP), 230–4
Castile, 207–8; Crown of, 207–8
Catalonia, 5, 10, 176, 207–36, 245, 249, 251, 255, 322n36, 322n41, 322n42, 322n45; Assemblea de Catalunya, 211; Assemblea Nacional Catalana (ANC), 223; *Bases de Manresa*, 210; Castillian language, 216, 218; Catalan language, 208–9, 211, 216, 218, 220; Centre Catalá, 210; Estat Catalá, 210; independence of, 10, 24, 176, 210, 213–15, 219–36, 249, 255, 322n41; Institut d'Estudis Autonòmics, 213–14; Mancomunitat of, 210; *Memorial de Greuges*, 210; Principality of, 207; *vegueries*, 214, 218, 322n45; 1932 Statute of Autonomy, 211; 2003 regional election, 213; 2014 European election, 229
Catalunya Sí Que Es Pot (CSQEP), 230–3
Cavour, Camillo Benso Count of, 57
Centre démocrate humaniste (CDH), 182, 185, 188–9, 192, 194–6
Charles, Archduke, 208
Charles I of Spain, 207

Chirac, Jacques, 104
Christelijke Volkspartij (CVP), 69–73, 75, 77–8, 80–1, 94, 96, 98, 114–15, 118, 121–4, 126, 129–30, 180–1
Christen-Democratisch en Vlaams (CD&V), 181–3, 185, 188–90, 193, 195–6
Ciutadans (Cs), 227–8, 230–5
cohesion policy [EU], 7, 33–5, 37–8, 47–8, 83, 113, 119–20, 133, 140, 145, 193, 247
Cold War, 60, 134, 178
Comitato di Liberazione Nazionale (CLN), 58
Committee of the Regions [EU], 37, 135, 140, 159
Common Agricultural Policy (CAP) [EU], 56, 133, 167, 313n1
Commonwealth, 86
Comparative Historical Analysis (CHA), 8, 29, 44–5, 54
Confederation of British Industry (CBI), 205
Conservative Party, 85, 87, 89–92, 136–7, 139–41, 143, 145–8, 150, 175, 200–3, 205–6
Constitutional Treaty [EU]. *See* Treaty establishing a Constitution for Europe
Convergència Democràtica de Catalunya (CDC), 230, 233, 251
Convergència i Unió (CiU), 213–16, 218–20, 222, 224–31, 233–5, 243, 246, 248–9, 251
Corsica, 106, 109. *See also* France
Council of Ministers [EU], 37, 47–8, 56, 88, 113, 128, 134, 144, 167
Council of the European Union. *See* Council of Ministers [EU]

Croatia, 320n1
Cyprus, 134
Czech Republic, 134

Dalyell, Tam, 147
Dansk Folkeparti (DF), 165–73
Davies, Ron, 197
De Gaulle, Charles, 103, 105
Debré, Michel, 107
de/centralization, 3, 6–7, 20–3,
    33–4, 57–9, 63, 71, 74–5, 102–3,
    105–7, 109, 115, 135, 154, 156,
    159–60, 163–4, 173–4, 211, 245,
    247
Delors, Jacques, 48, 113
democratic deficit [EU], 134, 155
Democrazia Cristiana (DC), 59–65,
    67, 151–4, 156, 175
Denmark, 9, 20, 23, 25, 27, 32, 47,
    49, 82, 132, 163–75, 242, 312n3,
    319n16, 320n20; Amtsråd-
    foreningen, 169; Dansk Industri,
    169; Strukturkommissionen,
    169–70, 174, 320n24; 2000
    referendum, 167
Der Spiegel, 4–5
Det Konservative Folkeparti (DKF),
    164–9, 171–3
Det Radikale Venstre (DRV), 165,
    167–72
Dewar, Donald, 147
Di Rupo, Elio, 196
Dini, Lamberto, 157
Draghi, Mario, 178

Ecolo, 123, 126, 128–30, 182, 185,
    188–9, 192, 194–6, 317n5
Economic and Monetary Union
    (EMU) [EU], 32, 36–7, 48, 96–7,
    119–20, 126, 128, 133, 145,
    158–9, 162, 175, 177–8, 236,
    244, 319n12
Economic and Social Committee
    [EU], 135
Economic planning, 32–3, 62–3,
    65–8, 73
The Economist, 5
Edinburgh, 84
England, 83, 198, 207, 257, 315n2;
    North-East 2004 referendum,
    198, 207; Regional Assemblies
    (Preparations) Act 2003, 198;
    regional development agencies,
    198
enlargement [EU], 47–48, 55, 82,
    112, 133–4, 145, 155, 158–9,
    167, 172, 177, 185–6
environmental policy [EU], 112,
    119, 187
Esquerra Republicana de Catalunya
    (ERC), 210, 213–22, 224–31,
    233–5, 243, 246, 248–9, 251
Estonia, 134
Europe of the Regions, 4–6, 36,
    75–6, 107, 111, 113, 120–1, 128,
    132, 135, 158, 180, 246, 256;
    Europe of the Peoples, 220–1;
    Europa der volkeren, 75, 97,
    127, 193
European Central Bank (ECB), 178,
    232
European Coal and Steel
    Community (ECSC), 47, 55
European Commission, 47–8, 56,
    97, 112–13, 118, 128, 133–4,
    144, 167, 171, 187–8, 193
European Council [EU], 37, 47–8,
    83, 112, 144, 177, 232, 245
European Court of Justice (ECJ),
    56, 127

European Monetary System (EMS), 47, 83, 96–7
European Parliament (EP), 47–8, 56, 83, 88–9, 96–7, 113, 119, 127–8, 134, 139, 144, 156, 159, 167, 177–8, 185, 187, 232, 313n2
European People's Party, 233
European Stability Mechanism, 178
Euskadi Ta Askatasuna (ETA), 211. *See also* Basque Country
Eyskens, Gaston, 73, 78, 315n37

Faroe Islands, 20
fascism, 58–9, 63
Federalism. *See* state structures; federalism
Finland, 21, 23, 48, 134, 311n21
Fiscal Stability Treaty, 178
Flanders, 68–73, 75–9, 93–4, 97–100, 114–17, 119, 121–30, 179–92, 194–7, 236, 243, 249–50, 314n31; Flemish movement, 68–9, 72, 315n39; independence of, 123, 125, 127–8, 180, 183–7, 190–1, 194–5, 197, 236, 243, 249–50. *See also* Belgium
Fontainebleau summit [EU], 82
Forcadell, Carme, 223
Forsyth, Michael, 143
Forza Italia (FI), 154–9
France, 9, 21, 23, 25, 27, 32, 47, 49, 59, 68, 82, 101–10, 133, 177, 208, 242, 311n23; Commissions de développement économique régional, 314n27; *départements*, 102, 105, 109; *intendants*, 101–2; Third Republic, 102; Vichy regime, 103; 1789 revolution, 102; 1969 referendum, 103; 2005 referendum, 177. *See also* Corsica
Franco, Francisco, 211, 223, 229, 234
Friuli-Julian Venetia, 60, 150, 313n11
Front démocratique des francophones (FDF), 95, 181, 315n43

Galicia, 210, 212
Germany, 21, 23, 37, 47–8, 57, 133, 231, 310n6, 313n5
Giolitti, Antonio, 63
Giolitti, Giovanni, 57
Giscard d'Estaing, Valéry, 104–5, 107–8, 316n27
Gladstone, William Ewart, 84
Glasgow Govan, 136
Greece, 48, 83
Greenland, 310n12
Groen!, 196. *See also* Agalev

Habsbourg, House of, 208
Hallstein, Walter, 56
Harmel Centre, 69
health care, 34, 163–4, 166, 170–3, 190
Heath, Edward, 87
historical institutionalism (HI), 24, 45
Homs, Francesc, 235
Hungary, 61, 134

Ibarretxe, Juan José, 212; Ibarretxe Plan, 213
independence, 4–5, 7, 9–10, 25, 32, 34–44, 51, 53–4, 59, 63, 69, 74, 86, 91, 123, 125, 127–8, 131–2, 136, 162, 175–6, 183–7, 190–1, 194–7, 200–7, 210, 213–14,

219–36, 244–5, 249–50, 253–5, 312n4, 312n5
Iniciativa per Catalunya Verds (ICV), 213–14, 216, 218, 220–2, 224–8, 230
International Monetary Fund (IMF), 177
Ireland, 21, 23, 33, 47, 82–4, 315n4
Italy, 9, 21–4, 27, 47, 49, 55, 57–68, 80–1, 132–3, 150–63, 174–5, 242, 244, 249–51, 253–4, 310–11n14, 313n4, 313n5, 313n6, 319n14; *centro-sinistra*, 60, 63, 65; Commissione Bicamerale, 161; constitution, 59; Constitutional Court, 66; German language, 58; Kingdom of, 57; *Risorgimento*, 57; resistance movement, 58; Slavic languages, 58; 1990 regional elections, 150; 2001 referendum, 161

Jones, Carwyn, 200
Julian Venetia, 58. See also Friuli-Julian Venetia
Junts pel Sí (JxS), 230–4

Kilbrandon Commission. See Royal Commission on the Constitution

Labour Party, 85–7, 89–92, 135–48, 150, 174, 198–203, 205–6, 316n7
Laporta, Joan, 221–2
Latvia, 134
Lega Nord, 24, 132, 150–60, 162, 174–5, 242–4, 249–51, 253
Leterme, Yves, 189

Liberal Party, 87, 137; Liberal Democrats, 148, 200–3, 205–6
Lithuania, 134
Lliga Regionalista, 210
local government, 19–23, 33, 58, 63, 66, 68, 71, 74–5, 84, 94, 102, 105–6, 109, 115, 122, 157, 161, 163–4, 166, 169–73, 179, 214, 231, 310n9
Lombardy, 150–1, 153, 159
London, 84
Luxembourg, 47
Luxembourg compromise [EU], 56

Maastricht Treaty. See Treaty on European Union
Maciá, Francesc, 210
Madeira, 22
Major, John, 139, 143, 146
Majorca, 207; Kingdom of, 207
Malta, 134
Maragall, Pasqual, 217
Marchais, Georges, 104
Martens, Wilfried, 117
Mas, Artur, 215, 217, 223, 234
Mauroy, Pierre, 108
Milan summit [EU], 111–12
Mitterrand, François, 104–6, 108
Montilla, José, 218
Moro, Aldo, 62, 65
Mouvement réformateur (MR), 182, 184–5, 188–9, 192–6
Mouvement wallon. See Wallonia; Walloon movement
Movimento Sociale Italiano (MSI), 66, 154
multilevel governance (MLG), 43–4, 247, 253

Napoleon I, 102, 208

Navarre, 208, 211–12, 214, 311n16
Nenni, Pietro, 62–4
The Netherlands, 22–3, 47, 125, 177; 2005 referendum, 177
Nieuw-Vlaamse Alliantie (N-VA), 181–3, 185–6, 188–91, 193–7, 243, 246, 248–50
North Atlantic Treaty Organization (NATO), 63–4, 127, 185, 187
Northern Ireland, 22, 197, 311n17, 311n18
Norway, 22–3, 173

Olivares, Gaspar de Guzmán, Count-Duke of, 208

Padania, 157–8, 160, 162, 250; independence of, 157, 160, 162
Paris, 103
Parti communiste français (PCF), 104, 106–8
Parti de la Liberté et du Progrès (PLP), 69–71, 74–5, 77, 79–81, 92–3, 98, 315n48
Parti des réformes et de la liberté de Wallonie (PRLW), 93, 95–6, 98, 316n8
Parti réformateur libéral (PRL), 93, 100, 114, 117, 120–1, 125, 128–9, 181
Parti social-chrétien (PSC), 69–71, 73–5, 77, 95–8, 114, 117–18, 120–2, 125, 128–30, 182
Parti socialiste (PS) [Belgium], 73, 93, 95–8, 114, 117, 120–3, 125, 128–30, 182, 184, 187, 189, 191, 193, 195–6
Parti socialiste (PSF) [France], 104, 106–8

Parti socialiste belge (PSB), 69–71, 73, 75, 77–8, 80–1, 93
Parti wallon des Travailleurs, 76
Partido Nacionalista Vasco/Euzko Alderdi Jeltzalea (PNV/EAJ), 209
Partido Popular (PP), 215–16, 223, 225, 232–3; Partido Popular de Cataluña (PP-C), 213–18, 220–2, 224, 226–8, 231–5
Partido Socialista Obrero Español (PSOE), 213, 215, 223
Partij voor Vrijheid en Vooruitgang (PVV), 93, 95–6, 98, 100, 114, 116, 119, 121, 124, 126, 129
Partit dels Socialistes de Catalunya (PS-C), 213–14, 216, 218–19, 221–2, 224–5, 227, 229, 231–3
Partito Comunista Italiano (PCI), 59–65, 67, 151, 153
Partito d'Azione, 58
Partito della Rifondazione Comunista (PRC), 151, 160
Partito Democratico della Sinistra (PDS), 151–7
Partito Liberale Italiano (PLI), 61, 63–6, 313n12
Partito Popolare Italiano (PPI), 58–9, 154–6
Partito Repubblicano Italiano (PRI), 61, 65, 313n12
Partito Sardo d'Azione, 58
Partito Socialista Democratico Italiano (PSDI), 61, 65, 313n12
Partito Socialista Italiano (PSI), 59–65, 67, 151–4
permissive consensus [EU], 56, 113
Philip IV of Spain, 208
Philip V of Spain, 208
Pi i Margall, Francesc, 209
Piedmont, 57, 150, 153

Plaid Cymru (PC), 84–6, 88–92, 136–42, 144–6, 148, 150, 199–200, 206, 243, 246, 248, 315n5
Podemos, 230
Poland, 134
Pompidou, Georges, 105
Portugal, 22–3, 48
Primo de Rivera, Miguel, 210
process tracing, 8–9, 44–6
Prodi, Romano, 160
Progress Party, 165

Qualified majority voting (QMV) [EU], 113, 128, 134, 159, 177, 187, 313n13, 324n1
Qualitative Comparative Analysis (QCA), 30, 52–3, 237–41

Rajoy, Mariano, 223
Rassemblement pour la République (RPR), 104–5, 107–8
Rassemblement wallon (RW), 70–2, 75–81, 92–4, 97–8, 100–1, 114, 118, 130, 249, 324n6
Rasmussen, Anders Fogh, 168–9, 172, 320n23
Rasmussen, Lars Løkke, 169
realist bargain, 8–9, 29–44, 46, 53–5, 81, 237–52, 254
Regional Authority Index (RAI), 17–23
Regional policy [EU]. *See* cohesion policy
Rodríguez Zapatero, José, 214–15, 217
Romania, 320n1
Royal Commission on the Constitution, 85
Russia, 178. *See also* Union of Soviet Socialist Republics

Salmond, Alex, 147, 200–1
Sardinia, 21, 58, 60
Schengen agreement [EU], 134, 167
Schuman Plan, 76
Scotland, 5, 9, 22, 25, 38, 82–91, 132, 136–50, 176, 198–207, 225, 236, 245, 250, 254–5, 257, 311n19, 315n2; business, 90, 147, 205–6, 243; Calman Commission, 201; Church of, 84; Claim of Right for, 136; Edinburgh agreement, 203, 225; independence of, 5, 25, 38, 86, 88, 136, 138–9, 141–4, 146–8, 150, 200–7, 236, 243, 254, 257; Scotland Act 1978, 87–8, 90, 136, 138; Scotland Act 1998, 148, 201; Scotland Act 2012, 202; Scotland Act 2016, 198, 206; Scottish Assembly, 86, 89–91, 136, 138; Scottish Covenant, 84–5; Scottish Office, 84, 138, 149; Scottish Parliament, 5, 25, 137–8, 140–2, 148–9; Smith Commission, 206; 1979 referendum, 87–91, 135, 138, 147–8; 1997 referendum, 143, 147–8; 2014 referendum, 176, 198, 204–7, 254–5, 257
Scottish Constitutional Convention, 137–8, 143, 149
Scottish Green Party, 204
Scottish National Party (SNP), 5, 37, 84–92, 110, 135–42, 144–50, 174–6, 198, 200–7, 243, 246, 248, 250, 255, 257
secession. *See* independence
Sicily, 21, 58–60
Silk Commission. *See* Commission on Devolution in Wales

Sillars, Jim, 136
Single European Act, 47, 112–13, 245
single market [EU], 36–7, 48, 111–13, 118–20, 133, 135, 141, 145, 164, 236, 244
Slovakia, 134
Slovenia, 134
Smith, John, 143
Social Democratic Party (SDP), 137
social policy [EU], 48, 97, 107, 112, 119, 126, 128, 132–3, 140, 145, 155, 187, 193, 232
Socialdemokraterne (DSD), 165–72
Socialistik Folkeparti (SF), 165, 167–8, 171–2
Socialistische Partij (SP), 73, 93, 95, 97–8, 114–15, 119, 121, 124, 126, 129–30, 181; Socialistische Partij-Anders (SP.A), 181, 184, 187–8, 190–1, 193, 195–6
Solidaritat Catalana per la Independència (SI), 221–2
South Tyrol, 58–9. *See also* Trentino-South Tyrol
Soviet Union. *See* Union of Soviet Socialist Republics
Spain, 10, 22–4, 36–7, 48, 49, 133, 176–7, 205, 207–36, 242, 245–6, 251, 256, 322n40, 322n43; Carlist Wars, 209, 322n38; Constitutional Court, 217–19, 222, 224, 228–9; Declaration of Barcelona, 212; First Republic, 209; Nueva Planta decrees, 208; Second Republic, 210–11; 1977 general election, 211; 1978 constitution, 212, 231; 2004 general election, 213; 2011 general election, 223. *See also* Catalonia

Spirit, 181, 184, 190
state structures, 3, 8–10, 11–28; a/symmetry, 12–23; confederalism, 123–5, 127, 157, 182–6, 190–1, 193–4, 196–7, 200, 207, 213, 226, 250, 256; constitutional un/incorporation, 19, 310n8; federalism, 3, 12–23, 39, 55, 57–9, 69, 71–6, 78–9, 94, 96, 100–1, 107, 111, 115–19, 123–8, 130–1, 149, 151–2, 154–8, 161–2, 179–80, 182–5, 187, 190–4, 196, 200, 208–10, 219–21, 225–7, 229, 231–2, 245, 250, 256; restructuring, bottom up and top down dynamics, 8–11, 26–29, 31–43, 49, 51, 54–5, 68, 80–2, 91, 109, 111, 131–2, 149, 162, 174, 176, 197, 206, 234, 236, 237–40, 251–2; restructuring, strong and weak forms, 8, 11, 23, 27, 32, 35, 68, 206–7; unitarism, 3, 12–23, 39, 57, 71, 73–4, 78, 93, 100, 131
Structural funds [EU]. *See* Cohesion policy
Sturzo, Luigi, 58
subsidiarity, 6, 34–6, 115, 127, 135, 141, 154–5, 158, 161, 186, 245
Sweden, 22–3, 48, 134
Switzerland, 22–3, 310n6

Tarradellas, Josep, 212
Thatcher, Margaret, 87, 136
Tindemans, Leo, 79, 92, 98
Treaty establishing a Constitution for Europe, 133–4, 167, 171–2, 177, 185–8, 220
Treaty of Amsterdam, 134

Treaty of Lisbon, 48, 177, 192–3, 202–3, 220
Treaty of Nice, 134
Treaty of Paris, 64, 313n3
Treaty of Rome, 56, 64, 113
Treaty on European Union, 34, 47, 111–12, 126–8, 132–5, 141, 145, 152, 155, 159, 167, 204–5; Social Charter of, 112, 141, 145
Trentino-South Tyrol, 21, 60, 150, 319n1. *See also* South Tyrol

Ukraine, 178; Crimea, 178
L'Ulivo, 157, 159–60, 163, 174
Unió Democràtica de Catalunya (UDC), 230
Union of Soviet Socialist Republics (USSR), 60–1, 97
Union pour la démocratie française (UDF), 104–5, 107–8
United Kingdom (UK), 9, 22–3, 37, 47, 49, 82–92, 110, 132, 135–50, 174–8, 197–207, 225, 242, 245–6, 250–1, 256–7; Brexit, 256–7, 1975 referendum, 88–9; 1979 general election, 90; 1987 general election, 136; 2016 referendum, 176–8, 205, 207, 257. *See also* England, Northern Ireland, Scotland, Wales
United States of America (USA), 32, 60, 97

Valencia, 207, 212; Kingdom of, 207
Van den Brande, Luc, 179
Van Rompuy, Herman, 189, 205
Veneto, 150, 153, 159, 250
Venstre (DV), 165–9, 171–2
Verhofstadt, Guy, 179, 187, 189

Vlaams Blok (VB), 93, 123–5, 127–9, 131, 180–1; Vlaams Belang (VB), 181, 186, 188, 190–2, 194–5, 243–4, 249, 321n10
Vlaamse Beweging. *See* Flanders; Flemish movement
Vlaamse Liberalen en Democraten (VLD), 124, 126, 181, 183, 318n34, 319n41; Open Vlaamse Liberalen en Democraten (O-VLD), 181, 183, 187–8, 190, 193, 195–6
Volksunie (VU), 70–2, 74–5, 77–81, 92–4, 97–8, 100–1, 110, 114, 116, 118, 121, 123–4, 126–7, 129–31, 180–1, 183, 243, 315n48; Volksunie Jongeren (VUJO), 97

Wales, 22, 25, 34, 82–91, 132, 137–50, 197–200, 206, 311n19, 316n7; Commission on Devolution in Wales, 199; Government of Wales Act 1998, 148–9; Government of Wales Act 2006, 199; independence of, 138–9, 142, 200; National Assembly for Wales, 25, 90–1, 139–40, 143–4, 148, 198, 206, 311n20, 321n34; Richard Commission, 198; Wales Act 1978, 87, 90–1, 136; Wales Act 2014, 199; Welsh Office, 84, 139; 1979 referendum, 88–91, 135, 148; 1997 referendum, 147–8; 2011 referendum, 199
Wallonia, 68–73, 76–9, 93–4, 96, 98–100, 114, 117, 121–5, 129, 179–80, 182, 184–6, 189, 191–2, 195; independence of, 180;

Walloon Movement, 69, 72, 76; Walloon National Congress, 76. *See also* Belgium
War of the Spanish Succession, 208, 322n42
Welsh Assembly. *See* Wales; National Assembly for Wales

Western Roman Empire, 57
Wilson, Gordon, 136
World War I, 57, 69
World War II, 3, 10

Yugoslavia, 135, 313n11